NEW PROCLAMATION

NEW PROCLAMATION
YEAR A, 2008

EASTER TO CHRIST THE KING

O. WESLEY ALLEN JR.
HOLLY HEARON
HANK J. LANGKNECHT
BEVERLY A. ZINK-SAWYER

DAVID B. LOTT, EDITOR

FORTRESS PRESS
MINNEAPOLIS

NEW PROCLAMATION
Year A, 2008
Easter to Christ the King

Library of Congress Cataloging-in-Publicatšn Data
The Library of Congress has catalogued this series as follows.
New proclamation year A, 2001–2002: Advent through Holy Week / Francis J. Moloney... [etal.].
    p. cm.
    Includes bibliographical references.
    ISBN 0-8006-4245-7 (alk. paper)
      1. Church year. I. Moloney, Francis J.
    BV30 .N48 2001
    251'.6—dc21   2001023746

New Proclamation: Year A, 2008 Easter to Christ the King
ISBN 978–0-8006-4259–4

The paper used in this publication meets the minimum requirements of American National Standard for Information Sciences—Permanence of Paper for Printed Library Materials, ANSI Z329.48-1984.

Manufactured in the U.S.A.
12   11   10   09   08   3   4   5   6   7   8   9   10

CONTENTS

The Season after Pentecost / Ordinary Time
Holly Hearon

The Season after Pentecost / Ordinary Time
Hank J. Langknecht

The Season after Pentecost / Ordinary Time
Beverly A. Zink–Sawyer

Calendar

PREFACE

For over three decades Fortress Press has offered an ecumenical preaching resource built around the three-year lectionary cycle that provides first-rate biblical exegetical insights and sermon helps, a tradition that this new edition of *New Proclamation* continues. Focused on the biblical texts assigned by the three primary lectionary traditions—the Revised Common Lectionary (RCL), the lectionary from the Episcopal Book of Common Prayer (BCP), and the Roman Catholic Lectionary for the Mass (LFM)—*New Proclamation* is grounded in the belief that a deeper understanding of the biblical pericopes in both their historical and liturgical contexts is the best means to inform and inspire preachers to deliver engaging and effective sermons. For this reason, the most capable North American biblical scholars and homileticians are invited to contribute to *New Proclamation*.

New Proclamation has always distinguished itself from most other lectionary resources by offering brand-new editions each year, dated according to the church year in which it will first be used, and featuring a fresh set of authors. Yet each edition is planned as a timeless resource that preachers will want to keep on their bookshelves for future reference for years to come. Both longtime users and those new to the series will also want to visit this volume's new companion Web site, www.NewProclamation.com, which offers access not only to this book's contents, but also commentary from earlier editions, up-to-the-minute thoughts on the connection between texts and current events, user forums, and other resources to help you develop your sermons and enhance your preaching.

This present volume of *New Proclamation* covers the lections for the second half of the church year for cycle A, from Easter morning through Reign of Christ Sunday, plus Thanksgiving. This volume also follows the time-honored series format, including the following elements and features:

- *New Proclamation* is published in two volumes per year, with a large, workbook-style page, a lay-flat binding, and space for making notes.
- Each writer offers an introduction to her or his commentary that provides insights into the background and spiritual significance of that season (or portion thereof), as well as ideas for planning one's preaching during that time.
- The application of biblical texts to contemporary situations is an important concern of each contributor. Exegetical work is concise, and thoughts on how the texts address today's world, congregational issues, and personal situations have a prominent role.
- Although each lectionary tradition assigns a psalm or other biblical text as a response to the first reading, rather than as a preaching text, brief comments on each responsive reading are included to help the preacher incorporate reflections on these in the sermon.
- Boxed quotations in the margins highlight themes from the text to stimulate the preaching imagination.
- A calendar at the end of the book will help preachers plan their worship and preaching schedules through the seasons of Easter and Ordinary Time.

As has become the custom of *New Proclamation,* the writers for this latest edition represent both a variety of Christian faith traditions and multiple academic disciplines. O. Wesley Allen Jr., a New Testament scholar and professor of homiletics, and editor of the Fortress Press Elements of Preaching series, brings his mastery of both disciplines to the Easter texts. Another New Testament professor, Holly Hearon, brings her broad knowledge of the biblical literature, particularly Matthew, to the opening weeks Ordinary Time. Hank Langknecht, a Lutheran professor of homiletics, continues the season of Pentecost with a creative approach that explores the linkages between the first, responsive, and Gospel readings. And Beverly Zink-Sawyer, a Presbyterian professor of preaching known especially for her historical work on women in the pulpit, guides preachers through the closing weeks Ordinary Time and to the celebration of Thanksgiving. We are grateful to each of these contributors for their insights and their commitment to effective Christian preaching, and are confident that you will find in this volume ideas, stimulation, and encouragement for your ministry of proclamation.

David B. Lott

THE SEASON OF EASTER [1]

O. WESLEY ALLEN JR.

The Great Fifty Days of Easter begin with the Easter Vigil [2] and culminate in the celebration of Pentecost. The length of the season is based on the chronology found in Acts 1–2, but this fact belies the complexity of the origins of Easter.

One of Christianity's earliest liturgical innovations (following perhaps only the move from worshiping on the Sabbath to worshiping on the day of resurrection—the Lord's Day) was the creation of the holy day *Pascha. Pascha* is the Greek word meaning "Passover" and "suffering." This name was used because the story of Christ's passion and resurrection is narrated as occurring at the time of Passover, and Christ was seen as the paschal lamb. This holy day in the early church was a unitive commemoration of Christ's crucifixion, resurrection, and exaltation. It was not until the fourth century that distinct celebrations evolved for each of these different moments of the story of the Christ event. The commemoration of the passion evolved backwards from *Pascha* into Good Friday and back further into Holy/Maundy Thursday and Holy Week. The resurrection was celebrated at the Easter Vigil (on Saturday evening) and on Easter Sunday. The celebration of the exaltation of Christ shifted forward to Pentecost (fifty days later, following the Jewish practice of celebrating Pentecost fifty days after the Feast of Unleavened Bread as described in the chronology of Acts). And, finally, the celebration of the Ascension later separated from Pentecost into its own solemnity ten days prior to Pentecost, again following the chronology of Acts 1. Thus Easter

Sunday functions as a hinge in the liturgical seasons of Lent and Easter. It is both the climax of Holy Week (or, more narrowly, of the Easter Triduum, that is, *the three days* of Holy Thursday, Good Friday, Easter Vigil/Sunday) and initiates the Great Fifty Days of Easter.

Before turning our attention to the lections for individual Sundays of Easter, it will be helpful to take note of some broad patterns found in the lectionaries' construction of the season. First, a word concerning Easter Sunday. During all three years of the lectionary cycle, the Gospel readings naturally focus on the discovery of the empty tomb. Each year, however, the RCL and BCP offer two options for the Gospel lection—the version from John 20 and the one from the Synoptic Gospel for the year. There are two related reasons for this approach, both of which invite continuity in liturgy and preaching with the services leading up to Easter Sunday. The first is that the choice on Easter allows the preacher to flow cumulatively from either the Gospel readings from Holy Week, which come from John, or from the extended Gospel readings for the previous Sunday (Palm/Passion Sunday), which come from the Synoptic Gospel of the year. The second reason is related to the readings for the Easter Vigil on Saturday night. In all three years, the readings for the Great Vigil remain the same with the exception of the Gospel lesson. It circulates each year among the Synoptic version of the empty-tomb story. The result of these two patterns for this year looks like the following:

- *Palm/Passion*—Matthew's version of the events in Jerusalem including the Last Supper and institution of the Lord's Supper, the crucifixion, and the burial.
- *Holy Week*—Johannine readings including Jesus' last meal with the disciples (washing their feet and commanding them to love one another), crucifixion, and burial.
- *Easter Vigil*—Matthew's version of the discovery of the empty tomb (the lectionary from *Evangelical Lutheran Worship* also offers the Johannine version).
- *Easter Day*—Either the Johannine or Matthean version of the discovery of the empty tomb.

For congregations that observe the Easter Vigil, it is obvious that the Gospel reading for Sunday morning should be John 20:1-18, since they just read the Synoptic choice the night before. (As noted, users of *Evangelical Lutheran Worship* who also observe the Vigil will likely want to use as their Sunday morning Gospel whichever reading they did not use the night before.) But for those who do not hold a vigil, the choice to be made is whether the best approach is to bring to completion for the congregation the Synoptic account of the events in Jerusalem from the previous Sunday or the Johannine account from Holy Thursday and Good Friday. The decision is often weighted toward John since the Gospel lections for most of the remainder of the Easter season (the exceptions in Year A are Easter Evening, the Third Sunday of Easter, and Ascension) come from the Fourth Gospel. But the Matthean version deserves consideration. Each Gospel offers a unique theology of the empty tomb through its version of the story, and over the years preachers should expose a congregation to the full range of theology of the resurrection found in the New Testament.

Turning from Easter Sunday to a broader view of Eastertide as a whole, a second pattern to be noted concerns the Gospel lections. The Gospel readings for the season divide into two sections (Easter 1–3 and Easter 5–7) with Easter 4 standing between them. The pattern unfolds in the following manner:

> Each Gospel offers a unique theology of the empty tomb through its version of the story, and over the years preachers should expose a congregation to the full range of theology of the resurrection found in the New Testament.

- Easter 1–3 focuses on the event of the resurrection and the resurrection appearances:

Easter	The empty tomb (John 20:1-18 or Matt. 28:1-10)
Easter Evening	The road to Emmaus (Luke 24:13-35)
Easter 2	The gift of the Spirit and the revelation to Thomas (John 20:19-31)
Easter 3	The road to Emmaus (Luke 24:13-35)

This focus invites an in-depth homiletical look at the meaning of Christ's resurrection.

- Easter 4 is Good Shepherd Sunday because every year the christological focus is on Jesus as the Good Shepherd, and the Gospel readings for all three years of the lectionary cycle are drawn from John 10. In Year A, the first ten verses of the passage comprise the reading. (Every year Psalm 23 is used on this Sunday as well.) This Sunday serves as a transitional day between the focus on resurrection on Easter 1–3 and what follows on Easter 5–7.

- The Gospel lections for Easter 5–7 each year are drawn from Jesus' farewell discourse (John 14–17) to his disciples in the Fourth Gospel, with Easter 7 coming from the great prayer in John 17. At first glance, reading Jesus' testament just before his death may seem like an odd liturgical practice for the season of Easter. It is important to remember, however, that when the Johannine Jesus speaks of his "departure" and "glorification" in this section, he is speaking of his crucifixion, resurrection, and exaltation as a unitive whole. Thus, while the tone of the readings may "feel" at odds with the celebratory tones of the season, the themes of the lections are quite appropriate and prepare worshipers for the celebrations of the Ascension and Pentecost.

Turning from the Gospel readings, another important pattern to recognize in the lections for Eastertide is that the First Testament readings are replaced with readings from Acts. (The BCP offers the worship planner the choice of substituting lessons from Acts for either the first or second reading.) Since Acts is neither a Gospel nor an epistle, Luke's second volume does not fit naturally into the normal categories of lectionary readings. While it is somewhat odd to displace the First Testament during this season, reading Acts during Eastertide is actually a practice that dates back to the fifth century. Moreover, the substitution is justified given that the chronology of Acts establishes the fifty-day celebration of the season of Easter and tells the story of the post-resurrection church—that is, the story of the shift from Jesus' preaching to the church's preaching about Jesus and of the transition from a band of followers in Galilee to an empirewide movement. Nevertheless, it cannot be denied that there is something uncomfortable about reading stories of the post-Pentecost church before we have celebrated Ascension and Pentecost in our liturgical cycle. (Indeed, the Acts readings for Easter 2–4 in Year A are taken from the Pentecost story itself!) All three lectionaries attempt to deal with this problem by assigning John 20:19-31 (the Fourth Gospel's version of Jesus giving the Spirit to the disciples) for Easter 2 each year.

> It is important to remember that when the Johannine Jesus speaks of his "departure" and "glorification," he is speaking of his crucifixion, resurrection, and exaltation as a unitive whole.

A final pattern to note involves the function of epistle readings during Eastertide. Instead of assigning epistle readings that are thematically related to the Gospel lection (as is the standard practice during the liturgical seasons, the epistle lections for the season of Easter are semicontinuous readings (similar to the practice during Ordinary Time). These texts are chosen because they are thematically appropriate for the season of Easter in general, but at times the individual lections do relate to the Gospel or Acts reading. During Year A, the epistle for Easter is 1 Peter.

It is unclear who wrote this letter that has been attributed to the apostle Peter, but it was likely composed in the late first century to churches in the region of the Roman Empire that is part of modern-day Turkey. Christians in this region were facing a significant level of persecution in the form of social ostracism caused in part by the fact that those Gentiles who converted to Christianity no longer participated in popular Greco-Roman religious activities. Such ostracism would have resulted in significant economic, emotional, and perhaps at times physical suffering. First Peter was written to offer comfort and hope to these Christians by reminding them that any suffering that they must endure is worth the reward they have received. While the reward is eschatological in nature, the author characterizes this reward less as some future state of existence and instead as being (presently) in (the resurrected) Christ and is consistently contrasted with the kind of lives the readers led before their conversion.

Preaching through the semicontinuous readings from 1 Peter on Easter 2–7 (or through Easter 6 if Ascension replaces Easter 7) holds much potential. While some key passages are missing from the choices for lections, preachers can easily fill in the gaps between lections each week thanks to the brevity of the letter. Preaching 1 Peter will give the congregation a chance to get to know the rich theological and pastoral content of a much-neglected epistle.

In the comments on individual Sundays that follow, primary emphasis will be placed on the Gospel lections early in the season and the Acts readings at the end, because these readings set the tone of the Eastertide. But special attention will also be given to the 1 Peter readings. The comments on the epistle lections will assume an adapted *lectio continua* approach to preaching through the Great Fifty Days by expanding the comments from focusing on the pericopae alone to using the flow from lection to lection as a lens for studying and preaching the letter as a whole.

> First Peter was written to offer comfort and hope to these Christians by reminding them that any suffering that they must endure is worth the reward they have received.

Notes

1. The material for this introduction is adapted from O. Wesley Allen Jr., *The Three Dimensions of the Lectionary* (St. Louis: Chalice, 2007).

2. The lessons for Easter Vigil 2007 have been covered by Melinda Quivik in the Holy Week section of *New Proclamation, 2007–2008, Advent through Easter Vigil* (Minneapolis: Fortress Press, 2007).

RESURRECTION OF THE LORD / EASTER DAY

MARCH 23, 2008

Revised Common (RCL)	Episcopal (BCP)	Roman Catholic (LFM)
Acts 10:34-43 or	Acts 10:34-43 or	Acts 10:34a, 37-43
Jer. 31:1-6	Exod. 14:10-14, 21-25; 15:20-21	
Ps. 118:1-2, 14-24	Ps. 118:14-29 or 118:14-17, 22-24	Ps. 118:1-2, 16-17, 22-23
Col. 3:1-4 or	Col. 3:1-4 or	Col. 3:1-4 or
Acts 10:34-43	Acts 10:34-43	1 Cor. 5:6b-8
John 20:1-18 or	John 20:1-10 (11-18)	John 20:1-9
Matt. 28:1-10	or Matt. 28:1-10	

FIRST READING
ACTS 10:34-43 (RCL, BCP)
ACTS 10:34A, 37-43 (LFM)

In the LFM, the reading from Acts for Easter Sunday replaces the First Testament lection, while the RCL and BCP allows worship planners to use the Acts lection for either the first or second reading.

The reading from Acts comes from the story of Peter and Cornelius being brought together by divine will. In the opening of the chapter (vv. 1-8), the story focuses on God instructing Cornelius, a centurion who is a Gentile God-fearer, to seek out Peter. The next scene (vv. 9-23a) focuses on Peter receiving a divine vision of God declaring all animals clean for consumption just as Cornelius's representatives arrive. The concluding scene (vv. 23b-48) is the climax of the story. Peter arrives and is greeted as a god. After quickly rejecting this greeting, he begins to preach about God's impartial love as manifested in Jesus Christ. While Peter is preaching, the Holy Spirit descends on Cornelius's household. Peter responds to the action of the Holy Spirit by baptizing the first Gentile converts to the faith.

Today's lection comes from Peter's sermon in the last scene. It is chosen for this day because at its core is the apostolic witness to the resurrection. The sermon summarizes the whole of Jesus' ministry from its beginning in Galilee, but verses 39-41 contain the central message. Throughout Acts, Luke presents apostles preaching the cross and resurrection using the same basic formula. When preaching in Judea, Peter's message had been: "You killed him, *but* God raised him, *and* we [the apostles] are witnesses to it." Now, preaching outside of Judea to Gentiles, the opening pronoun has changed from *you* to *they*, but otherwise the message is the same. This pattern reveals a key element of Lukan theology. While the cross was necessary, it was not God's doing. For Luke, the cross represents a necessary martyrdom but is not salvific in and of itself. As Peter's sermon makes clear, God is active in raising the One killed by human forces. This resurrection is the central act of God's salvation. Thus preaching this text would lead one to speak less of the event of the resurrection with a christological focus and more of the One who brought it about (God) and its results (as seen in the gift of the Holy Spirit and baptism).

For Luke, the cross represents a necessary martyrdom but is not salvific in and of itself.

JEREMIAH 31:1-6 (RCL ALT.)

Those who follow the RCL may choose to substitute the Acts lection for the second reading instead of using it as the first reading. This is not recommended since it breaks the pattern of replacing the first reading with Acts for the rest of Eastertide. Nevertheless, if one does so, the reading from Jeremiah 31 does offer a powerful vision of God's eschatological salvation. Opening with a covenant formula, this poem expresses hope after the exile with memories of Israel thriving after suffering in the wilderness and images of social, economic, and religious restoration.

EXODUS 14:10-14, 21-25; 15:20-21 (BCP ALT.)

Those who follow the BCP may choose to substitute the Acts lection for the second reading instead of using it as the first reading. Since the BCP offers this choice throughout Eastertide, it is best to determine a pattern for the season as a whole instead of Sunday by Sunday. The First Testament alternative for Easter Sunday involves selections from the story of the crossing of the Red Sea, the paradigmatic act of salvation in Israel's narratives. The text is offered as a typological foreshadowing of the salvation effected in the resurrection—as God brought the Israelites through the deadly waters to life on the other side, so God raised Jesus from the dead.

PSALM 118:1-2, 14-24 (RCL)
PSALM 118:14-29 OR
118:14-17, 2-24 (BCP)
PSALM 118:1-2, 16-17, 22-23 (LFM)

Psalm 118 is a liturgy of thanksgiving designed for one who makes a pilgrimage to the Temple. The portions the lectionary choices focus on emphasize God's salvific providence. Indeed, echoing themes of resurrection, verses 17-18 specifically speak of God protecting the psalmist from death. Even more important on this day, however, is verse 22. The early church understood Jesus to be the rejected stone (in the crucifixion) that God made into the cornerstone (through the resurrection). It is easy to see why the psalm has come to be associated with Eastertide.

SECOND READING
COLOSSIANS 3:1-4 (RCL, BCP, LFM)

The epistle lection is taken from the Deutero-Pauline letter to the Colossians. The primary reason for composing the letter seems to have been to counter what the author considers false teachings, especially those of a christological nature (see 2:8-23). The Colossians reading for Easter is taken from the paranetic portion of the letter (3:1—4:6) in which the author, in typical Pauline fashion, follows the main body of the letter with ethical exhortation. Our passage opens the paranetic section by calling the recipients of the letter to set their minds on the things that are above. Especially appropriate for Easter, this exhortation is grounded on the claim that Christians have died and risen with Christ. (Contrast this use of the present tense with Paul's future tense in Romans 6, where the apostle claims Christians have been buried with Christ in baptism so that we *will* be united with him in resurrection.)

1 CORINTHIANS 5:6B-8 (LFM)

This epistle lection is plucked out of context in the worst of ways. Chapter 5 of 1 Corinthians is dealing with sexual immorality in the Corinthian church, specifically the report Paul receives that a man is having relations with his stepmother. Paul is aghast that the Corinthian church would allow this to go on. The way the boundaries of this reading are set, however, gives congregants no sense of this context.

That said, it should also be noted that the language of this selection has a long tradition of being adopted in eucharistic liturgical settings to name the paschal mystery of Christ's sacrificial death that is lifted up by the postresurrection church every time it celebrates the Lord's Supper: "For our paschal lamb, Christ, has been sacrificed. Therefore, let us celebrate the festival . . ." (vv. 7b-8a).

ACTS 10:34-43 (RCL ALT., BCP ALT.)

See the comments on the first reading, above.

THE GOSPEL
JOHN 20:1-18 (RCL)
JOHN 20:1-10 (11-18) (BCP)
JOHN 20:1-9 (LFM)

The Fourth Gospel does not just end with the story of the resurrection. It is a Gospel in which the theme of resurrection plays an important role long before Jesus' final days draw near (for instance, see 2:1, 18-22; 3:13, 14; 5:21, 25-29; 6:62; 7:33; 8:14, 28; 12:23-26, 32; 13:1, 3, 33, 36; 14:2-7, 12, 28; 16:5-11, 16; 17:11). Nowhere is this more evident than in the extended scene where Jesus raises Lazarus from the dead (11:1-54). It is important to remember that in John, miracle stories are told less for how they show what Jesus can do and more because they are symbolic actions ("signs") revealing who Jesus is. The raising of Lazarus shows that Jesus *is* the Resurrection. This christological claim must be kept in mind as one turns to John's story of the empty tomb. After reading through the Gospel narrative, one realizes that the closing chapters are not simply about Jesus of Nazareth being raised from the dead. They are stories (or signs), if you will, of Resurrection being raised from the dead. Speaking less parabolically, John's stories of the empty tomb and the postresurrection appearances witness less to a moment of resuscitation in the past and more to the manifestation of resurrection itself among Christ's followers.

While John's version of the resurrection narrative comprises two chapters (although scholars debate who added chapter 21 as an epilogue), the lectionary is only concerned with the story of the empty tomb on Easter Sunday. John's story differs significantly from that found in the Synoptic Gospels. Jesus was buried with care (19:38-42), so Mary Magdalene comes not to complete his burial, but simply to mourn and honor Jesus. When she finds the stone rolled

> John's stories of the empty tomb and the postresurrection appearances witness less to a moment of resuscitation in the past and more to the manifestation of resurrection itself among Christ's followers.

away, she runs back to Simon and the beloved disciple claiming that they (whoever "they" may be) have taken Jesus' body. The two disciples run to the tomb,
find that Jesus' body has indeed disappeared, and discover that the cloths used to
wrap Jesus' body and head are now folded and laid in two different places. When
the beloved disciple sees this, he believes (although it is not entirely clear *what* he
believes). Meanwhile Mary Magdalene has returned to the graveyard and weeps
outside the tomb. When she looks in, she sees two angels who were not there
when the disciples had investigated the tomb. Unlike the figures at the tomb in
the other Gospels, these angels do not proclaim the resurrection but only ask
Mary why she is weeping. She responds by again claiming that "they" have taken
Jesus' body. Finally, the risen Jesus himself appears to Mary, but she does not
recognize him. When he repeats the angels' question, she, thinking him to be a
gardener, asks if he (presumably one of "them") has taken away the corpse. It is
only when Jesus calls Mary by name that she recognizes him (cf. 10:3). Jesus then
instructs Mary not to hold him because his ascension to God is not complete.
And the scene ends with Mary going and proclaiming to the disciples, "I have
seen the Lord."

That this passage is concerned with the manifestation of Resurrection itself to
Christ's followers can be found in the subtle connection between *seeing* on the
one hand and *knowing* and *believing* on the other. Mary *saw* the stone rolled away,
but did not *know* where they had taken her Lord (vv. 1-2). The disciple whom
Jesus loved *saw* the linen cloths from outside the tomb; then Peter entered and
saw them; and finally the beloved disciple, entered, *saw* and *believed* (vv. 6-9).
Mary *saw* the two angels but still did not *know* where they had taken the body
(vv. 12-13). When Mary first *saw* Jesus, she did not *know* it was him (v. 14). But finally when she proclaimed the good news of the resurrection to the
disciples, she used the words, "I have *seen* the Lord"
(v. 18). This connection between sight and knowl-
edge and faith runs through the Fourth Gospel (for example, 1:18, 50-51; 2:23;
3:3, 36; 6:2, 40, 62; 7:3; 9:1-41; 11:9, 40; 12:45; 14:7, 9, 17, 19; 16:10, 16-19,
22; 17:24; 19:35). Thus the resurrection does not change Jesus' status (how can a
resurrection change Resurrection?). Instead, it *reveals* Jesus as Lord, as Resurrection. Indeed, the story tells nothing about *how* Jesus was resurrected, but focuses
instead on how Mary *experienced* Jesus' resurrection. Likewise, sermons on this
text should focus on faith's reception of resurrection. The very reason we have
such large crowds on Easter Sunday is that they know that Jesus was raised and
that it is important. But the reason attendance at worship on the Second Sunday
of Easter is so low is that they did not truly experience resurrection themselves
the Sunday before.

> The story tells nothing about how Jesus was resurrected, but focuses instead on how Mary experienced Jesus' resurrection.

Matthew most likely used Mark as his primary source for writing his Gospel. Important keys to understanding Matthew's version of the story of the empty tomb, therefore, are found in the changes Matthew makes to Mark's version. Mark presents the empty tomb story (16:1-8) as a parabolic ending to a parabolic Gospel. After he died and the centurion recognized him as God's Son (15:33-39), Jesus had been buried in a rushed and disrespectful manner by a man who had participated in the unanimous condemnation of him by the Sanhedrin (14:64; 15:42-47). The women, seeing this, come to the tomb after the Sabbath has passed to care for the body properly. They are concerned about how they will move the stone, only to find that the stone has already been rolled away. When they enter the tomb, Jesus is gone but a young man (the same young man of 14:51?) proclaims to them that Jesus has been raised and they are to tell the disciples that the risen Jesus will meet them in Galilee. The women flee in fear and tell no one what they experienced. And this is how the Gospel of Mark ends—no resurrection appearances, no signs of eschatological glory, no instructions to the disciples. Only silence and fear.

Mark had intriguing theological and narrative reasons for ending his Gospel in this open-ended manner—he could assume that his original readers knew at least the basic story of the Christ event, and presents his parabolic narrative as a corrective to a misguided *Christus Victor* type of Christology. But it is easy to see why Matthew would want to alter this ending. Through the writing of his Gospel, Matthew edits and expands Mark in ways that make it clear that, while he may be dealing with some immediate

> The "scientific" *how* of the resurrection is not of concern to Matthew. The theological *what* is.

issues, he is attempting to create a document that will serve as a foundational narrative for his community for a while to come. This certainly would require a more fulfilling, complete ending.

Matthew begins this revision of the ending with an added detail at the crucifixion scene. When Jesus dies, there is an earthquake, and many of the saints (Gk: *hagio*) are raised from the dead. They wait until after Jesus' resurrection, however, to enter the city and appear to many (27:51-53). Whereas Mark wants to focus his readers' attention on the cross more than the resurrection, Matthew uses the story of the cross to foreshadow the resurrection.

Matthew then redeems Joseph of Arimathea and presents Jesus as being buried properly with the women watching (27:57-61). But then Matthew adds a major element to Mark's narrative—Jewish guards are placed at the tomb to keep the disciples from stealing Jesus' body and claiming he was raised from the dead (27:62-66). This is clearly an apologetic strategy used to counter those in Matthew's time who were claiming that Jesus' followers had indeed stolen his body.

When the women come to the tomb on the Sabbath, they are not coming to prepare the body. They are simply coming to mourn, so they are not concerned about the stone (28:1). When they arrive there is an earthquake, as there was at the crucifixion, and an angel (instead of a young man) descends and rolls the stone away (vv. 2-3). This is an intriguing detail and easily missed. In Mark the stone has already been rolled away so that Jesus could get out of the tomb. In Matthew the tomb is rolled away so that the women (and the readers) can get *in* to see that Jesus has already been raised, that the tomb is already empty. At this point the guards become frozen in their fear at what is happening (v. 4). Similar to Mark's young man, Matthew's angel then tells the scared women that Jesus has been raised and will meet the disciples back in Galilee (vv. 5-7). But the women's reaction is different here than in Mark: they do leave in fear but also in great joy, and they obediently run to tell the disciples what they have experienced (v. 8). But they are briefly delayed when the risen Jesus greets them along the way, they take hold of his feet and worship him, and he repeats the angel's message concerning meeting the disciples in Galilee (vv. 9-10). The scene at the tomb is then concluded with the guards reporting to the religious leaders what had happened and being paid off to lie and say that the disciples had stolen the body (vv. 11-14).

There are two theological issues to note here that are important for preaching on Matthew's unique perspective on the resurrection. The first concerns the nature of the resurrection as a bodily phenomenon. When the women meet Jesus they grab his feet. He is clearly not a spirit, but a physical being. Nevertheless, Jesus is raised and leaves the tomb *before* the stone has been removed from it. Matthew does not attempt to resolve the tension between asserting that Jesus left the tomb by passing through the physical reality of the stone walls (presumably as a spiritually raised being) and that Jesus can be physically touched. The "scientific" *how* of the resurrection is not of concern to Matthew. The theological *what* is. Matthew is concerned to interpret in a narrative manner *that* Jesus is raised and thus is present in his church. That presence (see 1:23 where Jesus is called Emmanuel, God with us, and 28:20 where the risen Jesus promises to be with the disciples until the end of the age) is as paradoxical as the story of the empty tomb.

> The resurrection of Jesus is a gift offered to those who seek out the risen Christ. It is an experience of faith, not a verifiable historical incident.

The second theological issue is brought to light by contrasting the women's and the guard's responses to what takes place at the tomb. The women greet the angel's news with joy and then when they meet Jesus on the road they worship him. This is new behavior in Matthew's Gospel. The preresurrection Jesus was not worshiped but is now (see also the response of the disciples on the mountain in Galilee, 28:17). The guards, in contrast, are not led to worship Jesus. Indeed, they conspire with the religious leaders to bear false witness concerning what happened. The point to be grasped here is that Matthew does not equate the resurrection with the empty tomb. The resurrection of Jesus is a gift offered to those who seek out the risen Christ. It is an experience of faith, not a verifiable historical incident. Even in the story, not all those who witnessed the epiphany at the empty tomb came to faith in Jesus as the risen Lord and Savior.

RESURRECTION OF THE LORD / EASTER EVENING

MARCH 23, 2008

Revised Common (RCL)	Episcopal (BCP)	Roman Catholic (LFM)
Isa. 25:6-9	Acts 5:29a, 30-32 or Dan. 12:1-3	Acts 10:34a, 37-43
Psalm 114	Psalm 114 or 136 or 118:14-17, 22-24	Ps. 118:1-2, 16-17, 22-23
1 Cor. 5:6b-8	1 Cor. 5:6b-8 or Acts 5:29a, 30-32	Col. 3:1-4 or 1 Cor. 5:6b-8
Luke 24:13-49	Luke 24:13-35	Luke 24:13-35

FIRST READING

ISAIAH 25:6-9 (RCL)

Although the RCL offers a reading from Acts rather than a First Testament lection throughout most of Easter, on Easter Evening it offers a reading from Isaiah. This passage is chosen to relate to the Gospel text, which tells of Jesus' resurrection appearance to the disciples on the road to Emmaus, and in the breaking of the bread in their house. Two primary images lie behind the connection of this Isaiah passage with Luke's Easter story—the messianic banquet that God provides for all nations at Zion (vv. 6-7) and God swallowing up death (v. 8).

Although this passage falls in the scope of material considered to be First Isaiah (Isaiah 1–39), some scholars argue that chapters 24–27 come from a later period—probably the sixth century B.C.E. Certainly the themes of hope and comfort found in the passage fit the messages of prophets of the exilic period. The image of celebrating a feast with God on Mount Zion at the accession of a new king is a powerful one for people who experienced their temple being destroyed, their king being dethroned, and being removed from their homeland. Following on the heels of a prayer celebrating salvation for the weak in the form of divine judgment against oppressors (25:1-5), this passage does indeed resonate with New Testament understandings of the resurrection as an eschatological event with sociopolitical implications.

DANIEL 12:1-3 (BCP ALT.)

The BCP offers this Daniel passage as an alternate to the Acts reading because it is one of the earliest Jewish references to bodily resurrection. In exilic prophets there are a number of references to the restoration of Judah using resurrection metaphors, but this passage from Daniel seems to go further than such metaphorical use by explicitly naming the expectation that "many" will be raised from the dead, some for everlasting life and others for everlasting contempt.

Although the language of Daniel 12 refers to the resurrection of individuals, one must be careful about too easily drawing conclusions about Jewish anthropology and views of life after death based on this passage. For one thing, Daniel is specifically addressing those persecuted by Antiochus Epiphanes and is not making general theological claims. For another, Daniel is thoroughly apocalyptic, and apocalyptic imagery is often not meant to be interpreted literally. In fact, it is important that the imagery in 12:1-3 be read in the context of (that is, as part of the conclusion to) chapters 10–12, which comprise a single apocalyptic vision. Being true to this text in a sermon will require a great deal of background explanation about apocalyptic in general and Daniel specifically. This may not be the best use of homiletic energy on Easter Evening.

ACTS 5:29A, 30-32 (BCP)

The BCP assigns these verses without regard for their narrative context. The full context is the story of the apostles being arrested by the religious authorities, being freed by the angel of the Lord and instructed to preach in the Temple, being rearrested by the authorities, and being tried by the authorities (5:17-42). The assigned verses are from Peter's defense before the council—notice how 29b is omitted so the reference to the broader context will not confuse the oral rendering of the selection.

That said, the verses chosen represent the core of the apostolic proclamation of the Gospel According to Luke. As noted in the commentary on Acts 10 for Easter Day, Peter repeatedly preaches: "You killed him, *but* God raised him, *and* we [the apostles] are witnesses to it." This formulaic expression is expanded here to include a description of Jesus' exaltation for the sake of Israel (an appropriate inclusion given Peter's audience) and a reference to the gift of the Holy Spirit.

> Peter repeatedly preaches: "You killed him, *but* God raised him, *and* we [the apostles] are witnesses to it."

ACTS 10:34A, 37-43 (LFM)

See the comments on the first reading for Easter Day, above.

Responsive Reading
PSALM 114 (RCL, BCP)

As Easter celebrates the core of the church's paradigmatic story of God's redemptive engagement with the world, so Psalm 114 celebrates the paradigmatic story of God's salvation in the First Testament—the exodus and delivery into the promised land. The psalm praises God for rescuing Judah from Egypt and residing with them, for the crossing of the sea (out of Egypt) and the Jordan River (into the promised land), and for providential care in the wilderness (water from the rock). The water imagery as a sign of God's salvific and providential care is especially appropriate for this evening, given that the Easter Vigil and Easter Sunday are traditional services for baptizing catechumens.

PSALM 118:14-17, 22-24 (BCP ALT.)
PSALM 118:1-2, 16-17, 22-23 (LFM)

See the comments on the responsive reading for Easter Day, above.

PSALM 136 (BCP ALT.)

The BCP offers Psalm 136 as one of two alternate psalter readings for Easter Evening. Thematically, it is very similar to the first choice, Psalm 114. It is a hymn of praise celebrating God's work in creating the world (vv. 1-9) and delivering the Israelites from Egypt and into the promised land (vv. 10-22). It then closes with general praise for God's remembering God's people (vv. 23-26). But what is striking about the song is the way that it functions as a litany. The first half of each verse, which celebrates some aspects of God's salvific action, was spoken by an individual voice leading the congregation in worship. The second half of each verse is a refrain—"for his steadfast love endures forever"—spoken by the people.

SECOND READING

1 CORINTHIANS 5:6B-8
(RCL, BCP, LFM ALT.)
COLOSSIANS 3:1-4 (LFM)

See the comments on the second reading for Easter Day, above.

ACTS 5:29A, 30-32 (BCP ALT.)

See the comments on the first reading, above.

THE GOSPEL

LUKE 24:13-49 (RCL)
LUKE 24:13-35 (BCP, LFM)

For congregations that have a service on Easter Evening, the Gospel lection should be the focus of the homily, for indeed, Luke's story is set on Sunday evening after the resurrection. It is this story that calls the church together on Easter Evening.

The scene in which Jesus encounters the disciples on the road to Emmaus is the lection for Easter 3 and is discussed in more detail in comments for that Sunday. It should be noted here, however, that the RCL extends the pericope beyond the boundary set by the BCP and LFM to include verses 36-49. These verses describe Jesus' appearance to a whole group of disciples later in the evening after having appeared to Simon (v. 34) as well as the disciples in Emmaus (vv. 13-32).

Three elements of this scene are worth noting. First, one of Luke's primary purposes in narrating this scene is to argue that Jesus' resurrection was a *bodily* resurrection. The fact that Jesus simply disappears after Cleopas and the unnamed disciple recognize him in the breaking of the bread (v. 31) could lead to a view of the resurrection as a purely spiritual event. While the story of the resurrection has mysterious elements to it, showing that Jesus is somewhat different after the resurrection, Luke wants to make perfectly clear that the disciples have not simply had a vision of the ghost of the still-dead Jesus. He can be touched (vv. 39-40). He eats (vv. 41-43). He is raised from the dead.

> Luke wants to make perfectly clear that the disciples have not simply had a vision of the ghost of the still-dead Jesus.

Second, Luke uses this scene to assert that all that has happened (both crucifixion and resurrection) were in accordance with God's providential plan as laid out in the whole (Law, Prophets, and Writings) of Scripture (vv. 44-47). (See the comments on Acts 2:14a, 22-32 for Easter 2, below.)

Third, Luke wants his readers to know that the resurrection is something that cannot be kept quiet. Indeed, beginning in Jerusalem the message spreads to all nations, that is, it spreads from Israel to all Gentiles. And those who are witnesses to the resurrection are the ones who, after being empowered by the promise of the Holy Spirit, are to proclaim the resurrection (vv. 48-49; cf. Acts 1:8). "Witness" here clearly has the double meaning of one who witnesses something as well

> Luke wants his readers to know that the resurrection is something that cannot be kept quiet.

as one who gives witness *to* something. Within Luke's narrative world, as seen in Acts, a witness is one who followed Jesus from his baptism through his resurrection (see 1:21-22). It is clear, however, that Luke is speaking also of the readers who have witnessed (through the narrative) all that Jesus has done, all that Jesus has said, and all that has happened to Jesus. The experience of the risen Christ is available, says Luke, to all who share the Eucharist. We must be careful not to import eisegetically later assertions about Christ's real presence in the elements of bread and wine into this passage. Nevertheless, it is clear that Luke believes we experience Christ in some way in the breaking of the bread. Resurrection cannot be kept secret because Christ makes it available to all. This event that was necessary, this resurrection of God's Child, must be proclaimed, and we, the ones who experience it in the meal, are the ones who must proclaim it.

SECOND SUNDAY OF EASTER

MARCH 30, 2008

Revised Common (RCL)	Episcopal (BCP)	Roman Catholic (LFM)
Acts 2:14a, 22-32	Acts 2:14a, 22-32 or Gen. 8:6-16; 9:8-16	Acts 2:42-47
Psalm 16	Psalm 111 or 118:19-24	Ps. 118:2-4, 13-15, 22-24
1 Peter 1:3-9	1 Peter 1:3-9 or Acts 2:14a, 22-32	1 Peter 1:3-9
John 20:19-31	John 20:19-31	John 20:19-31

FIRST LESSON

ACTS 2:14A, 22-32 (RCL, BCP)

Following the pattern of the readings from Acts for Easter Day and Easter Evening, this Acts lection for Easter 2 consists of Luke's formulaic account of the Christ event that appears in sermons throughout Luke's second volume. The pattern is, "You killed him, *but* God raised him, *and* we [the apostles] are witnesses to it."

Today's reading is part of Peter's extended Pentecost sermon, so this pattern is expanded and unpacked in ways that indicate much about Lukan theology. First, for the "Israelites" to crucify and kill Jesus, God had to "hand over" Jesus to them according to God's "definite plan and foreknowledge" (vv. 22-23). This Lukan theme of God's providential plan is signaled throughout the two volumes by the Greek word *dei*, usually translated as "must" or "is necessary." But in this passage, Peter is presented as naming this providential plan in explicit terms. The death of Christ is part of God's plan as a whole (that is, it was not a surprise to God or a defeat of God's salvific goals in Christ), but God did not cause Jesus' death. Peter says to the crowd, "*You* killed him." God is, however, directly active in the resurrection that overcomes human power to bring about death.

> God is directly active in the resurrection that overcomes human power to bring about death.

(Note: preachers must be careful in highlighting this element of Lukan theology not to present Luke as anti-Semitic. Luke is making a theological claim about God's knowledge and action. He is not condemning all Jews as Jesus-killers.)

Second, Luke is intentional about redefining messiahship in terms of resurrection by drawing on a contrast between David who died and stayed dead on the one hand and Jesus who was raised and exalted on the other. This theme actually continues through verse 36. At stake is countering the popular understanding of the Messiah as one who would redeem and rule over Israel with a theology of Jesus' exaltation to God's right hand—that is, Christ's heavenly rule over all creation.

ACTS 2:42-47 (LFM)

While the RCL and BCP choose an Acts text drawn from Peter's sermon at Pentecost, the LFM chooses to focus on the *results* of Peter's Pentecost sermon. Specifically, this text follows the baptism of the three thousand and describes the formation of the first Christian community in Jerusalem. It is an idealistic view—Luke holds up an ideal toward which the church should continue to strive. There is concern for the apostolic teaching and wonder-working, regular fellowship (including the breaking of bread, which may or may not refer to the Lord's Supper), prayer, a just use of economic resources, and evangelism. This short passage includes a whole seminary course on ecclesiology. (For more notes on this text, see my comments on the first reading for Easter 4.)

GENESIS 8:6-16; 9:8-16 (BCP)

The BCP offers excerpts from the Noah cycle as an alternative to the reading from Acts 2. The Genesis passages come from the end of the cycle, telling of the receding of the flood and of God establishing a new covenant with humanity. The story of the flood is one of judgment and re-creation. This cosmic "do-over" is a fitting narrative to accompany the theme of resurrection from the New Testament lections. Indeed, the early church used the flood imagery in association with baptism as resurrection to new life as is seen in the RCL epistle lesson for Easter 6, 1 Peter 3:13-22.

RESPONSIVE READING
PSALM 16 (RCL)

Psalm 16 is an individual's prayer expressing confidence in God in the face of distress. It is an appropriate prayer for Eastertide in that the psalmist claims God has rescued him from Sheol or the Pit, the abode of the dead. Evidently the one praying has experienced some near-death crisis and believes God kept him alive. This language resonates with the themes of resurrection of Eastertide.

PSALM 111 (BCP)

This is an acrostic (alphabetical) hymn of praise focusing primarily on God's powerful and providential works. This emphasis on divine works is a helpful lens through which to view resurrection. However, the psalm is chosen as much for its tone as its content. The grand expressions of praise are fitting for a season filled with Alleluias.

PSALM 118:19-24 (BCP ALT.)
PSALM 118:2-4, 13-15, 22-24 (LFM)

See the comments on the responsive reading for Easter Day, above.

SECOND READING
1 PETER 1:3-9 (RCL, BCP, LFM)

As is the case with other ancient letters found in the New Testament, 1 Peter opens with a salutation (1:1-2) that names the sender and the recipient. The sender is pseudonymously named as the apostle Peter. The recipients are named in reference to five regions of Asia Minor in the western half of the peninsula between the Mediterranean and Black Seas. This area is part of modern Turkey. More importantly, the author refers to the recipients as exiles of the Diaspora. This is a striking metaphor. In ancient use, "Diaspora" usually referred to ancient Jews living outside of their homeland of Judea. The origin of the Jews being dispersed was the Babylonian exile and continued through centuries of Palestine being subdued and ruled by the likes of Alexander the Great, the Seleucids, and the Romans. The author of 1 Peter transfers this label to the Gentile churches of Asia Minor. As becomes

> Obedience to Christ is a major theme of 1 Peter, specifically obedient suffering for the sake of the gospel.

clear later in the letter, these Gentile Christians are experiencing persecution in the form of social ostracism. Even though they have not moved geographically, their conversion to Christianity has turned them into resident aliens in their own homeland. (For more on exiles, see my comments on Isa. 43:1-12 on Easter 3.)

But this name of exiles is not the final word. In spite of their status in culture, the true or real status of their existence is determined by God. Society has rejected them, but God has chosen them, the Spirit has sanctified them, and the blood of Christ has been sprinkled upon them. The end result is obedience to Christ. This obedience is a major theme of 1 Peter, specifically obedient suffering for the sake of the gospel.

Following the salutation, most New Testament letters include a prayer of thanksgiving for the recipients. Instead, 1 Peter offers a doxological blessing celebrating God's gift of new birth. While the lection for today is 1:3-9, the actual blessing extends to verse 12. In fact, in Greek the blessing (vv. 3-12) can be construed as one convoluted, run-on sentence—a stylistic element found throughout 1 Peter. So the choice of verses 3-9 represents a sentence fragment. But contemporary translations break the Greek sentence into multiple English sentences. Indeed, the NRSV constructs six sentences (divided into two paragraphs!) out of the one-sentence blessing. This is a sentence that grammar students could spend a semester trying to diagram. This is a sentence of which Karl Barth could be proud. This is a sentence that easily equals two paragraphs or more.

Indeed, so much is here that a preacher will not be able to do the content justice in one sermon. Each clause works like a tangent that flows out from a word or concept from the previous clause. The sentence opens with praise of God. The next clause begins with God as the one who gives new birth to "you" (the letter's recipients). The next clause begins with the recipients as the subject of God's protection. And so forth and so on.

But taking a step back from the complex (and confusing) grammatical structure, there is a more easily determined rhetorical structure of the sentence that can help determine a homiletical focus. It is a sandwich structure.

- The opening clauses—*first piece of bread*—celebrate God's salvation. It is a realized and eschatological new birth wrought through the resurrection of Christ (vv. 3-5).
- The next few clauses—*the meat of the sandwich*—deals with the suffering of the recipients, suffering that is characterized as a testing of faith that is rewarded with salvation (vv. 6-9).
- The remaining clauses—*the final slice of bread*—return to discuss this salvation, specifically stating that the prophets of old were inspired by the spirit of Christ to speak of it (vv. 10-12).

Such structures are meant to lead readers to interpret the outer parts in relation to inner and vice versa. The use of this structure at the beginning of the letter reveals a major emphasis that runs throughout 1 Peter, one that is important to address at the beginning of a series of sermons on 1 Peter. It is perhaps the primary purpose for writing the letter. This claim is that the recipients' current suffering is given meaning by its relation to the salvation foretold in the past, experienced in the present, and brought to completion in the future. Their suffering for the faith does not raise questions about God's justice (theodicy) for 1 Peter. Indeed, the author assumes that suffering should be expected as part and parcel of salvation itself.

This is an interesting theology to struggle with in a North American context where freedom of religion is a paramount value so that few of us experience socioeconomic persecution because of our faith. Indeed, another paramount value—the right to pursue happiness—would make any of us question why we would want to embrace suffering as a *good*. As already mentioned, the kind of suffering described in 1 Peter is some level of social ostracism. Gentile Christians who once fit into society are presumably being pushed to the social, economic, and political margins. To claim this is part of salvation is an odd claim at best. A prominent aspect of the gospel preached today concerns overcoming the marginalization of racial-ethnic, gender, age, political, religious minorities.

> The recipients' current suffering is given meaning by its relation to the salvation foretold in the past, experienced in the present, and brought to completion in the future.

Indeed, even for those of us in the center of society, liberation and social gospel approaches to Christianity call us to be in solidarity with those who experience exile *in order that* we can hear their voices and help them be heard in the center, validate and learn from their experience, and widen our circle to include all who have been oppressed. There is plenty of justification for this orientation in the canon, but 1 Peter's message is different. It raises the question: If Christianity is not being marginalized, is it really experiencing/living out the fullness of God's salvation?

ACTS 2:14A, 22-32 (BCP ALT.)

See the comments on the first reading, above.

THE GOSPEL
JOHN 20:19-31 (RCL, BCP, LFM)

Today's reading from John is the Gospel lection for all three years of the lectionary cycle. This is due to the fact that the story is John's version of the gift of the Holy Spirit. Telling John's version of the reception of the Spirit at the beginning of the season justifies reading stories of the post-Pentecost church in Acts before the Feast of Pentecost is actually celebrated.

But there is more to this reading than that element alone. The lection is actually two closely related but nevertheless distinct pericopae followed by a Johannine summary. The first passage (vv. 19-23) tells of Jesus appearing to the group of disciples on Easter evening, breathing on them the Holy Spirit, and authorizing them to forgive sins. The second (vv. 24-29) flows out of the first in that the reason for telling it is that Thomas was missing from the first group and "doubts" what the disciples claim to have seen. The summary (vv. 30–31) may have been the original ending to the Gospel (that is, before chapter 21 was added) and names the purpose for the Gospel narrative as a whole as creating faith so that readers may have life. We will discuss the first two pericopae as possessing different homiletical possibilities.

Frankly, most preachers are attracted to the Thomas story more than the scene in verses 19-23. But the first scene holds some important theological claims to consider from the pulpit. First, Jesus' act of breathing the Spirit on the disciples clearly recalls God's breathing life into creatures at the beginning of the world (Gen. 2:7). Easter tells us that we are recreated through Christ's resurrection. Thus resurrection is not a past (*sui generis*) event so much as it is a current (continual) experience of new life in Christ available to all (a claim echoed in the summary mentioned above).

> Resurrection is not a past event so much as it is a current (continual) experience of new life in Christ available to all.

Second, John presents the gift of the Spirit as empowering or authorizing the disciples to forgive or not to forgive sins. This claim, of course, has been the focus of much ecclesiastical debate concerning the authority of and need for clergy to offer absolution to the laity. Apart from that specific issue, however, this text clearly indicates that those who have experienced Christ's resurrection and thus the gift of the Spirit (that is, the church) have a responsibility for the salvation of others. We cannot keep the Spirit to ourselves. We are gifted with it for the sake of others. God gives the church the spiritual gift of resurrection life *so that* the church will bring it to bear on the world.

Turning to the second pericope, Thomas often gets a bad rap by preachers. Indeed, calling him "doubting" Thomas is really an unfair characterization. Thomas does not doubt the disciples' assertions about Jesus in the manner that a scientific skeptic debates the historical veracity of Genesis 1. He is saying, "To believe as you believe, I need to have the same experience of the risen Jesus you had. I need to have the Spirit breathed into me. I need to *see* what you *saw*." (Consider how strongly

> God gives the church the spiritual gift of resurrection life so that the church will bring it to bear on the world.

seeing is connected to *believing* in John's version of the Easter narrative before the Thomas story: vv. 1, 5-8, 12, 14, 18, 20; see the commentary on John 20:1-9 on Easter Day, above.) And, in fact, Thomas does experience and see what the disciples experienced and saw. John presents Thomas's experience in a structure parallel to theirs:

Jesus appeared to the disciples behind a locked door (v. 19)	Jesus appeared to Thomas behind a locked door (v. 26)
Jesus said, "Peace be with you." (vv. 19, 21)	Jesus said, "Peace be with you." (v. 26)
Jesus showed his wounds (v. 20)	Jesus showed his wounds (v. 27)
The disciples responded with joy (v. 20)	Thomas responded with faith (v. 28)

So Thomas was not asking for anything that was not a basis for the other disciples' claim.

But the story does not end with the account of parallel experiences of the risen Christ. In verse 29, Jesus gets to deliver the punch line: "Have you believed because you have seen me? Blessed are those who have not seen and yet have come to believe." To read the question as a criticism of Thomas is too strong. It simply names what brought Thomas to faith—sight. But the emphasis is on the next sentence. This blessing is an affirmation of John's readers, of the later church, of us. This is John's way of praising those who have different (distant) experiences of the risen Christ and yet still have faith beyond the time of seeing Jesus in any literal fashion.

THIRD SUNDAY OF EASTER

APRIL 6, 2008

Revised Common (RCL)	Episcopal (BCP)	Roman Catholic (LFM)
Acts 2:14a, 36-41	Acts 2:14a, 36-47 or Isa. 43:1-12	Acts 2:14, 22-33
Ps. 116:1-4, 12-19	Psalm 116 or 116:10-17	Ps. 16:1-2a, 5, 7-8, 9-10, 11
1 Peter 1:17-23	1 Peter 1:17-23 or Acts 2:14a, 36-47	1 Peter 1:17-21
Luke 24:13-35	Luke 24:13-35	Luke 24:13-35

FIRST READING

ACTS 2:14A, 36-41 (RCL)
ACTS 2:14A, 36-47 (BCP)

On Easter 2 the reading from Acts was drawn from the core of Peter's Pentecost sermon. This week the reading starts with the conclusion to that sermon and then focuses on the crowd's response to the sermon. (See the comments on the first readings for Easter 2 and 4 for a discussion of verses 42-47).

This reading, of course, is often cited as the birth of the church. The conversion of three thousand and the beginnings of a new community gathered around the apostolic teaching and breaking of bread (word and table) certainly signals a new movement in Luke's schema of salvation history. Liturgically, however, we celebrate that moment on Pentecost in connection with the gift of the Spirit to those praying in the upper room.

Thus, for Easter 3, preachers would best serve this text read in this liturgical context by examining what it says about baptism. If baptism and confirmations occurred at the Easter Vigil or on Easter Day, it may seem odd to preach about baptism two weeks later. Yet this is exactly what the ancient tradition of mystagogical preaching did—interpret the Christian "mysteries" (that is, sacraments) to those who had just been initiated into the faith. For all the preparation leading up to these rituals of Christian initiation, congregations (and specifically the recently initiated) can hear a word about baptism differently in the wake of the

25

rippling waters of baptism than they could in the time of preparing for entering the waters. So one sound exegetical, homiletical, and liturgical approach to this text is to explore how Luke interprets baptism. There are a number of motifs that can be explored if one wishes to offer a teaching sermon.

First, repentance and baptism are linked for Luke (v. 38). Peter requires both when the crowd asks what they should do in response to his sermon.

Second, for Luke baptism is to be performed in the name of Jesus Christ (v. 38). Liturgically speaking, Matthew 28:19 won the day, and baptism using the trinitarian formula became the norm. But baptism in Jesus' name here is likely more than just a reflection of liturgical practice in Luke's community (although it is certainly that as well). It names *who* the baptizand follows. This is not the same as Paul's metaphor of (mystical?) participation in Christ's death and resurrection in baptism, but there is something similar in that one who is baptized in Jesus Christ's name becomes a part of the community of Christ's followers (v. 42). So baptism is initiation into the name of Christ.

Third, the purposes of baptism are twofold: the forgiveness of sins and the gift of the Holy Spirit. The relation of cleansing from sins to baptism has been hotly debated throughout church history, with interpretations ranging from the idea that baptism works *ex opere operato* to it being an ordained signifier of God's grace experienced elsewhere. The church has also debated and developed various rituals related to the question concerning how the Holy Spirit is active in baptism. Is water baptism and baptism of the Holy Spirit the same or two different things? What role does confirmation play in the gift of the Spirit? Indeed, even Luke confuses (perhaps intentionally?) the issues. In this passage and others it seems clear that water baptism results in the gift of the Spirit. But in the story of the conversion of Cornelius (read on Easter Day), water baptism is performed in *response* to the gift of the Spirit (10:44-48).

> Baptism in Jesus' name here is likely more than just a reflection of liturgical practice in Luke's community. It names who the baptizand follows.

One would not be far off the mark to claim that Acts 2:36-41 raises more questions about baptism than it settles. A sound doctrinal sermon would use this text to name some of the key issues and then move to how the particular theological tradition/denomination of the congregation has dealt with them.

ACTS 2:14, 22-33 (LFM)

See the comments on the first reading for Easter 2, above.

The Book of Common Prayer offers this Isaiah text as an alternative to the Acts reading. It is a poor division of the material in Isaiah 43 but is an appropriate passage for Eastertide. Deutero-Isaiah casts a vision of redemption from the exile at the hands of Cyrus by drawing on imagery from creation and the exodus and the gathering of God's dispersed people. They are images of redemption from oppression, powerlessness, and death. Moreover, similar to the flow of the sermonic material in Acts, the prophet declares that those redeemed are to be God's witnesses. In this case the testimony is that there is no other God, no other savior, than the One who saves the people from exile.

This lection relates well to 1 Peter in lifting up a view of those exiled in the world. Indeed, there are a number of theologians who find the biblical understanding of exile to be an important metaphor for many people in today's world. This understanding has much to say to the church in a post-Christian society. Perhaps more profoundly it can be applied to those in our society who are not considered full citizens, even by the post-Christian church. These may be women, persons of color, gays and lesbians, the elderly, the ill, and the poor. In early twenty-first-century North America, the best analogy may be between exiles and immigrants who come to the United States from the South or the East looking for a better life only to be resented for hoping our land is the promised land. These resident aliens have crosses burned in their yards and are told, "Maybe in my country, but not in my neighborhood." Isaiah of the exile calls Easter people to witness to God's redemption for exiles by practicing divine hospitality in which all God's people are gathered from the north, south, east, and west.

> Isaiah of the exile calls Easter people to witness to God's redemption for exiles by practicing divine hospitality in which all God's people are gathered from the north, south, east, and west.

RESPONSIVE READING
PSALM 116:1-4, 12-19 (RCL)
PSALM 116 OR 116:10-17 (BCP)

Psalm 116 is a hymn of thanksgiving for divine help in a time of need. It is unclear just what the character of the distress is, but the psalmist describes it in terms of being at the point of death. This claim is perhaps to be taken literally, but it may well simply be a powerful metaphor expressing both the depths of the pain or trouble the one praying has experienced and the greatness of God's salvific and providential care. Either way, it is a wonderful psalm for the season of Easter, for it allows all of us to claim resurrection not only as a past event but as a present and future reality we experience through God's grace.

PSALM 16:1-2A, 5, 7-8, 9-10, 11 (LFM)

See the comments on the responsive reading for Easter 2, above.

SECOND READING
1 PETER 1:17-23 (RCL, BCP)
1 PETER 1:17-21 (LFM)

Last week's lection (see the comments from Easter 2) from 1 Peter was a portion (1:3-9) of the doxological blessing (1:3-12) that follows the salutation at the opening of the letter. This blessing praises God for the gift of salvation, the new birth that comes through Christ's resurrection, and gives the recipients the strength to endure their current persecution.

A new section—the body of the letter—begins at verse 13. The tone shifts from the indicative to the imperative, from worship of God to exhortation of the church. But the two sections are not unrelated. The first word of verse 13 is "therefore" (Greek, *dio*). The tone shifts, but the imperative grows out of the indicative, the exhortation grows out of the worship. As the opening blessing theologically justifies suffering as part and parcel of God's salvation through Jesus Christ, so the exhortation is a call to live out one's salvation with obedience in a time of suffering.

The opening section of the body of the letter is composed of 1:13—2:10. If one is preaching through the 1 Peter lections in sequence, it is important to note that the lectionary gets out of sequence at this point. Next week's lection is 2:19/20b-25, chosen to connect with the themes of Good Shepherd Sunday, and then on Easter 5 the lectionaries return to 2:1-10, or some segment of these verses.

To complicate matters further, the NRSV obscures the structure of 1:13—2:10 by translating Greek participles as imperatives (for instance, prepare your minds, discipline yourselves, v. 13). This translation is not inappropriate; it simply clouds what the Greek establishes as primary (the actual imperatives) and secondary (the participial phrases). A more wooden translation of verse 13, which opens the section, illustrates the issue: "Therefore, girding up the loins of your mind [and] being self-controlled, set your hope totally in the grace being brought to you in the revelation of Jesus Christ." So "prepare your minds" and "discipline yourselves" in the NRSV should actually be understood as subordinate aspects of hoping.

All of this is to say that the structure of 1:13—2:10 is shaped by five Greek imperatives that do not stand out in the English, since the NRSV consistently translates participles in this section as imperatives. They are the commands:

- to hope (1:13),
- to be holy (1:14-21),
- to love one another (1:22-25),
- to long for spiritual milk (2:1-3),
- and to be built into a spiritual house (2:4-10).

This means that the three lectionaries under consideration at best choose to look at only part of one subsection (1:17-21, LFM) and at worst, two parts of two subsections (1:17-23, RCL, BCP). For the sake of preaching, I will focus on the imperative to be holy that shapes 1:14-21.

Similar to what we found with last week's lection from 1 Peter, 1:14-21 is composed of only two lengthy sentences with multiple clauses that the NRSV breaks into six sentences. The first Greek sentence takes up verses 14-16 and is the primary call to be holy. The second sentence (vv. 17-21) interprets broadly how this holiness is to be lived out in the midst of the recipients' experience of exile.

> For 1 Peter, we are not simply to be good, we are to be holy.

In the first sentence, the imperative to be holy is based primarily on a contrast between the recipients' pre- and post-baptismal existence. One who becomes Christian will not simply go about conducting their lives in the same way they did before they were Christian. Just adding worship and a little devotional reading to what everyone else does is not enough. Remember that for 1 Peter, salvation is new birth (1:3); it is not just an addendum to one's status quo. One becomes a new person through a new orientation. There are many voices out there— political, social, philosophical, economic, relational—telling us what it means to be a good person. Some of these are positive and others are not, but none of them are enough. For 1 Peter, we are not simply to be good, we are *to be holy*. This idea is extended later in the command to be built into a spiritual house and a holy priesthood. To be holy, sanctified, is to be set apart. To be set apart implies a *from* and a *for*. First Peter views the *from* in terms of the Gentile recipients' earlier form of existence, which is still lived out by the rest of society. To become holy, therefore, is to enter willingly into exile. The *for* is, simply put, God, the One who is Wholly Other. To

> Holiness is a way of being, God's way of being. The character of Christian holiness is found in God's holiness.

be holy is not some personal spiritual practice that we "take time" for, as the old hymn says. Holiness is a way of being, God's way of being. The character of

Christian holiness is found in God's holiness. This is certainly not a call to become gods, but to become godly in the deepest sense of that term. As God is Wholly Other, Christians are to be other than we were before we were Christian, other than the rest of the world.

Lest we interpret such being set apart as a call for monastic existence, we should be clear that there is a difference between exile and isolation. In verses 17-21, it is clear 1 Peter calls his audience to be holy *in the midst* of social existence. They are to live out the fear of God, a First Testament metaphor for a life of faith and awe before God, in the middle of the everyday-ness of life. Having been ransomed from the perishable inheritance of their society, they are to live out in this society the imperishable, undefiled, and unfading inheritance God has ransomed them into through Jesus Christ (cf. 1:4). Indeed, this inheritance is trustworthy, because God has raised and exalted Jesus Christ.

First Peter's exhortation to a holy exile is a hard word for the North American church to hear today. But it is a word we need to hear as we move further and further into a post-Christendom age. As noted in the comments on Isaiah 43:1-12 above, a number of scholars who have affinity for the postliberal school of thought—for instance, Stanley Hauerwas, Walter Brueggemann, William Willimon—claim exile as an important metaphor for the church's calling in today's world. Closely identifying with the center of society as occurred in the modern church only leads to a distortion of its message and practices. The post-modern church must reclaim its unique identity (that is, holiness) over against the greater culture.

> They are to live out the fear of God, a First Testament metaphor for a life of faith and awe before God, in the middle of the everyday-ness of life.

ACTS 2:14A, 36-47 (BCP ALT.)

See the comments on the first reading, above.

THE GOSPEL
LUKE 24:13-35 (RCL, BCP, LFM)

See the comments on the Gospel for Easter Evening, above.

FOURTH SUNDAY OF EASTER

APRIL 13, 2008

Revised Common (RCL)	Episcopal (BCP)	Roman Catholic (LFM)
Acts 2:42-47	Acts 6:1-9; 7:2a, 51-60 or Neh. 9:6-15	Acts 2:14a, 36-41
Psalm 23	Psalm 23	Ps. 23:1-3a, 3b-4, 5, 6
1 Peter 2:19-25	1 Peter 2:19-25 or Acts 6:1-9; 7:2a, 51-60	1 Peter 2:20b-25
John 10:1-10	John 10: 1-10	John 10:1-10

FIRST READING
ACTS 2:42-47 (RCL)

Acts 2:42-47 continues last week's lection from Acts in the RCL (and it was the lection for the LFM on Easter 2 and part of the Easter 3 lection in the BCP). While it is intimately connected with the response to Peter's Pentecost sermon depicted in 2:36-41, it is not inappropriate to separate it into a separate lection. Verses 36-41 detail the immediate response to Peter's proclamation of the gospel and verses 42-47 describe the ongoing, sustained response.

The opening verse (v. 42) is unpacked in those that follow and is almost a ready-made four-point sermon concerning piety in Christian community: study, fellowship, breaking of bread, and prayer.

The ideal in the passage that receives most comment involves verses 44-45. This view of selling one's possessions and the church distributing the proceeds to those in need fits with Luke's dealings with possessions in his Gospel. Jesus often draws a contrast between being rich and being a disciple (see, for example, the blessings and the woes, 6:20-26; the parable of the rich man and Lazarus, 16:19-31; or the rich ruler whom Jesus instructs to sell all he has, distribute the proceeds to the poor, and come follow him, 18:18-25). In Acts this theme is not highlighted with the same repeated vigor—at times the author seems to want to counter views that Christianity was only for the poor and uneducated (for instance, by pointing out that Lydia was a dealer of expensive purple cloth, 16:14). By narrating this theme at the beginning of the narrative and the point of the formation of the community, however, Luke makes it clear it is as much his vision for the church as it was his "memory" of the movement surrounding Jesus.

ACTS 6:1-9; 7:2A, 51-60 (BCP)

The BCP has selected portions of the lengthy scene in Acts dealing with the choosing of the Seven and the martyrdom of Stephen (one of the Seven). The way the text is divided is not ideal, but in all fairness this is a lengthy piece that is difficult to pare down. The opening verses (6:1-8) introduce the Seven who maintain the community by overseeing the ethic of communal possessions and distribution to the needy. They also introduce Stephen and the conflict surrounding him. In 6:9-15, the false accusations against Stephen are spelled out. 7:1 is where the high priest turns to Stephen to give him a chance to respond to the accusations. Stephen's lengthy speech (7:2-53) does not respond to the accusers directly but instead recounts the salvation history of Israel through the lens of Lukan theology. This salvation history is presented to show how Jesus is the fulfillment of the whole of Scripture. Scholars have especially attended to the way Luke presents Jesus as a prophet like Moses (v. 37) and Jesus' followers (including Stephen) as prophets like Jesus. The last section of the lection (7:51-53) closes out the salvation history and picks up where Stephen turns the accusation back on his accusers. This counteraccusation, however, makes little sense when read without any description of Stephen's sermon. The culmination of the scene is the stoning of Stephen as the first Christian martyr (vv. 54-60).

Stephen's faithful death serves as a reminder in Eastertide that the resurrection is not a happy-ever-after ending to the story of Jesus. It is a once-upon-a-time ending to Jesus' ministry and beginning of the church's ministry. As Jesus suffered and died, so will the church (if it is faithful to Jesus' prophetic mission). But as Jesus was raised from the dead and the church was called into being to continue his work, as each generation of the church passes another generation of prophets will be raised up to continue its work.

> Stephen's faithful death serves as a reminder in Eastertide that the resurrection is not a happy-ever-after ending to the story of Jesus.

ACTS 2:14A, 36-41 (LFM)

See the comments on the first reading for Easter 2.

The BCP offers a reading from Nehemiah as an alternative to the Acts lection just discussed. The lection from Nehemiah is part of a covenant ceremony detailed in chapters 8–10. Ezra gathers the people to hear the law read, celebrate the feast of booths, confess their apostasy, and recommit themselves in service to God.

The choice of this passage is intriguing. Instead of lifting up themes related to Good Shepherd Sunday, the text resonates with the part of Stephen's speech that is omitted in the above lection. The opening of Ezra's prayer of confession is today's lection. It rehearses salvation history, highlighting the covenant with Abraham and the exodus. Omitted from the lection is the rest of the prayer, which focuses on the people's apostasy as a response to God's faithfulness. Indeed, at the beginning of the omitted section Ezra names their ancestors as stiff-necked, a term Stephen used at the end of his speech, which is included in the above lection.

RESPONSIVE READING

PSALM 23 (RCL, BCP)
PSALM 23:1-3A, 3B-4, 5, 6 (LFM)

Psalm 23 is the psalter reading every year for the Fourth Sunday of Easter, Good Shepherd Sunday. Although the lectionary is not set up to encourage preaching on the psalter, one should preach the psalms occasionally. And there is no better occasion than Psalm 23 in the middle of the Great Fifty Days. This psalm is almost exclusively associated with funerals in our society, because of the traditional translation of verse 4 of walking "through the valley of the shadow of death." Given its association with rituals surrounding death, Psalm 23 can offer a powerful message in the midst of the season celebrating new life. Speaking of the valley of the shadow of death (or simply "the darkest valley") while basking in the light of the empty tomb offers much homiletical potential.

The psalm is chosen for this Sunday because of the imagery of God as shepherd employed in the first four verses. In verses 5-6, the metaphor shifts to one of God as host. But while the metaphors are mixed (and the voice changes from speaking about God in the third person to speaking to God in the second person), the theological worldview is consistent throughout the psalm. This hymn of trust proclaims divine providence. The basis of trust is set up in the first verse: if God is my shepherd,

> The basis of trust is set up in the first verse: if God is my shepherd, then I have no unmet need as God's sheep.

then I have no unmet need as God's sheep. God will provide for the basic necessities of life: food (vv. 2a, 5a), drink (vv. 2b, 5c), shelter (v. 6), and protection from danger (vv. 4, 5a).

But one must be careful not to interpret this to say that God provides for a carefree life. Even while the psalm proclaims God as a trustworthy provider and protector, it also names that this providential care does not preclude hardship in the form of dark valleys and enemies. The metaphors of providing and protecting are primarily ways of affirming God's providential presence in times good and bad. At the center of the psalm are the words, "for you are with me." This should be the center of the sermon as well.

RESPONSIVE READING

1 PETER 2:19-25 (RCL, BCP)
1 PETER 2:20B-25 (LFM)

The lectionaries make an odd epistle choice for this week. Because it is Good Shepherd Sunday, they have skipped ahead in chapter 2 to a passage that includes shepherd imagery in verse 25: "For you were going astray like sheep, but now you have returned to the shepherd and guardian of your souls." Next week, the lectionaries move backward to the beginning of the chapter (see the comments on the second reading for Easter 5), thus breaking the semicontinuous pattern and its potential for preaching through the letter in an unbroken *lectio continua* manner. Moreover, and more troubling, to make today's passage palatable, they lop off the opening line (v. 18), which names who is being addressed in this paragraph.

We must be careful not to confuse slavery during the Roman Empire with images of slavery in pre–Civil-War America.

The author is speaking to house slaves (*oiketai* instead of *douloi*, the more general Greek term for slaves), and offers instructions concerning their behavior toward their masters. Without the opening verse, the offense is removed. But this invites congregations to hear the passage out of its literary and historical context. Moreover, the offense is exactly where any exegetically sound sermon on this passage will begin. Thus our comments begin with slavery.

This passage is part of 1 Peter's household code. Household codes were common in ancient literature. They offered moral exhortation to different members of the household—parents, spouses, children, and, yes, slaves. New Testament writers picked up this convention and used it to offer moral exhortation to (1) Christian members of households and (2) house churches. First Peter's household code found in 2:13—3:12 addresses the relation to governing authorities (2:13-17), domestic slaves (2:18-25), and spouses (wives are exhorted in six verses and husbands in only one, 3:1-7), and closes with a word to all (3:8-12).

Biblical scholars are quick to remind modern readers that we must be careful not to confuse slavery during the Roman Empire with images of slavery in pre–Civil-War America. The slave industry was quite different in the ancient world. It was not at all based on race. One could be born into slavery, enter into slavery to satisfy a debt, or become a slave through military defeat. Slaves were often well educated and served as tutors of their master's children or managers of their master's business affairs. But in distinguishing ancient slavery from the slavery of African Americans, we must not go overboard in painting a rosy picture. Slaves were property back then just like they were in the eighteenth and nineteenth centuries. And as property they could be treated in any manner the master desired. Abuse and dehumanization was certainly a common element of the slave's experience.

First Peter acknowledges these circumstances in 2:18-25. The letter, like the other New Testament writers who mention slavery, however, fails to condemn slavery itself. Nowhere does the author address masters, calling on them to free their slaves or even just to treat them well. The author instead addresses household slaves and instructs them to accept the authority of their masters, whether they be fair or hard masters. They are willingly to accept their state of suffering. As offensive as this command sounds to our post–Civil-War ears and our liberation-theology-sensitive eyes (and it should!), we must recognize that the instruction is consistent with 1 Peter's view of the relation of suffering and salvation (see the comments on the second reading for Easter 2). The author is not calling upon the slaves to suffer as slaves. He is calling upon them to suffer as Christians, as all Christians are to suffer, as Jesus himself suffered as our model.

> The author is not calling upon the slaves to suffer as slaves. He is calling upon them to suffer as Christians, as all Christians are to suffer, as Jesus himself suffered as our model.

While the focus of the passage is clearly the willing suffering of house slaves as Christians, the theological climax is this christological foundation for such suffering (and all Christian suffering). Like any good preacher, the author quotes a hymn to close out his mini-sermon to the slaves. Verses 21-25 are considered by many scholars to be a piece of early Christian liturgy. In a manner that was conventional in the early church, the hymn interprets Christ's suffering through the lens of the suffering-servant tradition found in Isaiah, especially the opening verses of Isaiah 53.

How one preaches this text will be determined by a great extent to where one decides to locate the congregation in the text. Should they identify with the addressees, the house slaves? Or would this be too artificial? Should they identify with the implied masters? Should they identify with the author? This question of identity is difficult. How does today's church relate to this ancient scenario? While 1 Peter is discussing suffering as a Christian instead of suffering as a slave, and slavery was different in the ancient and modern worlds, the text still does not condemn slavery. Slavery is no longer a part of our society, but its residual effects are. Moreover, slavery has not disappeared from humanity altogether: sweatshops, prostitution, kidnapped soldiers. The best way to preach this text may be to name 1 Peter's perspective but then move beyond it in the name of the God who offers new life, who is at the center of 1 Peter's understanding of the gospel.

ACTS 6:1-9; 7:2A, 51-60 (BCP ALT.)

See the comments on the first reading, above.

THE GOSPEL

JOHN 10:1-10 (RCL, BCP, LFM)

Every year for Easter 4, Good Shepherd Sunday, the Gospel lection is taken from John 10. At first glance the chapter may seem like a convoluted mixture of shepherding metaphors. It might be more helpful to think of it as jazz improvisation—there is a common melody and rhythm all the musicians in the band share, but each one takes the melody and rhythm in different directions with her or his solos. At the core of the chapter is the claim that Jesus leads sheep who know his voice; but at different moments, John riffs on the melody in different ways.

Another thing to remember that will help readers get a handle on John 10:1-18 is that these verses are part of a larger literary unit beginning in 9:1. In chapter 9 Jesus heals a blind man and a controversy ensues. The narrative controversy likely plays out a real conflict in John's community: Christians are being cast out of the synagogue. After the man gains physical sight, he slowly comes to christological sight/insight. When he is first asked how he gained his sight, he tells his neighbors that "the man called Jesus" healed him (v. 11). Next, when the Pharisees ask him about what happened, he ends up declaring that Jesus is a prophet (v. 17).

> The imagery of the relation of the good shepherd and the sheep is meant to explain why some respond positively to Jesus and others do not.

When he is questioned by the religious authorities a second time, he is found claiming that Jesus is from God (v. 33). This results in his expulsion from the synagogue. When Jesus seeks him out after this, he finally worships Jesus as the Son of Man (vv. 35, 38).

But the story then turns with Jesus confronting the religious authorities and accusing them of being the ones who are actually blind (vv. 39, 41). The discourse in chapter 10 is part of this accusation against the religious authorities. Jesus is addressing them in 9:41, and 10:1 just keeps going. This is clear in 10:6-7: when the narrator speaks of "them," the reader is to assume it is still the religious authorities.

Thus the imagery of the relation of the good shepherd and the sheep is meant to explain why some respond positively to Jesus and others do not. Indeed, the authorities' inability to understand what Jesus is trying to say (v. 6) simply shows that they are not in the relationship being lifted up, for the sheep know the shepherd's voice. They claim to have religious knowledge (9:29), but are clearly not in the know. More importantly, however, as Jesus is the one who enters by the gate and calls the sheep by name, the religious leaders are the thieves in the figure of speech. They have gained their roles by illicit means and this is why the people are rejecting their leadership (as the sheep flee from voices they do not recognize).

One need not, of course, focus on this negative aspect to preach this text. Nor should one turn the sheep language into an exhortation to be faithful, meek followers (although this is not necessarily a bad message in and of itself). It is the positive relationship between Jesus and his followers that is to be affirmed. Specifically, the text invites a sermon that celebrates the revelation of Christ. We do not know Christ because we are bright or holy, but because God is gracious in revealing the Good Shepherd to us. Sheep do not initiate a relationship with the shepherd. The shepherd is in charge.

> We do not know Christ because we are bright or holy, but because God is gracious in revealing the Good Shepherd to us.

FIFTH SUNDAY OF EASTER

APRIL 20, 2008

Revised Common (RCL)	Episcopal (BCP)	Roman Catholic (LFM)
Acts 7:55-60	Acts 17:1-15 or Deut. 6:20-25	Acts 6:1-7
Ps. 31:1-5, 15-16	Ps. 66:1-11 or 66:1-8	Ps. 33:1-2, 4-5, 18-19
1 Peter 2:2-10	1 Peter 2:1-10 or Acts 17:1-15	1 Peter 2:4-9
John 14:1-14	John 14:1-14	John 14:1-12

FIRST READING

ACTS 17:1-15 (BCP)

Acts 17:1-15 is one of the few places where details in the Lukan narrative of Paul's ministry line up with those found in Paul's letters. There is a fair amount of overlap between this passage and details found in 1 Thessalonians concerning opposition to his gospel and his travel itinerary. If one is considering preaching on the semicontinuous series of texts from 1 Thessalonians at the end of the liturgical year (Propers 24–28), pausing over this passage in Acts now might leave hearers with a vague sliver of memory of Thessalonica.

The passage is not, however, filled with theological gems on which to preach. It is a small piece of a narrative quilt of Paul's itinerant ministry. The missionary journey as a whole is really the author's focus. But the passage is not without homiletical possibilities. It is a variation on a pattern found throughout the Pauline section of Acts: the apostle enters a new town, preaches at the local synagogue, finds some open to his message but many who resist, and then goes to Gentiles in the area. In this passage, Paul comes to Thessalonica, preaches in the synagogue, and persuades some Jews and some Gentile God-fearers. He is then run out of town by Jews who are against him and he finds a much more receptive audience among the Jews in nearby Beroea. However, when those opposed to him in Thessalonica hear of his success in Beroea, they follow him and cause trouble for him there as well.

There are two primary homiletical approaches to this passage: (1) By asking the congregation to identify with Paul, hearers are reminded that being faithful to one's calling and being assured of success are not synonymous. Responses to the gospel will always be mixed. Every time I step up into the pulpit I remember an older scholar telling me that unless someone is offended by what you say, you probably have not preached the gospel. (2) By asking the congregation to identify with those Paul was forced to leave behind, hearers are reminded that there is risk involved in being a Christian. When Paul left Thessalonica, those who had been hospitable to him and his message (Jason and some believers, vv. 5-9), were arrested, accused, and forced to post bail before being let go. Luke never returns to resolve the details of this scene, but the point is as clear as taking up your cross and following Jesus: being open to the gospel means we will at times be in opposition to the world or, better, that the world will sometimes be in opposition to us.

> Being open to the gospel means we will at times be in opposition to the world or, better, that the world will sometimes be in opposition to us.

ACTS 6:1-7 (LFM)
ACTS 7:55-60 (RCL)

See the comments on the first reading for Easter 4, above.

DEUTERONOMY 6:20-25 (BCP ALT.)

In Deuteronomy 6–8, Moses is presented as dealing with how the Israelites are to live out the covenant in the promised land. Today's lection, which the BCP offers as an alternative to reading Acts in the place of the First Testament during Easter, opens with a question concerning how to explain the rationale behind the ordinances Israel is to keep to future generations. The answer is simple: tell them the story of the exodus. But it is not that keeping the commandments is payback for God's deliverance. The commandments are part of the deliverance; they are salvation themselves. God *gave* them to Israel "for our lasting good, so as to keep us alive" (v. 24). In Christian pulpits, the "law" of the First Testament is too often incorrectly presented in legalistic terms. This text reminds us that the law is an example of God's grace.

RESPONSIVE READING
PSALM 31:1–5, 15–16 (RCL)

Psalm 31 is a prayer uttered by an individual in some form of distress described in terms of illness that is so horrific that enemies and friends alike scorn him or her. The portions of the psalm assigned by the RCL omit the detailed lament and focus only on the theme of prayer for deliverance from a trustworthy God.

PSALM 33:1–2, 4–5, 18–19 (LFM)

Psalm 33 is a hymn of praise. The opening verses (1–3) are a call to praise and the remaining verses offer the reasons God is to be praised—as the One who created the cosmos (vv. 4-9) and the One who reigns over creation (vv. 10-22).

PSALM 66:1–11 OR 66:1–8 (BCP)

This hymn of thanksgiving is offered as a response to the choice of Deut. 6:20-25 in the BCP. The opening verses from which the lection is drawn are a general call to praise and thanksgiving based on the exodus. The second half of the psalm (vv. 13-20) is presented as the prayer of an individual who has experienced God's goodness in his or her life. The message is clear: all individual blessings are to be understood in light of God's great act of salvation of liberation from slavery.

SECOND READING
1 PETER 2:2–10 (RCL)
1 PETER 2:1–10 (BCP)
1 PETER 2:4–9 (LFM)

Last week's reading from 1 Peter broke the semicontinuous pattern by jumping to the household code. This week the lection returns to an earlier section (1:13—2:10), which is shaped by five Greek imperatives:

- to hope (1:13),
- to be holy (1:14-21),
- to love one another (1:22-25),
- to long for spiritual milk (2:1-3),
- and to be built into a spiritual house (2:4-10).

As noted earlier (see the comments on the second reading for Easter 3), the NRSV translates many subordinate participles as imperatives, thus obscuring this structure. Today's reading includes the final two imperatives. The first exhortation (2:1-3) is one sentence in the Greek. The language of verse 1 sets up the focus in verse 2. A wooden translation highlights this focus:

> Then throwing off all wickedness,
>> and all deceit [dolon] and hypocrisy and envy and all slander,
> as newborn infants long for spiritual/rational, pure [adolon] milk,
>> so that by it you may grow into salvation if you tasted that the Lord
>> is good.

As noted in the discussion of our first reading from 1 Peter, the author views salvation as new birth (see the comments on the second reading for Easter 2). This metaphor (1:3, 23) refers to the difference between the Gentile recipients' pre- and post-baptismal existence. But this passage makes clear that birth is an appropriate metaphor in that it is not the end of salvation but the beginning of it. While new birth may mark a dramatic change from one's previous mode of existence, change is to continue as one grows in the faith and intentionally nurtures this growth.

> While new birth may mark a dramatic change from one's previous mode of existence, change is to continue as one grows in the faith and intentionally nurtures this growth.

In this instance, the author names the character of this growth in negative terms through the use of a vice list. Instead of listing virtues toward which the readers should aspire, he lists characteristics and behavior patterns that Christians should avoid. The verb translated above as "throwing off" is the term used for undressing, for casting away dirty clothes. This verb, added to the metaphor of new birth, has clear baptismal connotations. It was common in the early church for those being baptized to strip off their old clothes before entering the bath and to be clothed anew upon exiting the baptistery. This reclothing is symbolic not of something that has occurred in some completed fashion but something that has occurred eschatologically in baptism, and thus continues to occur (daily) throughout one's life as a baptized member of the Body of Christ. We must constantly strive in Christ to strip away those attitudes and actions that make us less than Christ calls us to be and has modeled for us. Preachers are not diminishing the good news of God's grace revealed in Jesus Christ by joining their voices with 1 Peter and calling our congregations to take stock of themselves and then do something about what they see there.

> We must constantly strive in Christ to strip away those attitudes and actions that make us less than Christ calls us to be and has modeled for us.

The message of the second exhortation in today's lection (2:4-10) is very similar to the first, except that it uses metaphors that speak to the community as a whole instead of to the individuals in the community. There is a mixture of corporate metaphors here that includes holy/royal priesthood, chosen race, holy nation, and God's own people. But the root metaphor of the passage is that the church should allow itself to be built (that is, allow God to build it) into a spiritual house made of living stones. This metaphor is central because it grows out of the use of First Testament cornerstone imagery (Isa. 28:16; Ps. 118:22; and Isa. 8:14) that was commonplace to interpret christologically. Indeed, Psalm 118 was offered as a choice for the psalter reading a number of times early in Eastertide. Christ is our living cornerstone, we are to be living stones built upon him into a spiritual house. (It is interesting that before 1 Peter begins to address individual members of the household in the household code of 2:13ff., a portion of which was read for Easter 4, that he first lifts up the idea of a spiritual house.)

As we have seen earlier, the call to be set apart, spiritual, holy uttered in both parts of this passage, is one of 1 Peter's primary themes (see the comments on the second reading for Easter 3). Christians, and certainly the church as a whole, should look and act differently than the rest of the world. This is what we have been saved for. This is what we have been saved into. This is salvation.

ACTS 17:1-15 (BCP ALT.)

See the comments on the first reading, above.

THE GOSPEL
JOHN 14:1-14 (RCL, BCP)
JOHN 14:1-12 (LFM)

It was common in ancient literature to close out a hero's life with a last testament. John 14–17 is Jesus' farewell discourse to his disciples. The first three chapters are the discourse proper and chapter 17 is Jesus' concluding prayer on their behalf. Each year the readings for Easter 5–6 are drawn from the discourse, and on Easter 7 the Gospel lection comes from the prayer.

> As Jesus offers final instructions to his disciples, John presents them as instructions to his postresurrection church.

As noted in the introduction to Easter, drawing on the Farewell Discourse may seem to be an odd practice for Easter. Chronologically it seems a better fit in Lent, before Jesus is crucified. Theologically, however, when John speaks of Jesus' departure he is speaking of Jesus' exaltation as well as passion. Moreover, as Jesus offers final instructions to his disciples, John presents them as instructions to his postresurrection church.

Today's lection is perhaps best known from funerals. Similar to Psalm 23 (see the comments on the responsive reading for Easter 4), this fact makes it an interesting text to preach during Easter. Instead of standing before a grave about to be filled, we stand outside a tomb that has been vacated. This radically different liturgical context offers a congregation a potentially different hearing of the passage and the language concerning many rooms in the Father's house.

Preaching on this text (and the Gospel lections for Easter 6 and 7) is difficult, however, because John's language and theology in the farewell discourse is dense and repetitive. The trouble is not finding something on which to preach, but selecting from the multiple possible directions the text invites one to follow. Instead of trying to preach the text as a whole, the preacher will do well to focus on one of the key Johannine themes referenced in the passage while keeping the context in mind to help interpret it. Some potential, interrelated Johannine themes that relate to current theological questions follow:

"In my Father's house there are many dwelling places." This theme is usually misread in terms of Jesus preparing space for his followers in heaven. But our contemporary concept of heaven as the abode of souls of believers was not shared by John. John's understanding of eternal life focuses on the present as much as the future. By "life" and "eternal life," John is less concerned with contemporary questions about what life after death is like and more concerned with the (existential) quality of life in relationship with Christ and one another. These relationships (and thus the quality of Christian existence) are determined by the intimate relationship of Jesus and God. In other words, Christology determines soteriology.

"No one comes to the Father except through me." Are only Christians saved? This has been a question of importance for Christian theology since the church's beginning as a movement within Judaism in the context of a multireligious Roman Empire. For many in the West the answer seemed as obvious as the dominance of Christendom from Constantine on. But in a postmodern world it is more difficult to hold on to an exclusivist understanding of salvation. Today, cultures and religions previously able to be demonized due to ignorance are better known through travel, television, education, and the Internet. Moreover, our next-door neighbors are more and more likely to be Jewish, Muslim, Hindu, or Buddhist than simply United Methodist, Lutheran, or Roman Catholic. Congregations want to hear their pastors' answer to this question. But be clear that what is at stake is not just *who* is saved, but *what* salvation actually is.

"Whoever has seen me has seen the Father." There are a number of Christologies in the New Testament and many variations have been proffered throughout

church history. Johannine language was the starting point for much of the trinitarian discussions that developed later in the church. This text invites readers to consider the proper understanding of who the historical Jesus of Nazareth was and who the Jesus Christ of faith is in relation to God. With Pentecost's emphasis on the Holy Spirit and Trinity Sunday just a few weeks away, preaching on this theme for this Sunday gives a congregation several opportunities to consider trinitarian issues.

SIXTH SUNDAY OF EASTER

APRIL 27, 2008

Revised Common (RCL)	Episcopal (BCP)	Roman Catholic (LFM)
Acts 17:22-31	Acts 17:22-31 or Isa. 41:17-20	Acts 8:5-8, 14-17
Ps. 66:8-20	Psalm 148 or 148:7-14	Ps. 66:1-3, 4-5, 6-7, 16, 20
1 Peter 3:13-22	1 Peter 3:8-18 or Acts 17:22-31	1 Peter 3:15-18
John 14:15-21	John 15:1-8	John 14:15-21

FIRST READING

ACTS 8:5-8, 14-17 (LFM)

At the beginning of Acts, Jesus declares that the disciples are to be his witnesses in Jerusalem, Judea, Samaria, and to the ends of the earth. However, it is only after the persecution that follows Stephen's martyrdom that the gospel is actually taken outside of Judea. Philip, one of the Seven along with Stephen, flees from persecution to Samaria where he preaches, exorcizes demons, heals the sick, converts and baptizes many. But for all his evangelistic success, he is unable to give them the Holy Spirit, for in Acts (or at least parts of Acts) this gift and responsibility is reserved for the apostles.

As Pentecost draws near, we should not be surprised to find lections raising issues related to the Holy Spirit. But in truth it is the part of the text that is omitted (vv. 9-13, 18-24) that best draws the passage's presentation of the Spirit into the spotlight. Simon the magician, who was considered great in Samaria, comes to believe, is baptized, and is amazed at Philip's wonder works. When he sees Peter and John laying hands on people with the result that they receive the Spirit, he attempts to buy the power to pass on the Spirit from the apostles.

Today people are constantly seeking spiritual experiences. Like Simon we attempt to buy, process, or manipulate the Spirit. The text affirms institutionalized approaches to passing on the Spirit, but absolutely rejects any idea that we can control the working of the Spirit. Such ideas call for repentance and humility.

ACTS 17:22-31 (RCL, BCP)

For the RCL, today's lection from Acts represents a great jump in the book of Acts. Last Sunday, the reading from Acts presented the stoning of Stephen with Saul approving. In today's reading, Saul has long since become Paul, persecutor has become missionary. But in the BCP, last week's lesson from Acts dealt with Paul being run off from Thessalonica and Beroea. He ran to Athens, where today's reading is set.

The reading is composed of Paul's speech at the Areopagus, so preachers will need to fill in the context by describing both the introduction and conclusion to the scene. But the focus should stay on the sermon and likely reflect on the strategy involved in the speech as much as the content. This scene, and especially the speech, is often regarded as one of Luke's most accomplished pieces of literature. He has moved from imitating the style of the Septuagint, the Greek translation of the First Testament, to using complex rhetorical strategies found in Hellenistic philosophical writing. For the sake of preaching, however, it is perhaps better to state this shift in terms of Luke's narrative and theology than in terms of socio-historical background.

Over and over again, readers of Acts have seen Paul, as well as those preachers in the narrative who precede him, do two things: (1) witness to the story of the Christ event, emphasizing the resurrection; and (2) base their interpretation of the Christ event in ancient Scripture. In this scene, Paul still witnesses to the resurrection (see 17:18), but because he is speaking to Gentiles, and philosophers in the center of philosophy at that, turning to the Scripture of the Jews will do him no good. It has no authority for this audience. Paul turns instead to religious practices/beliefs evident in the altars of the city (v. 23) and cites the philosophical tradition of his audience (v. 28).

> Paul still witnesses to the resurrection, but because he is speaking to Gentiles, turning to the Scripture of the Jews will do him no good. It has no authority for this audience.

This text has much to say to congregations struggling with what level of contemporary culture to welcome into church, especially worship. Paul identifies and analyzes the spiritual quest in his audience and attempts to proclaim how his understanding of God has addressed their situation. Instead of presenting salvation history as it is seen in the history of Israel, Paul names God the creator of all (that is, Jews and Gentiles) as the One they do not know but he does. Then he proceeds to the next step by claiming this creator of all humankind has appointed a day of judgment for all humankind through one person whom God appointed. Proof of this is found in the fact that God raised this person from the dead. (In the response to Paul's speech, the crowd does not debate the claim that they all have a common creator but that one was raised!) Some might claim that Paul has essentially changed the form of the message but kept the content the same. So the answer to how much of culture is to be invited into the church would be something like this: we should embrace cultural forms of communication (music, technology) only so long as the message is not altered. Others, however, will point out the dictum that form and function, medium and message, are not unrelated dimensions of communication. To change the form of a message is to change the message. Paul, in a real sense, does not preach the same gospel in this scene that he does elsewhere in Acts. By this reading, this scene would seem to justify attempts to adapt (and update) Christian theology to fit changing sociohistorical contexts.

> Paul claims this creator of all humankind has appointed a day of judgment for all humankind through one person whom God appointed.

To keep the use of this text balanced in relation to the question of the church and changing culture, it is important to remember that this is only one scene in the two-volume Luke-Acts. Luke is constantly concerned about showing the gospel relevance for various groups and individuals. However, the evangelist is also concerned with consistency, especially divine consistency. How do we hold on to this tension in the twenty-first-century church?

ISAIAH 41:17-20 (BCP ALT.)

Episcopal preachers have the option of reading from Isaiah instead of Acts. This beautiful passage comes from Second Isaiah—Isaiah of the exile. Thus when it opens with the words, "When the poor and needy seek water . . . I the LORD will answer them," it is not concerned with the poor and needy in general. The lection is part of a larger passage (41:11-20) in which God promises to accompany and protect the Jews who will return home through the wilderness from exile in Babylon. This text echoes themes of exile found in 1 Peter throughout the season of Easter.

RESPONSIVE READING
PSALM 148 OR 148:7-14 (BCP)

Psalm 148 is a hymn of praise. To be specific, it is a *call* to praise. In verses 1-6 the psalmist calls the heavens and those who reside there to praise their Creator. In verses 7-14 the psalmist calls the earth and its inhabitants (especially, all of Israel) to praise the God of power.

PSALM 66:8-20 (RCL)
PSALM 66:1-3, 4-5, 6-7, 16, 20 (LFM)

See the comments on the responsive reading for Easter 5.

Second Reading
1 PETER 3:8-18 (BCP)
1 PETER 3:13-22 (RCL)
1 PETER 3:15-18 (LFM)

All three lectionaries have chosen an epistle lesson from the same section of 1 Peter 3, but each has chosen different boundaries for the pericope, thus highlighting different aspects of 1 Peter's message in this part of the letter. Verses 8-12 are probably best understood as the closing to the household code (2:13—3:12; see the comments on the second reading for Easter 4)—a move from exhorting specific members of the household to a general exhortation for all in the household (in the church?). Verse 13 begins a new section. Thus the boundaries of the BCP are the least helpful. I will focus, therefore, on the RCL's division of the text since it begins at the opening of the new section and includes the whole of the LFM lesson.

While 3:13 clearly begins a new section, it does not introduce themes completely new to the letter. It returns to the issue of suffering. But now 1 Peter explicitly addresses the question of *unjust* suffering (vv. 13-17). But even with this added dimension, the author's perspective remains consistent. He does not turn to questions of theodicy, but simply assumes Christians are to suffer (see the comments on the second reading for Easter 2). Indeed, even unjust suffering is to be considered God's will (v. 17) in that suffering is part of living out God's gift of salvation.

> Even unjust suffering is to be considered God's will in that suffering is part of living out God's gift of salvation.

At other places in the epistle, the author bolsters the readers in their suffering by claiming that they are following the model of the suffering Christ (for instance, 2:21-24; see the comments on the second reading for Easter 4). This idea is certainly not absent from the christological material in verses 18-22, but it is not the primary point being made. The odd description of Jesus preaching to the spirits in prison certainly goes beyond a model for how we are to live out the Christian faith. This action is something we cannot emulate.

Moreover, this material is not something we fully understand in our modern context. The mythical imagery of a prison of spirits from the days of Noah to which Jesus proclaims the good news is foreign to us. We must be careful not to interpret anachronistically the reference through the lens of the creed in which

Jesus is said to have descended into hell between the crucifixion and resurrection. This creedal reference is clearly derivative of this passage and 4:6, but it is not clear that 1 Peter views this as happening in chronological relation to Jesus' death and exaltation.

Biblical scholars agree that verses 18-22 contain hymnic material, but disagree over how much of the material is traditional and how much comes from the author's pen. We need not be concerned with the details of this debate but should allow the author's use of traditional liturgical material to influence how we read the passage. Specifically, this material would likely have been familiar to the recipients. While we are confused about all that the mythical material imagines, the original readers would not have been.

The author is attempting to put the recipients' suffering in perspective by placing it in the context of the results of Jesus' suffering, using traditional material that they already claim as their own. Jesus suffered and died, the righteous for the unrighteous. This graceful act was so expansive that the unrighteous even included those of Noah's day, a generation that was so evil and sinful that God chose to destroy the earth by flood and start creation over again. Thus God's salvation wrought through Christ's suffering is much bigger than the immediate circumstances of the suffering the readers are experiencing. It is bigger than Asia Minor or the Roman Empire. It is cosmic. It even passes over the boundary between the living and the dead. Baptism is not only our reminder of this expansive suffering. It is through baptism that we participate in it.

> God's salvation wrought through Christ's suffering is much bigger than the immediate circumstances of the suffering the readers are experiencing.

ACTS 17:22-31 (BCP ALT.)

See the comments on the first reading, above.

THE GOSPEL
JOHN 14:15-21 (RCL, LFM)

The Gospel lection for the RCL and the LFM follows immediately after last week's lesson from John. However, there is a thematic shift between the two passages of the farewell discourse. Last week's lection (as the RCL delineated the text) ended with the promise,

"If in my name you ask me for anything,
I will do it" (14:14).

This week's passage opens (v. 15) with the same if-then structure, but the weight of responsibility has shifted from the speaker (Jesus) to the hearers (the disciples):

> "If you love me,
>   you will keep my commandments."

Promise gives way to exhortation. Yet behind the exhortation is another promise. The disciples will be able to keep Jesus' commandments *because* he will ask God to send the *Paraclete*, the Spirit of truth. While Jesus is telling his disciples that he is leaving them, he is promising that he will not leave them alone. He is both leaving them and coming to them (vv. 18-20).

This is a wonderful text on which to preach before Ascension, Pentecost, and Trinity Sunday. Its language resonates with themes that arise on these days—the departure of Jesus, the promise of the coming Spirit, how the Spirit functions, how the Spirit is related to the first two persons of the Trinity.

At the text's core is a double paradox. First is the theological tension between divine immanence and transcendence: Christ is both distant and silent on the one hand and present and comforting on the other. Once when I was a college chaplain, a nineteen-year-old student became very upset with me during a discussion group for claiming that God is often experienced as aloof. She argued that any such experience is caused by a lack of faith on our part. A year later our roles were switched. Her mother died and all she knew was a silent, inactive God, and I tried to affirm God's mysterious loving presence even in the midst of divine silence as a response to human suffering.

The second paradox is the tension between the text's abstract theology concerning divine transcendence and immanence and the explicit ethical exhortation to keep Christ's commands. Our theoretical understanding of the nature of God should translate into certain forms of praxis. If God were completely present and active, we would have no responsibility for the world. God could do all that needed to be done. If God were completely absent, we would have total responsibility. God as Wholly Other and utterly Immanuel calls us to keep Christ's commands, follow God's will, and *cooperate* with the movement of the Holy Spirit in living out Christ's love in the world.

> God as Wholly Other and utterly Immanuel calls us to keep Christ's commands, follow God's will, and cooperate with the movement of the Holy Spirit in living out Christ's love in the world.

JOHN 15:1-8 (BCP)

The BCP breaks with the other two lectionaries and has us read from the next section of the farewell discourse. The text's allegory of the true vine is Jesus' final and climatic "I am" statement in the Gospel of John. Its themes unfold from those found in last week's lection in chapter 14: the intimate relationship between God and Christ determines the intimate relationship between Christ and the disciples and, in turn, the ethic of the community of Jesus' followers.

In interpreting this passage it is important to remember that the image of the vineyard is common in the First Testament. Israel is God's vineyard. In John, the metaphor shifts. God is the farmer, Christ is the vine, and the disciples (the "you" is plural; thus Jesus is addressing the disciples as a community and not as individuals) are the fruit.

The metaphor would imply that the disciples (that is, *we*) are passive. We are Christ's fruit. But, actually, in the allegory, our role in this relationship is not guaranteed. We should not be surprised to find John mixing or, better, twisting metaphors. If we do not produce fruit, God will prune the vine.

> Where we reside—in whom we dwell—determines the quality of our life.

So how are we to produce fruit? In the following passage (vv. 9-13), the answer is summarized in the command to love one another as Christ has loved us. John, however, does not provide a checklist of moral and ethical behavior that unpacks this command. Instead, he presents Jesus as claiming simply that those who *abide* in Christ will produce abundantly. "Abide" is a key term for the Fourth Gospel. The Greek is *menō* and, in addition to "abide," can be translated as "remain, dwell." John uses the term to remind us that our heart is where our home is. Where we reside—in whom we dwell—determines the quality of our life.

ASCENSION OF THE LORD

MAY 1, 2008 / MAY 4, 2008

Revised Common (RCL)	Episcopal (BCP)	Roman Catholic (LFM)
Acts 1:1-11	Acts 1:1-11 or	Acts 1:1-11
	Dan. 7:9-14	Ps. 47:2-3, 6-7, 8-9
Psalm 47 or Psalm 93	Psalm 47 or 110:1-5	
Eph. 1:15-23	Eph 1:15-23 or	Eph. 1:17-23
	Acts 1:1-11	
Luke 24:44-53	Luke 24:49-53 or	Matt. 28:16-20
	Mark 16:9-15, 19-20	

While Ascension is found forty days after Easter Day in the liturgical calendar and thus always on a Thursday, most Protestant churches have the option of celebrating it on Easter 7. While the Easter 7 readings clearly flow out of the readings for Easter 6, if Ascension is not celebrated during the week, it should certainly be celebrated on the Seventh Sunday of Easter. Celebrating Pentecost without having paused to remember the ascension is like celebrating the resurrection without having paused at the cross.

FIRST READING
ACTS 1:1-11 (RCL, BCP, LFM)

While the Gospel reading anchors the set of lections on most Sundays, for Ascension and Pentecost the celebrations are rooted in opening chapters of the Acts narrative, which have also set the length of the season of Easter itself.

While today's Gospel lection from Luke is a quite different version of the ascension, although written by the same hand (see below), there are a number of elements that relate the opening scene in Acts to Luke's first volume. The passage, of course, opens with a reference to the first volume and has the same addressee (Theophilus) as the first (Luke 1:3). It recalls Jesus' command for the disciples to stay in Jerusalem to await the promise of the Father (Luke 24:49)—over against the other Synoptics, which present the risen Jesus appearing to the disciples in Galilee—and expands the call for the apostles to be Jesus' witnesses (Luke 24:48).

Most important for interpreting the story of the ascension for today is the reappearance of the two men in white clothes (v. 10). While Mark has a young man at the empty tomb and Matthew has an angel, Luke has two men in dazzling clothes appear to the women (Luke 24:4). Moreover, in his story of the transfiguration, Luke describes Moses and Elijah as "two men" and Jesus' clothes are "dazzling white" (9:29-30). There is some narrative rationale for arguing that Luke views the two men at the empty tomb and the ascension as Moses and Elijah. At the very least, the appearance of the two men at the ascension using similar language to that found at the transfiguration and the empty tomb is a signal to the reader that this scene is one of the central epiphanies of Luke's narrative. As these earlier scenes revealed something of Jesus' full significance, so does this story.

In terms of the plot of Luke-Acts, the story of the ascension is essential for setting up all that follows in Luke's second volume. To narrate the story of the early church that grew out of the Jesus movement, the author must get Jesus offstage. If Jesus rose from the dead, why is he still not present with the church (that is, in some physical manner) as he was immediately after the resurrection? This question of narrative logic is resolved with this scene.

But, as we saw with the connection to the transfiguration and resurrection, this scene has deeper theological import than simply clearing the stage for the apostolic church to begin. The ascension is the exclamation point on the exaltation of Christ that opens with the resurrection (see the second reading). But for Christ's exaltation (to the right hand of God in heaven) to be complete, Jesus must leave his followers. Exaltation, for all the power and glory it entails, also implies distance and otherness. Pentecost will be about immanence— the words of the two men about Jesus coming as he departed likely has a double meaning referring to both the parousia (Luke 21:27) and Pentecost. But ascension is about transcendence; Christ no longer

> The ascension is the exclamation point on the exaltation of Christ that opens with the resurrection.

present in an incarnational manner. The resurrection is fulfilled in both transcendence and immanence, both ascension and the gift of the Spirit.

There are two ways to preach the transcendence proclaimed in the ascension. The first is to emphasize the glory that is Christ's and to lead the congregation in praise (see the second reading, below, for more on this option). The second is to ask the congregation to identify with the disciples at that moment when they stand staring into the heavens. In the Gospel of Luke, the disciples return to the city after the ascension with great joy (Luke 24:52). But in Acts, Luke assigns no such emotion to the disciples. They did not get the answer they wished to their question about the restoration of Israel. And instead of a blessing (Luke 24:50), Jesus' last words to the disciples are instructions that will require of them much work and sacrifice (Acts 1:8). And then Jesus leaves. They stare off into the heavens, receive a word from the two men, and return to Jerusalem without speaking a word (or at least Luke mentions no expression).

In the context of the Acts scene, the staring into the sky is a moment of loss, not wonder or worship. To be sure, it is not the same kind of loss the disciples experienced in the crucifixion—they are now on the other side of the empty tomb and have been promised that the Father's promise (that is, the Holy Spirit) will come upon them soon. But it is still loss.

While theologically it may not be appropriate to separate divine transcendence and immanence as if they were different personality characteristics of the Godhead, Luke's narrative (and the liturgical year's) separation of the two speaks truth in experiential terms. People of faith know times when we experience Christ or the Spirit with us. But we also know times when we have experienced divine silence or distance. The difference between our experience of God's immanence and transcendence speaks to difference in our circumstances or our psyche, not in God. Nevertheless, the difference is real. Naming this in the pulpit is good news. Many parishioners are afraid to admit dark nights of the soul because they think it reveals flaws in their faith. Dispelling this misconception can be liberating.

> The difference between our experience of God's immanence and transcendence speaks to difference in our circumstances or our psyche, not in God.

A final note: while the two options for honoring the ascension—praise of the exalted Christ and naming the experience of divine "absence"—may not be able to be held together in the same sermon very well, they can be in the same service. Ascension can be celebrated with loud, strong hymns of praise of the exalted Christ while the sermon names that it is not always so easy to tell Christ is near to be praised.

DANIEL 7:9-14 (BCP ALT.)

The BCP alternate is chosen because the image of the son of man (NRSV: "human being") descending from the clouds of heaven (v. 13) is used in the Synoptic eschatological discourse (Mark 13:26 and parallels) to refer to Jesus returning in victory after the ascension. This image is fitting for a celebration of the Ascension.

The lection, however, is an excerpt from the apocalyptic vision that comprises 7:1-28. Although similar to Revelation, this type of apocalyptic, allegorical literature is foreign to modern ears and First World experience. With its strong religio-political tone, this is an important text to read and preach on in worship. But that message will be lost on Ascension of the Lord. It is better to use the Acts text on this feast day, and return to the Daniel text another Sunday.

PSALM 47 (RCL, BCP)
PSALM 47:2-3, 6-7, 8-9 (LFM)

Scholars have argued that Psalm 47 is an enthronement psalm that was used in festivals declaring God to be king over Israel or the cosmos. This hymn of praise calls worshipers to celebrate the reign of the One who subdued Israel's enemies (perhaps in the conquest). The overall tone of the song fits well with the celebration of Christ's exaltation to rule over the living and the dead at the right hand of God.

PSALM 93 (RCL)

Like Psalm 47 above, Psalm 93 is an enthronement psalm (see also Psalms 95–99). This psalm celebrates God's reign in relation to the divine victory over chaos in creation.

PSALM 110:1-5 (BCP)

Unlike Psalms 47 and 93 above, which declare God's royalty, Psalm 110 proclaims God's favor for the king. The opening verse of the psalm—"The LORD says to my lord, 'Sit at my right hand until I make your enemies your footstool'"— is referenced a number of times in the New Testament as referring to Jesus' exaltation (Acts 2:34-35; Rom. 8:34; and Eph. 1:20, part of today's second reading).

SECOND READING
EPHESIANS 1:15-23 (RCL, BCP)
EPHESIANS 1:17-23 (LFM)

The epistle lection for Ascension is part of the opening material of the Deutero-Pauline letter to the Ephesians. Following a salutation (1:1-2) and blessing (vv. 3-14), this section is a prayer of intercession for the recipients (vv. 15-23).

The author is praying that the readers might gain revelation and wisdom, that is, a deeper faith. But the content of the revelation is specified as knowledge of the hope to which the church is called, the inheritance God gives us, and God's power that is available to us. Mentioning power last leads the author to name the manner in which God's power has been revealed most clearly—in the resurrection and exaltation to God's right hand. The right hand of a king is a metaphor for the king's might.

It is important for modern ears to recognize that Ephesians describes this power in terms of a cosmic struggle between good and evil. Christ has been exalted over every "authority and power and dominion." This list refers to destructive powers—both demonic and human—that would resist God's reign over God's creation. Through the resurrection and ascension, God has given an eschatological victory to Christ and Christ's church.

In a twist on the Pauline metaphor of the church as the body of Christ (Romans 12; 1 Corinthians 12), the author of Ephesians describes the church as Christ's body, with Christ as the head. The exaltation gave Christ dominion over all things *and* made him head of the church (v. 22). These are not two separate acts, but one unified, redemptive act. Christ is head of the church by virtue of being the One who rules over all powers that attempt to rule over us.

> Through the resurrection and ascension, God has given an eschatological victory to Christ and Christ's church.

The tone of this description of the exaltation of Christ is very different from that found in today's readings from Acts and the Gospels. To preach this hymnic language is to preach about the eschatologically present reign/kingdom of God. While Christ's power is expressed in terms of transcendence, it is important to remember that the author describes Christ's exaltation as evidence of God's immeasurable power *for us who believe* (v. 19). Christ has been exalted to the heavens in order that God's power is accessible to us on earth.

This mythical language is the author's (and, in general, the early church's) way of asserting that all descriptions of the transcendent Christ is existentially significant. Descriptions of Christ "up there" are really parables about Christian life down here. Eschatologically speaking, in Christ, *we* are victorious over all authorities and powers and dominions. There are destructive, systemic forces in the world that assert themselves *on* us, but they never truly rule *over* us. Political systems, social structures, economic barriers, failing health, destructive relationships, violence, and mortality are all forces in the world with which we struggle individually and as the church. But preaching that reminds us that Christ sits at God's right hand instead of Caesar, Satan, cancer, poverty, war, or death is to offer hearers liberation. Ascension becomes an exorcism. We are freed from destructive

> Preaching that reminds us that Christ sits at God's right hand instead of Caesar, Satan, cancer, poverty, war, or death is to offer hearers liberation.

power by being placed under the providential power of God revealed in Christ's resurrection and exaltation.

LUKE 24:44-53 (RCL)
LUKE 24:49-53 (BCP)

As noted above in the discussion of the Acts lesson, there is much that Luke's version of the ascension in his first volume has in common with his version in the second. However, there are also key differences in the details. The scene is set in a different location: Bethany instead of the Mount of Olives. Different teaching surrounds the event: in Acts, the dialogue is eschatological in nature, focusing on the reign of God and the restoration of Israel, while in Luke the focus is on the death and resurrection as the fulfillment of Scripture. And the timing is different: in Acts the ascension occurs forty days after the resurrection, but in the Gospel it occurs on Easter evening. And, finally, whereas in Acts the disciples stand staring into the sky, in Luke after the ascension they worship Jesus and return to the city with joy.

These differences do not translate into a completely different perspective on the ascension, but do offer a different nuances to the Lukan perspective. Jesus is still gone and the disciples are in waiting mode— waiting for the promise of the Holy Spirit. Transcendence is emphasized, but because it is in the immediate shadow of the resurrection

> Jesus is still gone and the disciples are in waiting mode–waiting for the promise of the Holy Spirit.

it is a moment of celebration. Only with time does the divine distance become experientially troubling.

MARK 16:9-15, 19-20 (BCP ALT.)

New Testament scholars for the most part agree that 16:8 was the original ending of Mark. The few who do not agree argue that the ending must have been lost. This is to say that all agree that verses 9-20 comprise later scribal additions to the Markan manuscript. Thus the ending, verses 19-20, which speaks of the ascension is not part of Mark's narrative plot. As scribes felt the need to complete Mark's unresolved ending, they borrowed materials from the other Gospels. This material comes from Luke. Since the BCP offers the Lukan text as an option, that choice should be taken.

MATTHEW 28:16-20 (LFM)

The ending of Matthew is not an ascension story. It is the story of Jesus' sole resurrection appearance to his disciples in Galilee and his giving them the Great Commission. But it does echo the ascension stories in Luke-Acts. As the disciples are sent out to be witnesses to Jerusalem, Judea, Samaria, and the ends of the earth in Acts (1:8), so here they are sent to make disciples of all nations (that is, Gentiles). As the disciples are to wait for the promise of the Holy Spirit in Luke-Acts, here Jesus promises to be with the disciples until the end of the age. The promise is built on the fact that for Matthew's readers Jesus is no longer (physically) present. This scene emphasizes Jesus' immanence as an element of divine transcendence.

Two narrative connections are especially important for understanding the full significance this scene has for Matthew. The first concerns immanence. Matthew's Gospel begins with the promise that the Messiah to be born shall bear the name of Emmanuel, God with us (1:23). The promise of the risen Jesus to be with his disciples forever reiterates the opening prophecy (that is, God's promise) and shows that Jesus' exaltation does not mean God will renege on God's promise.

The second narrative connection involves the sending out of the Twelve in chapter 10 but is blurred by a translation discrepancy in the NRSV. At that point in the narrative, Jesus explicitly instructs the twelve apostles to go nowhere among the Gentiles (Greek, *ethnoi*) but only to the lost sheep of the house of Israel (10:5-6). It is only after the resurrection that Jesus extends the mission to include the Gentiles when he instructs the disciples to make disciples of all nations (Greek, *ethnoi*).

> The church is not simply proclaiming a Jesus of the past but is offering the world a Christ of the present.

These are not unrelated narrative connections. For Matthew, the Great Commission to make disciples and baptize is grounded in the promise of Jesus' continued (post-exaltation) presence. The church is not simply proclaiming a Jesus of the past but is offering the world a Christ of the present. Pentecost, the birth of the church, the gift of the Spirit, the celebration of the baptism of three thousand, witnesses to this very reality.

SEVENTH SUNDAY OF EASTER

MAY 4, 2008

Revised Common (RCL)	Episcopal (BCP)	Roman Catholic (LFM)
Acts 1:6-14	Acts 1:(1-7) 8-14 or Ezek. 39:21-29	Acts 1:12-14
Ps. 68:1-10, 32-35	Ps. 68:1-20 or Psalm 47	Ps. 27:1, 4, 7-8
1 Peter 4:12-14; 5:6-11	1 Peter 4:12-19 or Acts 1:(1-7) 8-14	1 Peter 4:13-16
John 17:1-11	John 17:1-11	John 17:1-11a

If Ascension is not celebrated on Thursday, it should be celebrated on the Seventh Sunday of Easter and the lections for Ascension used today. In that case, these readings will not be used during Eastertide. If, however, Ascension is celebrated on Thursday, these readings will be used on the Sunday in between Ascension and Pentecost. They continue the patterns found in the lections for Easter 2–6 as well as serve as a transition from Ascension to Pentecost.

FIRST READING

ACTS 1:6-14 (RCL)
ACTS 1:(1-7) 8-14 (BCP)
ACTS 1:12-14 (LFM)

The Acts reading for the RCL and BCP includes Jesus' ascension so that laity who did not attend worship on Thursday or churches that chose to celebrate Ascension neither on Thursday nor today at least hear the story proclaimed before Pentecost. (Because Ascension is a day of obligation for Roman Catholics, such repetition of the reading is not necessary in the LFM.) But the boundaries of the pericope are clearly constructed in such a way that the liturgical emphasis falls on the closing verses.

With these verses (as well as the remainder of Acts 1), Luke establishes what happens in between Jesus' departure and the gift of the Holy Spirit. Specifically, Luke establishes the disciples' mode of being after the ascension. Two key Lukan concepts are found in this passage.

59

1. *Prayer.* The importance of prayer in Luke-Acts can be seen by the fact that it is mentioned over fifty times in the two-volume narrative. Prayer serves two functions in Luke's narrative. First, prayer is found at key moments in the narrative. Before this scene, readers would have found Jesus praying at his baptism (Luke 3:21), when he appoints the Twelve (6:12), when Peter confesses him as Messiah (9:18), at the transfiguration (9:28), and just before Jesus' death (22:41-44). Luke's use of prayer in this scene signals a key moment is around the corner—Pentecost. The Holy Spirit comes upon those who pray.

Second, Luke presents prayer as a model of Christian devotion for his readers. As we have just seen, Jesus prays. He also teaches his disciples extensively about prayer in the Gospel (11:1ff. and 18:1ff.). So the community gathered in the upper room in this scene is following Jesus' example and prefigures the post-Pentecost church. Three thousand were baptized and devoted themselves to the apostles' teaching, the breaking of bread, and . . . prayer (Acts 2:42). And throughout the Acts narrative, the church continues praying. To be Christian, to be church, is to pray.

2. *Homothumadon.* This Greek word, which means something like "together," "in one accord," or "with one mind," appears only one time in the New Testament outside of Acts (Rom. 15:6). In Acts, however, Luke uses it ten times. It is an adverb/adjective that describes a group acting/existing together in unanimity. Luke uses it to refer both to riots against the Christian gospel (7:57; 18:12; 19:29) as well as positive actions of the Christian community (1:14; 2:46; 4:24; 5:12; 8:6; 12:20; 15:25). Luke held an ideal of the church living in complete unity under apostolic guidance.

To preach on this Acts passage, therefore, is to preach on the relation of ecclesiology (the nature of the church) and Christian practice (the behavior of the church). Luke presents the community of faith praying in one accord. This is not exactly, "The church that prays together stays together," but clearly Luke believes that the true church is marked by unity in prayer. The church, like the rest of society, can hardly agree on anything. We argue about the nature of sin and salvation, economic justice, who God is, military policy, worship styles, sex, inclusive language, and so forth and so on. But by God, or better, through Christ, we ought to be able to pray together. We may disagree about whether a certain war is just, but we ought to be able to pray in unison for peace. We may view God through different theological lenses—liberal, neoorthodox, process, liberation—but we all ought to be able to speak God's name together.

> We may disagree about whether a certain war is just, but we ought to be able to pray in unison for peace.

EZEKIEL 39:21-29 (BCP ALT.)

The BCP offers a passage from the middle of Ezekiel's restoration oracles as the First Testament alternative to the Acts lection. Ezekiel was a priest and prophet whose ministry took place during the exile. Indeed, Ezekiel himself was an exile. His view of the exile was that it was God's just judgment on Judah. But that is far from Ezekiel's last word.

Ezekiel believed and prophesied that God would restore Judah to its homeland. As sure as God punished Judah for its impurity, God would cleanse the people, return them home, rebuild their temple, and continue as always to be their God. Indeed, in today's reading this last promise is the punchline of the passage, spoken in words that the church hears during this season in terms of its experience of Pentecost, "I pour out my spirit upon the house of Israel."

RESPONSIVE READING
PSALM 27:1, 4, 7-8 (LFM)

The psalmist here expresses confidence in God as savior and protector in the face of opposition. Verses 1-6 speak *about* God, while verses 7-14 are supplication spoken *to* God.

PSALM 68:1-10, 32-35 (RCL)
PSALM 68:1-20 (BCP)

Psalm 68 is a complex composition. It reads more like a collection of loosely connected fragments than a unified poem. Broadly speaking, the psalm praises God for God's victorious self-revelation at different times in Israel's history.

PSALM 47 (BCP ALT.)

See the comments on the responsive reading for the Ascension, above.

SECOND READING

1 PETER 4:12-14; 5:6-11 (RCL)
1 PETER 4:12-19 (BCP)
1 PETER 4:13-16 (LFM)

This is the final lection from 1 Peter for the season of Easter. The boundaries of the epistle lesson in the RCL and LFM are poorly chosen. In fact, the RCL seems to want to get an extra reading in before the season closes. Preachers focusing on this reading will need a clear understanding of the full context to determine what message to offer a congregation. The structure of this portion of the letter is as follows:

> 4:12-19—Christian Suffering
> 5:1-11—Closing Exhortations
>> vv. 1-4—To elders (tend the flock)
>> v. 5:5a—To those who are younger (be subject to elders)
>> vv. 5b-11—To all (be humble)

The LFM lesson is a portion of the first section dealing with Christian suffering. Omitting the opening line concerning the fact that the readers should not be surprised at their persecution and starting with the call to rejoice dramatically changes the intended tone. The RCL offers portions of two sections, the opening of the section dealing with Christian suffering and the ending of the exhortation to all concerning humility. Sermons dealing with the RCL or LFM lessons will need to be expanded to focus on one of the whole sections. The following comments will deal with the first section since all three lectionaries hold it in common.

The content of the opening section (4:12-19) is neither completely new nor simply a repetition of the discussion of Christian suffering that readers have encountered earlier in the letter. There is both continuity and extension, especially as an *inclusio* related to our lection for Easter 2. The section begins with a claim that those who are being persecuted should not be surprised at their

> We should imagine here struggles in terms of social location and economic well-being instead of lions in the coliseum or being burned at the stake.

suffering. This relates to what we have seen before concerning the fact that for 1 Peter, suffering is part and parcel of salvation. The language here, however, is stronger than has been found so far in the letter: to suffer unjustly as a Christian is to *participate* in Christ's sufferings.

The language of "fiery ordeal" in verse 12 is, likewise, a more striking description of the persecution the recipients are experiencing than 1 Peter has used before. As the letter draws toward a close, the intensity of the discussion seems to be increasing. But we must be careful not to read great physical suffering into this term. As we have seen, scholars are generally agreed that clues in the letter point more to social marginalization as the primary form of persecution 1 Peter is addressing than a government-sponsored persecution leading to martyrdom. We should imagine struggles in terms of social location and economic well-being instead of lions in the coliseum or being burned at the stake. The use of "fiery" is related to two elements in 1 Peter's thought. First, the verse speaks of the readers undergoing fiery ordeal as part of their testing. We have seen the author use the metaphor of metal being tested by fire earlier to describe the suffering being experienced in Asia Minor (1:7). So fiery ordeal refers less to intensity of persecution and more to the testing of faith. Second, 1 Peter has consistently viewed persecution in an eschatological framework (see 1:3-5). Fire is imagery that was often associated with eschatology in ancient thought, especially eschatological judgment. This context is helpful for understanding the language about judgment in verses 17-18. First Peter's claims about judgment should not be read as either celebrating religious revenge (assuming God will get our enemies) or as escapism (through salvation we avoid judgment). The author is a realist at heart. All will be/are being judged, and 1 Peter wants the recipients to recognize that their suffering prepares them for judgment.

The newest element introduced in this passage is the cause given for the recipients' unjust suffering. They suffer for the "name of Christ" (v. 14) or, put differently, for being "Christian" (v. 16). First Peter is the only New Testament document other than Acts (11:26; 26:28) that uses the term *Christian*. While we claim this as an acceptable label for ourselves today, it likely originated as an insult thrust upon followers of Jesus in similar fashion to the terms *Methodist* or *Baptist* in the eighteenth century. But 1 Peter

> The author is a realist at heart. All will be/are being judged, and 1 Peter wants the recipients to recognize that their suffering prepares them for judgment.

does not dispute the name. Indeed, he says those in Asia Minor are suffering for the name of Christ, for the name of Christ given to them. In other words, they are not being punished for anything they do, but simply for the identity they have claimed, or better, for the identity that has claimed them. They are being persecuted for *whose* they are.

To preach this text to contemporary congregations, preachers need not call hearers to suffer, as if living out the gospel necessitates some kind of religious masochism. The sermon should, however, call hearers to claim an identity that sets Christians off from the world instead of allowing us to disappear into the crowd. Remember, the letter opens by identifying the recipients (us?) as exiles. We may not need to long for suffering at the edge of society to be Christian, but we may not be able to be Christian and exist comfortably in the center of society.

ACTS 1:(1-7) 8-14 (BCP alt.)

See the comments on the first reading, above.

The Gospel
JOHN 17:1-11 (RCL, BCP)
JOHN 17:1-11A (LFM)

Every year on the Seventh Sunday of Easter, the Gospel lection comes from John 17, Jesus' prayer for his disciples at the end of his farewell discourse. The setting is still the Last Supper (see 13:1-4). Traditionally labeled the Great Priestly Prayer, this prayer replaces the Gethsemane prayer found in the Synoptic Gospels. Unlike that prayer, however, Jesus here is not agonizing over the cross that he is about to face. Flowing out of the farewell discourse proper (chaps. 14–16), in which Jesus instructs the disciples about continuing on after his departure, this prayer asks God to protect the disciples after his glorification (vv. 11ff.).

Our reading for this Sunday includes the opening verses of the prayer. The division is awkward. In the first five verses, Jesus prays for himself. In verse 6, the focus shifts to his disciples. Noting the division of Gospel lections for the other two years of the lectionary cycle is helpful for seeing what is at work in the chapter. In Year B, the lection is John 17:6-19. This section focuses on Jesus' first disciples—that is, those with him in the narrative. In Year C, the lection is 17:20-26, where Jesus prays for those who will come to believe due to the witness of those first disciples—in other words, future disciples, including John's community and us. So in today's lection the focus is on verses 1-5. But the overlap with the lection for Year B should remind the preacher that Jesus' prayer for himself only makes sense as an *introduction* to the prayer for the church.

Even focusing on just the first five verses is no easy task. First of all, let's admit that if John turned this paragraph in to a teacher or an editor it would be sent back to him immediately for revision. His prose is repetitive and confusing. And John, as he often does, confuses the voice of Jesus with the voice of the narrator. Jesus not only prays for "me" but Jesus prays for the "Son" in the third person (vv. 1-2) and even for "Jesus Christ" by name (v. 3). Anyone who has been reading through John and especially through the farewell discourse, however, is used to these sorts of stylistic issues.

> By Jesus' true character being revealed in the cross, resurrection, and exaltation, God's true character will be revealed.

Underneath the confusing language are some key issues for Johannine theology. All of these have homiletical potential. The first is "glorification." The words *glory*, *glorify*, and *glorification* appear forty-two times in the Fourth Gospel. Eight of those occurrences are in chapter 17, and five in verses 1-5 (with a sixth in verse 10). Clearly it is central for this passage. This cluster of terms has multiple layers of meaning in John. At its simplest, it means to honor someone. When Jesus speaks of his own glorification, it refers to the events of the cross, resurrection, and exaltation. In this sense it is a term similar to the Johannine use of *departure* earlier in the farewell discourse. But the glorification of the Father (and of Jesus) also involves a revelatory character. To glorify is to reveal the true nature of God and/or Christ. Jesus offers this prayer as he heads toward his own glorification, which will glorify the Father—by Jesus' true character being revealed in the cross, resurrection, and exaltation, God's true character will be revealed. So Jesus' prayer that God glorify him is not a vain prayer, but a request that God be revealed through what lies ahead.

Central to what is revealed is that through Christ God gives eternal life to all whom God has given to Jesus. In a day when outside the church people try to attain eternal life with success, possessions, or power and inside the church we focus on achieving a reward in heaven after we die, it is important to hear what John really means by eternal life. Jesus has discussed this at other places in John (1:4; 3:14ff.; 4:10-14; 5:19-29; 6:27ff; 8:12; 10:27-28; 11:25; 12:25, 50; 14:6; 20:31), but never does he state the content of eternal life more explicitly than here. Too often those preaching on John have read the language of eternal life as future reward. Without denying an eschatological aspect to John's theology, the primary emphasis is eternal life *as* the quality of current existence. Here Jesus says, "And this is eternal life, that they may know you, the only true God, and Jesus Christ whom you have sent." It is not that knowledge of God and Christ leads to eternal life; knowledge of God and Christ *is* eternal life itself. This knowledge is the gift. Eternal life for John is less about lengthening the duration of one's life (a chronological, quantitative claim) and more about participating in God's eternal love and thus radically transforming life (an existential, qualitative claim).

> It is not that knowledge of God and Christ leads to eternal life; knowledge of God and Christ is eternal life itself.

DAY OF PENTECOST

Revised Common (RCL)	Episcopal (BCP)	Roman Catholic (LFM)
Acts 2:1-21 or	Acts 2:1-11 or	Acts 2:1-11
Num. 11:24-30	Ezek. 11:17-20	
Ps. 104:24-34, 35b	Ps. 104:25-37 or	Ps 104:1, 24, 29-30,
	104:25-32 or	31, 34
	33:12-15, 18-22	
1 Cor. 12:3b-13 or	1 Cor. 12:4-13 or	1 Cor. 12:3b-7, 12-13
Acts 2:1-21	Acts 2:1-11	
John 20:19-23 or	John 20:19-23 or	John 20:19-23
7:37-39	14:8-17	

First Reading
ACTS 2:1-21 (RCL)
ACTS 2:1-11 (BCP, LFM)

The Acts reading is, obviously, the central Scripture lesson for Pentecost. Luke's story of the gift of the Holy Spirit and the beginning of the church gives rise to this feast day.

First, a word about the background of the lesson. The Jewish feast of Pentecost came fiftieth (*pentēkostos*) day after Passover. It was originally a celebration of the first fruits of the harvest but evolved into a celebration of the gift of the law and the covenant God made with Israel. This covenant-making backdrop may serve to help interpret Luke's understanding of the gathering of a community of the newly baptized around the teaching of the apostles. We must be careful not to make too much of this connection, however, since the only explicit reason Luke mentions that it is Pentecost is to explain why Jews from so many different regions of the Roman Empire had gathered in Jerusalem.

Luke's story of Pentecost is structured in the following manner:

The miraculous gift of the Spirit (Acts 2:1-13)
    Gift of the Spirit and speaking in different languages (vv. 1-4)
    Surprise of the crowd (vv. 5-13)

66

Peter's sermon (2:14-36)

 Interpretation of reception of Spirit and speaking in different languages
 using Joel 2:28-32 (vv. 14-21)
 Interpretation of death and resurrection of Jesus using Psalm 16:8-11
 and Psalm 110:1 (vv. 22-36)
Immediate response to the miracle and the sermon (2:37-42)
Summary of continued response (2:43-46)

The BCP and LFM focus on the miracle of Pentecost alone, while the RCL extends the reading to include the opening of Peter's lengthy sermon. With both divisions, the relationship between the first postresurrection proclamation of the Christ event and the first baptizands into the faith need to be assumed (recall the lections for Easter 2 and 3) by the preacher, but the focus of the lection is on the phenomena that occur.

The phenomena that engage the senses of those gathered—the heavenly sound of rushing wind, tongues like fire, the speaking of different languages—all indicate that this scene is a major epiphany that grounds Luke's two-volume narrative. It stands alongside the angel Gabriel's appearances to Zechariah (Luke 1:11-20) and Mary (1:26-38), the Spirit coming upon Jesus after his baptism (3:21-22), the transfiguration (9:28-36), the resurrection appearance in Emmaus (24:13-35), the apostles (Acts 5:19-21) and later Paul and Silas (16:25-34) being freed from prison, Jesus' appearances to Stephen (7:54-56) and Saul (9:1-8), Cornelius and Peter's coinciding dreams (10:1-16), and Paul's vision during the storm at sea (27:23-24). These Lukan epiphanies present a God who is not an offstage object of the story. God is the author/director of the story who occasionally appears (that is, intervenes) on screen to help set the direction of the narrative. This is not Alfred Hitchcock just showing up in a crowd of extras as a signature gimmick of his movies. These epiphanic moments when God appears explicitly show that God is actually the main character of Luke's narrative, even when the spotlight seems to be pointed elsewhere. Luke's story is a story of salvation history, a history of a paradigmatic period of God's saving acts through Christ and the church.

> These epiphanic moments when God appears explicitly show that God is actually the main character of Luke's narrative, even when the spotlight seems to be pointed elsewhere.

As an epiphany, the story of Pentecost reveals the *manner* in which God is directing and starring in the story of salvation, the church's story, our story. God configures the work of the apostles and the nature of the church after the resurrection. The story is about divine immanence—God present with and through the community of faith after Jesus ascended. It is about *how* God is present in the church and the *results* of God's continual spiritual presence.

The story opens when "they" are all gathered together. Who "they" are is not completely clear. In the line immediately preceding the opening of the scene (1:26), the narrator refers to the newly constituted Twelve. But that reference is part of a passage in which the whole community of believers (about 120 men and women) are gathered (1:12-15). This distinction is important because in verse 4 "all of them" began speaking in other tongues. Are those speaking the Twelve or 120 people? The use of "all" might indicate the larger number, but the importance placed on replacing Judas just before the gift of the Spirit justifies arguing for the smaller number. Indeed, throughout the first half of Acts, the twelve apostles have a special responsibility for carrying and conveying the Spirit to others (for instance, when Philip baptizes converts in Samaria, Peter and John must come to lay hands on the new believers in order for them to receive the Spirit, 8:14-17). If "they" refers to the 120, the miracle is that so many were endowed with this spiritual gift in one event. If "they" refers to the Twelve, the miracle is that twelve people spoke in a manner understood by Jews from some many different nations. In this case, it is more a miracle of the ear than the mouth.

> The story is about divine immanence—God present with and through the community of faith after Jesus ascended.

Indeed, as important as the "they" who speak in different languages is the list of Jews and proselytes who hear them in their own languages. The list represents regions from around the Mediterranean Sea; from areas of Africa, the Middle East, and Europe; across the whole of the Roman Empire. While 1:8—". . . you will receive power when the Holy Spirit has come upon you; and you will be my witnesses in Jerusalem, in all Judea and Samaria, and to the ends of the earth"—serves as an outline for the whole of Acts, it is also, in foreshadowing fashion, fulfilled in this moment of Pentecost. The apostles (or the 120) proleptically witness to the ends of the earth by speaking to this wide variety of visitors.

Pentecost is a miracle of communication in which God breaks down the boundaries that divide all those whom God has created. The Holy Spirit connects people linguistically so that they can be joined in the faith, joined in the salvation of Jesus Christ.

> Pentecost is a miracle of communication in which God breaks down the boundaries that divide all those whom God has created.

How a congregation celebrates the feast of Pentecost depends greatly on where the preacher locates them in the story. The preacher can have them identify with either those speaking or those listening. To identify with the speakers is to celebrate that we (the church) are endowed with the spiritual gift of breaking down barriers that divide the world . . . or just the church. A sermon of this sort will be hortatory in nature. It will be a call to live up to the evangelistic ideal of church that Luke offers and which we have failed. Indeed, there will be a penitential element to the sermon, confessing that the church over the centuries has not and the church now is not living out God's presence as it was directed to at its inception. This is an extremely appropriate tone to set given that Peter in his sermon quotes from the end of Joel 2, which celebrates God's promise of redemption through the pouring out of God's prophetic spirit. This promise flows out of a call to repentance earlier in the chapter, from which the church reads every year on Ash Wednesday.

To identify with the hearers, on the other hand, is to lead the congregation in experiencing awe at the presence of God in the church and calling them to repent and be baptized or to remember their baptism. Pentecost is certainly an appropriate day to baptize people into the faith. But for churches that used Lent as a catechetical period leading up to baptism and confirmation on Easter Day, Pentecost serves as a celebration of all our baptisms as a way of celebrating the constitution of the church. The gift of the Spirit leads to the proclamation of the good news of Jesus Christ, which leads to repentance and baptism, which leads to the formation of a community gathered around apostolic teaching and the breaking of bread, which eventually leads to us. The ancient story of the reception of the Spirit and the baptism of three thousand is the story of *our* church today.

> The ancient story of the reception of the Spirit and the baptism of three thousand is the story of our church today.

NUMBERS 11:24-30 (RCL)

The RCL offers the option of using the Acts lection in the slot of either the first or second reading. If the lection from 1 Corinthians is not read, then this passage from Numbers will be used.

Leading up to this passage, the people have been complaining that they have no meat to eat in the wilderness, only manna. Moses is feeling the weight of their weariness and complains to the Lord. He is overwhelmed and asks God for relief. So God instructs Moses to gather seventy elders whom God will appoint to share Moses' load. In today's lection, God empowers the seventy by sharing with them the prophetic spirit given to Moses. This is the obvious thematic connection to Pentecost. Not only do Jesus' disciples receive the Holy Spirit, but in his sermon Peter cites Joel 2:28-32 as declaring that through the pouring out of God's Spirit, men and women, young and old, even slaves, will prophesy.

In our Numbers lection, as soon as they receive a portion of Moses' spirit, the seventy begin to prophesy. But then they immediately stop (11:25). In the next paragraph, it is clear that they do so out of respect for Moses, for when two of the seventy, Eldad and Medad, are prophesying in the camp, Joshua asks Moses to stop them. But Moses makes clear that his ego is not at issue. He would wish that all of God's people had the Lord's spirit upon them and were prophets! This is a Pentecost type of wish.

EZEKIEL 11:17-20 (BCP)

The BCP offers the option of using the Acts lection in the slot of either the first or second reading. If the lection from 1 Corinthians is not read, then this passage from Ezekiel will be used. But one should be careful how it is used. It is unlikely that the text can be heard on its own terms on Pentecost. The very choice of verses leads us to hear it eisegetically in a typological fashion.

The lection is chosen because of language that is similar to the Acts passage. Here God promises to "gather you from the peoples, and assemble you out of the countries where you have been scattered." This claim resembles the roll call of the nations from which Jews came to Jerusalem for the Pentecost festival (Acts 2:9-11). Ezekiel, however, is not referring to a general diaspora but to those Jews who have been taken from Judah into exile in Babylon. The oracle is an answer to those left in Judah who claim the land for themselves because those in exile have "gone far from the LORD" (11:15). Ezekiel is condemning such a claim and asserting that the land belongs to the exiles, whom God will return to the land. The exclamation point to this promise of restoration is when God says, "I will give them one [or "a new"] heart, and put a new spirit within them."

> The mention of the spirit resembles the Acts passage, but here it not a promise concerning God's own presence but of hope and restoration.

Again, the mention of the spirit resembles the Acts passage, but here it is not a promise concerning God's own presence but of hope and restoration.

RESPONSIVE READING

PSALM 104:24-34, 35B (RCL)
PSALM 104:25-37 OR 104:25-32 (BCP)
PS 104:1, 24, 29-30, 31, 34 (LFM)

Psalm 104 is a lengthy song of praise to God as creator. This psalm is chosen for Pentecost because of verses 29-30, a reference to our dependence on God for life itself, based on Genesis 2:7, in which God creates a human out of the dirt and breathes life into it. The NRSV confuses the text by translating the same word in two different ways:

[29] . . . when you take away their breath [*ruach*], they die
and return to their dust
[30] When you send forth your spirit [*ruach*], they are created;
and you renew the face of the ground.

The connection of the Holy Spirit in the Acts text with the spirit/breath/wind (all of which *ruach* can mean) of creation is an appropriate biblical and theological link to make. Indeed, on Trinity Sunday, the First Testament lection will be the first creation story, in which the *ruach* passes over the face of the formless void (Gen. 1:2).

PSALM 33:12-15, 18-22 (BCP ALT.)

The BCP offers verses from Psalm 33 as an alternative to the reading from Psalm 104. Like Psalm 104, this is also a song of praise to God the creator. The verses chosen, however, emphasize that God in heaven keeps a providential eye on God's children on earth. This text connects the theme of God's transcendence celebrated on Ascension with God's immanence celebrated on Pentecost.

SECOND READING

1 CORINTHIANS 12:3B-13 (RCL)
1 CORINTHIANS 12:3B-7, 12-13 (LFM)
1 CORINTHIANS 12:4-13 (BCP)

The epistle lection is especially appropriate for this feast day given contemporary use of the adjective *pentecostal*, referring to that movement that emphasizes speaking in tongues as a sign of being baptized by the Holy Spirit. Often contemporary readings mistakenly read the story of Pentecost as if it presents the apostles as speaking in tongues after having received the gift of the Holy Spirit. But according to Luke, the miracle of Pentecost is not that the apostles spoke in different languages but that those who spoke different languages could understand them.

In the background of this 1 Corinthians passage, however, Paul is concerned with speaking in tongues (or glossalalia) as a gift of the Spirit. The collection of house churches in Corinth was divided along socioeconomic lines. This schism manifested itself in a number of theological and ecclesiological ways—for instance, who was baptized by whom, the Lord's Supper, eating meat sacrificed to idols, and resurrection of the dead. Paul discusses the division concerning spiritual gifts in chapters 12–14. The Corinthians were arguing over a hierarchy of gifts, with some asserting that glossalalia is the most important gift. Our epistle text for today is the opening of Paul's extended discussion of these issues. Paul wants to avoid setting up a hierarchy by claiming that the one Spirit of God has endowed the

> Paul does offer one primary standard for evaluating spiritual gifts: they must be used for the upbuilding of the community.

church with a variety of gifts. That said, Paul does offer one primary standard for evaluating spiritual gifts: they must be used for the upbuilding of the community.

Given all of the divisions in the church today, this text can be an important point of focus for a contemporary Pentecost celebration.

ACTS 2:1-21 (RCL ALT.)
ACTS 2:1-11 (BCP ALT.)

See the comments on the first reading, above.

THE GOSPEL
JOHN 20:19-23 (RCL, BCP, LFM)

See the comments on the Gospel for Easter 2, above.

JOHN 7:37-39 (RCL ALT.)

The RCL offers this text as an alternative to John 20:19-23 since that lection was read on Easter 2. The repetition of that lesson, however, is appropriate and a better choice than this one since it narrates a different version of the gift of the Holy Spirit.

If this reading is chosen, the literary context needs to be filled in for the congregation. Jesus at first resisted going to Jerusalem for the Festival of Booths because the religious authorities were seeking to kill him (7:1); then he decided to go in secret (7:10); and finally he starts teaching in the Temple, the central locus of the authorities' power. The words Jesus speaks in this passage are his final words in the Temple, after the authorities have sent guards to arrest him.

The text is chosen less because of its primary focus—the invitation for those who thirst to come to Jesus—and more because of the narrator's interpretation of the water metaphor referring to the coming infusion of the Spirit in the community of faith. This theme fits well with Pentecost, but the future orientation of the passage feels more like a call to worship than it does the Gospel reading in the midst of the proclamation movement of the worship service.

JOHN 14:8-17 (BCP ALT.)

See the comments on the Gospel for Easter 5 and 6, above.

THE SEASON AFTER PENTECOST / ORDINARY TIME

TRINITY SUNDAY THROUGH PROPER 12

HOLLY HEARON

Following Pentecost, the lectionary moves into Ordinary Time. This can seem like a letdown after the excitement of Easter and Pentecost. Yet "ordinary time" also has its place in the rhythm of the Christian life. Saint Katherine Drexel puts it well: "Out of our common todays and yesterdays, we are building for eternity."[1] It is the patterns of faithfulness that we cultivate in our day-to-day existence that sustain us throughout the year, that let us fully enter into the joyful celebration of moments such as Christmas, Easter, and Pentecost, then gently hold us as we return to "ordinary time."

This portion of the lectionary begins with Holy Trinity Sunday. This is a fitting introduction because it roots all of our reflection in the nature and character of God, a theme that recurs throughout the texts that follow. We often talk about how we should respond to God; we less often reflect on the nature of God. Yet it is this which is the very basis of our faith: a God who is our Creator, who invites us into relationship, who has sustained us in the past, who has reached out to us most distinctly in Jesus Christ, who continues to call us into relationship, and whose grace compels us to witness to the kingdom of God, which even now is breaking into the world.

The lectionary is rich with possibilities during this period Ordinary Time. The Revised Common Lectionary follows the narrative of Genesis from creation to Jacob's dream. These texts focus on individuals, their encounters with God, and the unfolding of God's promises. One thread that preachers might follow is the

73

different ways people encounter God: for example, in creation, in covenant, in prayer, in oracles, in dreams. Another possibility is tracing the persistence and consistency of God in the midst of human foibles. Yet a third thread is the recurrence of the theme of blessing.

Beginning with the third Sunday after Pentecost, all three lectionaries follow Romans. Reading Romans can be likened to biting into a piece of fruitcake: it is rich, dense, and often surprising. It is most definitely challenging. One of the challenges, at times, is trying simply to understand Paul's language. For this reason some of my discussions are focused on trying to give clarity to Paul's line of thought. Another challenge is bringing the text down to earth. I have made an effort to include references to film and literature. Often these suggestions can apply to texts where no specific illustration is cited. Because each step in Paul's argument is so closely built on what has preceded, I recommend that those considering preaching on Romans read through all of the passages with their attendant discussions in a condensed period, rather than parceling them out week by week. This will help to show how the whole fits together and to experience the flow of its dramatic narrative.

The Gospel lections follow Matthew. Beginning in the Sermon on the Mount, they trace a thread through the missionary discourse (chap. 10), the identification of Jesus with Wisdom, and conclude with the chapter on parables (chap. 13). The theme running through the selected texts is discipleship. The lectionary does not back off of difficult passages. They challenge us to consider our loyalties, discern motives, examine the quality of our witness, and reflect on the discipleship of the community as well as the individual. A theme that emerges on the Eighth Sunday after Pentecost and following is hearing and seeing. This theme can be projected backwards into chapter 10 by considering what others hear and see as we witness to the kingdom.

Living with these texts week by week may reveal that Ordinary Time is not so ordinary. It is the time in which we discover day by day who God is, the mercies we enjoy because God is our Creator, and the joys and challenges of living in community as God's people. It affords us time to consider ways in which we have yet to grow in faith and commit ourselves in witness through action. It also offers us the time to find our rest in God.

Note

1. Quoted in *The Woman's Prayer Companion: Praying Life Events & Celebrating Women of Inspiration* (Indianapolis: Carmelite Monastery, 1995), 103.

HOLY TRINITY SUNDAY / FIRST SUNDAY AFTER PENTECOST

MAY 18, 2008

Revised Common (RCL)	Episcopal (BCP)	Roman Catholic (LFM)
Gen. 1:1—2:4a	Gen. 1:1—2:3	Exod. 34:4b-6, 8-9
Psalm 8	Psalm 150 or	Dan. 3:52, 53, 54, 55
	Canticle 2 or 13	
2 Cor. 13:11-13	2 Cor. 13: (5-10) 11-13	2 Cor. 13:11-13
Matt. 28:16-20	Matt. 28:16-20	John 3:16-18

FIRST READING

GENESIS 1:1—2:4A (RCL)
GENESIS 1:1—2:3 (BCP)

In the midst of debates over whether creationism should be taught in public schools alongside evolution, these verses take on a burden they were never meant to bear. The structure of the text invites us to hear this story of creation as poetry, a stunning declaration about the nature of God. Written at the time of the Babylonian exile (sixth century B.C.E.), it assures those who have been dislocated in time and space that God is more powerful than the chaos that has overtaken them; that nothing—whether exile, loneliness, illness, or unemployment—can separate them from God their Creator.

The NRSV offers an alternate translation of the opening words, "when God began to create." This alternate reading highlights that the Hebrew word *bereshit* refers to the beginning of a series of actions, rather than a first moment in time. Time is defined for us by the seasons that are one of God's acts of creation (1:14); in contrast, God's first creative action identifies God as the One who exists outside of time, outside of the created order, but who is known to us by the act of creation. God's creative actions are not limited to seven days; rather, they describe the very nature of God as One who is constantly engaged in the act of creation, whether it is a clean heart (Ps. 51:10) or a new creation (2 Cor. 5:17).

> God's creative actions are not limited to seven days; rather, they describe the very nature of God as One who is constantly engaged in the act of creation.

Indeed, God alone is the subject of the verb "create" (*bara*) in the Hebrew Bible.

75

The story unfolds in parallel structure: verses 1-5, 14-17 (days one and four) describe the creation of light that separates day from night; verses 6-9, 20-23 (days two and five), the separation of the waters and the creatures that inhabit them; verses 9-13, 24-25 (days three and six), the creation of land, its vegetation, and the creatures that inhabit it. The orderliness of creation contrasts with the chaos described by the watery void. It also points to the intentionality that informs God's acts of creation: they are not random, but come forth by the will of God who pronounces them good (1:4, 10, 12, 18, 21, 25, 31).

The greatest amount of narrative space is given to the creation of humankind, the act of creation that stands outside the parallel structure and the only one to receive God's blessing. The creation of one humankind (*ha'adam*), male and female, is a powerful commentary on the ways that we have found to create divisions of nation, gender, and race. Since the primary characteristic of God in the narrative is God's role as Creator, the image of God in which humankind is created may be described by humankind's capacity to create. This is by no means limited to procreation. Rather, just as God has created order out of chaos, a life-giving environment in which all of creation can thrive, so too humankind has the capacity to create an order within creation that is life-giving for the whole of creation. This is perhaps the best way to understand that language of "dominion": it is not intended to give us license to abuse creation; rather, we are to promote well-being. We may find ourselves challenged, in this regard, by the statement that God has given humankind "every green plant for food." The creation of humankind also tells us something about God. With the creation of humankind, God is no longer the only creative force in the universe. God's willingness to share this power with humankind is a remarkable invitation to partnership and an act of trust.

> "Dominion" is not intended to give us license to abuse creation; rather, we are to promote well-being.

EXODUS 34:4B-6, 8-9 (LFM)

These verses belong to the episode of the golden calf (chap. 32). The larger narrative context is a reminder of the many ways we stray from God, drawn in by the glitter of seemingly more tangible gods, gods we can shape to our own design. In the context of Trinity Sunday, the selected verses focus on the glory of God, revealed to Moses who intercedes on behalf of the people (see 33:12—34:9). The glory of God stands in stark contrast to the golden calf, whose glory can be melted away by the heat of fire.

The lectionary, by omitting verse 7, eliminates the reference to divine retribution, saving the preacher from the most theologically challenging verse (and avoiding conflicts with the LFM Gospel reading). We are not alone in our struggles with this verse; the words of verse 6 are found in eight other passages in the

Hebrew Bible (Num. 14:18; Neh. 9:17; Pss. 86:15; 103:8; 145:8; Joel 2:13; Jonah 4:2; Nah. 1:3), but only two include the idea of retribution found in verse 7. The adjectives "merciful and gracious" (*rahum* and *hannun*) are ascribed only to God in the Hebrew Bible. "Steadfast love" (*hesed;* "lovingkindness") is not unique to God, but distinguished by God's mercy, grace, and faithfulness. This description of God in the face of our iniquities complements the Gospel lection. Moses' response in worship models for us the appropriate response to this manifestation of God's glory.

RESPONSIVE READING
PSALM 8 (RCL)

Psalm 8 is well matched with the other lections for the day. With Genesis 1 it lifts up God's wondrous work in creation and the role that God has assigned humankind within creation. As a text for Trinity Sunday it draws attention to the glory of God as Creator. The psalm maintains a delicate balance, lifting up the honor bestowed on humankind by God while describing humankind's awe at the work of the Creator, and bracketing the whole with references to God's sovereignty.

PSALM 150 (BCP)

As a celebration of God, Psalm 150 is appropriately assigned to Trinity Sunday. It exhorts us twelve times to "Praise the LORD": in the sanctuary, where we worship God; in the heavens, where God reigns; for God's mighty deeds on behalf of creation; for God's surpassing greatness over all creation. The psalm ends with a great symphony of sound, and an invitation to every creature in the whole of creation to praise God.

DANIEL 3:52, 53, 54, 55 (LFM)

These verses come from that portion of the additions to the book of Daniel known as the "Song of the Three Jews." Within the book of Daniel, the song follows 3:23, heightening the drama of the event by describing how the well-stoked flames consumed the Chaldeans standing near the furnace, but left Azariah and his companions untouched. The three companions then lift up their voice in unison and exhort the whole of creation to bless God. Each verse may stand on its own; together the verses form a crescendo, as each part of creation lends its voice in praise. As one of the texts for Trinity Sunday, these verses emphasize the overwhelming majesty of God, who is worthy of creation's praise forever and ever.

2 CORINTHIANS 13:11-13 (RCL, LFM)
2 CORINTHIANS 13:(5-10) 11-13 (BCP)

Of all Paul's letters, only 2 Corinthians concludes with a tripartite formula. Normally, the benediction invokes the name of Christ alone. Why Paul steps out of pattern here is a mystery, yet in doing so he has provided us with a fulsome summary of faith, one that has become familiar to us through its repetition in liturgy. Whereas Jesus, in Matthew's Gospel, instructs the disciples to baptize in the name of the "Father, Son, and Holy Spirit," Paul begins his tripartite formula with Jesus Christ. Paul here does not refer to Jesus as "the Son," but instead speaks of "the grace of the Lord Jesus Christ." Christ is named first in, for Paul, it is through Christ that we come to know God's love for us because of God's gift of grace in Jesus Christ (see Rom. 5:17, 21). Scholars differ in their reading of the third part of the formula: it could be rendered *the sharing that comes from the Holy Spirit*, or *the sharing that we enjoy in the Holy Spirit*. This benediction is a kind of shorthand for the story of salvation. Each phrase offers us an opportunity to reflect on the ways in which God is present in our lives.

MATTHEW 28:16-20 (RCL, BCP)

Matthew 28:19 perhaps may be best described as a first impulse toward trinitarian theology. This, of course, makes it an appropriate text for Trinity Sunday. Nonetheless, we need to exercise care not to read our understanding of the Trinity, based on centuries of debate, into the text. Further, we do not know precisely what the relationship of this formula was to baptism. W. D. Davies and Dale Allison demonstrate that a variety of phrases were employed in connection with baptism and that only in the *Didache* (a late-first-century text) do we similarly encounter the triadic formula. The majority of texts indicate that baptism was performed in the name of Jesus.[1]

These cautions aside, it is worth exploring briefly Matthew's language regarding the Father, Son, and Holy Spirit. This can become an opportunity for comparing our own language and ideas with those of Matthew. "Father" is Matthew's standard title for God, sometimes qualified as "your father in heaven." It is this distinction that allows Matthew to say, "Call no one your father on earth . . ." (23:9); in Matthew God is the *pater familias* in the household of God (11:25). As this "head of the household" God knows what we need before we ask (6:8, 32) and is ready to give us good things (7:11). Nothing can happen to us of which

God is unaware (10:29). God is said to be perfect (5:48; *teleios* can also be translated as "mature" or "undivided"—that is, not of two minds; cf. 5:37). For all God's care of God's children, Matthew also says that God causes the sun to rise on both the good and the evil (5:45), without distinction. Verses close by instruct us to love our enemies (5:44) and to forgive our debtors, for as we forgive so shall God forgive us (6:14; 18:35).

Jesus is identified as Son of God, Son of David, and Son of Man, the latter being by far the most frequent title (although it is not always clear that it refers to Jesus). He is first declared "Son of God" by a voice from heaven at his baptism (3:17; cf. 17:5; 2:15). However, his birth by means of the Holy Spirit has earlier indicated his divine connection (1:20). The remaining references to Jesus as Son of God cluster around two significant texts: the temptation by the devil and the temptation at the cross. In each case, Jesus is taunted with the words, "If you are the Son of God . . .," and in each instance he shows himself to be obedient to God's purposes (4:1-11; 27:40, 43; see also 26:63). This purpose has been revealed at his birth, when the angel instructs Joseph to name the child "Jesus, for he will save his people from their sins" (1:20; 26:26-29). It is Jesus' obedience to the word of God that leads to the cross, and, beyond the cross, to the promise of God with us (1:21; 28:20), indicating the restoration of our relationship with God. The close relationship between Jesus and God is lifted up in 11:25-27 (see the discussion on the Gospel for Proper 9, July 6, below). These verses, like the birth narrative, reveal that Jesus is both distinct from God (as Son; see 24:36), yet as the obedient Son faithfully reflects the will and purposes of God.

> It is Jesus' obedience to the word of God that leads to the cross, and, beyond the cross, to the promise of God with us, indicating the restoration of our relationship with God.

The movement of the Holy Spirit, in Matthew, is closely aligned with the Father and the Son (cf. Luke-Acts where the Spirit blows where it will). At Jesus' baptism, for example, it is the Spirit *of God* who descends on Jesus (cf. 10:20). This is, by the way, the one other place in Matthew's Gospel apart from 28:19 where the Father, Son, and Spirit appear together in the text. Jesus is conceived by the power of the Holy Spirit (1:18, 20) and, in turn, John the Baptist declares that Jesus will baptize with the Holy Spirit (3:11). Yet it is by *God's* Spirit that Jesus casts out demons (12:28). It is difficult, therefore, to speak of the Spirit apart from God and Jesus. In the Gospel of Matthew, it has no independent mission within the life of the church.

The triadic formula occurs in the midst of Jesus' final words to the eleven disciples (minus Judas). The setting is significant: mountains are where revelatory moments occur (4:8; 5:1; 14:23; 15:29; 17:1; 24:3). Although not included in the lection, it is worth noting why the disciples go to the mountain: because the women, to whom Jesus also appeared, told them to go. Jesus announces that he has received all authority on heaven and earth. This echoes the temptation in chapter 4 where the devil promises to give Jesus "all the kingdoms of the world." Jesus, the obedient Son, rejects this offer. His obedience renders him far more authority: the authority that belongs alone to God. He instructs the disciples to go to "all nations." Although some interpret this as a mission to the Gentiles, it is almost certain that Matthew intends both Jews and Gentiles, all the world (cf. 25:32). Only now are the disciples instructed to teach "everything that I have commanded you." Jesus' teaching offers, for Matthew, the definitive interpretation of God's word, Torah. "I am with you always" brings us full circle, to 1:23, and reveals that risen Jesus and God are now one.

JOHN 3:16-18 (LFM)

These few verses offer a marvelous summary of John's rich and distinctive theology. According to John, the Son was with God in the beginning, so when John says God "gave" the Son (the Greek omits "his") we are reminded that Christ represents a self-giving act on the part of God. This is why John calls Christ the "only Son." We are all offered the opportunity to become children of God (1:12), yet Christ is the "only Son" because he is the One who has been sent from the very heart of God. This designation "the only Son" occurs in verses 16 and 18, so that the passage is framed by references to the revelatory nature of God.

> In the Gospel of Matthew, the Spirit has no independent mission within the life of the church.

In verse 17 John says that God sent the Son into the world. The world, in John's view, has rejected the ways and the truth of God (1:10); it is a place of chaos, not unlike the watery void in Genesis 1. We do not have to look far to see how John could reach such a conclusion. Yet the world is not, ultimately, irredeemable. From the beginning of the Gospel, God moves to restore the world, to draw it to Godself. God does this by sending God's only Son into the world—to us: a testimony of God's love and God's desire to give life (wholeness) to the world. The many actions performed by Jesus—the healings, the feeding of the multitude, the raising of Lazarus, the establishing of a community of friends—reveal that wholeness includes physical as well as spiritual well-being. The two are closely intertwined.

The difficult words are those that speak of condemnation for those who do not believe. On the one hand, John states that God's desire is not to condemn, but to save; on the other hand, those who do not believe are condemned already. This radical dualism (creating a "them" and an "us") is frightening because it is the language of zealots. It has the capacity to turn love into coercion, and make ends justify means. John, however, tells us that Jesus has "sheep that do not belong to this fold" (10:16). How the lines are drawn may not be self-evident. As those who believe, this text offers us a chance to explore how we make known God's love for the world as individuals and communities. As one of the texts for Trinity Sunday, it describes the close relationship of God and Christ, the heart of God reaching out to the world in love.

Notes

1. W. D. Davies and Dale C. Allison, *The Gospel According to Saint Matthew,* vol. 3; International Critical Commentary (London: T&T Clark, 1997), 685.

SECOND SUNDAY AFTER PENTECOST

EIGHTH SUNDAY IN ORDINARY TIME / PROPER 3

MAY 25, 2008

Revised Common (RCL)	Episcopal (BCP)	Roman Catholic (LFM)★
Isa. 49:8–16a	Isa. 49:8–18	Isa. 49:14–15
Psalm 131	Psalm 62 or 62:6–14	Ps. 62:2-3, 6-7, 8-9
1 Cor. 4:1-5	1 Cor. 4:1-5 (6-7) 8-13	1 Cor. 4:1-5
Matt. 6:24-34	Matt. 6:24-34	Matt. 6:24-34

FIRST READING

ISAIAH 49:8-16A (RCL)
ISAIAH 49:8-13 (BCP)
ISAIAH 49:14-15 (LFM)

This reading from Deutero-Isaiah describes the deliverance God has promised to those who were led into captivity in Babylon (597 and 598 B.C.E.) following the destruction of the Temple in Jerusalem (587 B.C.E.). Prior to this cataclysmic event, many had already been scattered at the time of the Assyrian conquest of the Northern Kingdom of Israel (730–722 B.C.E.). During the turbulent years in between these events, some fled from Judea to Egypt, some to other regions resulting in the beginning of what is known as the Jewish diaspora. In 539 B.C.E. Babylon was conquered by Cyrus, emperor of Persia, who subsequently allowed some of the exiles to return to Jerusalem.

If we focus on the joy in these verses without due attention to this background we may miss their impact. For those of us who have known only comfort the idea of exile is difficult to comprehend; it may feel like nothing more than being sent to our room as a child. Yet we do not need to look far, perhaps no further than our congregations, to meet those who have lost homes, families, jobs, and literally fled for their lives as armies have crossed their lands bringing unspeakable violence and destruction. Many of these have spent years in refugee camps,

★ In the Roman Catholic Church, the Sunday after Trinity Sunday is celebrated as the Solemnity of Corpus Christi (Body and Blood of Christ). Comments on the texts for that day may be found in *New Proclamation Commentary on Feasts: Holy Days and Other Celebrations,* ed. David B. Lott (Minneapolis: Fortress Press, 2007).

waiting for a word of hope: that the violence has ended and they may return. It is the fear and despair brought about by such a situation that we need to try and embrace in order to hear the words of hope spoken by Isaiah.

The verses begin with a fourfold declaration by God: "I have answered you," "I have helped you," "I have kept you," "I have given you." The first two declarations reveal the nature of God as one who hears the cry of those in distress and takes initiative on their behalf. The final two declarations reveal that God has preserved them for a purpose: that those who were once themselves without hope might become a hope to the nations. This is a remarkable vision. It goes beyond personal salvation, beyond restoration of the community, even, and calls on those who have been delivered to be concerned for the welfare of all peoples. In context, this would include even the Babylonians who were responsible for their exile in the first place. Following as they do on the second of the servant songs (Isa. 49:1-7), some hear the "you" in these verses as a reference to an individual, prophetic figure. Yet the servant role in Deutero-Isaiah is also filled by the corporate body, Israel. Further ambiguity is found in verses 9b-10: Is the one who has pity on the returning exiles the servant or God? In verses 11-12 the actor is clearly God, whose actions invite the praise of all creation.

> This remarkable vision goes beyond personal salvation, beyond restoration of the community, and calls on those who have been delivered to be concerned for the welfare of all peoples.

The language of these verses describes a new exodus. Those returning to Zion will come not only from Babylon, but from all those places to which the people Israel have been scattered. Syene likely refers to modern Aswan in southern Egypt. Klaus Baltzer observes a "sting" in these verses since Aswan is located opposite the island of Elephantine where Jews had established a temple (destroyed in 411 B.C.E.). The return of those from Syene to Jerusalem would give priority to the temple located there.[1] Particularly prominent is language evoking the image of the shepherd (vv. 9b-10; see Psalm 23). This image is recurrent in Scripture to describe the faithful leader (often identified as God or Jesus) who provides nourishment and safely guides those being led. To those who have had to scrape out a living from dust, the shepherd provides comfort and relief.

The closing verses (14-16a) signal that not everyone is rejoicing equally at the return of the exiles. Those who have remained in Zion wonder if God's comfort and compassion extends also to them. Ada María Isasi-Díaz, theologian and Cuban refugee, observes that such tension within fractured communities requires repentance and forgiveness on the part of the exiles as well as those who stayed behind so that the community may be restored. Otherwise, our hate and desire for revenge may become for us new places of exile.[2] Isaiah 49 is a reminder that this, too, is a part of our deliverance, so that we may fulfill our role as God's covenant with all peoples.

RESPONSIVE READING
PSALM 131 (RCL)

This psalm is "A Song of Ascents" and belongs to a series of psalms (120–134) that may have been sung by pilgrims as they journeyed toward Jerusalem for festal celebrations. The attitude of humility and trust expressed in the psalm is similar to that in the prayers we pray as we prepare to worship God. The heart refers to what we call the mind; thus the psalmist is not saying that her heart is downcast, but that her heart is not swollen with grand thoughts, things "too great and too marvelous for me." In the psalms, marvelous deeds are ascribed consistently to God. The psalmist not only acknowledges the limitations of human thought and deed, but recognizes that overvaluing our capacities can prevent us from placing our trust in God.

Among the pilgrims traveling to Jerusalem would have been women and children. The image in the psalm of God as a mother and the pilgrim as a "weaned child" would have readily spoken to this context. A weaned child was about three years old, old enough to wander off on its own and to ask questions that are beyond answer. In the arms of its mother, however, who has been its source of nurture, comfort, and sustenance, the child is calmed and quieted. This image echoes Isaiah 49:15 where the prophet declares that God is like a mother who does not fail to show compassion toward her child. The psalmist's concluding call to "hope in the Lord" speaks to the vulnerable child as well as the weary, returning exile.

PSALM 62 OR 62:6-14 (BCP)
PSALM 62:2-3, 6-7, 8-9 (LFM)

The opening words of this psalm speak to the quiet surety that comes from trust in God. It does not silence all internal voices: verses 3-4 lift up a cry of complaint against those who are false friends, who "bless with their mouths" and seek to bring down one who is already on the verge of collapse. Yet this cry is enclosed by words of confidence in God (vv. 1-2, 5-7), who is declared to be "my rock, my salvation, my fortress" and "my hope, my deliverance, my honor, my refuge." The repeated use of "my" underscores the confidence of the psalmist that "God alone" (vv. 1, 2, 5, 6) will not forsake even "the lone wild bird in lofty flight."[3]

In verse 8 the psalmist shifts from personal meditation to public proclamation. Reflecting on the human condition the psalmist observes that both great and small are "but a breath" (v. 9). Yet the constellation of language related to money and gain in verses 9-12 (balances used to weigh coins; extortion; robbery; riches; repay) suggests that a particular concern here is those who put their confidence in financial gain (anticipating the Gospel lection). Robbery need not refer to banditry; it was also used to describe the oppression of the poor by the rich through taxes, wages withheld, debts demanded. To seek to increase wealth was, effectively, to rob the poor. Addressing God directly in verses 11-12, the psalmist expresses confidence in God's steadfast love, which seeks the benefit of all, but also reminds God of the need for justice, to "repay to all according to their work."

Second Reading
1 CORINTHIANS 4:1-5 (RCL, LFM)
1 CORINTHIANS 4:1-5 (6-7) 8-13 (BCP)

These verses from 1 Corinthians drop us into the middle of a conversation and are difficult to untangle apart from the rest of the letter. Verses 8-13 give voice to a part of the conflict in Corinth: Paul accuses the Corinthians of having become "rich." Although social status may be one of the divisions among the Corinthians (11:17-22), Paul here is probably not referring to wealth, but to the elevated status some Corinthians claim because they have attained wisdom through Christ. This wisdom appears to be manifested in spiritual gifts, such as speaking in tongues or knowledge that allows them to eat meat offered to idols unharmed (1:4-7; 8:1-13). Paul sees this perceived elevated status as contrary to the Christian life. He lifts up the life of apostles (in reality, himself) as an example to them. Their every gain is countered by Paul's own deprivation and shameful status. The list of hardships that he claims for himself should not be taken literally for the most part, but as examples of hardship lists found in ancient literature.

It seems that the elevated status enjoyed by some Corinthians has led to ranking within the community based on manifestations of gifts and wisdom. Paul counters this view in verses 1-5, telling the Corinthians to think of him (*logizomai*, reckon or evaluate) as that of a "servant" (*hupēretēs*, a helper or assistant) and "steward" (often a slave who has supervision of the household). In either case, Paul is focused on the responsibilities entrusted to him ("mysteries" remain undefined, but may refer generally to God's providential plan for the salvation of the Gentiles) rather than the spiritual gifts manifested through him. He goes on to caution the Corinthians against pronouncing judgment before the end times. Such judging of one another can result in tearing the community apart rather than building it up. Paul

> Paul is focused on the responsibilities entrusted to him rather than the spiritual gifts manifested through him.

concludes that each will receive commendation ("praise") from God, thus suggesting the value of all gifts used for the life of the community.

THE GOSPEL
MATTHEW 6:24-34 (RCL, BCP, LFM)

These verses are both familiar and troubling. Anytime wealth or posses-sions are mentioned you can feel the discomfort in the pews. On the one hand are those who wonder: Am I not entitled to the things I have earned? Does the Gospel demand that I impoverish myself for the sake of others? On the other are those who ask: I've been unemployed for a year; is God going to pay my bills for me? The Gospel does not let us off the hook easily. Instead it invites us to struggle with these legitimate questions and to reevaluate our priorities again and again.

The language of the opening verse is embedded in a world described by mas-ters and slaves. The word for "master" is *kurios* and refers to those who have pos-sessions and authority. In other contexts it is translated as "lord" and is the title we use in reference to both God and Jesus. A slave is both the possession of and under the authority of the *kurios*. Paul (Rom. 1:1; Phil. 1:1) identifies himself as a slave of Jesus Christ, signaling to us how familiar and powerful this language was in the ancient world. The legacy of slavery in the United States can cause us to feel uncomfortable with this language. It should always be used with caution so that we do not unconsciously use it to justify abusive contexts. Here, the language of master and slave is used to punctuate the question of loyalties.

Verse 24 is anticipated by verse 21: "For where your treasure is, there your heart will be also." When we read in verse 24 that we cannot serve God and mammon, we understand that it is a question of loyalty, for we will "love the one and hate the other." We experience "love" and "hate" as emotions, and use this language to describe our attitude toward everything from food to family mem-bers. The too-free use of this language has come to render it almost meaning-less. The parallel line in this verse, however, offers us a different way to think about these two words: "love" is demonstrated as loyalty or commitment to another; "hate" is demonstrated by disregard or scorn. Neither word is concerned with how we feel about things so much as how we orient ourselves and, consequently, how we will behave.

> Here "love" is demonstrated as loyalty or com-mitment to another; "hate" is demonstrated by disregard or scorn.

Mammon refers broadly to wealth and property. The Gospel recognizes the allure of wealth, as powerful today as it was in the ancient world. We are sur-rounded by advertising that seeks to persuade us that we deserve everything we want and more. The sky is the limit. In the ancient world, limits to wealth were perceived as real. There was only so much land and only so many people could own it. There was only so much food and only so many people could have access to it. In such a world one person's gain was another person's loss. To serve mammon (literally, "be enslaved to," *douleuō*), then, had implications for how one behaved in relationship to others: to serve mammon, to seek personal gain was, effectively, to rob someone else. That someone was usually those who had little to lose in the first place.

The "therefore" in verse 25 signals that what follows is an explication of what has gone before: that is, "if you love God, then do not worry . . . ." The word for "worry" (*merimnaō*) can be rendered as "anxious" or "unduly apprehensive" (see also v. 34). This helps to put these verses in perspective. They do not say that food and clothing are unimportant. In the peasant society of the ancient world, these things were very important, representing the minimum of what was needed to get by: food on the table and clothing on your back. What the Gospel cautions against is letting our anxiety over having enough food or sufficient clothing so dominate our lives that it consumes all our energy, becoming the driving force of our behavior and ultimately claiming our loyalty.

The imagery of verses 25-29 describes a world populated by peasant farmers. In this subsistence economy, survival depended on the contributions of the entire household. Sowing and reaping were primarily, although not exclusively, the work of men. Spinning was a task carried out by women who were responsible for providing clothing for the household. These tasks consumed the days of peasant farmers. Yet the Gospel invites them to look up from their labors and observe the birds of the air that do not gather into barns, yet are fed by God, and the lilies of the field that do not toil or spin, yet are arrayed more gloriously than Solomon (who, for all his wisdom, was notorious for his gathering of wealth). In Matthew, the word for "toil" (*kopiaō*) occurs elsewhere only in 11:28, where Jesus declares, "Come to me all you that are weary [*kopiōntes,* "those exhausted from their toils"] and are carrying heavy burdens, and I will give you rest." This reference is often thought of in spiritual terms, but the link to chapter 6 indicates that it is also concerned with those who labor under heavy burdens just to survive.

At three points in these verses we are reminded that we are of more value: than the birds of the air, the lilies of the field, the grass that is alive today and burned tomorrow. This construction ("if the lesser, how much more the greater") is common in ancient literature. Although we are the ones who are said to be of "more value," these sayings are, perhaps, less about us and more about God. If God is concerned even for the transient things of the world, how much more will God care for transient humankind who are created in God's own image?

> If God is concerned even for the transient things of the world, how much more will God care for transient humankind who are created in God's own image?

God, who will not let a sparrow fall unnoticed, promises to lift the burdens from those who must toil for their sustenance and give them rest.

Verse 33 returns the focus to us with the admonition to "strive first for the kingdom of God and God's righteousness." This is an important verse because it is a reminder, once again, that this passage is not primarily about "God and me" but about how we live in relationship with God and with one another. If we serve mammon, it is too easy for our primary concern to become "me." If we serve God, then we are oriented toward the larger economy of God, the whole of creation, and to value each life in the same way that God has valued each of us.

Notes

1. Klaus Baltzer, *Deutero-Isaiah: A Commentary on Isaiah 40–55,* trans. Margaret Kohl, Hermeneia (Minneapolis: Fortress Press, 2001), 316.

2. Ada María Isasi-Díaz, "'By the Rivers of Babylon': Exile as a Way of Life," in *Reading from this Place, Vol. 1: Social Location and Biblical Interpretation in the United States,* ed. Fernando F. Segovia and Mary Ann Tolbert (Minneapolis: Fortress Press, 1995), 159.

3. Henry Richard McFadyen, "The Lone Wild Bird," in *The Presbyterian Hymnal: Hymns, Psalms, and Spiritual Songs* (Louisville: Westminster John Knox, 1990), #320.

THIRD SUNDAY AFTER PENTECOST

NINTH SUNDAY IN ORDINARY TIME / PROPER 4

June 1, 2008

Revised Common (RCL)	Episcopal (BCP)	Roman Catholic (LFM)
Gen. 6:9-22; 7:24; 8:14-19 or Deut. 11:18-21, 26-28	Deut. 11:18-21, 26-28	Deut. 11:18-21, 26-28, 32
Psalm 46 or 31:1-5, 19-24	Psalm 31 or 31:1-5, 19-24	Ps. 31:2-3a, 3b-4, 17, 25
Rom. 1:16-17; 3:22b-28 (29-31)	Rom. 3:21-25a, 28	Rom. 3:21-25, 28
Matt. 7:21-29	Matt. 7:21-27	Matt. 7:21-27

FIRST READING
GENESIS 6:9-22; 7:24; 8:14-19 (RCL)

This is not the stuff of children's books or vacation Bible schools. The story of the flood reveals God's internal struggle to honor the terms by which creation has been ordered, and sets in motion the first of many efforts by God (for instance, the sending of prophets, Jesus) to restore creation to the divine image. A troubling aspect of this narrative is God's decision to destroy what God created in what appears to be a fit of anger, followed by what sounds like repentance (9:11). We are left to wonder if God is struggling in this story to become reconciled to the earlier decision to allow human creatures to function as moral or immoral agents, able to act independently of their Creator.

The selected verses offer an abbreviated telling of the story. The lectionary follows the Priestly (P) version, as in the previous lection, so that we hear in these verses echoes of the creation story. The omission of significant portions of the story as told by P (see in addition, 7:6, 11, 13-16a, 18-21, 24; 8:1-2a, 3b-4, 13a; and especially 9:1-17) leaves gaps that the preacher may feel obliged to fill by the inclusion of additional verses.

The text begins with a threefold description of Noah. He is said to be righteous (a word also used to describe God; of humankind, one who is counted upright in the eyes of God: for instance, Pss. 1:6; 34:16; 55:22), blameless (for instance,

Pss. 15:2; 119:1), and to walk with God (an expression elsewhere used only of Enoch, Gen. 5:21-24). This description stands in contrast to the rest of the earth, which is said to be corrupt and filled with violence. Following on the creation story, this lection reveals that what God has created has somehow come to ruin. The violence and corruption that consume the earth clearly stand in contrast to God's intention that the earth continue to be engaged in life-giving acts of creation. This is underscored by the phrase, "And God saw the earth was corrupt" (v. 12), which echoes in counterpoint 1:31, "And God saw everything that he had made, and indeed, it was very good." How this ruination came about is not specified and it is striking that blame is not placed specifically on humankind. All of creation is caught in God's destruction (an image made more palpable by the South Asian tsunami of 2004). Nonetheless, just as humankind is given dominion over creation in Genesis 1, in Genesis 6 Noah is given responsibility for the remnant that is to be preserved. Noah does all that God has commanded, demonstrating his righteous character, worthy of being partner in God's covenant.

> The violence and corruption that consume the earth clearly stand in contrast to God's intention that the earth continue to be engaged in life-giving acts of creation.

DEUTERONOMY 11:18-21, 26-28 (RCL ALT., BCP) DEUTERONOMY 11:18, 26-28, 32 (LFM)

The Gospel lection offers a good illustration of the text from Deuteronomy: build your house on the rock, not on the sand. Deuteronomy puts it in terms of blessing and curse. This language may sound to our ears like something out of a fairytale, but it is rooted in an understanding of the consequences of human action. Barbara Kingsolver, in her novel *Prodigal Summer,* concludes, "Every choice is a world made new for the chosen."[1] Our choices often have unintended consequences and may have an impact on things and people we cannot see. Blessing and curse.

The word *obey* may also be translated "give heed to" (built on the root "to hear": *shama*). In either case, volition is required. Whether we read these words in the context of Deuteronomy or more broadly in relation to the Gospel we need to read (and heed) them as an expression of God's concern for just relations, with respect to both humans and the earth. A key phrase in this passage is the warning against following "other gods that you have not known" (v. 28). There is always the temptation that the view will look better from the other side of the fence. Yet

> Over and over again the Scriptures testify to the character of God as the One who demonstrates steadfast love, who protects the needy, who sets free the captive.

over and over again the Scriptures testify to the character of God as the One who demonstrates steadfast love (*hesed*), who protects the needy, who sets free the captive. Unknown gods are often the ones that we fashion after ourselves.

The words with which the lection begins are a repetition of the familiar *Shema* (Deut. 6:4-6). The instruction to "put these words of mine in your heart and soul" resonates with Jer. 31:33, and anticipates Jesus, showing that the intent of God's statutes has never been legalism, but mercy. The heart was viewed as the seat of volition; the soul (*nephesh*) as the life-breath: together they describe our whole being. Writing "these words" on the doorpost and gate is a way to remind us in our coming in and going out of the call to be a blessing in the land; teaching them to our children (a communal activity not restricted to parents) ensures that they will continue from generation to generation. These words are to fill our whole being, and inform the whole of our lives.

Responsive Reading
PSALM 46 (RCL)

This psalm complements the passages in both Genesis and with its roaring waters and desolations brought upon the earth. The context of the psalm, however, is warring among the nations. In the midst of this tumult, the psalmist asserts the presence of God "our refuge" and our "help in trouble." With confidence, the psalmist declares, "we will not fear." Perhaps aware that we, the hearers, may be less confident, the psalmist exhorts us to "behold the works of the LORD" as proof of God's capacity to save. God's voice, says the psalmist, is able to melt the earth; God makes wars to cease; when God is in our midst, we are not moved. Finally, we hear God's own voice, "Be still, and know that I am God." To be still in the midst of tumult is the greatest challenge.

PSALM 31 (BCP)
PSALM 31:1-5, 19-24 (RCL ALT., BCP ALT.)
PSALM 31:2-3A, 3B-4, 17, 25 (LFM)

Psalm 31 follows a pattern of personal prayers of petition, interspersed with expressions of confidence in God's deliverance. References to scheming (vv. 4, 13, 18, 20), accompanied by the cry "do not let me be put to shame" (vv. 1, 17), suggest that the psalmist is the victim of a social or political plot. The result is social isolation (vv. 11, 12); the effect is a life dashed against the rocks: "I have become like a broken vessel." Despite depths of despair, the psalmist rejoices in the surety of God's presence. Where others abandon their friends, God preserves those who trust in God.

SECOND READING

ROMANS 1:16-27; 3:22B-28 (29-31) (RCL)
ROMANS 3:21-25A, 28 (BCP)
ROMANS 3:21-25, 28 (LFM)

In Romans, Paul is writing to a community that he did not found and that he has never visited. The "why" of his writing is signaled in 15:22-24: Paul hopes the churches at Rome will support his mission to Spain. Because they do not know him, however, he must demonstrate to them that they are of one mind in the gospel. This accounts for Paul's lengthy explication that makes up the body of the letter. Although some have read Romans as if addressed to both Jews and Gentiles, more recent scholarship suggests that it was written exclusively to Gentiles (see 1:5-6, 14-15); the "Jewish voice" in the text, then, is rhetorical, included for the sake of argumentation. This has implications for how we read and interpret this letter. To read Romans as a polemic against Jews is to misconstrue its meaning. Rather, it is concerned with how the God of Israel has extended grace to the Gentiles.

The RCL begins the lection at 1:16-17 with what may be called Paul's "thesis statement": salvation is available to all who have faith. "Faith" (*pistis*) may be translated as "trust" or "confidence," but also "faithfulness." This introduces some ambiguity into the text. Does "through faith for faith" mean *through the faithfulness of God for our faith* or *through our faith for our faith?* In either case, faith has less to do with intellectual assent than loyalty. This is underscored in the verses that follow, where the cause of God's wrath is creation's refusal to recognize God as their Creator. In denying this role to God, human creatures have not only failed to acknowledge their relationship to God, but to give thanks for the benefits they have received from God. Creation has become self-serving (rather than serving God), leading to all manner of abuse. The abuses named are standard slanders rather than actual particulars, but nonetheless apt. Verses 26-27 should be understood in terms of gender hierarchies assumed to in the ancient world: for a man or a woman to have intercourse with a member of the same sex violates this hierarchy by requiring one member to assume the dominant or subordinate role, thus stepping out of their gendered place.

> In denying God as Creator, human creatures have not only failed to acknowledge their relationship to God, but to give thanks for the benefits they have received from God.

The BCP and LFM begin the lection at 3:21 (RCL, v. 22b). Here another translation question arises (see vv. 22, 26): is *pisteōs Iēsou Christou* best translated *faith in Jesus Christ* (that is, our trust in Jesus) or *faith of Jesus Christ* (that is, faith demonstrated by Jesus)? Verses 21-23 reiterate the point of 1:18-27, namely that all have sinned ("missed the mark"; see also vv. 27-31). Verses 24-26 are theologically loaded, but hardly self-explanatory. A number of terms deserve explanation: *grace* ("good will" or "favor") comes from the sphere of patronage and relates to God's role as creator and initiator in our salvation. *Redemption* refers to "manumission from slavery"; in the ancient world, everyone served some master, therefore sin is represented as an almost personal force. *Hilastērion* ("means of making amends") is likely a reference to the mercy seat in the Temple; combined with the statement "by his blood," it invites association with the Day of Atonement (Yom Kippur; see Leviticus 16). The blood is not a penalty paid but is an act of cleansing and reconsecration. The initiative in all of this resides with God: in Jesus Christ creation is reconsecrated to the Creator. The phrase "in Jesus Christ" (*en*) refers, for Paul, to a sphere in which we take on the very spirit of Christ.

The option to include verses 27-31 introduces the subject of the law. Verse 31 is the key: faith does not overthrow the law, which we continue to uphold. Yet it is our trust, demonstrated through acts of loyalty, in God's continuing favor that places us in right relationship with God.

THE GOSPEL
MATTHEW 7:21-29 (RCL)
MATTHEW 7:21-27 (BCP, LFM)

A pivotal scene in the film *Lawrence of Arabia* occurs when Lawrence crawls out of the desert (the one they said could not be crossed). Standing along the Suez Canal, he is spotted by a lone motorcyclist who, seeing this figure encrusted in sand, calls out, "Who are you?" This is, of course, the question: Who is Lawrence of Arabia? His story is one of many examples demonstrating our fascination with this question "Who are you?" The lives of the rich and famous, fictional characters such as Harry Potter, and even our own selves all fall under its scrutiny. It is, in many respects, the question that the Gospel lection for the day poses to us as well.

This lection brings to conclusion the Sermon on the Mount, the most extensive teaching passage in Matthew and filled with provocative illustrations of the values, behaviors, and attitudes that describe the transformative perspective of the realm of God. Having challenged us to see things in a new way, the Sermon concludes with a series of warnings, reminders that the realm of God is not something easily attained. Even some who think they have found their way may be surprised to discover themselves excluded. These warnings prompt us to ask of ourselves and one another, "Who are you?" and to ponder how it is that we know.

The lection falls into two parts. The first (vv. 21-23) describes those who have prophesied in Jesus' name, and cast out demons in his name and performed many acts of power in his name, yet whom Jesus refuses to recognize (Who are you?). We may think these people are easy to identify: they are the charlatans, all talk and glamour, who have television shows and make money off of the innocent faith of naïve people. But nothing in the text suggests they are, in fact, fake. Matthew has already issued a warning about false prophets (7:16-20), saying that "you shall know them by their fruits." In verses 21-23 we encounter prophets who apparently *are* producing good fruits; neither their prophecies nor mighty deeds of power are critiqued or rejected. Further, a close reading of Matthew suggests that the community may have viewed themselves as prophets (5:12; 10:41; 23:34). For the rest, Jesus himself performs mighty deeds (11:20-23; 13:54) and both Jesus and the disciples cast out demons (9:33; 10:8; 12:27-28). It is not the actions of these followers that are the cause of their exclusion. This moves the text closer to home. Do we not sometimes take prophetic stands in church or society, or perform mighty deeds in the name of Jesus? If being a prophet can be a positive role and deeds of power can be "good fruit," what, then, is at issue?

> Following Jesus' example, doing God's will requires identifying what we want in order to rightly discern what God wants.

Matthew responds, saying that only the one who does the will of God will enter the kingdom of heaven. We encounter this phrase numerous times in the Gospel. We are instructed to petition God in the Lord's Prayer, "thy will be done" (6:10), and Jesus himself, facing the time of trial, prays for God's will to be done (26:42). Following Jesus' example, doing God's will requires identifying what we want in order to rightly discern what God wants. We do not just imitate Jesus with this prayer; those who do the will of God are said to be Jesus' brothers and sisters (12:50). Doing the will of God draws us into relationship with Jesus and with one another. This is highlighted in 18:14 where Jesus says that it is *God's will* that not "one of these little ones should be lost." Doing the will of God means that we are to look out for one another, particularly those most lost and vulnerable. The final occurrence of this phrase is in a parable found only in the Gospel of Matthew: the parable of the two sons (21:28-32). The parable reveals that it is not what we say, but what we do that reveals whether we do the will of God.

> In our world, it all depends on us; in the realm of God, it depends on the word of God that called us into being.

So, perhaps these prophets claim to produce "good fruit" when they did not. Or perhaps they produced good fruit in the name of Jesus, but claimed the glory for themselves. Or perhaps they produced good fruit, but in doing so, fractured the community of faith. Or perhaps they produced good fruit without stopping to discern what was required; for example, when we go into communities in need and determine what the best solution is without first listening to the voices and insights of that community. The challenge is not to dismiss the prophets, but to see in them our own potential pitfalls.

The second part of the lection begins, like the first part, with an admonition followed by an illustration. The admonition not only to hear Jesus' words, but to do them, anticipates the aforementioned parable of the two sons. It is Jesus' words, interpreting the word of God as expressed in Torah, that form the foundation on which the house is to be built. To state, perhaps the obvious, the foundation is not us. In a culture that prizes self-sufficiency, this is counterintuitive. In our world, it all depends on us; in the realm of God, it depends on the word of God that, called us into being (see the above discussion of Romans). This brings us back to the question: "Who are you?" How we answer this question will also answer another important question: What is it that sustains us, that anchors us in a storm? And will we simply rest on this foundation, or, living out the word of God in action, will we build a life that does not crumble, but, like a house, is able to offer shelter and hospitality to others?

Note

1. Barbara Kingsolver, *Prodigal Summer* (New York: HarperCollins, 2000), 444.

FOURTH SUNDAY AFTER PENTECOST

Tenth Sunday in Ordinary Time / Proper 5
June 8, 2008

Revised Common (RCL)	Episcopal (BCP)	Roman Catholic (LFM)
Gen. 12:1-9 or	Hos. 5:15—6:6	Hos. 6:3-6
Hos. 5:15—6:6		
Ps. 33:1-2 or 50:7-15	Psalm 50 or 50:7-15	Ps. 50:1-8, 12-13, 14-15
Rom. 4:13-25	Rom. 4:13-18	Rom. 4:18-25
Matt. 9:9-13, 18-26	Matt. 9:9-13	Matt. 9:9-13

FIRST READING
GENESIS 12:1-9 (RCL)

Of all humankind, why did God choose Abram? Paul will make much of Abram's righteousness, but as yet he is an unknown quantity. This narrative sets in motion the first of many stories that will reveal his character. In this story we are introduced to Abram through his actions (notice that we never hear the voice of Abram in these verses). Abram goes, as God has commanded him, from his own country and family; at Shechem he builds an altar to the Lord "who had appeared to him"; he builds a second altar near Bethel and "invoked the name of the LORD." These few words suggest a shift in Abram's relationship to God: at Shechem Abram worships the One who has sought him out; at Bethel, Abram becomes the one who seeks ("invokes") God.

The character whose voice dominates the text is God. God commands Abram to leave his country and his father's house. In a culture where identity is lodged in kinship and group, this is a remarkable demand. Today, we move from place to place for work or a change of scene. Phones and computers ensure that we are never far from those we left behind. For Abram, such a step requires leaving behind the known world. Without family and social connections, Abram becomes dependent on God as the source of his identity and his sustenance. Nonetheless, Abram does not travel lightly. He takes with him his wife Sarai and nephew Lot (names we are intended to remember), along with all their possessions, dependents, and slaves. Abram is no Horatio Alger, starting from nothing.

God promises to make of Abram a great nation (or people) in a land of God's choosing. This promise is enfolded within multiple occurrences of the word *blessing* (five times in verses 2-3). We have encountered God's blessing earlier in the stories of the creation (1:22, 28, 31; 2:3) and Noah (9:1); it describes God's fundamental goodwill toward humankind, but even more, God's promise to sustain us in all circumstances. It is a word, however, that occurs only in relationship: to receive God's blessing we must seek the One who seeks us. The text also says that God will bless those who bless Abram and curse (or show contempt for) those who curse him. This is the language of patronage: God will protect Abram, whom God has adopted as a client and who, in turn, serves and honors God. The need for such protection points toward the challenges that lie ahead of Abram and

> It is the assurance of God's presence with Abram that makes it possible to step into the unknown.

his descendents before God's promises will be fulfilled. The future, therefore, still contains unknowns. It is the assurance of God's presence with Abram that makes it possible to step into the unknown.

HOSEA 5:15—6:6 (RCL ALT., BCP)
HOSEA 6:3-6 (LFM)

Hosea was a prophet of the Northern Kingdom, active during the eighth century B.C.E. The immediate literary context refers to a period of political intrigue in Israel, when they formed an alliance with Syria against Assyria (5:8-14). In an attempt to force Judah to join the alliance, they invaded Jerusalem; Judah later retaliated by invading Israel. The alliance failed and in 733 B.C.E. Israel became a client kingdom of Assyria. More broadly, Hosea rages against Israel's flirtation with other gods (4:12-15). Political intrigue and seeking after any god who will support one's causes often go hand in hand. Both point to a kind of desperation driven by loss of direction.

At 5:15 the text shifts from an oracle of judgment to a dialogue between God and Israel. God begins, stating the intention to withdraw until "they acknowledge their guilt and seek my face." In many churches a prayer of confession is lifted up each week, but this is not necessarily the same as accepting culpability. It is a hard thing to face our wrongs. In Hosea, God sits backs and waits.

Israel responds in 6:1-3. Their words echo the confidence expressed in the psalms: God will surely revive us and quickly. Yet there are telling signs that something is amiss in their perspective. They say, "it is God who has torn" and "struck down," but they offer no reflection on why this has happened. They move quickly to the solution without examining the problem. In verse 3 they exhort themselves to "know the LORD." If this were a psalm, they would go on to explain *why* they should know the Lord: "for God's steadfast love endures forever" or "God raises up the needy in distress." Instead, they look for a sign of God's appearing in nature.

God's response in 6:4 will sound familiar to anyone responsible for a wayward child: "What shall I do with you?" God discerns that their intentions have as much substance as a cloud. Verse 6 (quoted in Matthew 9:13 and echoed in Psalm 50) is so familiar to us that we may miss the radical nature of this declaration. Sacrifice was the way to worship God, as accepted as our celebration of the Lord's Supper. God's rejection of burnt offerings is like pulling away the curtain that masks the Wizard of Oz: it is an effort to see what really lies behind the gesture. What God seeks to find is *hesed,* steadfast love expressed in loyalty and informed by knowledge of God.

RESPONSIVE READING
PSALM 33:1–12 (RCL)

The reference in verse 12 to "the people whom he has chosen as his heritage" connects the psalm to God's promises to Abraham in Genesis. A lengthy introduction to the psalm (vv. 1-5) exhorts us to praise the Lord because God, whose word is upright and whose steadfast love fills the earth, is faithful, righteous, and just. We may think it obvious *why* God should receive our praise, but the psalmist invites us to reflect on *whom* and *what* we praise. Are they worthy? What attributes would we ascribe to them? Verses 6-10 focus on God's role as creator, and begin and end with references to God's word (see also v. 4). It is by God's word that creation came into being and it is by God's breath breathed into us that we have life. This description both underscores the power of God and our dependence on God as our creator. Verses 10-12 continue this theme, contrasting the counsel of nations (peoples), which is ephemeral, with the counsel of God, which stands forever.

> What God seeks to find is *hesed,* steadfast love expressed in loyalty and informed by knowledge of God.

PSALM 50 (BCP)
PSALM 50:7–15 (RCL ALT., BCP ALT.)
PSALM 50:1–8, 12–13, 14–15 (LFM)

What happens when we gather for worship? Psalm 50 challenges us to reflect on the attitudes that inform our practices. The opening verses describe God coming to judge the people. This need not be the end times; if the participle in verse 5 is rendered as contemporaneous action ("who are making a covenant"), the setting suggested is that of a covenant renewal ceremony. The psalm is divided between words to the faithful (v. 5) and words to the wicked (v. 16). The faithful God admonishes the people to offer sacrifices with thanksgiving for the ways in which God has delivered them (vv. 14-15). God does *not* rebuke the people for their sacrifices per se (v. 8), which are assumed to be the appropriate way to worship God. Rather, the implication is that God is challenging what are perhaps ever more lavish displays of sacrifice, as if God were hungry. God chastises them for entering into covenant renewal when their behavior toward others violates the covenant itself. It is assumed that how we treat others is a direct reflection on our relationship with God. The references to covenant and sacrifice link this psalm to both the Genesis and Hosea texts.

Second Reading

ROMANS 4:13-25 (RCL)
ROMANS 4:13-18 (BCP)
ROMANS 4:18-25 (LFM)

These verses revolve around the faith of Abraham, the promises of God, and us, describing a theology that is, at heart, relational. The figure of Abraham is central to Paul's argument because of the promise in Genesis 17:5 that he will be "the father of many nations." This promise is interpreted by Paul to point to God's plan of salvation for *all* humankind: Gentiles as well as Jews. (This vision is not exclusive to Paul; it is anticipated in texts such as Isaiah 2:2-4; 42:6-7; 60:1-3.) Yet it was a promise that was dependent on Abraham's trust (faith) in God, since all the presenting circumstances argued against Abraham and Sarah bearing children. Paul builds phrase upon phrase to demonstrate Abraham's faith: "he believed," "hoping against hope," "he did not weaken in faith," "no distrust made him waver," "he grew strong in faith," "being fully convinced." It is this unwavering confidence, this loyalty to God, that renders Abraham righteous, that is, in right relationship with God.

Abraham's faith (trust) is set in contrast to the law, which, says Paul, cannot bring us into right relationship with God. This must be understood in terms of Paul's larger argument regarding the law (see the discussion of Romans 7:15-25a for Proper 9, July 6, below). What is of importance here for Paul's argument is that Abraham demonstrated trust in God not only before the giving of the law, but before he received the sign of circumcision—that is, the marker that separates Jew from Gentile (4:10-12). Therefore it is through faith that Gentiles have access to the grace (favor) of God.

> We are invited to see ourselves in Abraham who does not yet know the end; to "hope against hope" and "give glory to God."

God is described in these verses as the One who initiates the promise to Abraham (note the repetition of "promise" in verses 13, 14, 16, 20, 21). The phrase, "who gives life to the dead and calls into existence the things that do not exist," points to the end of the Abraham story when God's promise is fulfilled, but may easily be heard in the context of our own lives. Within the context of these verses, we are invited to see ourselves in Abraham who does not yet know the end; to "hope against hope" and "give glory to God" (the appropriate response to the One who shows us favor).

In verse 23 Paul, in good sermonic fashion, draws together the horizon of the text and the horizon of his audience. The God who "gives life to the dead" is the same God who raised Jesus from the dead. Like Abraham, we are invited to trust that God's promise to us—that we have been restored to right relationship with God—is sure.

The Gospel
MATTHEW 9:9-13, 18-26 (RCL)
MATTHEW 9:9-13 (BCP, LFM)

There are two call narratives in the Gospel of Matthew. The first is the familiar calling of the fishermen, which occurs just before Jesus begins his public ministry (4:18-22). This second call narrative is strategically placed between two passages that describe the role of Jesus in relation to sin and sinners. In the story that precedes, the healing of the paralytic, Jesus declares that the Son of Man (here, understood to be Jesus) has authority on earth to forgive sins (in the same way as God in heaven). In the verses that follow, Jesus declares that he has come not to call the righteous, but sinners. The healing of the paralytic signals that he has the authority to do so. The call of Matthew (in Mark and Luke, the tax collector is identified as Levi) serves as a bridge between these two passages.

Tax collectors are consistently associated with sinners in the Gospels, indicating their status as outcasts. Matthew alone has Jesus instruct the disciples to shun, as if they were "a Gentile and a tax collector," those members of the community who, having sinned against another member, refuse to listen to the voice of the com-

> When Matthew, no respectable fisherman, but a tax collector, follows Jesus without hesitation, a new element enters the band of followers.

munity (18:15-17). Greco-Roman authors associated tax collectors with beggars, thieves, and robbers.[1] This suggests that tax collectors were viewed as no better than thieves, perhaps because they took more than was due in order to supplement their own income (see Luke 19:1-10). However, tax collectors were also servants of the occupying power, Rome. Taxes benefited Rome, not the people of the Galilee—specifically, taxes paid for the Roman soldiers who kept the Romans in power and who could bring destruction on a community in a moment. When Matthew, no respectable fisherman, but a tax collector, follows Jesus without hesitation, a new element enters the band of followers.

The tension created by the presence of persons such as Matthew among Jesus' followers provokes the discussion that follows. The question is raised by the Pharisees who, in the Gospel of Matthew, are portrayed as Jesus' antagonists. We need to apply caution in taking Matthew's characterization of the Pharisees at face value, particularly since many people equate "Pharisees" with "Jews," leading to a false impression of Judaism as a living faith today. Although the Pharisees are a historical group within first-century Judaism, it is probably best to view them as a character type within the Gospel of Matthew and one that we know from our own communities of faith—that is, people who are concerned with protecting the purity of the group. These are the people who become anxious when persons of a different social class, or racial-ethnic group, or family structure come to the church. We politely suggest that they won't fit in or feel at home in our midst. And it is very likely that they will not, because we will shun them—not in a formal sense, but simply by forgetting to greet them, or invite them to activities, or help them find ways to offer leadership.

Jesus' responds that he has come to call sinners, those who are in need of healing. These words are both familiar and a comfort. Who among us is not in need of forgiveness, of healing? Yet we tend to think of our sins as private; as long as other people don't know, then we can masquerade as a member of the redeemed. What happens, then, when someone whom we identify as a known sinner enters our midst, or worse, if our own failings (whether divorce, depression, or driving drunk) somehow become public knowledge? When the sinners are no longer faceless, but us? When we become identified as the "Matthew" in Jesus' band of followers? Do we flee to another congregation?

Matthew alone includes the quotation from Hosea in this passage. This is consistent with Matthew's emphasis on obedience to God's word (see Matt. 4:4) and on Jesus as the One who offers a definitive interpretation of God's word (5:17). The effect created by the inclusion of the quotation from Hosea is of a context in which two groups have come into conflict over the correct way to interpret Scripture: the Pharisees and Jesus. This is underscored by the Pharisee's identification of Jesus as "your teacher." This, too, is a setting familiar to many of us from our own congregations and denominations. The quote does not, ultimately, resolve the conflict, but raises the question: What does it mean to show mercy to sinners? This is one of the many questions raised in the profound film *Shakespeare Behind Bars*.

The RCL includes with this passage two stories intertwined that lift up examples of those in need of healing. These stories suggest that mercy is revealed in acts of compassion and restoration. Although the NRSV describes the man who approaches Jesus as a "leader of the synagogue," these words are not found in the Greek; he is simply a leader in the community, perhaps a civil servant. Just as Matthew follows Jesus, now Jesus follows the man who has interceded on his daughter's behalf. There is nothing surprising on the part of the man; there is ample evidence from the ancient world of men demonstrating great affection toward their daughters. What is surprising is that Jesus follows the man; normally, people follow Jesus. This action on Jesus' part shows his willingness to demonstrate mercy. As they are departing, a woman suffering from hemorrhages approaches Jesus and touches his cloak. It should not be assumed that "hemorrhages" refers to menstrual bleeding or that the woman is unclean. This issue is not raised

> What is surprising here is that Jesus follows the man; normally, people follow Jesus. This shows Jesus' willingness to demonstrate mercy.

by the text. More likely, the story invites comparison between the woman and the ruler: the ruler, a man of status, approaches Jesus in public and falls down before him; the woman, of no apparent status, approaches Jesus in secret, relying on her faith. The woman is praised for her faith (inviting a connection with the texts from Genesis and Romans). Nonetheless, both receive mercy and healing; Jesus makes no distinction between them.

Note

1. J. Andrew Overman, *Church and Community in Crisis: The Gospel According to Matthew,* The New Testament in Context (Valley Forge: Trinity Press International, 1996), 126.

FIFTH SUNDAY AFTER PENTECOST

ELEVENTH SUNDAY IN ORDINARY TIME / PROPER 6

JUNE 15, 2008

Revised Common (RCL)	Episcopal (BCP)	Roman Catholic (LFM)
Gen. 18:1-15, (21:1-7) or Exod. 19:2-8a	Exod. 19:2-8a	Exod. 19:2-6a
Ps. 116:1-2, 12-19 or Psalm 100	Psalm 100	Psalm 100:1-2, 3, 5
Rom. 5:1-8	Rom. 5:6-11	Rom. 5:6-11
Matt. 9:35—10:8 (9-23)	Matt. 9:35—10:8 (9-15)	Matt. 9:35—10:8

FIRST READING
GENESIS 18:1-15 (21:1-7) (RCL)

"What happens to a dream deferred? Does it dry up like a raisin in the sun?"[1] The story of Abraham and Sarah is the story of a dream deferred. God has promised that their offspring will endure for generations (12:7; 15:5; 17:7) and they have been waiting long years for this promise to bear fruit (15:2-4; 16:1; 17:17). But Sarah is now past menopause; at ninety her womb is shriveled and dry. Abraham, even older, has no seed left. Although we know this story is about to have a happy ending, it is important to hold on to the tension. It is our experience of dreams deferred that allows us to enter into the story, to recognize the strain that dreams deferred can place on a relationship and the kind of desperate acts to which they can drive us (witness Abraham and Sarah's effort to bear a surrogate child using the slave Hagar).

The tension also allows us to experience the confusion and wonder that happens when the Lord finally does appear to Abraham. Twice before the Lord has appeared (12:7; 17:1), each time announcing the promise of offspring. In this third appearance, the Lord announces that the promise is about to be fulfilled. Why God appears to Abraham as three men is a mystery. Abraham addresses them using the singular, "Lord," possibly a reference to God; in context it may identify one as the spokesperson for the three. The story builds slowly, its pace mirroring the pattern of hospitality that is expected and which Abraham provides. First the strangers are offered water with which to wash and shade in which to rest.

The shade is important because it will take time to prepare this meal. It is a feast. There is no indication that Abraham knows he is entertaining God in the guise of strangers; rather, his response indicates how strangers are to be welcomed: with generosity and no expectation of return.

The story takes a turn when the strangers inquire after Sarah. Although mentioned briefly in verse 6, Sarah has otherwise been absent from the story. The strangers Abraham has so graciously entertained have come with a purpose. When Sarah hears that she, who is wasted away, is to bear a son she laughs within herself. It is a private moment of mirth, in which Sarah contemplates an old woman once again enjoying sexual pleasure. We, after being reminded again that she and Abraham are old, are meant to laugh with her. Sarah's laughter brings her to the center of the scene. It also pulls aside the curtain to reveal the identity of the strangers as God.[2] It is the Lord who asks why Sarah laughed (cf. v. 9, "they" ask). Sarah's denial suggests that she recognizes with whom she is speaking. The response, "Oh yes, you did laugh," anticipates 21:1-7 where Sarah gives birth and the child is named Isaac, which means "laughter." There is no reproach here, but anticipation: Sarah should laugh, because her laughter will give way to laughter as God's promise is fulfilled, a dream deferred no more.

> Sarah should laugh, because her laughter will give way to laughter as God's promise is fulfilled, a dream deferred no more.

EXODUS 19:2-8A (RCL ALT., BCP)
EXODUS 19:1-6A (LFM)

Chapter 19 marks the beginning of the Sinai narratives, which describe the giving of the law. The opening verses of this chapter, however, build on memories of God's interactions with humankind narrated in earlier texts and are best understood within this larger context. In this sense they are a reminder that each new chapter in our interaction with God is rooted in memories of our previous encounters with God.

The lection begins with the arrival of the Israelites in the wilderness of Sinai. Preachers may find it helpful to include verse 1, which links this journey explicitly with the exodus from Egypt. This is the first of several memories evoked: it reminds us that this is a people recently enslaved. Their encampment at the foot of "the mountain" leads us to anticipate that an encounter with God is about to take place (see 3:1-2; 4:27; 15:17; 18:5). Moses' role as a mediator between God and the people is signaled by the opening phrase, "Thus you shall say." While Moses' role is significant, it is the relationship between God and the people that is the central concern of the text. (Note the switch to the plural "you" in verse 4.)

God addresses the people as the "house of Jacob," a reminder of who they were before they were enslaved in Egypt and of the root of their identity as Israelites (Gen. 35:1-15). Before extending to the people the invitation of covenant relationship, God reminds them of what God has done on their behalf. This is not a passive-aggressive gesture (that is, "you owe me"), but a reminder that they can depend on God. The image of being lifted up on eagle's wings points to God's fierce protection and tender care of those who are vulnerable (Deut. 32:11-14; Isa. 40:31).

"Obey" may sound harsh (an alternative translation is "hear"). In the ancient world, however, it was understood that everyone serves some master. The Israelites had served the Egyptians; now they are offered the opportunity to serve God. Yet there is a difference: they have the free will to decide whether or not they will serve. If they choose to serve God faithfully, they will be God's treasured possession, a priestly kingdom, a holy nation. These three phrases are interrelated, each building on the other: "Treasured possession" is more nearly "personal property," yet the intended sense is of something that belongs exclusively to God. Priests are those set apart to serve God; within a kingdom of priests, however, there is no hierarchy for all are called equally to serve God. "Holy nation" points less to manifest destiny than to the idea of corporate responsibility and accountability. God's covenant relationship is not with individuals but with communities of people.

> The image of being lifted up on eagle's wings points to God's fierce protection and tender care of those who are vulnerable.

RESPONSIVE READING
PSALM 116:1-2, 12-19 (RCL)

Psalm 116 echoes a theme that finds expression in each of the lectionary texts: "God has heard my voice and my supplications." The assurance of one who listens, who hears us when we speak, stands in contrast to what we know of ourselves: that we often listen, but do not hear. The affliction suffered by the psalmist brought her close to death (vv. 15-16). The psalmist responds by promising to give thanks to God in the presence of all God's people (vv. 14, 18). The references to the "cup of salvation" and "thanksgiving sacrifice" indicate that this public witness is expressed through participation in temple worship. So, too, our worship can become a declaration of thanksgiving in the presence of all God's people.

PSALM 100 (RCL ALT., BCP)
PSALM 100:1-2, 3, 5 (LFM)

The first four verses of this familiar psalm are punctuated by seven imperatives: "Make a joyful noise"; "Worship the LORD"; "come into his presence with singing"; "Know that the LORD is God"; "Enter his gates with thanksgiving"; "Give thanks to him"; "bless his name." The first and last three imperatives call us to worship. In the middle is a declaration of who God is (the Lord), yet the psalmist goes on immediately to describe God in relationship to creation. This addition identifies verse 3 as the "heart" of the psalm. It is the relationship described here that elicits our praise (which literally surrounds the declaration). The psalm concludes with a statement of God's attributes; the "for" shows this verse to be an explanation of why we should bless God.

SECOND READING

ROMANS 5:1-8 (RCL)
ROMANS 5:6-11 (BCP, LFM)

Verses 1-5 are a statement of confidence, each phrase building on the one that precedes it, leading up to outpouring of the Holy Spirit. "Justified" may be rendered "made righteous" (that is, restored to the image of the Creator, who is righteous); "by faith" may be interpreted *because of our trust in God* or *because of God's faithfulness*. It is on the basis of "justification by faith" that we have peace with God and access to God's favor through Jesus Christ (see 4:23-25). We should not misconstrue Christ's role as mediation; Paul never calls Jesus "mediator." Rather, we experience these things as we participate in Christ's spirit (Rom. 8:14-17; Gal. 4:4-6). It is this participation that offers us hope of sharing in God's glory (see 6:1-5). Yet on the "road to glory" we may encounter suffering. For Paul, this is an opportunity to grow, not in faith per se, but in character. "Character" (*dokimos*) was what distinguished a person in Paul's world and true character was proved through testing. This reference to character is one of the many ways Paul reminds us that faith is revealed in how we act in the world. We are sustained in our efforts, says Paul, by the love of God, which is not love in word only, but actively poured into our hearts through the Holy Spirit.

> God sets aside God's anger and reaches out to us so that we might be reconciled with one another, once for all and daily.

Verses 6-8 continue the theme of verse 5 with a powerful statement of how God "proves his love for us" (that is, demonstrates God's character). The proof is in Christ dying for us (not for God). Christ died for us not when we were in top form, feeding the hungry and performing random acts of kindness, but when we were at our lowest of lows (*asthenēs;* weak or sick), our angriest, our most impatient, our least kind—the kinds of people television crime shows tell us deserve to die. It is Christ who dies for us, Paul continues in verses 9-11, who saves us from the wrath of God. The wrath of God is a much misused concept, yet it is a reminder that God is relational: "wrath" assumes something or someone with which to be angry. For Paul, it ultimately underscores the radical nature of God's love: God sets aside God's anger and reaches out to us so that we might be reconciled with one another, once for all and daily.

THE GOSPEL
MATTHEW 9:35—10:8 (9-23) (RCL)
MATTHEW 9:35—10:8 (9-15) (BCP)
MATTHEW 9:35—10:8 (LFM)

Each of the Synoptic Gospels describes the naming of the Twelve differently: In Mark, Jesus goes up on a mountain and "called to him those whom he wanted" (3:13-19). In Luke, Jesus goes up on a mountain to pray and in the morning calls out twelve from among his disciples (6:12-16). Matthew differs from Mark and Luke in two significant ways. First, although 10:1 is the first time Matthew refers to the Twelve, the language of the text ("he summoned his twelve disciples") suggests that this group was already established. Thus in Matthew this text is a commissioning rather than an appointing of the apostles. (Matthew follows Mark in including Thaddaeus, who is replaced in Luke by Simon the Zealot. Only Matthew identifies the apostle Matthew as a tax collector.) Second, Matthew includes a lengthy introduction that places the naming of the Twelve in a specific context. This is a reminder that ministry always takes place in specific contexts, in response to specific needs.

The context described by Matthew includes the cities and villages of the Lower Galilee. It is estimated that Capernaum, the center of Jesus' ministry in Matthew's Gospel, had a population of ten thousand. The region fell along a major trade route, which would have exposed residents to goods and ideas passing from east to west. Tiberius, built in honor of the emperor along the southwest edge of the sea, was a reminder of the all-embracing presence of Rome, to whom they paid taxes, and whose troops they supported.[3] It is in this context that Jesus teaches in synagogues, proclaims the good news of the kingdom, and cures every disease and sickness. Although the Gospel of Matthew is often thought of as a

> Although Matthew is often thought of as a "teaching" Gospel, Jesus' teaching and proclamation always occur in close proximity to physical healing.

"teaching" Gospel, Jesus' teaching and proclamation always occur in close prox-imity to physical healing. This underscores that the reign of God is not simply a spiritual reality, but is explicitly concerned with physical well-being. In the ancient world, with poor sanitation and limited access to clean water (except in a very few locations), disease would have been rampant.

The threefold summary of Jesus' ministry echoes 4:23 where we encounter almost the same words as introduction to Jesus' public ministry. Already, then, we anticipate that the ministry of the disciples will imitate that of Jesus, and it does, with one exception: the disciples are not commissioned to teach until after Jesus' resurrection (28:20). At this point, they still have more to learn. Jesus calls together the Twelve to send them out because he has compassion on the crowds who are "harassed and helpless, like sheep without a shepherd." The language is intentionally evocative. "Harassed and helpless" conjures up the image of those who are caught between competing forces; they have no power of their own to affect their circumstances and no advocate to intercede for them. The image of the "shepherd" describes both God (Psalms 23 and 100; Isa. 40:11) and those who lead the people, yet these leaders are more often shown to be faithless (Jer. 10:21; Zech. 10:3; Ezek. 34:5) because they do not have at heart the concerns of the people (a warning to us as well). Jesus, in contrast, has compassion (*splagchnizomai*) on them. The translation does not really do this word justice: it refers to the kind of gut-wrenching feeling that twists the bowels.

When Jesus sends out the disciples, he forbids them from going among the Gentiles and the Samaritans; rather, they are to go only to "the lost sheep of the house of Israel." This ethnocentrism may strike us as puzzling although un-questionably the mission of the historical Jesus was among his own people, Israel. Only here does Matthew mention the Samaritans. (Both Luke and John offer evidence of contact with the Samaritans, but when is unclear.) Historically, there was animosity between the Samaritans and the Jews stemming from questions such as where the right place to worship God is or whether the Writings and the Prophets should carry the same authority as the Pentateuch. The Gentiles refers to all non-Jews. Later, Jesus will commission the disciples to go to "all the nations" (see the discussion of Matthew 28:16-20 on Holy Trinity Sunday, above). From a narrative perspective, the turning point comes in 15:21-28 when Jesus encounters a Canaanite woman. Although first rejecting her plea for help with the words, "I was sent only to the lost sheep of the house of Israel," Jesus is converted by her demonstration of faith. This movement toward the inclusion of the Gentiles in fact begins earlier in the Gospel, with the mention of Rahab, Tamar, and Ruth (Bathsheba was an Israelite), the presentation of the Magi, and the centurion whose slave Jesus heals, but it is not fully embraced until after the resurrection. It is not difficult to hear in this narrative progression the stories of churches today as they struggle to move beyond the racial, cultural, and class boundaries that define them.

The last line of the lection (v. 8b) serves as the introduction to one of the options for expansion, verses 8-15. These verses have been the inspiration for a few rare individuals, such as St. Francis and St. Clare, and the communities of faith they inspired, but for most of us they are difficult to hear. Some have found in these verses similarities to the practices of the Cynics, but such asceticism was not limited to them. In the context of Matthew, these commands echo earlier admonitions regarding, for example, serving God and mammon (see the discussion of Matthew 6:24-34 from Proper 3, May 25, above). They also invite us to consider that the proclamation of the good news does not invite security, title, or status. Rather, it requires vulnerability and a willingness to depend upon the hospitality of others—to travel with open hands. If they do not welcome you, judgment remains with God; it is not our prerogative.

A second possible extension includes verses 16-23. The very things that Jesus says the disciples can expect to encounter are the things that Jesus himself encounters in the Gospel (see vv. 24-25a). He is rejected by his family, handed over to the council, dragged before the governor. Yet each word of warning about the challenges that lie ahead is followed by a word of encouragement (vv. 19-20, 22b-23). These words of encouragement do not preclude persecution, but offer hope for those who endure. The Son of man here refers to Jesus' eventual return to judge the nations (13:41; 19:28; 24:27-31).

> These words of encouragement do not preclude persecution, but offer hope for those who endure.

Notes

1. Langston Hughes, "Montage of a Dream Deferred," in *Selected Poems* (New York: Vintage, 1974), 268. Lorraine Hansberry draws on this poem for her powerful play *A Raisin in the Sun,* which describes the effects of dreams deferred on one family.

2. Gina Hens-Piazza, "Why Did Sarah Laugh?" in *Distant Voices Drawing Near: Essays in Honor of Antoinette Clark Wire,* ed. Holly E. Hearon (Collegeville, Minn.: Liturgical, 2004), 66.

3. J. Andrew Overman, *Church and Community in Crisis: The Gospel According to Matthew,* The New Testament in Context (Valley Forge: Trinity Press International, 1996), 58–64.

SIXTH SUNDAY AFTER PENTECOST

TWELFTH SUNDAY IN ORDINARY TIME / PROPER 7

JUNE 22, 2008

Revised Common (RCL)	Episcopal (BCP)	Roman Catholic (LFM)
Gen. 21:8-21 or Jer. 20:7-13	Jer. 20:7-13	Jer. 20:10-13
Ps. 86:1-10, 16-17 or 69:7-10 (11-15) 16-18	Ps. 69:1-18 or 69:7-10, 16-18	Ps. 69:8-10, 14, 17, 33-35
Rom. 6:1b-11	Rom. 5:15b-19	Rom. 5:12-15
Matt. 10:24-29	Matt. 10:(16-23) 24-33	Matt. 10:26-33

FIRST READING
GENESIS 21:8-21 (RCL)

Do the promises of God to Sarah and Abraham mean that others can legitimately be cast aside? If one person receives the blessing of God, does that mean that another person is deprived of God's blessing? Does my being blessed by God mean that I can claim a special status for myself? What rights and responsibilities accompany the blessings of God? These are a few of the questions raised by this unsettling story.

Isaac is now about three years old, the age at which children were weaned, and Abraham is giving a feast. The joy of this event is quickly poisoned by bitter rivalry. Sarah sees Abraham's other son, born to Hagar, playing with her son Isaac. The word *play* is built on the same root as Isaac's name and may be translated as "derisive laughter." Robert Alter suggests that when Sarah sees Ishmael "laugh," she believes he is trying to usurp the role of the legitimate heir, Isaac ("laughter").[1] Since Ishmael is somewhere around seventeen years old (see 17:13), this concern is not unfounded.

Although there are three primary characters in this first part of the story (vv. 8-13), we only hear the voices of two, Sarah and God, both of whom instruct Abraham to send away the slave woman and her child. Caught between these two voices is Abraham, the father of two sons. Sarah seeks to protect the inheritance of her son, Isaac; God affirms that the inheritance belongs to Isaac. Yet God goes on to assure Abraham that his other son will also benefit from the promises made to Abraham by God and become a nation. In the midst of this discussion, Ishmael and Hagar remain on the periphery. Notably, Ishmael is never mentioned by name. Hagar is named only in verse 9 (highlighting her role as Sarah's rival) and thereafter is referred to as the slave-woman. While Ishmael has some rights as Abraham's son, Hagar has none. She is chattel.

Hagar is named a second time in verse 14 and from this point on she is no longer chattel, but the protagonist in the story. The provisions offered by Abraham to Hagar stand in stark contrast to the feast offered on behalf of Isaac. In the wilderness, the water does not last long, and soon Hagar sees her parched and hungry child on the brink of death. We know the face of Ishmael from the photos of hungry children around the world. Casting him under some bushes, she departs a bowshot's distance (that is, within eye distance). Her words are heard by many as a lament, but it is also possible that they are a prayer for the rescue of the child.[2] It was a practice in the ancient world to abandon children where they might be picked up by traders or merchants.[3] It most probably meant a life of slavery, but it did mean life. Rather than merchants, the one who hears the voice of the boy is God, who calls out to Hagar and tells her to hold the boy fast in her hand. One can imagine the intensity of the embrace as Hagar reclaims Ishmael as her own child. God declares that a *great* nation (cf. v. 13, "nation" only) will arise from him and brings proof to this promise by providing the water that will restore him to life. In the closing line of the story, Hagar, assuming the role of head of household, finds a wife for Ishmael, pointing the way to the descendents who will follow.

> Rather than merchants, the one who hears the voice of the boy is God, who calls out to Hagar and tells her to hold the boy fast in her hand.

JEREMIAH 20:7-13 (RCL, BCP)
JEREMIAH 20:10-13 (LFM)

These verses offer us a glimpse into the soul of Jeremiah. Prophesying in Judah during the tumultuous years that lead up to the Babylonian, exile he finds himself compelled again and again to speak a word that runs counter to the prevailing winds. In the verses immediately preceding the lection, Jeremiah has been placed in the stocks by Pashhur, a priest in the house of the Lord. Opening his heart to God in complaint, Jeremiah describes how God lured him in. "Entice" captures the seductive edge of this word (*pathah*), but covers up the harsher possibility of "rape" (see Exod. 22:16-17), suggested by the "violence and destruction" Jeremiah experiences when the word of the Lord comes upon him. In either case, Jeremiah declares that God has "overpowered" him and "prevailed." Yet while Jeremiah may feel he has been seduced by God, he confesses that when he tries to ignore God, he is filled with a burning fire that compels him to speak.

The difficulty is that when Jeremiah speaks he is met with derision. No status accrues to him as a prophet of God. Even his friends threaten to denounce him. Echoing the opening verse, they ponder whether Jeremiah can be "enticed" and they might "prevail" against him in order to take revenge. Yet they do not stand a chance next to God. At this point the text turns (v. 11) and Jeremiah's lament becomes a word of confidence in God who will defend him against his adversaries "like a dread warrior." He concludes (v. 13) by praising God who delivers those in need from those plotting evil against them.

Few of us would claim to be a Jeremiah, but he offers us a compelling example of someone who is so drawn to God that he cannot resist and yet dreads that which God asks him to do. The opening line of this lection appears in the film *Into Great Silence,* which documents the lives of Carthusian monks in France. It is an apt description of being called to live face to face with God, confessing our fears, confiding in God's grace, and remaining confident that God will continue to be our courage and our strength.[4]

> Jeremiah offers us a compelling example of someone who is so drawn to God that he cannot resist and yet dreads that which God asks him to do.

RESPONSIVE READING
PSALM 86:1-10, 16-17 (RCL)

See the discussion of the responsive reading on the Tenth Sunday after Pentecost (Sixteenth Sunday in Ordinary Time/Proper 11), July 20, 2008, below.

PSALM 69:7-10 (11-15) 16-18 (RCL ALT.)
PSALM 69:1-18 OR 69:7-10, 16-18 (BCP)
PSALM 69:8-10, 14, 17, 33-35 (LFM)

This psalm speaks words that we may be reluctant to pray. Waiting for God to act, the psalmist declares that there is no longer any foothold; that the flood is already here. The unstated implication is that God has abandoned the psalmist, who has no hidden faults, but is consumed with zeal for God's house. Although the psalmist will ultimately affirm God's deliverance (vv. 33-35), the psalm gives voice to those moments when God feels far from us. We may hear in the psalm the voice of Hagar or Jeremiah or followers of Jesus as they encounter opposition. The persistence of the psalmist's voice offers us encouragement to be relentless in our prayers and to speak openly from the heart.

ROMANS 6:1B-11 (RCL)

The main character in Edward P. Jones's story "Old Boys, Old Girls" is an ex-convict struggling to find his way in the outside world. He is transformed through the death of a friend; by entering into her death he rises to a new life.[5] This, says Paul, is what happens when we are baptized. In baptism we die with Jesus, and in doing so break the grip that sin has had on our lives. By "sin" Paul is not speaking of an itemized list of our character flaws or misdeeds. Paul means that powerful force that keeps us walking down the same street over and over again and falling into the same hole. It is what human beings do when we strive so hard to be in control of our own lives that we forget that we have been created for relationship with God and with one another, or when we strive so hard to control those relationships that we insist on the path that must be followed.

Having passed through the waters of death, Paul says, we have risen with Christ to newness of life now, and the future hope of resurrection. Death symbolizes for Paul the power of sin. We know what it is to die while our bodies live, when we find ourselves assaulted by grief or despair, depression or desperation. Recognizing that Christ's death becomes our death in baptism, we discover that we are not alone.

> Recognizing that Christ's death becomes our death in baptism, we discover that we are not alone.

When Christ rises, we rise with him, and become alive to God and God's presence with us. It may not be to a new life, but it offers us a new way to live.

ROMANS 5:15B-19 (BCP)

In the film *Groundhog Day* the main character keeps waking up to the same day over and over again. Even if we are not waking up to the same moment, it can feel as if our lives are caught in a vicious cycle of repetition as we encounter the same routine, the same pressures, the same mistakes. While repetition can offer a sense of stability, it can also leave us with a sense of despair. For Paul humanity is caught in a cycle of despair set in motion by Adam. Adam is associated with the words "trespass" (*paraptōma:* false step; also *hamartanō:* miss the mark), "condemnation," "death": the result of his disobedience (*parakoē:* refusal to hear [in context, the voice of God]). In contrast, Christ is associated with the words "grace" (*charis:* favor, benefaction), "free gift," "righteousness," "justification": the result of his obedience (*hupakoē:* hear with favor [in context, the voice of God]). Christ, says Paul, breaks the cycle of despair and offers us the opportunity to receive (as an exercise of our free will) the free gift of righteousness, with the result that we will "exercise dominion [*basileuō*] in life." This may refer to the power of the risen Christ at work in us (see 1 Cor. 4:8, where the Corinthians are accused of "reigning" already).

ROMANS 5:12-15 (LFM)

The universality of sin, as described by Paul in this passage, should caution us against pointing a finger at any individual or group as more sinful than others. So Paul also tells us in this passage. Drawing on Genesis 3, Paul takes up a tradition that holds Adam responsible for sin entering the world. Yet Adam's role in this is less that of "originator" than of "type." Adam represents creation in rebellion against God because it has assumed the role of creator for itself (see Romans 1). Therefore, Paul claims *all* have sinned, even those who lived when there was no law to tell them what sin was (see Rom. 7:7). Paul asserts that the "type" (mold or impression) established by Adam anticipates "the one who [is] to come": that is, Adam, the first creation, anticipates Christ the new creation (2 Cor. 5:17; Gal. 6:14-15). However, both the old and new creation belong to the same "type," that is, humanity living in relationship to God. Christ, the New Creation, offers us the opportunity, as creation, to renew a right relationship with the Creator. This, ultimately, reveals a positive view of humanity and invites us to see in each person the promises of God in Christ at work. Such a lesson is learned by a small community in Maine in the film *The Spitfire Grill*.

THE GOSPEL
MATTHEW 10:24-33 (RCL)
MATTHEW 10:(16-23) 24-33 (BCP)
MATTHEW 10:26-33 (LFM)

Following the commissioning of the Twelve, Jesus speaks to them words of warning: "See, I am sending you out like sheep into the midst of wolves; so be wise as serpents and innocent as doves" (10:16). Today's lection picks up in the middle of this discourse where it makes a transition from warning to encouragement (for comments on verses 16-23, see the Gospel for Proper 6, June 15, above). Nonetheless, these verses, too, are full of intimations that followers of Jesus can expect to encounter dangerous circumstances (not unlike Jeremiah). Indeed, the references to words told in secret, bodies killed, and oaths of loyalty sound like they belong in an espionage film. In the ancient world they belong to the language of apocalypticism, used by groups that experience themselves as oppressed and whose vindication resides in the hands of God.

Contrary to popular belief, there is no evidence that Christians experienced anything other than local persecutions during the first century C.E. The Romans, on the whole, exercised tolerance toward religion; as polytheists they considered monotheists, such as the Jews, to be peculiar but not a threat. The casting of Christians into the lions' dens, producing a movement of martyrs, did not begin until the middle of the second century. Yet it is clear from Matthew's text that followers of Jesus expected to encounter opposition. What evidence we do have indicates that Christians met social opposition, such as name calling, shunning, imprisonment (if they were viewed as disrupting the peace; witness Paul), destruction of property, and on some occasions, death. This invites us to ask, Why? Was it because they proclaimed Jesus as Messiah? In part: there is no question that the term *Messiah* had political overtones since it could refer to the king of Israel. "Son of God" was potentially even more threatening, since the emperor was also called "Son of God" (Zeus). Yet it is also likely that the opposition they encountered had to do with the degree to which they lived out their vision of a society driven by values consistent with the reign of God. This led Christians to eschew certain public rituals and challenge social structures. Such values threatened to mark them as antisocial, going against the accepted norm, undermining the structures of society and, in particular, the stability of the family (see 10:21-22a, 35-36).

> The opposition Christians encountered had to do with the degree to which they lived out their vision of a society driven by values consistent with the reign of God.

Jesus warns the disciples that they are not above their teacher; if even the teacher, who deserves respect, is maligned, how much more should "those of his household" expect to suffer (vv. 24-25). Yet the disciples are told not to fear! Here, "household" becomes an important word. It tells us something about how early Christians understood the community of Jesus' followers: they were family and, in the ancient world, your loyalty was owed above all else to your family. This meant that disciples were expected to support one another, and, in the face of opposition, to rally round. The head of this household was God. As members of the household, disciples could expect protection and support from God in their time of need (see 10:19-20).

> The word *household* tells us the community of Jesus' followers were family and, in the ancient world, your loyalty was owed above all else to your family.

Verses 26-31 offer to disciples words of encouragement. Verses 26-27 urge them to proclaim the gospel boldly ("what I say to you in the dark"), without fear of "them." The "them" remains unspecified, not because Jesus is speaking in code, but because Jesus is speaking in broad strokes: "them" refers to anyone who has the power and authority to suppress others. When we consider these verses in our own context, they raise important questions: What does suppression of the Gospel look like? Who has the power and authority to suppress others? Do *we* have the power and authority to suppress others and, if so, to what degree can we legitimately consider ourselves suppressed? "What is told in secret" is drawing on the language of apocalypticism, where secrets hidden since the beginning are publicly declared at a propitious moment (see 5:14-16).

Verses 28-31 encourage disciples not to fear those who can kill the body, but rather those who can kill the soul. These words have proved true words of encouragement to many Christians in diverse circumstances. We hear them in hymns, from "A Mighty Fortress Is Our God" to "His Eye Is on the Sparrow." They are echoed in the poetry of Julia Esquival: "I am no longer afraid of death, I know well its dark and cold corridors leading to life. . . . I am afraid of my fear and even more the fear of others . . . who continue clinging to what they consider to be life which we know to be death!"[6] We find them in the witness of people such as Dietrich Bonhoeffer and Nelson Mandela. They also raise for us the questions: What are we clinging to? What is it that we fear? What stands in the way of our proclaiming the gospel boldly?

The closing verses can best be described as a loyalty oath. They are unwavering in their expectation, yet as we read to the end of Matthew's Gospel we learn of how Peter denies Jesus three times, and the disciples flee at the first sign of danger. Nonetheless these are the very same disciples Jesus will send out into the world following the resurrection. Life in the household of God is not without its rocky moments. These verses raise yet more questions: What does denial of Jesus look like? How many times can we be forgiven? What does it look like to acknowledge Jesus before others? How can we support each other as members of the household of God?

Notes

1. Robert Alter, *Genesis: Translation and Commentary* (New York: Norton, 1996), 106.

2. Patrick D. Miller, *They Cried to the LORD: The Form and Theology of Biblical Prayer* (Minneapolis: Fortress Press, 1994), 88, 234–36; J. Gerald Janzen, "Did Hagar Give Ishmael up for Dead? Gen. xxi 14-21 Re-visited" (unpublished paper, cited with permission), 2–11.

3. Janzen, "Did Hagar Give Ishmael up for Dead?" 11–20.

4. Adapted from "Prayer of Confession (1)," in *The Book of Common Worship* (Louisville: Westminster John Knox, 1993), 87.

5. Edward P. Jones, *All Aunt Hagar's Children* (New York: Amistad, 2006), 75–102.

6. Julia Esquivel, "I am not afraid of death," in *Threatened with Resurrection: Prayers and Poems from an Exiled Guatemalan* (Elgin, Ill.: Brethren Press, 1982), 65.

SEVENTH SUNDAY
AFTER PENTECOST

THIRTEENTH SUNDAY IN ORDINARY TIME / PROPER 8
JUNE 29, 2008

Revised Common (RCL)	Episcopal (BCP)	Roman Catholic (LFM)
Gen. 22:1-14 or Jer. 28:5-9	Isa. 2:10-17	2 Kgs. 4:8-11, 14-16a
Psalm 13 or 89:1-4, 15-18	Ps. 89:1-18 or 89:1-4, 15-18	Ps. 89:2-3, 16-17, 18-19
Rom. 6:12-23	Rom. 6:3-11	Rom. 6:2-3, 8-11
Matt. 10:40-42	Matt. 10:34-42	Matt. 10:37-42

FIRST READING
GENESIS 22:1-14 (RCL)

Too frequently we hear in the news about the deaths of innocent children at the hands of their parents or guardians. For some, this story of God commanding Abraham to sacrifice his son may be difficult to hear. It may raise memories of authority abused, or questions about the kind of faith demanded by God. Although it concludes with a "happy ending," this remains a troubling story that does not lend itself to easy resolution.

The opening verse prepares us for what lies ahead by stating that God tested Abraham. Why God needed to test Abraham we are not told. It may be helpful to think of the test in the context of relationship. Human relationships go through tests all the time; sometimes these tests are fair, sometimes they are not, yet they are a way in which we discover the degree to which we can trust one another.

The test comes after Abraham has already been asked to send away his other son, Ishmael. In brutally straightforward language, Abraham is told to take his son, his *only* son, Isaac, the *one whom he loves,* and to offer him as a burnt sacrifice to God. The phrase "go to the land" (22:2) repeats the language of 12:1, when God commands Abram to "go [lek-lĕkā] from your country." In both cases, Abraham is asked to step out into an unknown world. Just as Abraham acted without question in chapter 12, he again sets off to carry out God's command. At no point are we given any insight into Abraham's internal thoughts. Many have suggested that Abraham knew that God would, ultimately, prevent him from committing this horrifying act. Yet the text does not indicate this and to read it into the text is to rob the story of its dramatic force.

At three points the text is punctuated by the words, "Here I am," each time spoken by Abraham in response to someone calling his name. The first and last time Abraham is responding to the voice of God. In the last instance, Abraham's name is called twice; there is some urgency here to stay Abraham's hand as he is about to kill his son. In between, Abraham speaks these words in response to his son Isaac, who then asks, "Where is the lamb for a burnt offering?" This is the only time we hear Isaac's voice. Readers will hear Isaac's question differently: Is it a question from innocence and trust? Does it suggest a growing premonition? Just as in the case of Abraham, the text tells us nothing of what Isaac is feeling. It is unclear how to hear Abraham's response. Is it a sign of trust in God? Is it an attempt to protect Isaac from the truth? Is it intended as irony? This exchange with Isaac is bracketed by the words "the two of them walked on together" (vv. 6, 8), suggesting that whatever lies ahead, they must face it side by side. These verses are, in turn, bracketed by God calling to Abraham: at first to command him to sacrifice his son; then to stay his hand. The providence of God surrounds Abraham and Isaac as they journey toward the unknown.

> The providence of God surrounds Abraham and Isaac as they journey toward the unknown.

The story concludes with Abraham's affirmation that God will provide. However, there is an earlier statement that is equally significant: in verse 12 God says to Abraham, "Now I know that you fear God." In the story of the birth of Isaac (18:14), the question is asked, "Is anything too wonderful [difficult] for the LORD?" Here the question is, "Is anything too difficult for Abraham?" Gerald Janzen observes that, in the end, Abraham has sacrificed Isaac by entrusting him utterly to God. He goes on to say, "God waits until we have acted before knowing our response (v. 12). If this has been Abraham's severest test of trust in God, it has been no less an occasion in which . . . God has trusted the human partner in the covenant."[1]

JEREMIAH 28:5-9 (RCL ALT.)

This passage anticipates the Gospel lection, with its reference to prophets. In the Gospel of Matthew, prophets receive a mixed review (see Matt. 7:15-20). This passage in Jeremiah presents the problem precisely: How do you know when the prophet speaks a true word? The episode with Hananiah takes up the whole of chapter 28. These few verses are Jeremiah's response to Hananiah's prophesy that the yoke of Babylon is about to be broken and the exiles returned. Yet in chapter 27 Jeremiah has placed a yoke around his neck (as instructed by God) to symbolize that it is God who has given Judah into the hands of the king of Babylon. The two prophets now come face to face, prophecy to prophecy. Jeremiah's opening words (v. 6) may be heard as a genuine prayer, or as dripping with sarcasm. He then reminds Hananiah that it is a rare prophet who brings good news. Yet, whether prophesying peace or war, the truth of a prophet's word can be known only in retrospect, when that which is prophesied comes to pass.

ISAIAH 2:10-17 (BCP)

This passage from Isaiah is loosely linked with those from Matthew and Romans in that all three stress commitment to the ways of God. The Isaiah passage brings a word of judgment against humankind for their hubris. Verse 10 functions as an introduction to the passage, and establishes the great distance between the Lord and humankind, who are urged to hide in trembling from the glory of God's majesty. The remaining verses are bracketed by references to the people, whose haughtiness will be brought low and pride will be humbled, while "the LORD alone will be exalted on that day" (vv. 11, 17). In between (vv. 12-16), we read of God's judgment (God "has a day"), punctuated by a series of declarations, each beginning with the word *against*. Bashan and Lebanon may be references to rival kingdoms, while Tarshish was a major trade center. All the things that humans point to as signs of their power and pride, says Isaiah, will be brought low, for none can stand before the glory of God.

2 KINGS 4:8-11, 14-16A (LFM)

This text offers an example of a woman receiving a prophet's reward (see the Gospel lection, below). Verses 8-10 tell the story of a wealthy woman who offers hospitality to Elisha. Although she has a husband (who is old [v. 14]), it is the woman who takes the initiative and opens their home to the prophet. This is culturally consistent since women were in charge of household management. She is attentive and looks to Elijah's every need.

The omission of verses 12-13 robs the story of its humor. Elijah, looking for an opportunity to reward the woman for her hospitality, proposes speaking on her behalf to a king or commander of an army. Since the woman is wealthy, she circulates in circles where such a connection could prove advantageous. Yet he overlooks what his servant sees: the woman's personal grief at the lack of a son (the text does not say whether she has a daughter). In the ancient world, a woman's social standing also depended on her ability to produce a son who would have primary responsibility for the care of his mother. This woman already had wealth and power (demonstrated by her initiative); Elijah, enlightened by his servant, rewards her with the one thing she lacks: a male child.

RESPONSIVE READING
PSALM 13 (RCL)

This short psalm gives voice to the despair that threatens when we fear God has forgotten us. Four times the psalmist cries out "How long?"; each successive phrase adds another dimension to the waiting. In verse 3 the lament turns to petition. "Consider" may be rendered more actively as "look up"; the psalmist is asking God not simply to reflect upon but to take notice. This is punctuated by the psalmist's warning that without God's intervention death is surely at hand. The final verses turn to expressions of confidence in God. The use of "I" statements reveals the psalmist's transition from despair to rejoicing, yet both the despair (the cry for help) and the rejoicing reveal the psalmist's confidence in God.

PSALM 89:1-4, 15-18 (RCL ALT., BCP ALT.)
PSALM 89:1-18 (BCP)
PSALM 89:2-3, 16-17, 18-19 (LFM)

Psalm 89 celebrates God's covenant with David (see 2 Sam. 7:8-16) and, by extension, those whom David rules (vv. 15-18). The psalm describes God in much the same terms that one might describe David: as a warrior (vv. 10, 13, 18) who protects with a mighty arm and rules with righteousness and justice (v. 14). In every generation we draw on the images that are familiar to us to try and describe God, knowing always the limitations of the language we use. The psalm emphasizes God's steadfast love and faithfulness (vv. 1, 2, 5, 8, 14) as the One who rules both the heavens and the earth.

SECOND READING
ROMANS 6:12-23 (RCL)

For Paul, there are two ways to be in the world: as slaves of sin or slaves of righteousness. We tend to think in less dualistic terms: people are capable of both bad and good; which impulse we act on may depend on the configuration of events on any one day. Paul would not deny this. When we read his other letters we encounter countless instances of human failings. Paul himself recognizes that he is on a journey that has not yet reached its end (Phil. 3:12).

Another way to think of Paul's dualistic language is in terms of the choices we make day by day. If these choices are driven by resentment, anger, self-pity, ingratitude, Paul would say we are under the power of sin. The path of sin leads to wickedness (literally "unrighteousness" [v. 13]; since God is righteous, sin represents the opposite of God), impurity ("unclean" [v. 19]; this refers to something that is out of place like garden dirt in the living room), iniquity (literally "lawlessness" [v. 19]), shame (that which dishonors), and death. In contrast, the path of God sets us on a journey that leads to life now and, ultimately, eternal life. Although Paul uses the language of slavery in relation to this path, he says that it is a path chosen freely rather than under coercion, "obedient from the heart" (v. 17). In the ancient world, the heart was considered the seat of thought and will, rather than emotions. Choosing the path of God requires attentiveness.

The phrase that follows, "to the form of teaching to which you were entrusted," is unique in Paul and therefore a puzzle. It may refer to the *typos* or pattern represented by Christ (see 5:14).

> The path of God sets us on a journey that leads to life now and, ultimately, eternal life.

The path offered by God leads to our sanctification ("being set apart for God" [vv. 19, 22]). This is a freighted word. For some it can mean a misplaced piety that creates a hierarchy in the community faith. This is far from what Paul intends. For Paul it means that we are fully embraced by the grace of God, no longer a slave to sin, but free to participate in God's life-giving activities on behalf of creation.

ROMANS 6:3-11 (BCP)
ROMANS 6:3-4, 8-11 (LFM)

See the discussion of the second reading for the Sixth Sunday after Pentecost (Twelfth Sunday in Ordinary Time/Proper 7), June 22, 2008, above.

THE GOSPEL
MATTHEW 10:40-42 (RCL)
MATTHEW 10:34-42 (BCP)
MATTHEW 10:37-42 (LFM)

This lection brings to conclusion what is called Matthew's missionary discourse. It opens with words that sound shocking to our ears. The repetition of "I have not come to bring peace" indicates that Matthew understands the difficulty we will have hearing them. The only other place we hear the word *peace* is in Matthew 10:13; it is a word associated specifically with the proclamation of the Gospel. "Sword" represents division rather than violence. This word appears again during Jesus' arrest (26:47); yet Jesus warns his followers against taking up the sword (26:51-52) and tells his captors that he will not resist them (26:55). This perhaps makes these words even more challenging, for they say we must learn to stand by our witness, our "yes" (5:37), and be prepared to live with the division and conflict that may result.

The disruption of the household described in verses 35-36 (see Micah 7:6) would have been heard as undermining the very fabric of society. In the ancient world, the patriarchal household served as a model for the Empire. The emperor was called "father" while the citizens of the empire were his "children" upon whom he bestowed favor and whom he was obligated to protect. To disrupt the household was to attack the stability of the Empire. These verses, then, likely refer to more than just the domestic household; they speak to the variety of relationships that hold society together. "Love" is less about emotion than it is loyalty. Verse 37 can be heard as a reprise of Matthew 6:24, but this time in reference to human relationships rather than mammon. This is perhaps the most difficult part for us to hear. It is important to recognize that we are not being called to break off all human relationships or necessarily leave our families. Elsewhere, Jesus affirms the importance of family obligations (see 15:1-9). Yet the gospel can lead to conflict, even with the very fabric of society, as we struggle to live a true and genuine response to what we believe the gospel asks of us. The admonition to "take up our cross" is a reminder of the level of commitment asked: to be willing to experience degradation, shame, abuse,

> The admonition to "take up our cross" is a reminder of the level of commitment asked: to be willing to experience degradation, shame, abuse, humiliation—without resistance.

humiliation—without resistance. Verse 39 echoes Matthew 6:25 and underscores the call to give ourselves over wholly to the care of God.

A different kind of illustration of these verses is offered in Mark Salzman's novel *Lying Awake*. The main character is a Carmelite nun, a woman who has dedicated her life to God. She is blessed with visions, which she expresses in beautiful poetry. However, she is more and more troubled by the powerful headaches that accompany her visions. Learning that these headaches are a serious threat to her health, she must decide whether to have surgery, potentially losing her visions and the gift that accompanies them. It is a compelling story because it represents a conflict of goods. What does it mean to be faithful to the gospel in this context? What divisions are created within the community (her family) by her gift and its potential loss? What does forsaking life and taking up the cross look like when confronted with these choices? Often the choices we face in our efforts to live out the gospel are just of this kind; discerning the way of the cross is rarely clear cut and challenges us to sift through competing values and claims, and ultimately, to trust in God.

Verse 40, addressed to the newly commissioned disciples, describes the unity of their mission with that of Jesus, and, ultimately, with God. This verse can also be heard as a challenge: Is our mission consistent with the mission of Jesus and with the kingdom of God? In verses 41-42 Matthew turns to the ones who receive those who proclaim the gospel. We might expect Matthew to end with a word about the rewards those proclaiming the gospel, who have endured all the various hardships described in chapter 10, are going to receive. That the evangelist does not tells us that disciples need to keep their focus on the cross, not on rewards and acclamations. The reward goes, instead, to those who welcome those whose words and deeds proclaim the kingdom of heaven (10:11-13). This opens up reflection on individuals and groups who are only tangentially associated with the church or its larger mission, but offer support in different ways.

The designations *prophet*, *righteous person*, and *little one* do not likely refer to formal offices within the Matthean community, but to different kinds of informal roles that individuals acted out in the community. Prophets may be described as those who bring the word of God to bear on the life of the community in self-critical ways; this would seem to be consistent with how Matthew identifies Jesus (that is, as the One who rightly interprets God's word). In the Sermon on the Mount, the final beatitude calls those who are persecuted blessed, "for in the same way they persecuted the prophets who were before you"

> The way of the cross is rarely clear cut and challenges us to sift through competing values and claims, and ultimately, to trust in God.

(5:10-11), suggesting that the Matthean community may have understood themselves to stand in the line of prophets (cf. 7:15-20). "The righteous" are those who belong to the kingdom (13:49; as an example see 1:19), but always qualified by the reminder that Jesus came to call sinners, not the righteous (9:13; see also 23:28). "Little ones" seems to describe those members of the community who are most vulnerable; this could be due to age (young or old), illness, isolation, pressure, uncertainty. The "little ones" appear again in chapter 18 (vv. 6, 10, 14), where they are shown to be the recipients of God's special care, and for whom the community is held accountable.

Note

1. J. Gerald Janzen, *Abraham and All the Families of the Earth: A Commentary on the Book of Genesis 12–50* (Grand Rapids: Eerdmans, 1993), 80, 81.

EIGHTH SUNDAY AFTER PENTECOST

FOURTEENTH SUNDAY IN ORDINARY TIME / PROPER 9

JULY 6, 2008

Revised Common (RCL)	Episcopal (BCP)	Roman Catholic (LFM)
Gen. 24:34-38, 42-49, 58-67 or Zech. 9:9-12	Zech. 9:9-12	Zech. 9:9-10
Ps. 45:10-17 or Song of Sol. 2:8-13 or Ps. 145:8-14	Psalm 145 or 145:8-14	Ps. 145:1-2, 8-9, 10-11, 13-14
Rom. 7:15-25a	Rom. 7:21—8:6	Rom. 8:9, 11-13
Matt. 11:16-19, 25-30	Matt. 11:25-30	Matt. 11:25-30

FIRST READING

GENESIS 24:34-38, 42-49, 58-67 (RCL)

After the anxiety caused by the previous lection, Genesis 24 comes as a relief. Everyone loves a wedding. Yet the marriage of Isaac and Rebekah can leave us perplexed, so distant is it from our cultural expectations. In the film *Monsoon Wedding* we glimpse how one contemporary community negotiates an arranged marriage. The film highlights how individuals are embedded in extended family systems and how the entire family must work together for the happiness and well-being of each individual.

The marriage of Isaac and Rebekah is an arranged marriage. The story takes up the whole of chapter 24 and is narrated between the deaths of Sarah and Abraham. This placement is strategic: the marriage of Isaac fulfills Abraham's final wishes, and looks forward to the fulfillment of God's promise of progeny. It also signals the passage from one generation to another of God's promises. The careful reader will observe that the servant is identified as Abraham's servant until verse 65, where he identifies himself as the servant of Isaac. When Isaac installs Rebekah in the tent of Sarah we understand that Isaac and Rebekah have stepped into the role of Abraham and Sarah as the recipients of God's blessing.

The lection focuses on the voice of the servant as he recounts his mission before Laban. A different configuration of verses would bring to the fore the complex family dynamics involved in the negotiation of the marriage. The servant describes how Abraham, a man blessed by God with considerable wealth (which has been promised to Isaac, making him a most eligible bachelor), commanded him to seek a wife for Abraham's son from among his kin. The rejection of a Canaanite wife anticipates future tensions around marriage with women outside the kinship group. The servant then describes his encounter with Rebekah at the well, an encounter that is clearly guided by God. Yet God's intervention here is far more subtle than in previous lections. It is made evident through the servant's prayers; we do not hear the voice of God nor does God take direct action. We might describe this as God's providential care. The success of the venture rests ultimately on Rebekah, who, as yet, has not met the God of Abraham. Yet like Abraham before her, she steps out into the unknown, and willingly agrees to go with Abraham's servant. At the very least she has some assurance that she will not suffer poverty, and marrying kin means that there will be someone looking out for her interests. Isaac takes Rebekah as his wife and, the text says, he loved her. This suggests we are to understand that this arranged marriage has been arranged with care, for the well-being of those involved.

> God's intervention is made evident through the servant's prayers; we do not hear the voice of God nor does God take direct action.

ZECHARIAH 9:9-12 (RCL ALT.; BCP)
ZECHARIAH 9:9-10 (LFM)

Although the opening verse conjures up the story of Jesus' entry into Jerusalem, there is something to be gained by hearing the text in its own suggested context. Chapter 9 belongs to what is called Deutero-Zechariah and dates from the postexilic period. Not surprisingly, the theme of restoration is prominent. The phrase "daughter of Zion" occurs with some frequency in the Hebrew Bible (see esp. Zech. 2:10); in contrast, "daughter of Jerusalem" occurs only a few times. Both phrases dominate Lamentations 2 (vv. 1, 4, 13, 15), describing the degradation experienced by Jerusalem at the time of the Babylonian destruction. Carol and Eric Meyers comment that the "daughter" language "is particularly suggestive of helplessness and dependency, with respect to the status of prisoners . . . ."[1] Certainly unmarried daughters would be vulnerable to sexual violation. This description helps us to hear the powerful reversal of fortune being proclaimed by Zechariah.

There is no indication that the king of verses 9-10 should be identified as a messianic figure. Nonetheless, this is one whose "dominion shall be from sea to sea" and who will establish peace among the nations. "Triumphant" (*tsadiq*) may be better translated as righteous or just. "Humble" (*'ani*) refers to those who are poor or afflicted (see, for instance, Pss. 9:12; 14:6; 40:17; 70:5; 107:10). The latter indicates that this is a king who identifies with those who are the victims of war. He establishes peace by first disarming his own (Ephraim and Jerusalem); only then does he command peace to the nations, thus ruling by example.

In verses 11–12 the text shifts from third person ("the king") to first person ("I") representing the voice of God. The language "blood of my covenant" is found elsewhere in the Hebrew Bible only in Exodus 24:8. In that text, the blood, cast on the people, serves to bind the parties of the covenant together. In this context, it is the strong bond represented by the covenant that assures those who have been prisoners in exile of the surety of their release. This is underscored by the phrase "prisoners of hope." The seeming contradiction (prisoner/hope) directs attention to the one in whom the prisoners find their hope. The closing line, "I will restore to you double," assures those who have suffered much that their afflictions are recognized and that they will receive what is needed to restore them to wholeness.

> It is the strong bond represented by the covenant that assures those who have been prisoners in exile of the surety of their release.

RESPONSIVE READING
PSALM 45:10–17 (RCL)

The theme of marriage is picked up in Psalm 45, which describes the splendor and pageantry of a royal wedding. Verse 10 is addressed to the woman, who, like Rebekah, must leave her people and her father's house to be joined to that of her husband. In verses 16 and 17 the promises of progeny and prominence of name are lifted up, echoing these important themes in the Abraham cycle.

SONG OF SOLOMON 2:8–13 (RCL ALT.)

Although often read as allegory, the Song of Songs is a celebration of human love expressed between lover and beloved. The text alternates between the voice of the woman and that of the man, representing the mutual passion that exists between them. The unbridled enthusiasm on the part of both echoes the willingness of Isaac and Rebekah to embrace each other as husband and wife, and reminds us of the joy that may be found in the binding together of human lives.

PSALM 145 (BCP)
PSALM 145:8-14 (RCL ALT., BCP ALT.)
PSALM 145:1-2, 8-9, 10-11, 13-17 (LFM)

Although the effect is lost in English, the psalm is composed as an acrostic—each verse beginning with a successive letter of the Hebrew alphabet. The psalm is a hymn of praise from beginning to end. Verses 1-2 serve as an introduction and employ the "I" voice of the psalmist. The remainder of the psalm alternates between the voices of the faithful declaring God's power and glory (vv. 4-7, 10-13), and descriptions of God (vv. 8-9), which serve as a summary of God's attributes and enumerate God's deeds (vv. 13b-20). Notably, the emphasis is not on God's work as Creator, as in other psalms, but on God's mercies toward humankind. In verse 5, the "I" voice of the psalmist again pops out, declaring "on your wondrous works I will meditate," an invitation to us to follow this example (see also v. 6).

SECOND READING
ROMANS 7:15-25A (RCL)
ROMANS 7:21—8:6 (BCP)

The division of verses by the lectionaries creates overlapping texts. This shows how carefully Paul's argument is constructed, verse upon verse, but creates a challenge for this writer. Because a natural division occurs at 8:1, those following the BCP must see the discussion on July 13 for 8:1-6. However, I will indicate the connection to earlier verses.

The use of the first-person singular throughout 7:15-25 has led past interpreters to view this passage as an autobiographical statement revealing Paul's internal struggles. However, more recent studies of Romans recognize the "I" voice to be speaking as a kind of "everyman," not unlike medieval morality plays where a single character represents the struggles encountered by all humans. In the context of Romans, this figure would be Adam (see 5:12-21). This "voice" of Adam reveals that Paul is not speaking about current life, but of life prior to the experience of being raised with Christ to walk in newness of life (6:4). In this respect, an apt title for the passage would be "The Life We Left Behind."

There are a number of challenges in these verses, not least tracing Paul's line of thought. This can be aided by focusing on transition words. "For" introduces statements revealing the struggle of the human condition: on the one hand, "I do not do what I want" (vv. 15, 19) and "nothing good dwells within me"; on the other hand, "for I delight in the law of God in my inmost self" (v. 22).

"Now" introduces statements that begin "if I do what I do not want," but which conclude differently: "the law is good" (v. 16) and "sin . . . dwells in me" (v. 20). It is important to recognize that Paul is *not* saying that the law is sin (see 7:7); to the contrary, the law is holy (7:12) and spiritual (7:14). Indeed, it is the law that shows us what it is to sin (7:7b). Paul is contrasting the goodness of the law with the power of sin to pervert our best intentions. This is signaled by clauses beginning with "but." These follow on positive statements ("the law is good" [v. 16]; "I delight in the law of God in my inmost self" [v. 22]), but point to the power of sin that holds humankind captive and that is manifested by the distortion of our relationship to God as our Creator (see Romans 1, commented on for Proper 4, June 1, above). The potential confusion created by the repetition of the word *law* in verses 22–23, 25 is removed if it is remembered that "law" (*nomos*) refers also in general to a principle or rule.

> Paul is contrasting the goodness of the law with the power of sin to pervert our best intentions.

A difficulty with this passage is Paul's apparently negative view of humankind. The phrase "nothing good dwells within me" can be heard as "I am worthless." Yet heard in context, Paul clearly recognizes that the impulse to do good (*agathos:* that which is useful, beneficial) is present in every human being. In Paul's eyes, no human is worthless, but every human is in need of being rescued (*rhuomai*) from the powerful urge to live as if we were the rulers of the universe.

ROMANS 8:9, 11–13 (LFM)

See the discussion of the second reading for the Ninth Sunday after Pentecost (Fifteenth Sunday in Ordinary Time/Proper 10), July 13, 2008, below.

THE GOSPEL
MATTHEW 11:16–19, 25–30 (RCL)
MATTHEW 11:25–30 (BCP, LFM)

The previous Gospel lection left off with the promise of reward to the ones who welcome those who come in the name of Jesus. This week's lection (RCL) begins with a passage describing those who are less welcoming. "This generation" is uniformly condemned in Matthew's Gospel (for instance, 12:41–42; 23:36). Although the religious leaders, as Jesus' opponents, are most often identified with "this generation," in 17:17 the disciples appear to be included in Jesus' expression of exasperation for their little faith (a phrase only ever used of the disciples). "This generation," then, are those within immediate hearing and seeing who are just not quite sure of what it is they are hearing and seeing. How do you know when a prophet is a true prophet? When the church down the street offers a true witness? Sometimes this results in rejection; sometimes in doubt (28:17).

The image of children playing in the marketplace is familiar: some want to play the flute and dance (a marriage game), while others want to wail and mourn (a funeral game); in both cases their playmates do not cooperate, with the result that everyone sulks and no one gets to play. This is likened to responses to John the Baptist and Jesus: on the one hand, an ascetic who is said to be demon-possessed; on the other hand, a glutton and drunkard who hangs out with disreputable company. In neither case is "this generation" satisfied with what they are hearing and seeing. Perhaps they want something in between? We know too well this kind

> "This generation" are those within immediate hearing and seeing who are just not quite sure of what it is they are hearing and seeing.

of response, where it is clear what is *not* wanted and one thing after another is rejected. Unfortunately, we can become so locked into this kind of negative response that we miss the real thing.

Matthew suggests that this is precisely what has happened with the concluding verse: "Yet wisdom is vindicated by her deeds" (v. 19). The association of Jesus with the figure of Wisdom adds layer upon layer to Matthew's description of Jesus. In the Wisdom of Solomon, Wisdom is described "a spotless mirror of the working of God" (7:26b) and "an initiate in the knowledge of God" (8:4). In Proverbs, Wisdom is described crying out to the people in the street, "Come, eat of my bread and drink of the wine I have mixed [cf. Matt. 11:19]. Lay aside immaturity, and live, and walk in the way of insight" (Prov. 9:5-6; see Proverbs 8–9). This language anticipates Matthew 11:25-30. It also looks back to 11:2-6 where Jesus responds to John's disciples, inquiring whether he is the one to come or not: "Go and tell John what you hear and see . . ." (11:4). It is a reminder to us that the response to our witness will depend on what people hear and see.

The lection continues with a revelatory statement by Jesus declaring his identity. A parallel version to verses 25-27 is found in Luke 10:21-22; verses 28-30 are found only in Matthew. Jesus names God as "Father, Lord of heaven and earth." "Father" is Jesus' standard designation for God in the Gospel of Matthew (*patēr,* not *abba*). This language reflects the patriarchal household and reveals God as a generous parent who knows our every need (6:32; 7:11). The designation *Father* is also important for revealing Jesus' relationship to God. In the patriarchal household the eldest son is the one who is able to represent the father because he is considered to be the very image of the father, in word and deed. Thus "no one knows the Father except the Son and anyone to whom the Son chooses to reveal him" (11:27). This, again, goes to the question of "How do you know the real thing when you see it?" For Matthew, Jesus, like Wisdom, is "an initiate in the knowledge of God" (Wis. 8:4).

Jesus' prayer of thanksgiving because God has "hidden these things from the wise and intelligent and revealed them to infants" requires some comment. The only other reference to the "wise" in Matthew is in 23:34, where they are named along with prophets as those sent by God to Israel. We misinterpret the text, then, if we categorically dismiss the wise and intelligent (*sunetos:* sensible) and assume an anti-intellectual stance. In Matthew, the argument is against those who assume knowledge, but misapply it (for instance, the Pharisees whose interpretation of Torah Jesus challenges). This is a failing in the wise as well as the simple and it is a failing of character rather than intelligence. There is no virtue in ignorance. A second reference to "infants" occurs in 21:16 (another verse found only in Matthew). Here children raise their voices in praise when Jesus heals the blind and lame in the Temple. "Infants," then, are those who know what they hear and see (never mind that in reality children may speak from a lively imagination). They do not have a stake in the argument or a position to protect.

Verses 28-29, well known as they are, continue to speak powerfully. Is there a single person who is not desirous of rest? Whether it is the toil of day-to-day responsibilities, stresses that arise from work or family, or overwhelming burdens that send us into the spin of clinical depression, we all, at some point, feel indescribably weary (*kopiaō*: weariness from toil or struggle; cf. 6:28). "Yoke" has multiple referents. It can be heard as a referent to Torah (Jer. 5:5; Sirach 51); the reference to the "heavy burdens" or requirements of Pharisaic interpretation of the law (as opposed to the law per se) seems to point in that direction (23:4). We, too, are capable of turning God's Word into a rulebook or "how–to" manual, rather than viewing obedience to God's commandments as an instinctive and joyful response to God's grace. Another and more common use of "yoke" is as reference to the power of one nation over another (for example, Isa. 9:4; Jer. 27:8). The latter invites a contrast of the reign of God with the reign of Rome. Jesus, like the figure in Zechariah 9 and in contrast to the emperor in Rome, is humble in heart, and gentle (*praus:* meek; see also 5:5). "Rest for your souls" is drawn from Jeremiah 6:16, which underscores the path of God as the way that leads to rest. When this is our experience, we have both heard and seen.

> "Infants" are those who know what they hear and see. They do not have a stake in the argument or a position to protect.

Note

1. Carol L. Meyers and Eric M. Meyers, *Zechariah 9–14,* Anchor Bible (New York: Doubleday, 1993), 138.

NINTH SUNDAY AFTER PENTECOST

FIFTEENTH SUNDAY IN ORDINARY TIME / PROPER 10

JULY 13, 2008

Revised Common (RCL)	Episcopal (BCP)	Roman Catholic (LFM)
Gen. 25:19-34 or Isa. 55:10-13	Isa. 55:1-5, 10-13	Isa. 49:14-15
Ps. 119:105-112 or 65:(1-8) 9-13	Psalm 65 or 65:9-14	Ps. 65:10, 11, 12-13, 14
Rom. 8:1-11	Rom. 8:9-17	Rom. 8:18-23
Matt. 13:1-9, 18-23	Matt. 13:1-9, 18-23	Matt. 13:1-23 or 13:1-9

FIRST READING
GENESIS 25:19-34 (RCL)

Who needs reality television shows when we have the Bible? Greed, rivalry, deception, favoritism, they are all here revealing how we are driven by the needs and desires of our narrow frame of reference. The difference is that the Bible frames our behavior within the larger narrative of God and invites us to see our behavior in relation to this Other who is also active in the world.

The lection unfolds in two related episodes (vv. 19-28, 29-34). The first episode begins with the recurrent theme of barrenness. The earlier story of Sarah has prepared us to expect a positive resolution and we are not disappointed: Isaac's prayer is answered. The story quickly turns to the infants struggling within Rebekah's womb. A more literal translation of "struggle" (*ratsats*) would be "crashed." It is little wonder Rebekah wonders whether she will die of pain. Where Isaac prayed to God with a request, Rebekah asks of God a question and receives an oracle. The oracle reveals that the crashing about in her womb is a rivalry between two nations about to be birthed. The oracle is confirmed when the younger child, Jacob, is born grasping at the heel of his elder brother, Esau, and fueled as each parent favors one child over the other (a familiar family narrative). These domestic events anticipate future events to be played out on the world stage. However, they should be viewed less as predictions than perhaps a playing out of human character in dialogue with the larger narrative of God.

In episode two, the oracle is moved closer to fulfillment. This episode is filled with irony: Esau, a skillful hunter, is unable to recognize when he is being made the prey; Jacob, a "quiet man" (*tam:* morally innocent), is shown to be a ruthless schemer. Both are driven by their wants. Esau's want is food. Boorishly, he demands some of the "red stuff" and inhales it ('*akal:* "eat" can also mean "consume like an animal"). Jacob wants the birthright. As younger son he is expected to serve his elder brother all his life, but Jacob is more ambitious. So the brothers exchange want for want: food for birthright. There is nothing noble in Jacob's ambition: in seeking the power and material gain that accompanies the status of elder child, he is just as self-serving as Esau. The question remains how God will be able to work with such characters in bringing to fulfillment the promises and vision of God. The preacher may well ask, How is God able to work with us?

ISAIAH 55:10-13 (RCL ALT., LFM)
ISAIAH 55:1-5, 10-13 (BCP)

The reference to the sower in verse 10 creates an explicit link between Isaiah and the Gospel lection. A thematic connection between the texts also exists: the Isaiah passage issues an invitation to hear in order that we may live; the parable of the sower describes how different people hear and respond to the word. In each case, the focus is almost exclusively on the hearing, a reminder that "hearing" requires an openness of spirit so that we do not judge what we hear before we have heard it, an open mind to listen genuinely to what is being said, and an open heart to allow the possibility of being transformed by the word. In a world of multitasking, we have become too adept at half-hearing.

> There is nothing noble in Jacob's ambition: in seeking the power and material gain that accompanies the status of elder child, he is just as self-serving as Esau.

The opening words of the Isaiah passage echo the voice of Wisdom (Prov. 9:1-6), a figure present with God at creation (Prov. 8:22-31), who instructs humankind in God's ways (Prov. 8:32-36). This combination of Wisdom with prophecy allows Isaiah to address the future while adopting a more universal perspective. This is signaled in verse 1 with the address to "everyone who thirsts" and "those who have no money" to "come, buy and eat" (note the reversal of Isa. 3:1; 30:20; 50:2). No money or status is required to feast at the table of God (see the thematic development in 12:3; 33:16; 41:17; 43:20). We should not assume an exclusively spiritualized context here, since elsewhere it is clear that the word, the rich food that satisfies, demands of us concern for the physical well-being of the vulnerable. Two admonitions to "listen" are followed by two declarations, marked by "See." The first "see" recalls how God made David ruler over all Israel; the second "see" shifts the covenant God made with David to all Israel, who, by their example will draw even those whom they do not know to the voice of Wisdom, the way of God.

In verses 10-11 the cycle of rain to earth to seed to bread is similar to the pattern described in the parable of the sower, but here is intended to assure us that the word of God is utterly reliable. The phrase "it shall not return to me empty" recalls the power of God's word at creation. The passage concludes with a joyous procession involving the whole of creation. The thorns and the briers that can choke out the word or become a cause of stumbling are replaced by the cypress and the myrtle. Maintaining the universal voice of Wisdom, in God's everlasting covenant all of creation will be transformed.

RESPONSIVE READING
PSALM 119:105-112 (RCL)

The longest of the psalms, Psalm 119 consists of twenty-two stanzas, each stanza beginning with a successive letter of the alphabet, and each line of the stanza beginning with the same letter. Verses 105-112 are a meditation on Torah (within the psalm called "righteous ordinances," "decrees," and "statutes"). The stanza begins and ends with the psalmist's praise of Torah: it is a lamp to the feet and a light to the path (v. 105), the psalmist's heritage and a joy to the heart (v. 111). This praise is followed in each case by the psalmist's promise and willing desire to observe God's word (vv. 106, 112). In between, the psalmist speaks of afflictions brought about by evildoers. Nonetheless, the psalmist continues to hold fast to God's word for it lays a sure foundation. The psalm anticipates the parable of the sower in Matthew with its emphasis on the word.

> Maintaining the universal voice of Wisdom, in God's everlasting covenant all of creation will be transformed.

PSALM 65:(1-8) 9-13 (RCL ALT.)
PSALM 65 OR 65:9-14 (BCP)
PSALM 65:10, 11, 12-13, 14 (LFM)

This psalm is a celebration of God who forgives our transgressions, who delivers us in the midst of tumult, and who blesses the earth with a bountiful harvest so that we might be sustained. Although this may sound like a catch-all, the psalmist recognizes that it is our transgressions that lead us away from the presence of God and draw us into tumult and thus our need for deliverance, and that deliverance means not simply escape from danger but the capacity to live without want. Throughout, God is the One who provides. Particularly striking is the universal reach of God's salvation, who is the "hope of all the ends of the earth" (v. 5), to whom all flesh will come (v. 2), whom even the pastures and the valleys will praise (vv. 12–13).

SECOND READING

ROMANS 8:1–11 (RCL)
ROMANS 8:9–17 (BCP)

These verses are anticipated in 7:24-25 and develop Paul's answer to the question, "Who will rescue me from this body of death?" The first part of the lection, verses 1–8, is written in the third person ("those who . . ."). It begins with a positive statement in verse 1 ("therefore"), which is followed by four explanatory statements ("for," vv. 2, 3, 5, 7). In preaching these could be framed in a question-and-answer format ("why?" "for . . .").

As in the previous lection, it is helpful to recall that "law" has multiple referents: in verses 1–2, it is best understood as "principle"; in verses 3–4 as the Mosaic law. The Mosaic law, says Paul, lacks the power to make us right before God. This is not because of a failing on the part of the law (which Paul views as holy), but because human beings (Adam) confound the Mosaic law, being under the "law of sin that dwells in [our] members" (7:23). Paul associates this "law of sin" with life in the flesh, here meaning our willful tendency to declare our independence from God (so Romans 1).

God, who sent the law, now sends the Son in "the likeness of sinful flesh." The *typos* Adam is transformed into the *typos* Christ (see 5:14). A possible translation of the phrase "to deal with sin" (*peri hamartias*) is "to atone for sin," referring to Christ's role in reconsecrating humankind to the service of God (see the discussion of Romans 3 for Proper 4 on June 1, above). "The just requirement of the law" in verse 4 does not refer to a penalty or condemnation, but to the righteousness that describes God and which we are called to mani-fest when we live in relationship with the Creator. Verses 5–8 reveal that God's action through Christ does not deprive us of free will. We can continue to set our minds on "the flesh" (that is, to live in a way that is antithetical to God's law, which is sum-marized in the commandment to love one another [13:8]), or, because Christ has overcome the power of sin, we can set our minds on the Spirit (whether this is the Holy Spirit, the Spirit of Christ, or the Spirit of God is difficult to pin down).

> Although we have been set free to choose between life in the flesh and life in the Spirit, both the initiative and results are gracious gifts of God.

At verse 9 Paul shifts to the second-person plural, addressing his audience directly: "But you are not in the flesh; you are in the Spirit." The use of the plural is a reminder that Paul rarely speaks of the individual's relationship to Christ; he speaks almost exclusively of the individual in the context of community. This underscores the ethical component of all Paul's teachings. Although we have been set free to choose between life in the flesh and life in the Spirit, both the initiative and results are gracious gifts of God (vv. 3, 10, 11). The phrase "because of righteousness" likely has a double meaning, referring both to the righteousness of God and the righteous acts that may result when we embrace the Spirit, which is life. These are theologically loaded verses, but speak to the profound transformation that occurs in how we think and act toward one another when we receive the gift of God in Christ.

Again, the division of verses by the lectionaries creates overlapping texts. Those following the BCP will need to see the discussion on 8:12-17 for Proper 11, July 20, below.

ROMANS 8:18-23 (LFM)

See the discussion of the second reading for the Tenth Sunday after Pentecost (Sixteenth Sunday in Ordinary Time/Proper 11), July 20, 2008, below.

THE GOSPEL

MATTHEW 13:1-9, 18-23 (RCL, BCP)
MATTHEW 13:1-23 OR 13:1-9 (LFM)

Anyone who is a farmer or gardener knows the many pitfalls that await seed once scattered in the soil. Those who are not may identify with the sower who seems to scatter seed at will and hope for the best. The wonderful imagery in this familiar parable offers possibilities for dramatic presentation and the potential for two very different presentations. One might play up the humor of the text; however, another possibility is to portray the parable from the perspective of a subsistence farmer. For this individual, the seed snatched away is a catastrophe, leading to further indebtedness and potential loss of land. In contrast, the hundredfold produced by the seed in good soil represents about ten times what was the average yield. The more engaged we are with the story, the greater impact its interpretation will have.

Although the parable speaks about how people respond to the gospel, we might use the parable as an opportunity to reflect on the different ways we respond to different parts of Scripture and why. This is also one of the few lections that lines up well with both the first reading (Isaiah) and the second reading (Romans). For example, the Isaiah passage speaks to the necessity of preparing ourselves to hear the word of God. The Romans text expands on the significance of the gospel for our lives, and encourages us, also, to seek the way of God.

The parable and its interpretation are found in all three Synoptic Gospels, but each telling and interpretation is a little different. Matthew's version of the parable is tidier and more concise than Mark's version. This has the effect of making the images stand out in staccato fashion. In Matthew, the "seed" becomes plural ("seeds"), which will be important for Matthew's interpretation of the parable. Matthew also reverses the order of the grain brought forth, beginning with the hundredfold and decreasing to thirty (13:8; cf. Mark 4:8). The conclusion "Let anyone who has ears listen!" punctuates the end of the parable and invites our attention. Since minds may have drifted during the telling of the parable ("I've heard it before"), the preacher may not want to overlook the possibilities suggested by this line for getting the congregation's attention.

The distinctiveness of Matthew's version leaps out in the interpretation of the parable. Matthew's Jesus does not begin with a question, but a statement: "Hear then the parable of the sower." As it turns out, it is not really a parable about the sower, but the seeds. In Mark, the sower sows the word; in Matthew, the seeds are those who hear the word. We are the seed (see 13:24-30). That which is heard is specified as "the word of the kingdom." This anticipates each of the parables that are to follow ("the kingdom of heaven is like . . ."), but also invites us to reflect on what we have heard and seen in relation to the kingdom up to this point.

> It is those who do not understand the word who are vulnerable to the evil one who snatches what has been sown "in the heart," which is the seat of discernment.

It is those who do not understand the word who are vulnerable to the evil one who snatches what has been sown "in the heart," which is the seat of discernment. They have not yet been able to discern what it is they have heard. Has there been no one to teach them? Or have they simply been too lazy to spend time meditating on and studying the word? The seed that falls on rocky ground, like the seed in Mark's version, has no root and falls away when trouble begins brewing. Whole treatises have been written on the importance of the root system for the life of plants.

> Disciples are those who strive for the kingdom of God, rather than worrying about what they will eat or what they will wear.

Some plants have been able to adapt to clinging to rocky places, but most need deep soil, filled with nutrients and earthworms, and access to a steady supply of water. We, similarly, need inner resources (deep roots) and community (nutrients and water) when trouble arises, as it surely will. The missionary discourse (chap. 10) tells us that discipleship is not for the faint of heart. The seeds that fall among thorns are choked by cares of the world (*merimna:* worries, anxieties) and lure (*apatē*: seduction or deceitfulness) of wealth (see the NIV for this translation). Disciples, in contrast, are those who strive for the kingdom of God, rather than worrying about what they will eat or what they will wear (6:24-34). Notably, most of the seed proves unfruitful. Those eager for congregational growth will be disappointed. The parable, much as it may have to teach us about discipleship, also offers explanations for why people do not respond to the word. This was as much a puzzlement then as it can be now: Why is what is so obvious to us not obvious to everyone? The tremendous yield by the seed that falls in good soil is intended to offset discouragement. Why Matthew begins with a hundredfold is unclear, but the effect should be to astound the audience.

In between the parable and its interpretation, the disciples come to Jesus and ask why he speaks in parables. The explanation continues to address the question of why so few are drawn to the kingdom of heaven. These verses may be difficult to hear, particularly verse 12 with its harsh declaration: "but from those who have nothing, even what they have will be taken away." It is important to hear these words in their literary context. Jesus is not speaking about those who are impoverished physically or financially. Heard in dialogue with the parable of the sower, those who have nothing are the ones who lack understanding, or roots, or are lured away. It is these who will lose what little they have. The disciples receive the "secrets of the kingdom" because they both see and hear (11:2-6). These, like the good seed that yields a hundredfold, will receive even more in the way of understanding (13:51). Parables both reveal and conceal. To those who have ears to hear, they offer even greater insight; to those who have no will to hear, there is no learning to be gained. We should not necessarily exclude ourselves from the latter group—particularly if we think we have already heard the parable one too many times.

TENTH SUNDAY AFTER PENTECOST

Revised Common (RCL)	Episcopal (BCP)	Roman Catholic (LFM)
Gen. 28:10-19a or Isa. 44:6-8 or Wisd. of Sol. 12:13, 16-19	Wisd. of Sol. 12:13, 16-19	Wisd. of Sol. 12:13, 16-19
Ps. 139:1-12, 23-24 or 86:11-17	Psalm 86 or 86:11-17	Ps. 86:5-6, 9-10, 15-16
Rom. 8:12-25	Rom. 8:18-25	Rom. 8:26-27
Matt. 13:24-30, 36-43	Matt. 13:24-30, 36-43	Matt. 13:24-43 or 13:24-30

FIRST READING

GENESIS 28:10-19A (RCL)

The domestic tensions that marked the beginning of the Jacob cycle have continued. Esau is beginning to rue the loss of his birthright, so Jacob is sent to his mother's brother, Laban, for safekeeping and to seek a wife from among his mother's people. He is, in effect, a man on the run. On his way to Haran, Jacob pauses for the night and has a dream. Because they represent a liminal state between waking and sleeping, dreams were believed to be a space in which one might encounter God. We also often think of dreams as places of special vision: consider Martin Luther King Jr.'s "I Have a Dream" speech or the song made popular by Peter, Paul, and Mary, "Last Night I Had the Strangest Dream." Dreams offer a space suspended from time and place where harsh realities can be re-visioned. When they are fully embraced, these dreams have the potential, in turn, to transform reality.

Within the narrative, the liminality of the space is suggested by its initial ambiguous description as "a certain place." When, following the dream, Jacob renames the place *beth-el* ("house of God") he describes it as "the gate of heaven," a liminal space where earth and heaven meet. It is, as Jacob says, an "awesome place." We should hear in this the contemporary "Wow!" coupled with respect and even fear of that which is beyond our understanding. Jacob's dream is punctuated at four points by the word *behold* (omitted in the English): "behold, a ladder [more likely, staircase or ramp]," "behold, angels of God," "behold, the LORD stood beside him," "behold, know that I am with you." These markers draw Jacob in to the presence of God and the reassurance of the presence of God with him. Whatever else is said in the dream, it is this presence of God with him upon which the surety of all other promises is built.

God is identified as "the God of Abraham your father and the God of Isaac." God is not associated, ultimately, with place, but in relationship and promise. This description of God also firmly associates God with the promises made first to Abraham, then to his descendent, Isaac. The appearance by God to Jacob reveals that it is through Jacob the fugitive that the working out of God's promises is to be continued. It

> Whatever else is said in the dream, it is the presence of God with Jacob upon which the surety of all other promises is built.

is striking, therefore, that the promise revolves around land, for, at the moment, Jacob is a man dispossessed of land. God also promises offspring "like the dust of the earth" to a man as yet unmarried. Yet by this point in Genesis, we should be used to God whose vision is beyond what we can see immediately before us and who comes to us in dreams that hold out hope of transforming our reality.

ISAIAH 44:6-8 (RCL ALT.)

This short passage is an oracle ("Thus says the LORD"), spoken in the context of a judicial case ("Who is like me?"). The oracle concerns the one God versus the many gods that surround the exiles in Babylon (see 47:10). In the ancient world, where no division existed between religion and state, the power of the gods was closely aligned with nationalistic aims. This was true also of the one God, and presents one of the challenges of this text for preachers. How do we understand the power of the one God in a multireligious context built on the premise that there will be "no law respecting an establishment of religion"?[1]

The nationalistic dimension of God is evident in the titles of verse 6: "King of Israel," "Israel's Redeemer," "LORD of hosts [warriors]." Yet there are indications that this one God transcends national boundaries in the claim that God is the first and the last, "besides me there is no god." In historical context, the latter does not mean there are no other gods, but that they are of no account when compared with the one God. Verses 7a and 8 offer a word of assurance to those in exile by claiming that the whole of history is in the hands of God. This need not nec-essarily mean that God controls every movement of

> God's providence is at work in, through, and with the created order.

history like a puppet-master, but that God's providence is at work in, through, and with the created order. "You are my witnesses!" invites us to remember the story of God with us.

WISDOM OF SOLOMON 12:13, 16-19
(RCL ALT., BCP, LFM)

These verses belong to a larger literary unit that represents an effort to come to terms with a troubling aspect of Israel's past: the conquest of the Canaanites. The challenge of this task is great because the events have been previously described as the will of God. It is a task with which we may be uncomfortably familiar if we have had the courage to examine our own past with a critical eye. The approach taken is a common one: the Canaanites are shown to be deserving of their fate.

The verses chosen for the lection sidestep this larger polemic and focus instead on the sovereignty and majesty of God. The more adventurous preacher could consider how we sometimes use Scripture for our own ends, or project onto God justification for our deeds. However, the verses can also stand alone as testimony to the character of God.

> There are times when we can so overemphasize the tender nature of God that we lose sight of the sovereignty of God.

There are times when we can so overemphasize the tender nature of God ("God is my best friend") that we lose sight of the sovereignty of God. These verses alternate between declarations of God's power (vv. 12, 17) and affirmations of God's grace (vv. 16, 18). In this way, they provide a balance of perspective, allowing God to be God, while witnessing to God's mercy toward humankind. The closing verse, "you have taught your people that the righteous must be kind," is a poignant reminder that our relationship with God extends beyond us and should be reflected in how we live with other people, for we are all in need of repentance and live in need of the "good hope" God grants to us.

RESPONSIVE READING
PSALM 139:1-12, 23-24 (RCL)

The theme of God's intimate knowledge of our very being fits particularly well with the Genesis and Romans texts. For many, this is a psalm of comfort, offering assurance of God's presence, regardless. For some, it may be a fearful psalm; victims of abuse are often threatened with the words, "no matter where you go I will find you." It is important, therefore, to bear witness to the character of God, who seeks our well-being in all things and in every place.

Interspersed with prayers of supplication are testimonies to God's faithfulness, goodness, mercy, and grace. By affirming the nature and character of God, the psalmist names for us the One who hears our cries and who is able to deliver us. Verses 8-10 complement the Isaiah text as well as the Wisdom of Solomon ("There is none like you").

SECOND READING

ROMANS 8:12–25 (RCL)
ROMANS 8:18–25 (BCP)

The thick theology of the previous lections gives way here to an abundance of evocative images: adoption as children of God, the groaning of creation, hope for what we cannot yet see. With these verses Paul is bringing full circle his narrative on the salvation of humankind: from Adam to Christ, from dying to rising, from enslavement to sin to newness of life. Paul now grounds our identity in an eschatological context, revealing his discourse to have moved from the beginning of time (creation) and covenant (Abraham) to the end of time.

Verses 12-13 serve as a conclusion ("so then") to 8:1-11, repeating in second-person plural what was described in third-person plural in 8:5-8. This has the effect of making what was abstract personal: the choice is yours. To help his audience choose, Paul, like many great composers and songwriters, borrows one of his own familiar themes in verses 14-17 (see Gal. 4:5-7). Adoption was not uncommon in the ancient world; even slaves could be adopted as heirs. The effect of Paul's words is illustrated well in Barbara Kingsolver's novel *The Bean Trees*. The main character, showing her new daughter her adoption certificate, explains: "This means you're my kid . . . and I'm your mother, and nobody can say it isn't so. I'll keep that paper for you till you're older, but it's yours. So you'll always know who you are."[2] Paul wants his audience to know who they are; the Spirit serves as their adoption certificate bearing witness that "nobody can say it isn't so."

Verses 17-18 briefly introduce the subject of suffering. Elsewhere Paul develops this theme more thoroughly (for instance, 2 Cor. 1:3-11; 11:16-33; Phil. 3:7-11). Here it is simply a reminder that to be "in Christ" means not only justification; to be led by the Spirit of God may also enjoin us to participate in suffering with Christ. Suffering, however, is recognized as a prelude to glory (salvation), and, from an apocalyptic perspective, a sign that the end is soon to be revealed. Implicit in this view is the belief that history does not simply repeat itself, but is moving toward a moment of completion. Verses 19-22 are unique in Paul, for only here does he describe the inclusion of all of creation in this act of restoration. What is particularly striking is the way in which creation is described waiting "with eager longing for the revealing of the children of God" and "groaning in labor pains" alongside of us. There is, in Paul's mind, a bond between humankind and creation as, together, they await the moment when both will obtain freedom from "bondage to decay" ("the redemption of our bodies"). This might invite reflection on the ways in which we are discovering how all of the created order is interrelated and dependent upon one another.

> Suffering is recognized as a prelude to glory (salvation), and, from an apocalyptic perspective, a sign that the end is soon to be revealed.

The lection concludes with Paul's familiar words on hope. These verses bring us back to Abraham, where the theme of hope is first introduced (see also 5:2, 4, 5). God's promise to Abraham that he would be a "father of many nations" required him to hope in that which he could not see. Just as God's promise to Abraham is being fulfilled as the Gentiles are brought to salvation, so too we are invited to hope in that which we cannot yet see: the time of redemption when all of creation will be restored.

ROMANS 8:26-27 (LFM)

See the discussion of the second reading for the Eleventh Sunday after Pentecost (Seventeenth Sunday in Ordinary Time/Proper 12), July 27, 2008, below.

THE GOSPEL
MATTHEW 13:24-30, 36-43 (RCL, BCP)
MATTHEW 13:24-43 OR 13:24-30 (LFM)

"I don't go to church because it is full of hypocrites." "I love going to church; it's the people I can't stand." "Those people are trying to ruin our church." These declarations are all too familiar to anyone engaged in congregational life. Apparently they were known to the Matthean community as well. Continuing the theme of "sowing the seed," Matthew inserts a parable that is found only in this Gospel, commonly referred to as the wheat and the tares (weeds). Material that is unique to Matthew generally points to themes that are distinct to that Gospel, and that is the case here.

The parable likens the kingdom of heaven to someone who sows good seed in his field. The word for "someone" is *anthrōpos* (a human being as opposed to an animal), rooting the parable firmly in a human context (although the explanation will shift the parable to a cosmic context). The man is further identified as a householder with slaves who work his fields. This is a man of some status and wealth. Like a good farmer, he sows "good seed" in his field. "Good" (*kalos*) describes that which is useful; here, seed that will produce good fruit, a common description in the Gospel of those who walk in the ways of God (3:10; 7:1-18; 12:33; see also 5:16; 26:10). By extension, then, it refers to those who act in a way that is praiseworthy or noble: descriptive in the ancient world of a moral life.

An enemy comes along and sows weeds among the wheat. The NIV is more accurate here, including the pronoun specifying "his" enemy. This is no random enemy; this is personal. Nonetheless, nothing more is said about the enemy, signaling that the "who" or "why" are not important to the story. It is, however, interesting to consider what Jesus has said earlier about enemies: "love your enemy" (5:43-44), and "one's foes will be members of one's own household" (10:36). The first statement may offer some insight into the householder's response to the situation. The second refers to conflict within the domestic household as a result of following Jesus, but it is not too much of a stretch to hear it as a reference to conflict within the fictive household created by brothers and sisters in Christ (see 10:25).

The extended dialogue between the householder and the slaves forms the primary focus of the parable. The householder recognizes immediately who is responsible for the weeds; nonetheless, nothing is said about destroying the enemy. Further, when asked whether the weeds should be removed, the householder instructs the slaves to let the weeds grow alongside the wheat until the harvest. This is a puzzling response. What if the weeds, like the thistles in the previous parable, choke out the wheat? The householder holds back, he says, for fear that some of the wheat might be uprooted along with the weeds. Yet this leaves the wheat, later identified as children of the kingdom (v. 38), in a precarious position: it means they must rub shoulders day by day with those who clearly do not belong in the field. Matthew's Jesus, however, has earlier declared that God sends both sun and rain on the righteous and the unrighteous alike (5:45b). If God shows such generosity of spirit, can the householder do any less?

> God sends both sun and rain on the righteous and the unrighteous alike. If God shows such generosity of spirit, can the householder do any less?

The explanation of the parable is separated from the parable itself by two additional parables (see the discussion of the Gospel for Proper 12 on July 27, below). These, like the parable that precedes them, pick up on the theme of growth. They may be heard as words of encouragement to a beleaguered community who feel beset upon by enemies or at least surrounded by weeds. They also testify to the presence of the kingdom although it may not always seem visible. This may perhaps be a comment on the wheat and the weeds: is the householder concerned that, at least in the early stages of growth, it may not be wholly possible to discern what is wheat and what is a weed?

Verses 34-35 mark a transition to verse 36 where Jesus leaves behind the crowds and enters a house. It is the disciples only, then, who hear the explanation of the parable of the wheat and the weeds. The crowds are left to ponder its various possible meanings. The disciple's question of Jesus is worth noting: they ask him to explain the "parable of the weeds in the field." In the parable itself, the householder is concerned about the wheat; in contrast, the disciples focus on the weeds. Jesus identifies the one who sows the wheat as the Son of Man. In Matthew, the title "Son of Man" refers to Jesus in his earthly ministry (for instance, 9:6; 11:19; 20:18), and to the one who comes to judge (for example, 10:23; 19:28; 25:31). Both roles seem to be in view here. The good seed is identified with the children of the kingdom, while the weeds are identified as the children of the evil one, the devil (vv. 38c-39). On what constitutes evil see 5:37; 15:19; 18:32; note that all of these behaviors in one way or another break the trust that is the basis for human relationships.

The harvest is a common image for the judgment that accompanies the end of the ages (see 4:12). The furnace of fire conjures up both images of destruction (Mal. 3:1) and the refiner's fire (Mal. 3:2; 1 Pet. 1:7). Just as the weeds are collected at the end of the harvest, so the Son of Man will collect out of the kingdom (that is, the whole world) "all causes of sin and all evildoers." Here the NASV (1995) offers the closer translation: "all stumbling blocks and those who commit lawlessness." The word for "stumbling blocks" is *skandala,* from which we get our word "scandal." It refers to those who create obstacles or place temptations in the way of others (see 16:23; 18:7). Combined with "lawlessness" it echoes Matthew 5:19: "Therefore, whoever breaks one of the least of these commandments, and teaches others to do the same, will be called least in the kingdom of heaven . . . ." This verse suggests that until the judgment, stumbling blocks still have a place in the kingdom, for the time being anyway.

> The parable of the wheat and the weeds is a reminder that, until the judgment comes, we all grow up together, side by side.

For the disciples, who are concerned about the weeds rather than the wheat (cf. 9:37-38), it is perhaps reassuring to know that, in the end, all causes of stumbling will be swept away. It may be so for us as well. Dependent as we are on grace, we also want to remain confident of God's justice, and, ultimately, this requires judgment. We just prefer it when it is others, rather than ourselves, who are judged. The parable of the wheat and the weeds is a reminder that, until the judgment comes, we all grow up together, side by side.

Notes

1. U.S. Constitution, the Bill of Rights, Amendment 1.
2. Barbara Kingsolver, *The Bean Trees* (New York: HarperTorch, 1988), 311.

ELEVENTH SUNDAY AFTER PENTECOST

SEVENTEENTH SUNDAY IN ORDINARY TIME / PROPER 12

JULY 27, 2008

Revised Common (RCL)	Episcopal (BCP)	Roman Catholic (LFM)
Gen. 29:15-18 or 1 Kgs. 3:5-12	1 Kgs. 3:5-12	1 Kgs. 3:5, 7-12
Ps. 105:1-11, 45b or Psalm 128 or Ps. 119:129-136	Ps. 119:121-136 or 129-136	Ps. 119:57, 72, 76-77, 127-128, 129-130
Rom. 8:26-39	Rom. 8:26-34	Rom. 8:28-30
Matt. 13:31-33, 45-52	Matt. 13:31-33, 44-49a	Matt. 13:44-52 or 13:44-46

FIRST READING
GENESIS 29:15-28 (RCL)

After a sequence of narratives that revolve around the promises of God, the lection produces a text that makes no mention of God whatsoever. It is a story about Jacob's comeuppance. The younger son who cheated his elder brother out of his birthright is, in turn, cheated of his chosen wife, the younger daughter, in favor of the elder. Jacob eventually gets what he wants, Rachel, but the pattern of competition and strife that he experienced with his twin brother seems destined to follow him into his married life as his two wives compete for favor. One wonders if this is a case of destiny produced by character.

It is perhaps helpful to recall that, at this point, Jacob is on his own. When Abraham sought a bride for Isaac, he sent his servant along with gifts to negotiate the contract. Jacob, in contrast, has no one to speak on his behalf, to provide the required bride-price, or to protect him from unscrupulous relatives. Why God is absent at this point, despite God's promises to be with Jacob in last week's lection, is a matter of pure speculation. Does God think Jacob deserves what he gets or that this a matter simply beyond God's concern? The text is silent on these matters. It is possible that the narrative is intended to highlight Jacob's

> Although the promises of God will prevail in the end, Jacob is not spared from the vicissitudes of life, at least some of which are of his own making.

vulnerability as a fugitive from the home of his father. Although the promises of God will prevail in the end, Jacob is not spared from the vicissitudes of life, at least some of which are of his own making. When, ultimately, the promises of God are shown to be sure we understand that God has been with Jacob all along. Yet this text suggests that God is not standing by ready to rescue him from every twist of fate. It seems more a case of recognizing the presence of God in all our circumstances.

Laban's character is called into question when, after taking Jacob the fugitive into his home, he raises the matter of wages. One the one hand, he seems to be doing the honorable thing by offering to pay Jacob for his labor; on the other hand, by raising the subject at all, Laban implies that Jacob is somehow beholden to him, as a laborer is to the one who pays him the wages. This shifts the relationship out of the realm of kinship into the realm of master-hired worker. When Laban switches daughters on Jacob, therefore, he is assuming the role of master and the right to determine the wages. Laban's appeal to custom provides a thin cover for the deceit. Throughout this interaction, the two women are silent and described to us only in terms of their appearance. Although we are told that Jacob loved Rachel (as Isaac loved Rebekah), neither Rachel nor Leah, at his point, is given an opportunity to exercise volition.

1 KINGS 3:5-12 (RCL ALT., BCP)
1 KINGS 3:5, 7-12 (LFM)

The story of Solomon's dream at Gibeon is one of several narratives legitimating his reign. First Kings opens with David on his deathbed and Adonijah, Solomon's elder brother, ready to declare himself king. David, however, has other plans. Sending the prophet Nathan and the priest Zadok, he fulfills his promise to Bathsheba and has Solomon anointed king. Upon David's death, Solomon sets about to secure his throne. He kills Adonijah, who had requested marriage to one of David's concubines, Abishag, a move viewed by Solomon as an attempt to usurp what now belongs to Solomon. He also kills Adonijah's supporter, including another brother Joab.

> God grants Solomon's request, for he has asked for that which is most needful, not for his own gain.

Chapter 2 concludes, "So the kingdom was established in the hand of Solomon." Nonetheless, it leaves open the question of what kind of a king Solomon will prove to be.

Because the Temple had not yet been built, Solomon worships God at one of the "high places," Gibeon, located near Jerusalem. Solomon has probably slept at Gibeon in the hope of encountering God in a dream, a common practice in the ancient world. God indeed appears and inquires what Solomon desires. Solomon's response is a masterpiece of diplomacy. He begins with great praise for the love shown by God to David, who walked before God in faithfulness. Solomon then states that it is God who has given David a son to sit on his throne (God never confirms this). Solomon identifies himself as God's servant, a mere child (that is, humble, dependent, vulnerable) and describes how large is his task. Only then does he make his request: for an "understanding mind ['hearing heart'] to govern your people." God grants Solomon's request, for he has asked for that which is most needful (see Deut. 17:14-20 on the proper comportment of a king), not for his own gain. Although we no longer live in an age of divine kings, we recognize the challenges of governing rightly, whether our own lives or the lives of other people. This story of Solomon invites comparison with verses 44-45 in the Gospel lection, both texts raising the questions: What do we desire most? What is of most value? What are we prepared to do in order to obtain it?

RESPONSIVE READING
PSALM 105:1-11 (RCL)

This psalm complements the Genesis reading, celebrating the faithfulness of God's promises to Abraham, Isaac, and Jacob. It is a reminder of the importance of remembering these stories of the past, for they are one of the ways that we know God. It is because of God's faithfulness in the past that we seek the presence of God now, giving thanks and singing God's praises.

PSALM 128 (RCL ALT.)

The psalm associates domestic stability and prosperity with walking in the ways of God. While we recognize life is rarely this simple, the psalm invites us to reflect on who and what it is that guides our daily living, and is the source of our happiness. It reminds us that it is not enough to have a relationship with God, but that this must transform our actions and attitudes at home.

PSALM 119:121-136 (BCP)
PSALM 119:129-136 (RCL ALT., BCP ALT.)

Psalm 119 celebrates God's law. Woven into these two stanzas are pleas for protection from those who break God's commandments (v. 126), resulting in human oppression (vv. 121, 133, 134). This reminds us that the focus of God's law is the building up of human community on the basis of justice. The references to God as the one who shows steadfast love, who directs our steps, who imparts understanding, who protects and redeems, reveal the integral relationship between the character of God and the content of God's word.

PSALM 119:57, 72, 76–77, 127–128, 129–130 (LFM)

These verses form a hymn in praise of God's word. It is described as better than silver or gold (vv. 72, 127), a delight to the soul (v. 77), giving light and imparting understanding to the simple (v. 130). The psalmist, in response, promises to keep God's words (v. 57, 129), and walk in their way (v. 128). In between, the psalmist asks for God's steadfast love and mercy, which, in context, are revealed through God's word. The phrase, "the unfolding of your words," points to the continuously revelatory nature of this word (v. 130).

SECOND READING

ROMANS 8:26–39 (RCL)
ROMANS 8:26–34 (BCP)
ROMANS 8:28–30 (LFM)

Paul brings chapter 8 to a dramatic conclusion with words intended to bring deep comfort and encouragement. Since Paul, in Romans, is not addressing specific conflicts (in contrast to his other letters) this suggests Paul recognizes that every human life is confronted with disappointments, fears, and challenges, as are the churches to which we belong. In this lection, Paul offers three reminders of the ways in which God takes initiative on our behalf. Verses 26–27 describe how the Spirit intercedes for us in prayer. It is not that we are unworthy to approach God and therefore need intercession; rather, we often do not know what it is for which we should pray (here the NIV offers a better translation). "With sighs too deep for words" signals that these are not petty concerns, but those buried deep in our hearts. Paul says we are not on our own when we pray, but God is with us even as we search for the words to speak.

> The litany of catastrophes is a reminder of the fragility of human life, and the kinds of destruction for which we ourselves are often responsible.

Verses 28–30 offer the assurance that whatever befalls us we belong to God. In the context of chapter 8, "all things" likely refers to the sufferings of the present time (see vv. 17–18). The "good," then, is salvation (vv. 18–25, 29–30) rather than happy outcomes or security. How we hear the language of foreknowledge and predestination will depend on our theological tradition and understanding of God. Questions to ask include: Whom among humankind does God not know? What is God's intent for humankind? What is the role of free will? The word "glorified" (*doxazō*) brings narrative closure to chapters 1–8; in 1:21 creation fails to glorify God; now it is God who glorifies creation (see also 15:6, 9 where the Gentiles glorify God). This language is a reminder that this is a story about relationship.

The closing verses of chapter 8 are almost overwhelming in their declaration of God's love for us. Although a description of ultimate realities, they are addressed to us as we struggle through our day-to-day realities. The litany of catastrophes in verse 35 (hardship, distress, persecution, famine, nakedness, peril, sword) describes the worst that life on earth can muster against us. They are also a reminder of the fragility of human life, and the kinds of destruction for which we ourselves are often responsible. It is at these moments that we may feel most alone, most isolated, most forgotten. Yet Paul assures us that there is no power or principality that can separate those who are known, named, and called by God from God's love, which we have not earned, but which God has freely given to us and made known to us in Jesus Christ.

THE GOSPEL
MATTHEW 13:31-33, 44-52 (RCL)
MATTHEW 13:31-33, 44-49A (BCP)
MATTHEW 13:44-52 OR 13:44-46 (LFM)

"Have you understood all this?" Jesus asks the disciples at the end of this passage. The question follows the telling of seven parables, each describing some aspect of the kingdom of heaven. The disciples confidently respond "yes," yet it is clear from their earlier question in verse 10 that parables are not easily understood. They are a little like looking through a kaleidoscope: depending on how you turn them, you see different images and patterns of color. They provoke a different way of seeing and things leave room for questions.

> Parables are a little like looking through a kaleidoscope: depending on how you turn them, you see different images and patterns of color.

There are five parables in this lection; four appear to form matched sets. The first two are spoken openly to the crowds. The parable of the mustard seed and the parable of the bakerwoman both assume the peasant context of rural Galilee. Men took primary responsibility for fieldwork while women were in charge of baking, spinning, and weaving. In the subsistence economy of the ancient world, both were necessary participants for the survival of the household. The next three parables are spoken only to the disciples (v. 36). The parable of the treasure and the parable of the pearl more nearly reflect urban life. The person in search of hidden treasure may describe someone who traveled the empire in search of booty and quick gain; others suggest a day laborer who stumbles upon the treasure. The merchant in the parable that follows is more discriminating: he knows what he is looking for and patiently seeks it out. Both reflect the potential for gain that were possible as trade and safe travel increased within the Roman Empire. The final parable draws on the image that began the ministry of Jesus: fishing for people. Although this parable draws on another image from everyday life, the active fishing trade along the Sea of Galilee, the agent is not human but divine. This links this parable with the parable of the weeds, where the agent is identified as the Son of Man.

In the first parable, the kingdom is likened to a small seed. In Matthew 17:20, this same small seed gives way to great faith. Its description as the smallest of all seeds is poetic—there are other seeds just as small. The description of its growth is also poetic: mustard is a shrub (*lachanon:* garden herb) rather than a tree (*dendron*); it is not sturdy enough to sustain nesting birds. The reference to the tree, however, may be an effort to associate the parable with God's act of restoration (see Ezek. 17:22-24). Intended to evoke our imaginations through its vivid imagery the parable gives way to questions, for instance: When have you been surprised by a small gesture, a small vision, a small donation giving life to more than you expected? What does the image of sowing the kingdom in a field suggest to you? Who are the birds and what is it about this tree that invites them to nest (*kataskēnoō:* dwell, set up tent) in its branches?

A seed is placed in soil and relies on sun and rain for growth. In the next parable, a woman takes a growth agent, leaven, and mixes (literally "hides") it with flour until all of the flour has been mingled with the leaven. Although leaven is often understood as a metaphor for evil (Matt. 16:5-12), three positive references to leaven are found in the First Testament in connection with ritual contexts: the Thank Offering (Lev. 7:13; Amos 4:5), and the Elevation Offering, associated with the festival of the first fruits (Lev. 23:17). Heard in conjunction with these references, the parable of the bakerwoman celebrates the bounty of God's earth for the benefit of humankind. This echoes other images of bread in the Gospel of Matthew (6:11; 14:13-21; 15:21-28, 32-39). The amount of flour leavened reflects a context in which bread was baked for more than one family.[1]

> The parable of the bakerwoman celebrates the bounty of God's earth for the benefit of humankind.

Emilie Carles, a peasant who grew up in the Alps of France, recalls how the community gathered together to bake large quantities of bread, which had to last them through the winter.[2] What does it feel like to knead leaven into dough? How is this different from planting a seed? Why leavened bread rather than unleavened bread?

The parable of the bakerwoman is linked to the parable of the treasure by the repetition of the verb "hide" (*kruptō*). A treasure hidden in a field is found by someone who hides it in another location until, selling all he has, he is able to purchase the field and so claim the treasure. Burying treasure was not

152

THE SEASON
AFTER
PENTECOST
─────
HOLLY HEARON

uncommon; only the wealthy could afford a treasure house, and hiding treasure could be safer. The "hidden treasure" echoes the description of parables in verse 35, as that "which has been hidden from the foundation of the world"; within the context of chapter 13, this is understood as "the secrets of the kingdom of heaven" (13:11). It is these secrets of the kingdom that, like the treasure, are to be sought above all else (see also 6:19-21, 33; 19:21). What sort of person is it who finds the treasure? What would be hardest for you to sell in order to buy the field? For what would you be willing to sell everything?

The parable of the pearl presents a close parallel to the previous parable, but it is not identical. The agent is identified as a merchant, one of those who traveled the numerous trade routes of the Roman Empire.

> "The secrets of the kingdom of heaven," like the treasure, are to be sought above all else.

The treasure is specified as a pearl. Pearls were luxury items, associated with gold and precious stones (1 Tim. 2:9; Rev. 17:4; 18:12, 16). Earlier in Matthew, Jesus has warned against casting pearls before swine (7:6). This person, too, sells all he has for the one pearl. How is the pearl different from the treasure hidden in a field? How is the merchant different from the man who finds the treasure? What do all of these parables suggest about how people experience the kingdom of heaven?

The final parable marks a shift; it moves from everyday time to the end of time. It also differs from the previous four in that it is interpreted for us (vv. 49-50).

> The gathering of "fish of every kind" indicates that all are drawn into the kingdom; yet at the end of time the evil will be separated from the righteous.

The gathering of "fish of every kind" indicates that all are drawn into the kingdom; yet at the end of time the evil (see 15:18-19: evil may be described as that which violates the trust on which relationships are built) will be separated from the righteous (see 25:37-45). Do we expect God's grace while ignoring God's justice? Why does God wait until the end of time to sort out the fish? What emotions does this text evoke: Fear? Compassion? Hope?

Verse 52 catches our attention by the positive reference to a scribe. "Trained" (*mathēteuō*) may also be translated "discipled." "Bringing out old and new" indicates that Jesus both draws on the traditions of Israel (so 5:17-20) and offers new interpretations of the tradition. Do we know the traditions of Israel? Are we prepared to hear new interpretations?

Notes

1. Luise Schottroff, *Lydia's Impatient Sisters: A Feminist Social History of Early Christianity* (Louisville: Westminster John Knox, 1995), 80.

2. Emilie Carles, *A Life of Her Own* (New York: Penguin, 1992), 15–17.

THE SEASON AFTER PENTECOST / ORDINARY TIME

PROPER 13 THROUGH PROPER 22

HANK J. LANGKNECHT

As the lector reads the appointed lectionary texts, the Bible's vocabulary and imagery enter the mind, memory, and imagination of the worshiping community. Gathered in worship is a wide range of listeners: everyone from cradle-to-not-yet-grave Christians to skeptical first-time visitors; from the absorbed to the bored. As the reading unfolds, each listener is receiving the elements of the passages—the characters, actions, images, and unfolding plots—and is working to assemble those elements into something sensible and relevant. What influences this attempt to make sense and meaning? Everything: the day's liturgy (including the other Bible readings), Sunday school lessons, common sense, hymns, this morning's news, *Evan Almighty's* Noah, Charlton Heston's Moses, insights from private prayer, cubicle conversations at work, last night's diary entry, the latest IMHO from a favorite chat room, today's weather, and even the dynamite sermon the pastor preached on this same passage three years ago. Everything. If there is a baptism today or someone has just died or the congregation is breaking ground or the United States of America is bracing itself for (or enjoying!) two national political conventions and the Olympic Summer Games in Beijing, then as the Bible is read people may be hearing words as never before, identifying with characters heretofore ignored, finding meaning in hitherto overlooked details.

This is the gift preachers receive when they rise to preach: the Bible's words, images, and stories are strewn across various species and conditions of rock, thistle, path, and soil. And this is the challenge preachers accept when they rise

154

THE SEASON
AFTER
PENTECOST

HANK J.
LANGKNECHT

to preach: before the texts' materials are properly sorted, labeled, and stowed by the well-catechized minds of the faithful or discarded as irrelevant and archaic by the skeptics, the sermon will gather some of those elements and give testimony to how *these* passages read to *this* gathering at *this* incomparable moment in time help carry revelation from God.

What is most surprising and wonderful is that this chaotic context is where Scripture is quintessentially Scripture: read aloud to God's complex people gathered for worship. What is most disappointing is how often preachers choose to talk the Bible down from the precarious ledge whence new revelation might take flight and urge Scripture back into the safer confines of "the broader literary context" or the church's traditional interpretation or the reconstructed historical circumstances of the supposed human author.

These literary, canonical, and historical contexts are appropriate and are to be valued in their place. But they are not the *only* appropriate contexts for passages of the Bible; and they are not the most important contexts for preachers. Here is an article of faith that guides what follows: how the Bible bursts on the scene in its oral performance in worship is of fundamental theological importance for preaching because this is the church receiving its Scripture. We may lament a lot of things—biblical illiteracy, naïve accommodation of appealing verses, or the lectionary's clumsy editing—but this is still the church of Jesus Christ receiving its Scripture. You are allowed to *wish for* perfect Christian hearers; but you are not allowed to *preach among* them because they don't exist—and they never have. Time spent in the sermon explaining the experience a first-century listener might have had when hearing a parable is time spent ignoring and devaluing the living experience of the church hearing the parable now—a hearing just as inspired and guided by the Holy Spirit as the original.

The context in which a majority of congregations (likely including the one to which you preach) receive Scripture is the appropriate context of a set of lectionary readings. In all three of the lectionaries considered in *New Proclamation,* the Gospel reading sets the Sunday's primary tone or images: during Ordinary Time, the Gospel readings are arranged in canonical order so that over the weeks there is some sense of the unfolding narrative. Then a First Testament reading is selected to complement the Gospel in some way. Finally a psalm is chosen that resonates with the First Testament selection. In each of the chapters that follow, I will begin by discussing the principal themes, images, and ideas that this Gospel—First Testament—psalm grouping raises. During Ordinary Time, the epistle reading is independent of the Gospel—First Testament—psalm grouping and is instead part of a several-week-long continuous reading of the epistle (*lectio continua*). In addition, the Revised Common Lectionary (RCL) provides an alternative *lectio continua* First Testament lesson (with complementary psalm) that is an episode in a weeks-long anthology of some major sweeps of Hebrew Bible literature. After dealing with the principal themes I will treat the epistle and then the alternative First Testament-psalm pairing separately.

Before I turn to the first Sunday I want to acknowledge two providential bits of timing. During the time I was doing initial planning for this project I was teaching a course called "Hermeneutics for Preaching" at Trinity Lutheran Seminary. Near the end of each class session we read aloud the Gospel—First Testament—psalm groupings assigned to me in this volume. Many of the insights in the following chapters came from the discussions that followed those readings; I thank the students of that class for their reading and hearing. I also want to thank Pastor Jennifer P. Weetman who was able to give time to help with exegetical research and homiletical brainstorming.

155

THE SEASON
AFTER
PENTECOST
———
HANK J.
LANGKNECHT

TWELFTH SUNDAY AFTER PENTECOST

EIGHTEENTH SUNDAY IN ORDINARY TIME / PROPER 13

AUGUST 3, 2008

Revised Common (RCL)	Episcopal (BCP)	Roman Catholic (LFM)
Gen. 32:22-31 or Isa. 55:1-5	Neh. 9:16-20	Isa. 55:1-3
Ps. 17:1-7, 15 or 145:8-9, 14-21	Ps. 78:1-29 or 78:14-20, 23-25	Ps. 145:8-9, 15-16, 17-18
Rom. 9:1-5	Rom. 8:35-39	Rom. 8:35, 37-39
Matt. 14:13-21	Matt. 14:13-21	Matt. 14:13-21

PRINCIPAL LECTIONARY THEMES

ISAIAH 55:1-5 (RCL)
PSALM 145:8-9, 14-21 (RCL)
ISAIAH 55:1-3 (LFM)
PSALM 145:8-9, 15-16, 17-18 (LFM)
MATTHEW 14:13-21 (RCL, BCP, LFM)

The first reading sets the tone with a quaint-sounding "Ho!" followed by the lovely invitation to come and have thirst and hunger quenched. And where the Nehemiah reading from BCP sets the feeding imagery in the context of exodus and manna, Isaiah evokes the lavish eschatological banquet and invites us to read Matthew with the Eucharist in mind. This connection is strengthened as the provision of food and drink is connected to the invitation to hear God and obey, and to God's covenant and steadfast love expressed through David.

Following the opening invitation Isaiah plays simultaneously on universal poverty and universal consumerism: the invitation is for those without money (v. 1) who are scolded for using their money (that they don't have) for that which does not nourish (v. 2). This may not be the strongest biblical text for addressing vacuous consumerism, but the starkness (and familiarity) of the question, "Why do you spend your money for that which is not bread . . . ?" warrants consideration of the issue.

The psalm echoes the Isaiah themes, but now from the point of view of one recounting God's wonderful deeds. Verse 15, "The eyes of all look to you, and you give them their food in due season," is familiar and reinforces the feast imagery. Similarly, the universal scope of God's reign and God's openhanded lovingkindness—especially to those who are falling and bowed down—speaks of the relief that God's reign will be for many. The next-to-last verse sounds a brief note of judgment against the wicked, though the final verse returns to a more universal expectation.

Isaiah and the psalm combined with the familiarity of the feeding of the five thousand will lead most hearers to meditation on meal imagery, but the first verses of the Matthew passage contain some elements that might raise questions. If what "Jesus heard" (v. 13) is of the death of John the Baptist, then there may be a connection between John's death and his desire to be alone to pray. There is also a curious fold in the chronology of the narrative since the death of John the Baptist is recounted in 14:3ff. as though it had happened in the past (a recollection prompted

> If what "Jesus heard" is of the death of John the Baptist then there may be a connection between John's death and his desire to be alone to pray.

by Herod's hearing things about Jesus). This suggests that the events of 14:3ff. (including the feeding of the five thousand) actually take place prior to the events leading up to and ending at 14:2. Matthew also leaves some ambiguity as to what the crowds heard (v. 13). The plain narrative sense is that the crowds heard that Jesus was going into the mountains, but it is possible that what they heard was of John's death. This latter possibility also makes a different kind of sense out of Jesus' compassion for the crowds (v. 14). As curious as these things are, mentioning the death of John the Baptist or the details thereof (even in passing) could derail a sermon that intends to focus on the feeding.

As we move into the feeding story, the disciples play almost directly into the wordplay in Isaiah about having no money and yet inviting people into commerce. The disciples want Jesus to send the crowds away to buy food that does not satisfy. In response, Jesus throws down the test, "You give them something to eat" (v. 16). One fruitful angle on this story is to identify contemporary Christians or the church with the disciples. They (we) assess what they've (we've) got determine that it is not enough but Jesus blesses it gives it back to them (us) and it is more than enough. At a time when mainline Christian denominations are in decline and may assess their resources as "not enough," the narrative trajectory of this feeding miracle is encouraging.

> At a time when mainline Christian denominations are in decline and may assess their resources as "not enough," the narrative trajectory of this feeding miracle is encouraging.

The feast imagery invites connections to the Eucharist, of course. But there is potential here to speak to material issues as well. Isaiah invites a connection between the feast, the rich life of covenant obedience, and concern for the poor. But turning to material hunger means coming to grips with the miracle.

158

THE SEASON
AFTER
PENTECOST

HANK J.
LANGKNECHT

Explaining it away as a remnant of an ancient worldview is glib; eclipsing the material provision of bread for the hungry with promises of spiritual nourishment is faithful but slippery. If Jesus' power does not literally multiply bread and fish then exactly what *does* it do? Here is the challenge for the preacher to be as concrete as possible about God's movement and action in the world. One homiletical possibility would be to have the sermon shift the congregation's identification to the three main players. When are *we* the crowd, hungry and willing to be fed? When are *we* the disciples who look at what we've got, declare it insufficient, give it over to Jesus, get it back and distribute it (with our fingers crossed the whole time)? When are *we* the church, the Body of Christ, confidently telling the crowds to sit down and be fed?

NEHEMIAH 9:16-20 (BCP)
PSALM 78:1-29 or 78:14-20, 23-25 (BCP)

As noted above, the Nehemiah text enters the feeding imagery from the point of view of God's provision of manna in the wilderness and in doing so establishes a bit of a harder edge by recalling the stiff necks of the people. The power of this passage is the starkness of the people's disobedience and intransigence (against which the disciples' hesitation about the five loaves and two fish seems reasonable) with God's slowness to anger and steadfast love. Even when they desire a return to slavery and to turn to idols, God elects to provide. The psalm picks this up by redundantly recounting with excruciating specificity the sins of the people. And yet, and yet, and yet, and yet, God elects to provide. A wonderful line from the psalm (recalling the opening to Psalm 137) is in verse 19: "Can God spread a table in the wilderness?" Yes.

Semicontinuous Readings
GENESIS 32:22-31 (RCL)
PSALM 17:1-7, 15 (RCL)

The story of Jacob wrestling at Peniel is sandwiched between two scenes that deal with Jacob's estrangement from his brother, Esau. Having departed from Laban whom he outsmarted, Jacob is about to meet Esau whom he cheated. Jacob has sent presents to Esau as a peace offering of sorts; Jacob's messengers return to him with the news that Esau is coming to visit, with a contingent of four hundred men. Jacob is afraid, prays to God for his safety and the safety of his family, and arranges another present of large numbers of livestock to be sent ahead to Esau on the way. Again, Jacob is still afraid. Then comes the night at the Jabbok. Following this encounter, Esau arrives and he and Jacob have an emotional reunion (that foreshadows a similar reunion that will occur later in this stretch of the lectionary between Joseph and his brothers).

In terms of Jacob's own life story, this is finally a fair fight. No taking advantage of a hungry brother or a blind father or having to outsmart a wily father-in-law. Here it is Jacob wrestling to an honest draw; a busted hip in exchange for a blessing and the legacy of a people who strive with God and with humans and who prevail.

The only hint we get from the story that the wrestler is a divine figure is (perhaps) in the stranger's refusal to give a name. But Jacob (as is clear from the naming) knows that this was God. It is interesting that the stranger's assessment of Jacob's wrestling is better than Jacob's own; the stranger says Jacob has prevailed, Jacob himself settles for having his life preserved. The psalm picks up the theme of wrestling in the night and the joy of wakening to see God's likeness. The tension between the psalm and the Jacob story is that the psalm is spoken from the point of view of a person who sees himself or herself as righteous, the apple of God's eye, as one needing vindication.

> This is finally a fair fight: Jacob wrestling to an honest draw; a busted hip in exchange for a blessing and the legacy of a people who strive with God and with humans and who prevail.

I doubt that I am the only person who wakes up at three in the morning panicked and wrestling with things done and left undone, with thoughts of an insecure future for my nation, my family, myself. It would not do to reduce Jacob's story to just this, but perhaps it would do to elevate our striving by connecting it to a God who blesses and claims us. It is not always the case—though it is often enough—that our blessings come at the cost of a limp. A sermon that could give voice to anguished questions about justice or war would be powerful testimony that Christians are also free to strive with God.

SECOND READING
ROMANS 9:1-5 (RCL)

For the next three Sundays the RCL appoints passages from Romans 9–11 where Paul tackles the "Jewish question" head-on. While there is no way to bring a sermon audience totally up to speed on the complex arguments of Romans, it can be noted that both Gentile and Jew express in their lived communities the brokenness of creation: the Gentiles by their idolatry, the Jews by their disobedience to the Torah.

160

THE SEASON
AFTER
PENTECOST

HANK J.
LANGKNECHT

One of the challenges for preachers is to account for and deal thoughtfully with conflicting point of view and reference. The word *Jew* in the text will be taken by most hearers to refer unambiguously to contemporary Jews; this is not totally inappropriate but must be attended to with care. What is difficult is that as the text is read hearers will find it easy generally to identify with Paul, who comes across as passionate and caring and who is, more generally, a model Christian missionary and theologian! But in the scheme of Romans, Paul is a Jew while contemporary Christian hearers are Gentiles. So while it is fine for contemporary Christians to identify with Paul and feel compassion and care for the Jews, it is not appropriate for them to identify with Paul when he is doing rhetorical battle with the Jews; that is the stuff of an internal lovers' quarrel.

> Preachers who elect to preach on this passage will want to make it clear that we are observing the aspect of the lovers' quarrel as outsiders.

Preachers who elect to preach on this passage will want to make it clear that we are observing the aspect of the lovers' quarrel as outsiders. Perhaps analogy can be made to intramural strife in the Christian household, lifting up Paul's general attitude of agonizing love—a love that leads him to contemplate the kind of kenotic love that we will hear about in a few weeks when the lectionary turns to Philippians.

A more general challenge obliquely related to this passage is the challenge for Christians to learn to articulate *from the others' perspective* persuasive reasons for having faith in Jesus Christ. We know the reasons from our perspective; but how do we enter into the life struggles and worldviews of others, give them credence as from an insider (modeling after Paul's lavish appreciation for the Jew's blessings in verses 4-5), and then invite them into consideration of the Christian faith?

ROMANS 8:35-39 (BCP)
ROMANS 8:35, 37-39 (LFM)

See the second reading for the Eleventh Sunday after Pentecost, Proper 12 (July 27, 2008), above.

THIRTEENTH SUNDAY AFTER PENTECOST

NINETEENTH SUNDAY IN ORDINARY TIME / PROPER 14
AUGUST 10, 2008

Revised Common (RCL)	Episcopal (BCP)	Roman Catholic (LFM)
Gen. 37:1-4, 12-28 or 1 Kgs. 19:9-18	Jonah 2:1-9	1 Kgs. 19:9a, 11-13a
Ps. 105:1-6, 16-22, 45b or 85:8-13	Psalm 29	Ps. 85:9a, 10, 11-12, 13-14
Rom. 10:5-15	Rom. 9:1-5	Rom. 9:1-5
Matt. 14:22-33	Matt. 14:22-33	Matt. 14:22-33

PRINCIPAL LECTIONARY THEMES

1 KINGS 19:9-18 (RCL)
PSALM 85:8-13 (RCL)
1 KINGS 19:9A, 11-13A (LFM)
PSALM 85:9A, 10, 11-12, 13-14 (LFM)
MATTHEW 14:22-33 (RCL, BCP, LFM)

In the first reading for this day we enter into the story of Elijah the prophet. The reading itself gives only faint clues as to what has come before (and that only from Elijah's jaded point of view!), so the preacher will have to discern how much narrative context will be helpful without derailing the sermon. One exciting element of this text is the lector's privilege of giving tone of voice to both Elijah and God. Shall Elijah sound angry, weary, defeated, or like an overworked church leader with a martyr complex? Shall God be patronizing, gentle, or stern? Dialogue gives the reader manifold opportunities to provide tone of voice for Elijah and God. How weary, how defiant, how patronizing, how angry? Decisions on these questions will influence how hearers identify themselves in the story and could lead to insights into how we understand our own dialogue or debate with God.

Another homiletical choice is whether to cast this story as being about Elijah or God. An Elijah-focused sermon will highlight themes about the cost of prophetic word and action and could draw analogies to the mission of the whole church, the pastor's life (probably a dangerous self-indulgence!), or to any strong

162

THE SEASON
AFTER
PENTECOST

HANK J.
LANGKNECHT

contemporary Christian voice, especially when that voice faces persecution. A God-focused sermon might testify to how God resolves to be present to servants who face despair by giving them God's own presence, clear mission directives, and—most important—wry assurance that God meets us where God sends us in the form of an already-present remnant. God's mission is secure even when we are not.

The shorter reading (from LFM) sharpens the focus on God's presence in the stark stillness that comes after the terror of the storms. Elijah is drawn out of the cave by the silence just as the disciples are moved to worship Jesus when the wind ceases. This could suggest a sermon about God's presence in believers' lives, though care should be taken not to be overly sentimental about the importance of silence. A sermon that builds on both Elijah's and the disciples' stories could note that God's presence comes to both the self-pitying and the fearful.

> A sermon that builds on both Elijah's and the disciples' stories could note that God's presence comes to both the self-pitying and the fearful.

The psalm's resonance with the Elijah story is in the assurance to God's people that God will speak and that God's mission is a lock—salvation, glory, steadfast love, faithfulness, righteousness, and peace will be given. The psalm also assures that those who listen to God's voice will hear in God's word a path for their steps.

The story from the Gospel of Matthew follows directly after last week's feeding miracle. Jesus is finally able to find quiet time to pray after dismissing the crowds, this time with apparent ease. One of the plotlines running through the whole Gospel of Matthew—and certainly in the feeding of the five thousand and this story—is the maturing of the disciples' understanding of their faith and their call. In the previous passage Jesus allowed himself to be distracted from prayer by his compassion for the crowds. Here he is not distracted, even though the disciples have to flop around in the storm all night. But Jesus' relationship to the crowds is different from what it is to the disciples; the crowds are in need of direct ministry and care, the disciples need to be schooled in the relationship between fear, trust, and God.

Although the storm and the walking on water draw our attention to the exchange between Peter and Jesus and invite us to consider the storm and stillness theme, another minor theme is possible. The 1 Kings story (especially the shorter version in LFM) and the opening verses of the Matthew reading might lead us to consider two prophetic leaders, Elijah and Jesus, taking time to be alone. Preachers must avoid the temptation, however, of turning this into a warrant or justification for their personal downtime. There are appropriate texts and contexts to support preaching on the importance of self-care, prayer, and sabbath; such is not the case here. The one angle that might work—provided it aligns with the lived experience of the preacher and congregation—is to identify the congregation with the faithful remnant who stand ready to take up God's cause with a renewed and restored leader.

The obvious draw of the Matthew story is Peter's bid to walk on the water with Jesus. Depending on how the preacher moves the sermon from the text to the world there are many enticing details to explore. Peter is fine until he *notices* the wind; then he is afraid and sinks. It is not the chaotic power of wind and wave (principalities and powers) that present the danger, but only the fear of them. Jesus' compassionate action is to catch Peter but not to eliminate the danger by stilling the wind. If the congregation is invited to identify with Peter then it must be that we cannot wait for circumstances to be ideal before we step out; it is sufficient to know that Jesus is present and potentially in control of the chaos even if the chaos is allowed, for a time, to rage. Only after the danger is over and everyone is in the boat does the storm stop. A sermon focused on Peter must be careful not to over-sentimentalize the "as long as Peter looked toward Jesus he was fine" angle. Like many trite sermon angles, it has an element of truth but suffers in that it emphasizes our ability to stay focused rather than Jesus' power to save. Matthew's wording in verse 31, "You of little faith, why did you doubt?" is characteristically less harsh than the rebuke in Mark's Gospel ("Have you still no faith?" Mark 4:40). It also serves the theme of discipleship development as well as suggests that faith and doubt are not mutually exclusive but are, rather, in tension.

> It is not chaotic power of wind and wave (principalities and powers) that present the danger, but only the fear of them.

A speculative, but fun, play on biblical imagery would be to suppose that "walking on water" is a reference to the great promise of Revelation that the chaotic, demonic sea will be turned into crystal (though, admittedly, not "stormy" crystal). Perhaps Peter (assuming he was steeped in that symbolism) thought that the end times had come. But even if not, there is homiletical mileage to be made in imagining why, of all the stunning acts of Jesus a disciple might want to emulate, Peter chose this one: to walk on water. And what was is that convinced Peter that it was Jesus on the sea and not a ghost? Apparently just the word, "Come."

> There is homiletical mileage to be made in imagining why, of all the stunning acts of Jesus a disciple might want to emulate, Peter chose this one: to walk on water.

It is common to suppose that in the Gospel of Matthew the boat represents the church. In this passage that move can be a bit dangerous if it encourages Christians that eventually we will all be safe together on the calm sea. Contrast this with the longer version of the Elijah story (RCL, BCP) where what comes from the peaceful silence is not worship and calm but the clarification of Elijah's commission. Another parallel between these two passages is that both readings follow feeding stories. In 1 Kings, Elijah is fed bread

164

THE SEASON
AFTER
PENTECOST

HANK J.
LANGKNECHT

and water, just enough for his journey, by an angel who encourages him not to be afraid. So in both readings, the chaos of storm and the appearance of God in stillness follow a divine meal.

JONAH 2:1-9 (BCP)
PSALM 29 (BCP)

The success of pairing the Gospel story with the passage from Jonah depends on hearers' ability to import details from the first chapter of Jonah, especially his call, the storm, the crew's fear (though not Jonah's fear, he was sleeping), and the stilling of the storm that leads to worship (though again, not Jonah's worship, but that of the pagan crew). Without those intertextual connections, the reading might merely evoke the disciples' (likely) feelings of fear or despair after spending all night in a storm and (especially imagining Peter's thoughts as he sinks) the terror at being sucked under the water. A contrasting connection is that Jonah is sunk because he has little faith that leads him to disobey, while Peter ("son of Jonah") is sinking because he has little faith, which nonetheless is enough to lead him to risk obedience.

The Jonah reading is the prayer that Jonah speaks from the belly of the fish. The first part could be read as an extended embellishment of Peter's one line, "Lord, save me!" Then Jonah 2:6ff. recounts how God (similar to Jesus in Matthew) reaches down and brings Jonah out of the Pit.

It is debatable whether or not we can trust Jonah's prayer, knowing the unrepentant disobedience that comes before and the acrimony toward God's mercy that comes after. Jesus talks about the "sign of Jonah" in reference to death and resurrection. Perhaps the real sign of Jonah is the church we too often know—judgmental, pokey, evasive when it comes to mission, and much more skimpy and sensible than God when it comes to giving out mercy. And yet, God's mission continues to include the church.

> It is debatable whether or not we can trust Jonah's prayer, knowing the unrepentant disobedience that comes before and the acrimony toward God's mercy that comes after.

Psalm 29 leans the readings toward God's dominion over all the powers in the world: the waters of chaos, cedars, the wilderness, and oak trees. This invites a connection to Jonah's deliverance from the sea and to the quieting of the waves and wind in Matthew.

SEMICONTINUOUS READINGS

165

THIRTEENTH
SUNDAY AFTER
PENTECOST

AUGUST 10

GENESIS 37:1-4, 12-28 (RCL)
PSALM 105:1-6, 16-22, 45B (RCL)

Here we have the first of two readings from the saga of Jacob's family, specifically Joseph and his brothers. Note that while this and next week's readings are from the semicontinuous alternative reading in RCL, we also hear a piece of the saga in the Gospel-related First Testament reading in Proper 19. This offers an opportunity to spend some extended sermon time developing the images and themes of the Joseph story.

Joseph, the favorite son of the favorite wife of Jacob, is hated by his brothers both because he is the favorite and because of his dreams of dominion. One would think that Jacob would be cautious about favoritism considering what was wrought in his family of origin. While I am generally inclined to honor the lectionary, here it might be worth reading the omitted verses since they give some context for the brothers' anger about the "dreams" of this "dreamer."

On the one hand, this week's portion of the story opens the door to discussion about family dysfunction. A sermon that moves in that direction can succeed if it makes the connection with Jacob's clan and then moves into a more theological or pastoral consideration of the issue. But next week we will hear of the joyful, tearful reunion, and in the reading for Proper 19 we will hear Joseph's testimony that "Even though you intended to do harm to me, God intended it for good" (Gen. 50:20). It is reckless for preachers explicitly or implicitly to promise such outcomes for contemporary families.

Even if the preacher elects not to preach on this Genesis reading, Psalm 105 gives us some hint that God's purposes are being worked out even in the machinations of the brothers. The psalm is a recounting of Israel's history from the covenant to Abraham through the promise to Isaac, the giving of the land, and then (in the appointed verses) the story of Joseph's being sold into slavery to serve God's good ends. The psalm continues by remembering the plagues, several events in the wilderness, and finally the settling in the promised land.

SECOND READING
ROMANS 10:5-15 (RCL)

Paul here is recalling, in fact quoting, the sermon of Moses in Deuteronomy 30. The twist that Paul offers is that he replaces our ability to follow the law (the concern of Moses) with Christ himself. Both sermons end with the visceral promise involving heart and mouth. Both belief and speech are lifted up here for

166

THE SEASON
AFTER
PENTECOST

HANK J.
LANGKNECHT

reasons that are celebrated in the soaring anadiplosis in verses 14 and 15 (preachers, even if you do not preach on Romans 10, look for a chance to employ the rhetorical chain where the climax is built by repeating the end of each sentence at the beginning of the next!).

As Paul moves to the climax of Romans, Christ will be identified as the solution to both the Greek problem (of idolatry) and the Jewish problem (of disobedience). While the historical details of those two problems are of interest for us today, they are not gripping sermon material. Here is the greater sermon challenge for today: How is Christ the answer for the problems and longings represented across the contemporary spiritual landscape? And how are we to craft the message so that it sounds like good news to those who hear it (rather than a caricatured tent-revival ultimatum?). That is, rather than preaching about the details of Paul's situation, the preacher can hold Paul up as a model for us as we attempt to persuade the contemporary world about the Gospel so that our feet may be declared "beautiful."

The sublime rhetoric of verses 14 and 15 offers a chance to meditate on the fragile power of the spoken word. From the point of view of the speaker, the connection between heart and mouth is this: until you speak your faith, your claim to know your faith is suspect. My undergraduate degree was in music composition and I can remember going to composition lessons with, literally and figuratively, a song in my heart. I would sit down at the piano and my teacher would say, "Okay then, let's hear it!" and I would discover that the song in my heart had no outlet in my fingers. He would then say, "If you can't play it, it isn't music." Paul's corollary might be, "Until you say it, it isn't belief." It is hard work to express our faith, our heart—every Christian knows this. But the promise of "beautiful feet" is ours for the effort.

> How is Christ the answer for the problems and longings represented across the contemporary spiritual landscape?

From the point of view of the exchange between the one who proclaims and the one who receives the proclamation, we know that the power of the spoken word is wedded to its fragility. Speech is evanescent; borne on the breath of the speaker it immediately decays and dissipates. It is an organic connection prone to misinterpretation and "I said/you heard" confusion; and it is the vehicle God has chosen to deliver the news that God has answered every longing.

ROMANS 9:1-5 (BCP, LFM)

See the second reading for the Twelfth Sunday after Pentecost, Proper 13 (August 3, 2008), above.

FOURTEENTH SUNDAY AFTER PENTECOST

Revised Common (RCL)	Episcopal (BCP)	Roman Catholic (LFM)
Gen. 45:1-15 or Isa. 56:1, 6-8	Isa. 56:1, (2-5) 6-7	Isa. 56:1, 6-7
Psalm 133 or 67	Psalm 67	Ps. 67:2-3, 5, 6, 8
Rom. 11:1-2a, 29-32	Rom. 11:13-15, 29-32	Rom. 11:13-15, 29-32
Matt. 15: (10-20) 21-28	Matt. 15:21-28	Matt. 15:21-28

PRINCIPAL LECTIONARY THEMES

ISAIAH 56:1, 6-8 (RCL)
ISAIAH 56:1, (2-5) 6-7 (BCP)
ISAIAH 56:1, 6-7 (LFM)
PSALM 67 (RCL, BCP)
PSALM 67:2-3, 5, 6, 8 (LFM)
MATTHEW 15:(10-20) 21-28 (RCL)
MATTHEW 15:21-28 (BCP, LFM)

Taken in its most expansive version (which the BCP comes closest to rendering with the inclusion of verses 2-5), Isaiah's prophecy offers a striking invitation on God's behalf to outsiders—foreigners and eunuchs—who, the text suggests, will become "better than sons and daughters." Verse 8 (RCL only) then adds the cryptic parallelism that suggests that after the outsiders have been gathered, then others—outsiders who are even more outside the outsiders?—will be added. But even the sparest version (LFM) promises a joyous celebration of multinational prayer in the house of God. Read in the context of Isaiah's prophecy, Psalm 67 will also be heard as a celebration of universal worship as God's ways are made known to all the earth and "all nations" and "all people" will praise and sing with gladness. Given that this is the week of the Olympic Summer Games in Beijing, China, there should be available to the preacher vivid and colorful images of more secular (but no less significant or radical) inclusion and mutual celebration among nations.

168

THE SEASON
AFTER
PENTECOST

HANK J.
LANGKNECHT

There is blessing and curse for Christian preachers in Isaiah's expansive and inclusive language, largely depending on how adventurous we wish to be in extending the reference of the terms *foreigner*, *nation*, and—perhaps especially—*eunuch*. Few would quibble about homiletical treatments that envisioned God's house of prayer with people of many national, ethnic, or racial identities; but Isaiah's inclusion of eunuchs offers intriguing possibilities. The exclusion of eunuchs likely relates to issues of holiness and ritual purity related to sexual potency (as the "dry tree" reference of verse 3 suggests), but preachers should be aware that some contemporary interpreters—including advocates for sexual minorities—identify eunuchs in Scripture with persons of homosexual orientation.

The Gospel reading is in two parts in the RCL (vv. 10-20 are optional and vv. 21-28); both the optional and the stipulated sections contain vivid and preachable notions and images. In the context of Isaiah 56, however, the second, stipulated section will likely draw most hearers' attention as it involves Jesus' encounter with a Canaanite woman: a foreigner and an outcast.

Verses 10-20 do deserve some comment. Here is the resolution (at least from Jesus' side) of a debate between Jesus and the Pharisees that began with their criticism of Jesus' disciples for not washing their hands before eating. Jesus responded to their criticism by accusing the Pharisees of hypocrisy for their disobedience to the command to honor father and mother when they divert family funds to the Temple treasury. Jesus' central teaching in and through this debate—and everyone will hear and understand this—is that charitable, merciful speech is more pleasing to God than whether food (or the process by which it is eaten) is ritually clean.

> Jesus' central teaching in and through this debate is that charitable, merciful speech is more pleasing to God than whether food is ritually clean.

Whether the bathroom language he uses is meant to convey the same vehemence it would in our age is debatable; it may still surprise some hearers. The sidebar comment about God uprooting plants and leaving the blind guides to lead the blind into the pit is also quite harsh. Preachers dealing with this section should adhere to the rule that if anyone is set up as a villain in a sermon (even historical or literary characters such as the Pharisees), it is important that the preacher and the preacher's community be identified with that villain and not with the hero (in this case, Jesus). Using the sermon to set up and knock down characters (even patently evil or sinful characters) makes the preacher look like a bully and leaves the community feeling smug.

At the end of this optional section, Jesus explains again to the disciples what he had plainly said to the crowd: it is word and action that determine our cleanliness, not obedience to the law. If repetition (even of an obvious point) suggests importance, what are to make of this? Does this invite preaching about the prophetic theme of God desiring mercy more than ritual purity? Or could a sermon develop the idea that personal ethical/moral speech is of more interest to God than right ritual? Most of us preachers have more than enough examples we could tell on ourselves (note how this identifies us with the Pharisees!) about uncharitable thoughts we've harbored about "differently dressed" or "clearly outsider" worshipers even as we stand ready to distribute to them the elements of the sacrament. Given the vividness of the story of the Canaanite woman in the stipulated portion of the pericope and the way it resonates with Isaiah and the psalm, most preachers likely will not deal with verses 10-20, but some contexts might demand or invite it.

The encounter between Jesus and the Canaanite woman ends well but it still remains a hard text for its narration of Jesus' scandalous lack of mercy toward this mother of a stricken daughter. There is no way to soften the blow of the passage (even a convincing explanation will come *after* the dog is out of the bag). Some suggest that Jesus was muttering his thoughts or conveying them only to the disciples. Some suggest that he really meant "puppies" rather than "dogs." But the thoughts are still Jesus' and it's hard to imagine that "dog" is ever heard as a charitable reference to another adult human—no matter how cute the dog.

> The encounter between Jesus and the Canaanite woman ends well but it still remains a hard text for its narration of Jesus' scandalous lack of mercy toward this mother of a stricken daughter.

It's curious to wonder what the "food" is here; is it healing power or the mercy of being included in God's realm? And if Jesus' ministry is to the lost sheep of Israel, what is he doing in Tyre and Sidon (Lebanon) in the first place, and why has he so glibly consigned some of those lost sheep to the pit under the leadership of "blind guides" in verse 14?

Because the passage involves dialogue, the lector of the Gospel is challenged to consider what tone of voice the woman and Jesus will have. Is Jesus in anguish over the limitation of his ministry or is he committed to it? Is he angry, impatient, or stressed as he addresses the woman? Or will the lector decide that he was muttering an aside? Is the woman humble or defiant in her quick-witted replies? How does she articulate the designation "Son of David"? And, for that matter, if she is an outsider, why is that appellation on her lips? Often, answering these questions and executing the reading accordingly helps determine the course of the sermon.

What Jesus celebrates in the story is the woman's faith. Whether her poise and pluck is bred of necessity out of concern for her daughter's health or from the real-world wits many must cultivate through years of ill treatment, she knows that Jesus has what she wants and needs and she will have it. A question worth pondering (even if discarded) is whether the woman truly changes Jesus' priorities for mission. In any event the sermon might celebrate the universal scope of God's mission.

170

THE SEASON
AFTER
PENTECOST

HANK J.
LANGKNECHT

A more challenging direction might be to ponder whether Christians ask or expect enough of their faith. Would most of us emulate this woman's determination or quick-wittedness in arguing for more access to God's blessings, more frequent celebration of the communion, or the chance to hear God's Word?

Semicontinuous Readings
GENESIS 45:1-15 (RCL)
PSALM 133 (RCL)

Joseph is reunited and finally reconciled to his brothers. Much has happened since Joseph was sold into slavery (and his death faked). Without some narrative background, the reconciliation loses punch; with too much narrative background, the sermon loses steam. We heard the story of the brothers' horrid offense just last week, but in Joseph's world years have passed; years during which bitterness on Joseph's part, regret on the brothers' part, and grief on Jacob's part have had the opportunity to grow.

Joseph is initially successful in Egypt ("The LORD was with him"); then he is falsely accused of sexual assault and thrown into jail (but the Lord is still with him); his power to dream and interpret dreams figures prominently in his life (he even interprets Pharaoh's dreams); Pharaoh appoints Joseph to administer Egypt's economic affairs (Joseph's wisdom is rewarded); the famine comes as per Joseph's interpretation of Pharaoh's dream; Joseph's brothers (minus Benjamin) come to buy grain and Joseph recognizes them but they don't recognize him; Joseph treats them harshly and throws them in prison (note that they interpret this as divine punishment for what they've done); after they confess, Joseph weeps and puts their money in the sacks along with the grain and sends them home; when the brothers discover the money, they fear they'll be accused of theft (and again, they would interpret this as God's punishment); the brothers make a return trip, this time with Benjamin; Joseph is overcome with emotion at the sight of his full brother (this is quite a scene: Joseph retreats to a "private room" to weep, washes his face, regains "control" of himself, and returns); he invites the brothers (who still do not recognize him) to a banquet; Joseph frames Benjamin for "stealing" a silver cup and uses that as a pretext for keeping Benjamin behind; Judah tells Joseph that Jacob will die if Benjamin doesn't return (there is that cloud of favoritism again)—and then the events in today's reading occur!

Joseph reveals himself to his brothers, his brothers are "dismayed" at his presence, Joseph asks about his father, and (curiously) tells his brothers not to be upset with themselves, because God sent him to Egypt so that he would be there to sell them grain when the famine came. He "weeps upon" his brothers (especially

Benjamin). There is resolution and forgiveness of a sort, but at this point it is one-sided, initiated and maintained by Joseph who was, after all, the clearly wronged party (the facts that your younger brother is father's favorite and has a fancy coat and brags about his dreams of family domination do not justify selling him into slavery and faking his death).

The brothers' inability to enter fully into the joy of reunion is understandable. They remain skeptical and fearful because the one whom they betrayed is in a position of life-and-death authority over them. Even Reuben and Judah—who hatched the schemes that at least preserved Joseph's life—have little hope now for mercy. If we were more naïve about family dynamics, the scene would be a lovely prototype for family reconciliation. But as noted in the comments about last week's lesson, encouraging victims to see "God's plan" in the abuse perpetrated on them is irresponsible pastoral care. However, when it happens truly—when forgiveness is granted as an uncoerced gift to the perpetrator from the victim (as in the case, for example, of the Crucified One)—a moment of divine love transpires.

> When forgiveness is granted as an uncoerced gift to the perpetrator from the victim, a moment of divine love transpires.

Another approach to preaching the Joseph saga is to use it as a model for a community rather than a single family (this is more appropriate to its role as Scripture). A congregation or faith community could take Israel's lead and reflect on the ways in which God has sustained and prospered it even through stony roads, human brokenness, and bizarre ironies.

The psalm is a very short celebration of family unity. It is an odd experience to hear or recite this psalm because one of the two central images (having oil poured on one's head and running down the beard and clothes) is so celebrated by the psalmist as rich and good. And because we hear the psalm through the psalmist's heart, we know it to be an image of celebration. But that insider reader's knowledge is at odds with the fact that, to contemporary Western ears, the idea of oil on our skin and clothes feels so unpleasant. Do contemporary preachers and audiences have a way into that image? I just don't know.

SECOND READING
ROMANS 11:1-2A, 29-32 (RCL)
ROMANS 11:13-15, 29-32 (BCP, LFM)

It is critical to recall again that Paul's point of view is as a member of the Jewish people and so he sees them as full siblings in the faith. His claims, concerns, and criticisms are not ours to make, even though we easily identify with him as we read and hear his writings (this is especially important for the BCP and LFM

172

THE SEASON
AFTER
PENTECOST

___

HANK J.
LANGKNECHT

readings, which include verses 13-15). In terms of lectionary juxtapositions, it is too bad that verses 2b-5 are omitted since they are Paul's reference to the same Elijah story from 1 Kings some of us heard last week. But even without those verses read aloud, the notion of remnant can be drawn by implication from the reading. Recalling that the rhetoric of Romans is constantly contrasting and paralleling the Gentile and Jewish communities, Paul simultaneously celebrates God's ability to bring life to and from a community that seems to have rejected God (or at least a remnant of it) and warns (in this passage he warns the Gentiles) from jumping to the conclusion that because things are going so well for us in the Lord, we can claim that God's promises to them (in this case the Jews) have been eclipsed.

Paul makes it clear that all are in disobedience and God is merciful to all. The context of Romans and the specificity with which Paul names the Jews and Gentiles may constrain the scope of contemporary imagination and application, but there are contexts where Paul's line of reasoning and the theology behind it would be of help to us. For example, in communities where established congregations feel threatened by fast-growing evangelical community churches, a word from Romans might be that God's mission is not to sustain one community at the expense of the other but rather to establish whatever avenues lead to mercy expressed to the widest range of people. We may be diminished for a while, but that does not mean that God has turned away from us forever. A repeated theme sentence for such a sermon could be the strong assertion in verse 29: "the gifts and calling of God are irrevocable."

> Paul makes it clear that all are in disobedience and God is merciful to all.

FIFTEENTH SUNDAY AFTER PENTECOST

TWENTY-FIRST SUNDAY IN ORDINARY TIME /
PROPER 16
AUGUST 24, 2008

Revised Common (RCL)	Episcopal (BCP)	Roman Catholic (LFM)
Exod. 1:8—2:10 or Isa. 51:1-6	Isa. 51:1-6	Isa. 22:19-23
Psalm 124 or 138	Psalm 138	Psalm 138:1-2a, 2b-3, 6, 8
Rom. 12:1-8	Rom. 11:33-36	Rom. 11:33-36
Matt. 16:13-20	Matt. 16:13-20	Matt. 16:13-20

PRINCIPAL LECTIONARY THEMES
ISAIAH 51:1-6 (RCL, BCP)
PSALM 138 (RCL, BCP)
ISAIAH 22:19-23 (LFM)
PSALM 138:1-2A, 2B-3, 6, 8 (LFM)
MATTHEW 16:13-20 (RCL, BCP, LFM)

The prophecy in Isaiah 51 is addressed to those of God's people who pursue righteousness and who seek the Lord. It promises three things: that God will restore Zion; that from Zion God's justice, fruitfulness, and teaching will extend to all peoples; and that God's salvation and deliverance are permanent even though creation itself will pass away. The troubling circumstances that call for these comforts and promises are not specified in the passage. Most interpreters suppose that they relate to the insecurity of exile and the longing for the return to the land. Some preachers will be preaching in contexts where the use of the phrase "exile in Babylon" will immediately orient hearers to the historical and spiritual plights of Israel. Others will have to weigh the costs and benefits of using sermon time to lay the necessary groundwork so that the promises might be heard in relationship to "historical" Zion.

The imagery of the prophecy moves in a striking direction from rock to garden to disintegration. The people are called to remember that they are hewn from rock, which here seems to refer to the covenant God made with Abraham and Sarah. The rock metaphor also provides a connection to the day's Gospel lesson from Matthew 16. While there are liabilities to rock and foundation metaphors

174

THE SEASON
AFTER
PENTECOST

———————

HANK J.
LANGKNECHT

when it comes to being a pilgrim people, there are times when some sense of rootedness, stability, or even firm footing on the journey is a necessary comfort. In this passage the foundation will give way to something more secure still. The people are asked to believe that God's past covenant fidelity is adequate seed for hope that God, though at times indiscernible, continues to be faithful into their future. Once the foundation for that future is anchored and God has restored the wastelands of Zion, the people will see Eden reborn. Then, from that home, God's teaching, justice, and salvation will spread to the world. A sermon focused on Isaiah could give lavish time to describing first the solid-rock foundation of God's covenant promises (especially as they relate to the possession of the land and God's presence in the Temple). The preacher could then turn to imagine contrast of colors and textures as the desolation of wasteland slowly blossoms into Eden reborn. What a place to live!

The purpose of that lavish description would be to cast this prophecy's stunning turnaround in stark relief. As wonderful as the promise of new growth from solid foundations is, it will all pass away. And beyond that disintegration, God's salvation goes on forever. In the context of exile, the idea that the current world's destruction might be a comfort seems sensible, and it is true that God's realm of salvation is more permanent than the earth and universe—which we know are in a process of decay. But getting excited about the tail end of this prophecy takes a bit of doing.

> The people are asked to believe that God's past covenant fidelity is adequate seed for hope that God, though at times indiscernible, continues to be faithful into their future.

This trajectory could be taken as a way of chiding the people for only being able to muster hope for restoration to the way things once were and could be again *for them and theirs,* when in fact, God's vision and mission are pointed beyond—way beyond—any narrow national hopes, even the hopes of Israel (or the church!). This understanding of God's breadth of vision helps to make sense of the metaphor of the gnats. It isn't that God hates gnats; God loves gnats. But as lovely as a gnat's dreams may be for the gnat, they tend to include a relatively short-term view.

Psalm 138 is a prayer of thanksgiving from one who has called out to God and been answered. God is greater than any other heavenly being (or idol), greater than any earthly ruler precisely because, despite God's highness, God has deigned to stoop and consider the low.

The Matthew text tells the story of Peter's proclaiming Jesus' true identity as Messiah and Son of the living God. There is a strong irony here, in that this identification is made in Caesarea Philippi, a seat of power for pagan rulers and gods. Preachers must be aware, though, that a good deal of sermon time might be needed to bring the full impact of that irony to bear. That time would be well spent if the sermon invited us to consider how our confession of Jesus' identity is constantly surrounded by a dominant culture to which he is, at best, a key historical religious figure. But to note the irony in passing would not serve.

The disciples' initial response to Jesus' question—John the Baptist, Elijah, Jeremiah, or one of the prophets—indicates that Jesus' ministry is notable, that people have thought about it, and that they see his work as in continuity with these major figures of history. But these are flesh-and-blood insights comparable in our day to people saying, "Sure, Jesus was a great religious teacher like Mohammed and Gandhi and Martin Luther King Jr., but I don't believe he was God." The power of Peter's confession is that it involves a leap over a theological and intuitive chasm that no human can make.

Only God can reveal who Jesus is. This is as true now as it was then. The chasm is still there. Resurrection language and formulas about Christ's two natures slip off Christian tongues week after week. But when pushed, even many churchgoers would admit that they really understand Jesus merely to be a remarkable human teacher and that talk of resurrection is poetic hyperbole. Only God can reveal who Jesus is because his identity as God's Word and Anointed One continues to be scandal and mystery. The fun challenge for preachers at this point is to imagine how to push current Christian disciples beyond our favorite ways of referring to Jesus. That is, one aspect of the theology of the cross is the recognition that our language about Jesus and God is prone to become the equivalent of "Some say John the Baptist, but others Elijah . . . ." A sermon that could contain the preacher's personal testimony or the testimony of others who have had insight into what it means for Jesus to be God's Son (second person of the Trinity) could be powerful.

> Only God can reveal who Jesus is because his identity as God's Word and Anointed One continues to be scandal and mystery.

Jesus celebrates Peter's confession by calling Peter (or the confession—both the Greek and the English allow for some ambiguity of reference) the rock on which the church will be built. We can recall Isaiah's call to Israel to look to the rock from which she was hewn for a connection, though the metaphor operates differently in the two lessons. It has been noted so often that it is almost a cliché, but it is still apt to note—given the church's often-defensive posture in relation to principalities and powers—that the rock here is an offensive tool. The promise is not that we are safe from attack but rather that we are assured victory in mission. Gates are the defensive weapons here. So the "rock" to which Jesus refers is the foundation from which God's mission sets out; we hope that God wishes to take the church along.

The church in our age needs no encouragement from construction metaphors. Many congregations are burdened with buildings whose upkeep drains resources that could be used in staffing and programming. Jesus as cornerstone and other construction imagery notwithstanding, we are in a time when our foundations

176

THE SEASON
AFTER
PENTECOST

HANK J.
LANGKNECHT

must allow for nimbleness, creativity, and flexibility. Isaiah's development is helpful here—the rock of our foundation will sustain us and will pass away. Deep down, our foundation is God and Jesus Christ, and the Word of God that the apostolic ministry supports and preserves. Perhaps lyricist Ira Gershwin's song "Our Love Is Here to Stay" is prophetic: "In time the Rockies may crumble / Gibraltar may tumble / they're only made of clay / but [and here we would want to substitute "God's" for "our"] love is here to stay." It has become a sort of slogan in the church that it's not so much that God's church has a mission as that God's mission has a church. Isaiah's prophecy helps the people see that, in God's sight, even the bedrocks of covenant and creation are only made of clay and will give way to a security found only in a relationship to the God who saves. Peter and the disciples will learn that discipleship involves a similar adjustment of the zoom lens because God's mission extends well beyond Jesus' and their own deaths.

The Matthew reading also introduces the office of the keys. Different theological traditions will interpret the range of this power to bind and loose in different ways. Jesus states clearly that he did not come to overturn the Torah but to see that it is applied rightly; that it be received as gift rather than burden for God's people. At the least, Jesus is giving Peter and the church the authority to interpret the law so that where it becomes unbearable it may be loosened and where its presence in the community is a blessing it may be bound. Binding and loosing will appear again in the Gospel reading for Proper 18 and the meaning of the keys will be unfolded in the kingdom parables to which the Gospel of Matthew now turns. Binding and loosing is the interpretive key to dealing with law and tradition in such a way that the kingdom of God is advanced rather than stymied by lifeless legalism (and the Messiah says so).

> Jesus is giving Peter and the church the authority to interpret the law so that where it becomes unbearable it may be loosened and where its presence in the community is a blessing it may be bound.

The final line of the passage contains Jesus' stern warning that the disciples should not tell anyone that he is the Messiah. On the narrative front, this may be to protect the disciples from charges of blasphemy or insurrection. On the theological front, this may be Jesus' strategy for waiting until his identity is fully disclosed through his passion, death, and resurrection. In either event, despite the zeal with which contemporary Christians honor the command to keep silent, it is clearly eclipsed by the Great Commission in Matthew 28.

The Isaiah 22 reading directs our focus directly on the metaphor of keys. The reading spans two oracles against Shebna and Eliakim, stewards of the Temple. The keys to the Temple are taken from Shebna—who is guilty of self-aggrandizement and self-promotion—and given to Eliakim, son of Hilkiah, who in verse 23 is honored for being a secure "tent peg." Verse 24 reveals, however, that he turns out to be a wall peg that gets pulled out from the weight of the family emblems that he tries to hang on it (in other words, nepotism replaces justice). Stopping at verse 23 certainly provides some shading to the Gospel reading's granting of the keys to Peter, but while inclusion of verses 24-25 might invite a more ambiguous understanding of the Gospel reading, it is strangely congruent. As we will hear in next Sunday's Gospel reading, Peter, like Eliakim, will go from honor to shame, from celebrated confessor to demonic impediment.

SEMICONTINUOUS READINGS
EXODUS 1:8—2:10 (RCL)
PSALM 124 (RCL)

The Exodus passage picks up the patriarchal narrative just a few verses but many years after the death of Joseph. A new Pharaoh, who does not remember what a blessing Joseph was, has taken the throne. The Israelites, who began their lives in Egypt as welcome guests under royal protection, have prospered. The new Pharaoh conspires to enslave them because of his fear that because Israel is large and prosperous they could be a threat, if not on their own terms then certainly should some enemy of Egypt seek Israel out as an ally. This is a curious logic that is repeated over and over among world leaders even to our own day. Would it not have made more sense to keep the stories of Joseph alive among both nations and treat the Israelites with respect and largess and thereby assure their loyalty? Evidently the Pharaoh thinks not and so fear leads to oppression. We are given a hint that God's eye is on the situation, though, for the more ruthless Egypt becomes, the more Israel prospers and multiplies.

> We are given a hint that God's eye is on the situation, for the more ruthless Egypt becomes, the more Israel prospers and multiplies.

Pharaoh first instructs the Hebrew midwives to kill all the boy babies (a foreshadowing of the final plague that God will visit on Egypt), but the midwives fear God more than Pharaoh and refuse—though they elect not to pay the consequence for their civil disobedience, instead lying about why Hebrew boys continue to be born and to thrive. God rewards this conspiracy by granting the midwives their own families. Pharaoh in turn instructs his own people to toss Hebrew babies into the Nile.

This is a great piece of storytelling, coherent with the stories we have been hearing in the previous semicontinuous readings. In spite of incredible hardship God finds a way; through conspiring midwives and then the creative quick thinking of Moses' sister, another Israelite finds his way into Pharaoh's household whence he will further God's plan for God's people. Psalm 124 celebrates this attribute of God: "If it had not been the LORD who was on our side . . . ," boy, would he have been in trouble!

178

THE SEASON
AFTER
PENTECOST

HANK J.
LANGKNECHT

A sermon focusing on the women of this narrative could be powerful. If Pharaoh and Egypt are identified with any nation or people of our "world" who fear the prosperity and industry of God's people, then Shiphrah and Puah stand for all the faithful women (and men) who find ways to bear and nurture that prosperity knowing that God's mission and intent is secure. Similarly, the risk taken by Moses' mother and the ingenuity displayed by Moses' sister elegantly manage and manipulate the daughter of power. Such risk and ingenuity could be a metaphor for activist women (and men) who from the margins have found ways to lodge God's word and work in the political and public arenas. As the Democratic Party begins its national convention (with the Republican Party to follow next month), perhaps stories of such shrewd actions in the cause of justice are available to the preacher.

A harder direction for a sermon on this text would be to explore how powerful, rich nations like America can be as blind and foolish as Pharaoh when dealing with populations from other cultures. Without supposing that Mexican, Central American, Asian, or African immigrants are analogous to Israel in terms of their role in salvation history, we are still invited to marvel at how the rich and powerful suppose that migrant workers pose a "risk" to their prosperity and therefore become consumed with their control and oppression.

SECOND READING
ROMANS 11:33-36 (BCP, LFM)

This brief doxology emphasizes the inscrutability and otherness of God. No one gives God advice; no one gives gifts to God thinking that God will feel beholden. This passage reminds us that we are not God's peers. The passage accommodates well to preaching about God's nature and character even apart from its connection to either all of Romans to this point or to the recent discussion of the Jewish question in chapters 9–11.

ROMANS 12:1-8 (RCL)

The passage from Romans 12 presents the preacher with the decisions of how to deal with an opening "therefore." First the preacher has to decide if the implications that Paul spells out here spin out from the whole of the book or just its last section. Then comes the decision of how much precious sermon time and hearer energy can be spent summarizing the preceding material. That decision is further complicated by the fact that some of the phrases from these verses are fairly well known and could stand on their own. At the least, the preacher should note that the preceding has established that all are sinners and all are within the scope of God's mercy and redemption.

Living sacrifice is a wonderful oxymoron. In the context of Temple worship, sacrificial victims die; we have died in baptism, have been resurrected, and live as echoes of the lamb who, though slaughtered, reigns. Congruent with the sacrifice metaphor is the call to present our bodies, an invitation to consider that we are talking about a spirituality of the whole of our beings. The invitation to be moved from conformation to the world toward transformation and renewal is not an invitation for us to focus on our lives in and of themselves. Rather, we trust that by being in the right places at the right times—the places where God has promised to be—God will transform. This "presenting" of ourselves might therefore be accomplished through the classic disciplines of the church (almsgiving, fasting, prayer) or their contemporary extensions (service, worship, daily devotion). This is hope for renewal on a different scope than simple resolutions or promises to do better because here the hope is not that our resolve will hold but that God's resolve will hold.

> Congruent with the sacrifice metaphor is the call to present our bodies, an invitation to consider that we are talking about a spirituality of the whole of our beings.

The final verses of this passage make available to the preacher some candid talk about vocation. Part of the fabric of the American psyche is the frontiers-person ideal of self-sufficiency and individual multi-competency. But the fact that the pastor has background in accounting is not warrant for her to exercise that gift in the congregation. The fact that the theater professor from the local community college is a better public speaker than the pastor is not warrant for him to usurp the pulpit. Gifts and functions work together in mysterious ways in God's household economics. Paul's concern here is with gifts and vocations within the church, but congregations, even in times when tight budgets tempt them to do things themselves, can witness to differing gifts by supporting local economies and those who live out their vocations through craft and trade.

SIXTEENTH SUNDAY AFTER PENTECOST

TWENTY-SECOND SUNDAY IN ORDINARY
TIME / PROPER 17
AUGUST 31, 2008

Revised Common (RCL)	Episcopal (BCP)	Roman Catholic (LFM)
Exod. 3:1-15 or Jer. 15:15-21	Jer. 15:15-21	Jer. 20:7-9
Ps. 105:1-6, 23-26, 45c or 26:1-18	Psalm 26 or 26:1-8	Ps. 63:2, 3-4, 5-6, 8-9
Rom. 12:9-21	Rom. 12:1-8	Rom. 12:1-2
Matt. 16:21-28	Matt. 16:21-27	Matt. 16:21-27

PRINCIPAL LECTIONARY THEMES

JEREMIAH 15:15-21 (RCL, BCP)
PSALM 26:1-8 (RCL, BCP ALT.)
PSALM 26 (BCP)
MATTHEW 16:21-28 (RCL)
MATTHEW 16:21-27 (BCP, LFM)

The Jeremiah reading is a powerful and passionate narration of the interior life of the prophet that also gives voice to the frustrations and joys of Christian discipleship. The lector who is assigned this reading should be forewarned that it spans a range of emotions on the part of two speakers: the prophet and God. A totally flat reading or, worse, a reading whose tones are in dissonance with the words will not do. The prophet begins by calling on his old friend God in lament, asking for vindication by reminding God that it is specifically because of the speaker's ministry in God's name that he or she suffers. Then the prophet changes tone and remembers with joy the days of conversion. The metaphor is vivid: the prophet finds the words of God and eats them and they become "the delight of my heart." In addition, the call of God gives a sense of security and joy. Many hearers will have had something of this experience of euphoria in the story of their relationship to God, and a preacher would do well to develop this metaphor, especially in light of the contrasts that follow.

Then in verse 17 the prophet turns slightly self-righteous. After having digested God's word, indignation sets in (the first time I read the passage I was sure it said indigestion!). Jeremiah recalls how he confidently turned his back on the inadequate revelry and pleasures of the world, secure in his belief that the word of God would be ecstasy enough. But at some point the pleasures of indignation cease to be satisfying and the climactic question spews forth: "Why is my pain unceasing, my wound incurable, refusing to be healed?"

Then the prophet gets personal against God. The metaphor family of rivers, brooks, and flowing water usually connote God's lavish provision and promise for abundant life in the wilderness, but here God is a deceitful brook—the terrain is promising, but the waterway fails. Jeremiah here experiences what many Christians experience in their walk of faith. In light of the world's apathy toward God and its apparent ability to live happily without God, the promise of cozy contentment *inferred* by the prophet (even if not made by God) must feel like a double deceit. That is, not only am I not as happy with this word as I expected to be, the world revels in pleasures even without the word.

Now God responds. Jeremiah, with whom hearers will have been identifying, has been speaking from the point of view of a faithful prophet and disciple. But, surprise! God's first words are, "*if* you turn back." But where did the speaker go wrong? It isn't clear, though it seems likely that the prophet's mistake was taking those sweet, sweet words of God and allowing them to go "undigested" into indignation rather than digested and then spoken out into the world. The promise of God is that when the precious words are spoken, the people "will turn to you, not you . . . to them." When you open your mouth to testify to the sweetness that you remember, you will be a fortified wall of bronze, and though your own people may fight against you, they will not prevail.

> It seems likely that the prophet's mistake was taking those sweet, sweet words of God and allowing them to go "undigested" into indignation rather than digested and then spoken out into the world.

This relationship between God, Jeremiah, and Jeremiah's audience could be overlaid on many different relationships in our world. Assuming that God remains God in any case, Jeremiah's lament could reflect the preacher's relationship to his or her call or the Christian's relationship to an apathetic world. The flow of Jeremiah's lament mirrors the call- and faith-stories of many: heady early days of infatuation with God and God's Word, the resolution to live a different kind of life in response, disillusion, and finally cynicism and anger. Whichever way the preacher plays it, the point must not be lost that God does *not* honor the prophet's frustration, indignation, or self-pitying.

The mystery of the word—whether expressed orally in preaching or literally in writing—is that God's promise is true. Turn back. Testify to what you have experienced in God. The sweetness of God's words is still within you and that sweetness is restored in the telling. Any words will do; even words of anger and lament—if they are spoken aloud—will start the stream flowing. Keep testifying to your life in God and the sweetness returns and people will listen.

182

THE SEASON
AFTER
PENTECOST

HANK J.
LANGKNECHT

Psalm 26 echoes the Jeremiah trajectory (vindicate me, I have been faithful, I feast on you, I do not consort with hypocrites) but the psalmist has not yet come to the place of lament or anger. In fact, the psalmist is in that wonderful stage of "liturgi-philia" where worship is pure joy.

The trajectory of the first lesson casts an interesting shadow on the Gospel reading. On the one hand, it is possible to compare Jeremiah's prophetic trajectory to the life of Jesus—here is the point at which Jesus turns away from the world and toward Jerusalem, the cross, and death. Jesus's cry of lament from the cross (Matt. 27:46) would then echo Jeremiah's cry for vindication of his innocent faithful suffering (although Jesus is not portrayed in the Gospel as having Jeremiah's bitter feelings toward God or the world). On the other hand, it is also possible to overlay Jeremiah's prophetic trajectory onto Peter who, like Jeremiah, misunderstands what God is up to and will be called upon to repent.

While either trajectory is possible, Peter's story is compelling and sermon audiences may find it easier to identify with Peter and the disciples than with Jesus. We know that this reading follows directly after Jesus' celebration and honoring of Peter's confession that Jesus is the Messiah. What is striking is that the first assumption the keeper of the keys makes about Jesus' messiahship is wrong, satanic even. This is the heart of the theology of the cross: it always scandalizes us. Whenever we feel we have found a secure understanding about Jesus and his relationship to us, to God, or the world, our next step is likely to be wrong and we must return to our rightful place—behind Jesus rather than in front trying to guide Jesus. As an aside, it is curious that the phrase "get behind me, Satan," uttered here, fails to shock us.

> It is possible to overlay Jeremiah's prophetic trajectory onto Peter who, like Jeremiah, misunderstands what God is up to and will be called upon to repent.

Jesus makes it clear that Peter's confession in verse 17 was only possible because God had revealed Jesus' identity. So, too, understanding what Jesus' ministry—and finally our ministry—involves must be revealed to us by God through the Spirit. We would never stumble across true doctrine or the heart of true discipleship on our own. In this sense, Peter's enthusiastic misstep invites the preacher to develop the idea that the denial of self, while certainly full of implications for living in ethical relationship to the world, also calls for modesty in theology and moral deliberation.

> Understanding what Jesus' ministry—and finally our ministry—involves must be revealed to us by God through the Spirit.

It takes a lifetime to grow into full understanding of God's mission, purpose, and methodology, and the road to that understanding (as Jeremiah and Peter can attest) is full of missteps and misunderstandings. And contrary to our best efforts to define carefully what we believe, to cement biblical interpretation rooted in historical surety, God will always confound us.

For Jeremiah and Peter and us, what God demands is ongoing, complete reorientation. Even acknowledging that God does shape us into disciples over time, Martin Luther understood that repentance was a matter of daily baptism. Or to put it another way, Christians are always only "one day old"—as much in need of being "put behind Jesus" (so as to follow him) on this day as on any other.

The repayment language in verse 27 and the promise that the Son of Man will come before some standing there die (v. 28) are odd and challenging words. The dressing-down both Jeremiah and Peter received should warn us off thinking that our faithful discipleship puts us in line for reward. At the least we are reminded here that the road to the cross is also the road to the resurrection.

JEREMIAH 20:7-9 (LFM)
PSALM 63:2, 3-4, 5-6, 8-9 (LFM)

Jeremiah 20 is similar in tone to Jeremiah 15 and could be brought into relationship to Matthew 16 in similar ways. In this reading, however, Jeremiah didn't discover the sweetness of God's word on his own; rather, God actively enticed the prophet into the ministry—overpowered him. And now he is a laughingstock. The words are not sweet here; they are violence and destruction. But the Jeremiah of this passage has at least learned a part of the lesson God sought to teach: he now knows that not to speak results in a full-body burn, not just heartburn or indigestion. Psalm 63 is a striking contrast to Jeremiah 20, for here the psalmist rejoices to praise and pray and call on God's name not in order to avoid indigestion, but in response to the rich feast and the deliverance God gives from enemies.

SEMICONTINUOUS READINGS
EXODUS 3:1-15 (RCL)
PSALM 105:1-6, 23-26 (RCL)

What a surprise that when God searches out a leader, God elects a shepherd: in this case, Moses. This passage narrates the call of Moses and contains the iconic scenes of the burning bush and the revelation of the mysterious name of God. As prominent as those parts of the scene are, the key to the passage is God's self-revelation as the kind of deity who hears the people's misery and responds with deliverance. They will have their own land, a land flowing with milk and honey (a preacher could do a lot worse with this passage than to contrast any current misery with the rich sensory joys of milk and honey!).

184

THE SEASON
AFTER
PENTECOST

HANK J.
LANGKNECHT

Moses, with good reason, questions the call: "Who am I?" We know from the story in Exodus that Moses is an adopted son of the oppressor and a murderer on the lam. God's response is to ignore the implied objection and move directly to the strong promise of God's own presence with Moses. The sign that seals the agreement is the promise that the people will worship God on this same mountain (Horeb/Sinai) after they have been freed from Egypt.

The name of God is elusive, all-inclusive, mysterious, and, as even God recognizes, likely ineffective as a rallying cry for the Israelites. So, in the end, God instructs Moses to draw on the rich history of God's covenant faithfulness to Abraham, Isaac, and Jacob. Similarly for us, speculation about all the things that "I am who I am" might mean gives way to testimony about the God whom we have experienced in our lives, the church, and the world—supremely through the resurrection of Jesus from the dead.

> The name of God is elusive, all-inclusive, mysterious, and, as even God recognizes, likely ineffective as a rallying cry for the Israelites.

Psalm 105 calls for the people of God to give thanks by recalling the covenant to Abraham, retelling the story of Joseph, and then, in the section selected for singing today, how Israel came to Egypt, grew strong, and inspired the crafty oppression of the Egyptians, which in turn prompted God to send Moses and Aaron.

Second Reading
ROMANS 12:9-21 (RCL)

This section of Romans comes across as a collection of proverbial or catechetical instruction. The words *love* and *hate* draw our attention and give some sense of organization, though it is more intuited than heard in the reading. Those who have been hearing the continuous reading of Romans over the last several weeks may recognize that this way of "genuine love" is possible for us because we are redeemed sinners—whether we are Jews or Gentiles. Redemption rather than election or adoption is the ground for our discipleship. That is to say, the law here functions as gracious instruction, not requirement for salvation.

A sermon that tries to gather all of the exhortations—hate evil, hold fast to good, love with mutual affection, show honor, be zealous, have hope, be patient in suffering, persevere in prayer—into a general picture of life is a possibility. An alternative would be for the preacher to select just one or two of the exhortations that relate specifically to stories and challenges within the communities to which he or she preaches.

Or, given that the Republican national convention will take place in the coming week, perhaps portions of Paul's instruction about "genuine love" can be shown to be in resonance or contrast with emerging political platforms or national policies. Is our nation or church casting itself in the role of the persecuted? Then Paul has an exhortation: "Bless persecutors." Or is our nation or church recognizing the extent of its influence, wealth, or power with respect to the world? Then again, Paul has an exhortation: "Do not be haughty . . . associate with the lowly."

A sermon on this section must not become a tirade, as though the preacher or the people are faithful in doing these things while others fail. Christians are not allowed the indulgence of having enemies or permission to assume that we are right. God sorts out right and wrong; God decides who is deserving of vindication. The phrase "heap burning coals on their heads" will be heard in different ways. Some will hear, "Be nice to your enemies, it will drive them crazy and make them angry at you." In other words, niceness becomes an offensive weapon. More in keeping with the tone of Romans is the connection between ashes and repentance. Paul is suggesting that our charity toward enemies will cause them to reconsider their stance toward us. That is, if we act as friend to our enemies, our repentance and the charitable actions it inspires may bring about repentance from our enemies.

> Christians are not allowed the indulgence of having enemies or permission to assume that we are right. God sorts out right and wrong; God decides who is deserving of vindication.

ROMANS 12:1-8 (BCP)
ROMANS 12:1-2 (LFM)

See the second reading for the Fifteenth Sunday after Pentecost, Proper 16 (August 24, 2008), above.

SEVENTEENTH SUNDAY AFTER PENTECOST

Twenty-Third Sunday in Ordinary Time / Proper 18

September 7, 2008

Revised Common (RCL)	Episcopal (BCP)	Roman Catholic (LFM)
Exod. 12:1-14 or Ezek. 33:7-11	Ezek. 33:(1-6) 7-11	Ezek. 33:7-9
Psalm 149 or 119:33-40	Ps. 119:33-48 or 119:33-40	Ps. 95:1-2, 6-7, 8-9
Rom. 13:8-14	Rom. 12:9-21	Rom. 13:8-10
Matt. 18:15-20	Matt. 18:15-20	Matt. 18:15-20

PRINCIPAL LECTIONARY THEMES

EZEKIEL 33:7-11 (RCL)
EZEKIEL 33:(1-6) 7-11 (BCP)
EZEKIEL 33:7-9 (LFM)
PSALM 119:33-40 (RCL, BCP ALT.)
PSALM 119:33-48 (BCP)
PSALM 95:1-2, 6-7, 8-9 (LCM)
MATTHEW 18:15-20 (RCL, BCP, LFM)

The longest version (vv. 1-11, BCP opt.) of the Ezekiel passage is repetitive but elegant in its clarity. Sentinels must sound the alarm when they see danger coming. If they issue the warning but their words are unheeded, they are not blamed for the disaster, but if they fail to issue the warning, blame for the tragedy (no matter who is responsible for provoking the disaster) is pinned on them. The shorter version of the passage also makes this clear and specifies that in the case at hand, the sword is being drawn specifically because of the people's iniquity (in this sense it is like Jonah's message to the Ninevites, "repent or be destroyed").

For all its clarity, though, the passage is enigmatic in application to real communities. First of all, who in our culture is comfortable with the notion that anyone should pay for the wrongdoing of another? It makes sense for the sentinel to be punished for failing in the discrete act of giving warning (though a curmudgeon might grumble that even such obvious accountability is rare in our culture), but adding to that punishment the penalty of all those who are (after all) being *justly punished* is unfair.

Second, what is the danger here? The sentinel metaphor is rooted in the language of a city under military attack and in danger of being destroyed (vv. 1-6)—clearly a dire situation in which the sentinel's warning is a matter of life and death. In the application of the metaphor to the prophet's ministry (vv. 7-9), the "city" is the "people of God"; the "outside attack" is God's word of reproach and judgment; and again, it is a matter of life and death. The people will die if they do not repent (though "die" will likely be heard as a metaphor for spiritual separation from God rather than physical death). But what claims are Christian preachers willing to make here? What is the "sword" for us and what is at stake if it falls? Most preachers will likely shy away even from eschatological consequences (if we don't repent we go to hell), let alone any imminent demise. And is the community of faith so easily divided into the "wicked" and the "not wicked" or the "repentant" and "not repentant"?

An additional challenge here is deciding how the church should enter into Ezekiel's metaphor in the first place. Is the preacher the sentinel for the church? Or is the church the sentinel for the world? Dire warnings abound; how are we to know the voice of the appointed sentinel from other words of warning? Scientists remain divided about the causes and consequences of global warming; full inclusion of gay and lesbian persons into the life of the church will either permanently tear the moral fabric or be a sign of God's radical intent to include everyone. And most mysterious and troubling: If we are the sentinel and we *do* sound the warning, but those in our care die (spiritually or physically), is there really any comfort in knowing we're off the hook?

Where the lectionary reading includes verses 10-11, there is help (perhaps) in knowing some particulars. The message that Ezekiel is given to deliver is for Israel to repent. Note carefully that in this case, the people *know* that their sins are causing them trouble but in their misery and anxiety they are blinded to any options—they don't know what to do. Though the sentinel's words are hard and filled with law, to the extent that they offer the people a concrete response they are also a grace. Preachers who choose to grapple with the reading and are willing to name the "sin," the "sword," and the avenue of repentance would invite hearers to consider that the stakes for Christian life are higher than we often suppose.

> Though the sentinel's words are hard and filled with law, to the extent that they offer the people a concrete response they are also a grace.

The portion of Psalm 119 appointed for this day sounds like the plea that might be on the lips of the people in their duress, though here in the psalm they seem to know exactly what they need and where to find it. They need God's word, commandments, and decrees, and they need God to take the initiative to teach them. They need to look away from vain things and empty promises. Here again,

188

THE SEASON
AFTER
PENTECOST

HANK J.
LANGKNECHT

if the preacher can concretely describe our state of sin, the promise of God's relief will come as good news. The portion of Psalm 95 appointed by LCM enters at a different point in relation to the Ezekiel reading. Here the psalm speaks from the point of view of the sentinel, imploring the people to listen and to turn away from hard-heartedness and their tendency to put God to the test.

Where the reading from Ezekiel focuses on the sentinel's responsibility in relationship to the people and their God, Jesus in Matthew moves from the public herald to truth-telling in relationships within the community of faith. And while the stakes are different, they are still high. In Ezekiel, the stakes are between some form of life and death; here they have to do with remaining in communion or being excommunicated. Like the passage from Ezekiel, this section of Matthew is clear but difficult in application, honored more in the breach than the obeying (even though Jesus' steps are iterated nearly verbatim in the internal discipline section of many congregation constitutions). What do we make of this? Again, the preacher's challenge is the untangling of the various associations and identifications hearers make with the various entities in the text. The first couple of steps seem to accommodate themselves easily to all situations: one person sins against another, the sinned-against party gently confronts the sinner. If that doesn't work, then a meeting with one or two other members of the community is arranged. But, if that doesn't work, then what? Does "telling it to the church" mean a public announcement in worship, a bulletin blurb, or agenda time at the next congregation meeting?

This is hard but real. It is tempting to suppose (as we do when we read in Acts 4:32ff. about believers sharing all their possessions) that while the naïve early Christian community could actually embrace Jesus' policy suggestions, they are unworkable in our age of autonomous sophistication. But a preacher willing to peel back our assumptions about the relationship between Christian community and contemporary American culture might be the sentinel we need—*not* in this case to save the community from destruction but to point out that there is real balm for our culture's frantic anxiety right here where two or three are gathered in Christ's name. Sadly, most congregations are laissez-faire when it comes to holding brothers and sisters in Christ to account for sin. Most of us would *never* tell another person when he or she has sinned against us; being much more inclined toward apathy, gossip, or the silent indignation that lies behind the ubiquitous "whatever." These are times when the ability to speak and listen with the depth required seems beyond imagining; all the more reason why, today, the preacher might be called to sentinel duty.

These are times when the ability to speak and listen with the depth required seems beyond imagining; all the more reason why, today, the preacher might be called to sentinel duty.

One intriguing possibility for a sermon would be to walk the congregation through a test case—of course, one that ends with reconciliation! It could be a fictional member-against-member situation (though with enough verisimilitude that it would have some squirm factor) or, better, a real case from the community's life (especially if it involves the preacher himself or herself in the role of the "sinner" who is regained through candid, loving confrontation). The power for such a sermon must be fueled by the conviction that God empowers and directs the process and that the joy of "regaining that one" more than balances the agony of the process.

We must also recall that we do not rely on this passage alone for our practices of church discipline. Earlier in this same chapter of Matthew Jesus talks about not putting a stumbling block up for little ones. But what if the one who sins against you is one such "little one"—does the disciplinary process kick in? In Romans 14 (the second reading for Proper 19), Paul admonishes "strong" Christians to defer to "weak" Christians. We are to turn the other cheek; leave the speck in the other's eye and tend to the log in our own; love our enemies; and bless our persecutors. A sermon on Matthew 18 should be careful about putting too much procedural weight on this one response to community brokenness.

> We are to turn the other cheek; leave the speck in the other's eye and tend to the log in our own; love our enemies; and bless our persecutors.

A fanciful approach to this text might pretend that Jesus is talking to himself here since, in the end, he is the One against whom all have sinned. In this scheme, Jesus comes to us first alone, then embodied in one or two members of the community, and then Jesus surrounds us with loved ones who desire our repentance. And even though the plain sense of verse 17 is that those who fail to repent are excommunicated (becoming to the community as tax collectors or Gentiles), in the reading for Proper 21 Jesus will tell us that tax collectors are entering the kingdom ahead of the righteous. So if it is true that in our refusal to repent we become as Gentiles and tax collectors, it is clear that we then become special objects of Jesus' attention and mercy.

Semicontinuous Readings
EXODUS 12:1-14 (RCL)
PSALM 149 (RCL)

This section of Exodus 12 serves double duty. Its placement in the Exodus narrative suggests that it is the eleventh-hour instruction from Moses and Aaron for how the Israelites can survive the horror of the impending visit of the angel of death, the final plague. But the tone and language of the reading

190

THE SEASON
AFTER
PENTECOST

HANK J.
LANGKNECHT

are devoid of any urgency; it sounds more like a passage from the manual on the liturgy for Passover Seders. Preachers might want to compare the tone of this passage with the narrative that immediately surrounds it (see chapter 11 and also Exod. 12:29ff.). What is clear from this passage is that the lasting icons of this act of God's deliverance are the blood on the doorposts (lamb's blood will become important to Christian imagery as well), the directive to prepare only enough food for this day's needs (foreshadowing the daily bread of manna and quail), the ban on leavening since there will not be time for the dough to rise, and the vivid image of people eating with their overcoats and hats on (perhaps a modern analogy would be the harried commuter shoveling in an omelet and toast while standing over the kitchen sink because the bus will be at the stop at the corner less than three minutes from now). These are people ready to make a break for it and begin the journey as soon as God gives the signal.

Indeed, the first forty-one Passovers were commemorated and observed while the Israelites were on the road: pilgrim people in a concrete physical sense. After they possess the promised land they must have wrestled just as contemporary Christians do with the dual identity of "pilgrim people" and "settled community." Preachers electing to preach into the Exodus passage might help Christians grapple with this dual identity. Since it is unlikely that many congregations will sell the building and buy a traveling tent, the challenge is both to identify clearly the danger from which we would flee if we did flee (similar to the challenge of identifying the danger in the Ezekiel passage above) and to picture vividly the better land toward which we journey. This is hard. Even before the Israelites are out of the territory of Egypt they yearn to be back in the "comfort" of oppressive physical hardship and slavery (Exod. 14:12). How much more will we resist wilderness wandering in favor of our comfortable "slavery" to culture.

> After the Israelites possess the promised land they must have wrestled just as contemporary Christians do with the dual identity of "pilgrim people" and "settled community."

Another aspect of the story of the Exodus that clouds its application is the portrayal of Egypt as a land of unmitigated evil. But this is the story as told; it is not the historical reality (and the story itself suggests as much as it recalls the mercy that Pharaoh's daughter shows to the baby Moses). Whether the sermon is a good time for unpacking the difference in the way the "other" is portrayed between national story and disinterested history is questionable, but unless the preacher is willing to empathize with the "other" in a sermon, he or she should not characterize any living group as Egypt. The exception to that rule (and an interesting possibility in some contexts) would be either to cast our own nation or our own church in the role of Egypt or to acknowledge that our slavery is self-imposed and not the fault of such vague "straw Pharaohs" as "secularism" or "popular culture."

Psalm 149 celebrates the victory of God over the nations whom God must judge (in this case, we think of Egypt). In verse 5 there is an evocation of a settled people (called to give praise from their couches).

SECOND READING
ROMANS 13:8-14 (RCL)
ROMANS 13:8-10 (LFM)

This passage from Romans continues in much the same tone as the reading from Romans 12:9-21, with additional exhortations about living in Christian community. Here Paul reviews portions of the Ten Commandments and gives the same summary as Jesus does in the Gospels: the fulfillment of the law is to "love your neighbor as yourself." Then in a tone that raises some of the same issues of immediacy as our discussion of the Exodus passage, Paul urges urgency: "You know what time it is . . . salvation is nearer." According to Paul, the Christian community has been languishing in the dark where lowlifes reign. Now is the time to come into the light and live daytime lives of honor. As was the case when dwelling in the Ezekiel and Exodus texts, the preacher must be prepared to be concrete and real about trying to claim and communicate this same urgency in today's "settled" church. It is one thing to teach that Paul is driven by his belief that the Day of the Lord was imminent; it is quite another to articulate why—both in his day and ours, given the dependence of both Jew and Gentile on God's grace—that the nearness of that day necessitates putting aside the flesh and its desires. How do we articulate any comparable sense of urgency for this day and time? Paul's rhetoric is compelling and inspiring; it is up to the contemporary preacher to rearticulate the promises (or the threats) that invite us to open ourselves to repentance and conversion. Now!

> According to Paul, the Christian community has been languishing in the dark where low-lifes reign. Now is the time to come into the light and live daytime lives of honor.

ROMANS 12:9-21 (BCP)

See the second reading for the Sixteenth Sunday after Pentecost, Proper 17 (August 31, 2008), above.

EIGHTEENTH SUNDAY AFTER PENTECOST

Twenty-Fourth Sunday in Ordinary Time / Proper 19
September 14, 2008

Revised Common (RCL)	Episcopal (BCP)	Roman Catholic (LFM)
Exod. 14:19-31 or Gen. 50:15-21	Sir. 27:30—28:7	Sir. 27:30—28:7
Psalm 114 or Exod. 15:1b-11, 20-21 or Ps. 103:(1-7), 8-13	Psalm 103 or 103:8-13	Ps. 103:1-2, 3-4, 9-10, 11-12
Rom. 14:1-12	Rom. 14:5-12	Rom. 14:7-9
Matt. 18:21-35	Matt. 18:21-35	Matt. 18:21-35

PRINCIPAL LECTIONARY THEMES

GENESIS 50:15-21 (RCL)
PSALM 103:(1-7), 8-13
SIRACH 27:30—28:7 (BCP, LFM)
PSALM 103 OR 103:8-13 (BCP)
PSALM 103:1-2, 3-4, 9-10, 11-12 (LFM)
MATTHEW 18:21-35 (RCL, BCP, LFM)

The reading from Genesis gives us an unvarnished look into the hearts of the caught and guilty; it is not a pretty picture. The brothers of Joseph, assuming that he may want to avenge being sold into slavery and deprived of his family, throw themselves at his mercy and resort to one of the most greasy and manipulative family tricks: quoting the dead to their own advantage. During the long Joseph saga, Joseph has wrestled with his feelings toward his brothers (for example, he accuses his scheming brothers of spying, puts them in prison, and frames Benjamin for the theft of Joseph's silver cup). It is worth wondering how the brothers reevaluate the way Joseph has treated them on their trips to Egypt now that they realize he knew who they were all along. Perhaps they have good reason to be afraid.

But in a scene oddly reminiscent of the father's reception of the prodigal son (Luke 15:21ff.), Joseph will have none of their talk of being slaves to him. The decision to forgive is Joseph's alone and the text offers three insights into what informs the decision. First is the brothers' false testimony about Jacob's wishes; one hopes that Joseph is not leaning on that reason too heavily. Second is Joseph's realization that in spite of his near-divine status in Egypt, he is not God and is therefore not the one to make final judgment of guilt or innocence. Here Joseph's reasoning that mortals are bound to forgive rather than judge resonates with the optional section of Psalm 103 (BCP), the reading from Sirach (BCP and LFM), and the parable Jesus will tell in the Gospel lesson. Third, Joseph puts the whole unhappy business into the context of God's divine plan.

In fact, in spite of the personal terror and torment he has faced over the course of the saga, Joseph proclaims that the hand of God has guided every event. The motives of the brothers—and Joseph candidly names them as malevolent—are secondary. This is not a theodicy for all times and situations, and while Christians do celebrate providence in some events, we also seek to name—for the purpose of forgiveness—sin and evil. Joseph's decision to reconcile with his brothers comes only after he has passed through a crucible—some of that agonizing journey is narrated in the saga, some is not. Finally, Joseph should also be credited with resisting the temptation to say, "I told you guys that one day your sheaves would bow to my sheaf." (For additional comments on the Joseph saga, see the notes for the semicontinuous reading in Proper 15 above.)

> In spite of the personal terror and torment he has faced over the course of the saga, Joseph proclaims that the hand of God has guided every event.

Psalm 103 resonates with the Genesis text, especially in verses 8-11 where God's forgiveness is celebrated. God is slow to anger and even when angered, God does not hold a grudge and does not consider our sins when dealing with us. In God's atlas, our sins are as distant from us as east is from west (and no, it is not a globe—they do not meet again on the other side!). Those who recite the whole psalm (BCP, opt.) will hear that God's mercy comes from intimate knowledge of our makeup. God knows we are mortal, evanescent, and that our short view means that our lives and actions issue from a skewed perspective.

The reading from Matthew 18 is in two parts. First, Peter seeks and receives from Jesus clarification about the rules for forgiveness, here having to do with quantity: the number of times one must forgive. Second, Jesus tells a parable that deals with a different quantitative aspect of forgiveness (the severity of the debt forgiven), but on a deeper level examines the qualitative difference between divine and human forgiveness and the contagious quality that God's forgiveness is intended to have. God's ideal is that we will pass along to others even a fraction of what we have received from God. We are still close—in both lectionary and canonical terms—to Peter's confession, and Jesus through teachings and parables is

> God's ideal is that we will pass along to others even a fraction of what we have received from God.

194

THE SEASON
AFTER
PENTECOST

HANK J.
LANGKNECHT

unpacking what discipleship means under his messianic reign. This reading from Matthew is the first of five lectionary Gospel readings in which Jesus tells illustrative parables (Propers 19–23).

In last week's Gospel reading we heard that sinners who do not repent are to become to us as tax collectors and Gentiles. Here, Peter presses the point and we learn that before they become as tax collectors and Gentiles we have to forgive them seventy-seven times (or 490 times, depending on how one renders the Greek mathematics). The previous teaching had a human sensibility and human scale to it; it was all about rules and processes. And Peter's magnanimity here in offering six "second chances" still represents a human scale of forgiveness. Jesus' answer to Peter does two related things. First, Jesus establishes a scale for forgiveness that is divine rather than human, for whether the number is seven plus seventy or seven times seventy, it is beyond human accounting. Second, the reply shows that Peter still has not come to grips with what it means that the age being ushered in will be under the terms established by *this* Messiah: Jesus. And to the extent that we identify with Peter, it's likely that we also fail to understand the full implications, even after two millennia of church life and growth. An interesting sermon on this portion of the text might try to bring to light the patience required to forgive someone the same sin seventy-seven times. Then the preacher could muse on how God forgives us the same sins minute by minute by minute of our entire lives.

The parable in the second part of the reading approaches the accounting procedures for forgiveness a bit differently but also demonstrates that Jesus is calling disciples to forgiveness on a divine scale. God's hope is for the exponential reconciliation that a "pay it forward" ethic would produce, where the incomparable joy of being let off the divine hook inspires us to regard the indebtedness of others to us as the insignificant mortal denarii that it is. The parable sets up two transactions: the ridiculously huge debt a slave owes his king and the modest debt one slave owes another. Don't waste sermon time trying to nail down contemporary equivalents for the amounts; the plain sense of the text makes it sufficiently clear that the king's forgiveness was big and what the fellow slave asked for was small. Although legally the two transactions have nothing to do with each other, Jesus, in his telling, connects them through the so-called "unforgiving" slave, who features in both transactions.

> Jesus' last line tells us that this is a matter of the heart, of repentance, of conversion, and not just action.

If Jesus had not added a "moral" ("So my heavenly Father will also do to . . . you, if you do not forgive . . . from your heart") this parable would be more manageable. Everyone gets the simple point of the story. The slaves in the parable are so mad about the forgiven slave's failure to forgive that they report him to the king; the king is so mad that he rescinds grace and throws the bum into prison; and Jesus could "pull a Nathan"—on the disciples or on us—and return our indignation to us by saying, "you are the unforgiving servant" (see 2 Sam. 12:1ff.). But Jesus' last line tells us that this is a matter of the heart, of repentance, of conversion, and not just action.

Profitable preaching on this parable means heading directly to the hard question: Why does God's forgiveness of our ridiculously huge debt *not* inspire in us a joy and relief that results in our magnanimity to all fellow debtors? And what does it mean that Jesus knows that it will not (a knowledge that prompts the telling of the parable in the first place)? Is God's grace-based initiative finally an unworkable motivation for God's desired community because where God expects a responsive heart there is, in us, only a self-absorbed vacuum? We know what is in the slave's heart when he pleads for mercy from the king (anguish over the punishment that will be leveled at him and his family and the intent to repay the debt), but the text gives us no inkling of what is in his heart *after* grace is shown. We only see what he does next: he fails to express any gratitude to the king and he lowers the boom on a fellow slave.

But our entry into the parable depends on understanding what happens in his heart as he moves from one encounter to the next—Jesus says as much in verse 35—and so we are left to examine our own hearts for clues. Perhaps the slave had come, as we all come, to consider that the life he had built with borrowed resources was his due and so the king's forgiveness puts him where he had already imagined himself to be (a nondependent owner entitled to his wealth) and therefore warranted no thanks. Perhaps the slave left the king's presence perplexed over the *new* debt that he owes the king. That is, his financial debt was absurdly large but there was a certain comfort in the clarity and familiarity of the mechanics of repayment (handy coupon book or garnisheed wages). But now he has been given grace, relief, and freedom and his confusion about being in an unfamiliar relationship to wealth and king makes him cranky and he reverts back to simple accounting at the first opportunity. Or maybe in a strange way the slave has interpreted the king's largess as a sign of favor or special status and so feels justified in calling his fellow slave to account. It is a risk to supply motivations where the text is mute, but the parable's silence on this (and Jesus' "moral") invites us there in this case. Preachers will also have to account for the fact that few Christians spend time worrying about going to "debtor's prison" (would that be purgatory?) and so perhaps neither the king's largess or the threat of punishment carries enough weight to force our identification with the forgiven unforgiving slave.

> Our entry into the parable depends on understanding what happens in his heart as he moves from one encounter to the next, and so we are left to examine our own hearts for clues.

196

THE SEASON
AFTER
PENTECOST

HANK J.
LANGKNECHT

The reading from Sirach (BCP and LFM) addresses the issue of forgiveness through a series of sayings and exhortations. The prerogative for anger belongs to God alone; anger in anyone else is an abomination! The relationship between divine and human forgiveness is reversed in Sirach from that implied in Matthew; here you are forgiven as you forgive (v. 2) where in Matthew you are to forgive as you have been forgiven. Sirach (vv. 4ff.) with Psalm 103 (especially vv. 14ff.) also invites us to consider how the social status (king = God; slave = mortal) of the characters affects the story. Sirach asks, "If one has no mercy on another like himself, can he then seek pardon for his own sins?" The suggestion from this perspective is that we mortals are much more alike than different. Mutual empathy should prompt mercy, knowing as we do the mixed motives, the pressures, the limits, and the sheer complexity that we grapple with as we deal with one

> Mutual empathy should prompt mercy, knowing as we do the mixed motives, the pressures, the limits, and the sheer complexity that we grapple with as we deal with one another.

another. God alone stands in a position to see the complete landscape (God the "most high," that is); all judgment shall be deferred to God. Even among the thick family dynamics of the Genesis reading Joseph hints at this when he asks, "Am I in the place of God?" As the election season enters the home stretch, candidates, media pundits, and ordinarily tolerant Christians will be seeking the high ground from which to identify important moral distinctions. But as Sirach and the parable both suggest, even when confronted with the millionaire mercy of God, we of single-digit righteousness cannot resist sorting ourselves, making fine distinctions according to sins committed at the fifth decimal point.

SEMICONTINUOUS READINGS

EXODUS 14:19-31 (RCL) PSALM 114 OR EXODUS 15:1B-11, 20-21 (RCL)

The strange pre-Exodus drama is drawing to a close. This drama has been dominated by the tug of war between God—represented by Moses and Aaron—and the Pharaoh, who acts from the point of view of national self-interest and with a heart hardened by God. The plagues have worn Pharaoh and the Egyptians down and have impressed upon the Hebrew people that God's considerable power is being waged on their behalf. Finally, after the tenth plague, Pharaoh relents and lets the people go and the people finally muster up the faith to actually go. The passage appointed for today picks up the story on the eve of the journey through the Red Sea.

The power of this story is not in its faithfulness to geography or history (as we noted in last week's reflections, there is no way that the "real" Pharaoh or the "real" Egypt were so one-dimensionally evil). Pointing to known meteorological or oceanic phenomenon in an attempt to make the story plausible has the unintended consequence of making the Israelites look credulous and naïve (and us, by comparison, skeptical and sophisticated). Reducing the story to historical plausibility also misrepresents our faith: it is not the historical events *behind* the Bible that are inspired; it is the Bible that is inspired. This story only has power when it is shared and celebrated by people who have their own testimony about God's powerful action in their lives; people such as us see in this story evidence of a kindred testimony.

Christians often make that testimonial connection by telling the story of the Red Sea crossing when they recall what God does in baptism. A faithful sermon might develop the grand shared metaphors between exodus and baptism: slavery (to Egypt or to sin), deliverance (through the Red Sea or through the waters of baptism), and new freedom (to be God's obedient people). A mischievous (and perhaps more deeply faithful) sermon might explore some of the quirky details of the narrative. For example, in Exodus 13:17 we learn that God elects not to lead the Israelites by the most direct route for fear that if their first encounter as a free people is with the bellicose Philistines, they will ask to return to slavery (a hunch of God's that will be confirmed in next week's lesson). In Exod. 14:1 we learn that God is not yet done with Pharaoh. God has the Israelites wander aimlessly for a bit knowing that Pharaoh will interpret this as a chance to reclaim them. An important aspect of the Christian exodus is that it begins in baptism where we get wet and are drowned. Ironically, in this prototypical story in Exodus 14, it is the Egyptians who get wet and drown, not the people of God. None of these elements of the story scuttle the traditional wedding of Red Sea and baptism, but they provide sensory details that invite us to testify to the reality that life with God is not only a matter of marching forward with unswerving unambiguous confidence.

> An important aspect of the Christian exodus is that it begins in baptism where we get wet and are drowned.

Psalm 114 is a lovely celebration of God's mastery of nature. Riffing on the parting of the sea, the psalm also plays with the image of Jordan (the river) running uphill, and the mountains and hills skipping about. Why does nature act in such exuberant ways? Simply because God is present. The alternative response is the song sung by Miriam, Moses, and the Israelites on the far shore of the Red Sea. Taken strictly historically, it is a hard text that gets a bit overzealous when relishing the death of horse and riders thrown into the sea and sinking like rocks (which is, of course, not strictly how Exodus 14 and 15 tell it). Taken poetically, it is a wild celebration of freedom, poignant when we remember that after just

198

THE SEASON
AFTER
PENTECOST

HANK J.
LANGKNECHT

a few weeks of wandering in the wilderness anyone humming the song would likely be told, "Can it, will you? We haven't had a decent meal since we left Egypt!"

SECOND READING

ROMANS 14:1-12 (RCL)
ROMANS 14:5-12 (BCP)
ROMANS 14:7-9 (LFM)

It is not always the case that the second lesson resonates with the principal lectionary themes, but here in Romans 14 Paul touches on the roles of forgiveness and judgment in community life. The teaching in this section grows out of the central teaching of the book that Gentiles and Jews alike witness to human separation from God (Gentiles because they have been left to lawlessness; Jews because they have failed to properly follow the Torah) even as both groups are objects of God's mercy and redemption.

What Paul recognizes in chapter 14 is that when people from diverse backgrounds attempt to live together in community there are bound to be clashes of piety and practice. In the longer reading (vv. 1-6, RCL) Paul lays out a couple of cases: a dispute about whether Christians should abstain from certain foods (probably meat) and a dispute about how to honor certain days of the week. His simple instruction is that each group should allow the other its piety and practice even as it adheres to its own. However, Paul is not quite suggesting that the two sides in such a clash of pieties are spiritually equivalent. He is addressing the "strong" and exhorting them to welcome and express tolerance for the "weak." The "weak" are those who favor the stricter application of rules—"Some [the strong?] believe in eating anything, while the weak eat only vegetables" (v. 2). This distinction resonates with Paul's teaching in other places in Romans where he pushes to a more "spiritual" application than literal or physical application of the law.

Paul gives two rationales for his instruction. First, in verses 7-9, he attempts to raise people's sights so that they cease to focus on the particulars of difference but instead on the one Lord whom all people are seeking to serve. At its best, a community maintaining diverse pieties under one Lord is a rich tapestry of diversity and conviction with respect; at its worst, though, it denies the hard edges of difference, hiding them behind tolerant clichés (for instance, "it doesn't matter what you practice, as long as you're sincere").

At its best, a community maintaining diverse pieties under one Lord is a rich tapestry of diversity and conviction with respect; at its worst, it denies the hard edges of difference.

Then, in verses 10-12 Paul echoes Sirach by reminding the members of the community that as great as our differences seem to be from the day-to-day human perspective, they dissolve when we consider human difference from God and our equal need of mercy and redemption. What preacher could not do a whole sermon on the question in verse 10 ("Why do you pass judgment on your brother or sister?"), especially if the preacher treats it as a serious—in addition to being a rhetorical—question?

Paul is arguing from the point of view of one "strong in faith," and one goal of Paul's effective rhetoric is to invite "weak" hearers to identify with him. The difficult judgment a preacher must make is to decide what "cases" in our context appropriately fall under Paul's method. Even if we assume that for the Romans meat versus vegetables and the honoring of particular days were matters of life and death, most of us are beyond such "blue law" concerns. How do we apply Paul's reasoning to such internal conflicts as appropriate music in worship or the ordination of homosexual persons in committed relationships? Who is "weak" and who is "strong" in these and other contemporary cases? Is it tenable community practice to be tolerant in all things? The preacher must also realize that not every "weak" believer will accept that stricter obedience *is* a sign of weakness or that tolerance is always a sign of "strength." If it can be done without over-burdening the sermon, the preacher may want to note that in the next section of Romans (14:13ff.) Paul admonishes the "strong" not to flaunt their freedom to eat whatever they want but rather to conform their practices (at least their visible practices) to those of the weak.

NINETEENTH SUNDAY AFTER PENTECOST

Twenty-Fifth Sunday in Ordinary Time / Proper 20

September 21, 2008

Revised Common (RCL)	Episcopal (BCP)	Roman Catholic (LFM)
Exod. 16:2-15 or Jonah 3:10—4:11	Jonah 3:10—4:11	Isa. 55:6-9
Ps. 105:1-6, 37-45 or 145:1-8	Psalm 145 or 145:1-8	Ps. 145:2-3, 8-9, 17-18
Phil. 1:21-30	Phil. 1:21-27	Phil. 1:20c-24, 27a
Matt. 20:1-16	Matt. 20:1-16	Matt. 20:1-16a

PRINCIPAL LECTIONARY THEMES

JONAH 3:10—4:11 (RCL, BCP)
PSALM 145:1-8 (RCL, BCP ALT.)
PSALM 145 (BCP)
ISAIAH 55:6-9 (LFM)
PSALM 145:2-3, 8-9, 17-18 (LFM)
MATTHEW 20:1-16 (RCL, BCP)
MATTHEW 20:1-16A (LFM)

God has spared Nineveh because all the residents of the city, including the animals, have dressed themselves in sackcloth and poured on the ashes. This universal repentance was inspired by Jonah's brief sermon. Jonah is angry at God's change of heart and retreats to the east of the city to watch and see what happens—one wonders, though, to see what happens to whom . . . Nineveh or Jonah? Behind the scenes of this passage are several interesting questions. The first is implicit in Jonah's anger at God's decision to spare Nineveh: How hard is it supposed to be to receive God's mercy? Jonah's quarrel is not with God's mercy as such, only with God's decision to lavish it on Nineveh, the capital of Assyria, Israel's mortal enemy, on the basis of Nineveh's "deathbed repentance."

A second curiosity is that Jonah seems to assume that he is entitled to mercy. This despite the fact that his actions reflect a stubborn disobedience to God's command, followed by grudging obedience (bringing to mind the parable of the two sons from next week's Gospel reading) and—even more troubling—Jonah's apparent belief that he knows better than God how to dispense mercy. One theme from last week's Gospel lesson was God's hope that mercy extended to God's people would be passed on in kind. Jonah witnesses to the tendency on the part of God's people (including Christians) to be instead an impediment to that extension of mercy. What is it that turns us so quickly from glad recipients of God's blessing to cunning judges over the rights of others to receive the same?

A third wonderment of the Jonah story involves a bit of imagination about the scene in Nineveh. The book of Jonah gives only the text of Jonah's sermon: "Forty days more, and Nineveh shall be overthrown." But given Jonah's lack of enthusiasm for the task in the first place and his displeasure over the results, it is likely not Jonah's eloquence, passion, or persuasiveness that inspires Nineveh's repentance. There is a seed here for a reminder that, as important as we earthen vessels are in the proclamation of God's word, the word itself is efficacious sometimes in spite of its mistreatment in the hands of those of us who proclaim it.

> As important as we earthen vessels are in the proclamation of God's word, the word itself is efficacious sometimes in spite of its mistreatment in the hands of those of us who proclaim it.

The description of Jonah's action and the nature of his dialogue with God invite us to consider Jonah's frame of mind, his anger, and his twice-expressed death wish. Anger about mercy extended to an enemy, while wrong, is understandable; Jonah's death wish is harder to fathom. His story is not Elijah's; there is no Jezebel waiting to take his life. Is he saying that he doesn't want to live in a world where this kind of God holds sway? Or maybe he is worried that God will punish him for his intransigence, though this would suggest that Jonah is pretty obtuse given that God has just now spared the life of evil Nineveh. Or is he just *that* angry? The picture we get is of a prophet who would be right at home in too many Christian communities: red-faced, posturing, belligerent, and resentful of any suggestion that the mercies of God extend much beyond the walls of the church.

Preachers should be careful when using imagination to fill in details about Jonah's troubled state of mind. Of course we do this and should do this; the point is to be sure that the preacher himself or herself sympathizes with Jonah rather than setting Jonah up as any kind of straw man to be dismissed. If we suppose that Jonah is ranting or pouting or despairing, we must identify with him rather than ridicule him. Casting anyone in a bad light from the pulpit makes the preacher look either like a bully or as one who considers himself or herself (and perhaps the congregation) as holier than another.

The episode with the bush and the worm is extremely odd. The people of Nineveh might well be celebrating their deliverance from wrath with celebrations and tears and worship of God, but the narrative focuses on this petty, drawn-out

202

THE SEASON
AFTER
PENTECOST

HANK J.
LANGKNECHT

mini-drama. What sense we make of it comes from realizing that it is a parable of sorts told to remind us of the extreme variance between God's concerns and ours. Humans muse and whim about local trivialities, especially when they immediately touch our lives or affect our comfort—or even when they merely seem to. Jonah's interest in the bush might be compared to any one of the scores of stories that will captivate national attention and demand twenty-four-hour cable news coverage. God's concern extends deeply because (by implication) God knows everything about the creation, for God has labored over it all.

Psalm 145 responds to Jonah by providing the verses that Jonah himself cites: God is "slow to anger and abounding in steadfast love . . . good to all." God's compassion is "over all that God has made" and God delights in forgiving. What a stunning testimony to God's character—the same character that is revealed in God's ability to look with compassion on Nineveh. However, where Jonah resents, the psalm celebrates that character of God, inviting the faithful to bless God and to speak the glory of God's realm.

Matching the parable in Matthew 20 with the Jonah story has us hearing themes of fairness and worthiness. Jonah has been working in the vineyard for a while (though hardly enthusiastically) and resents that Nineveh comes in late but gets the same reward. And by extension, God's response to Jonah is not unlike the response of the landowner in the parable (is mercy not God's to grant?). Both the parable and Jonah's story pick up the indignation some feel toward those to whom God grants "less-deserved" mercy; the parable, however, does not have the complicating overtones of Jonah where God's mercy is extended to God's enemies. Except for their length of service in the vineyard, none of the laborers are enemies of the landowner.

On its own terms, the parable gets us every time because we can appreciate both the grumbling of the early workers (whether we count ourselves among their number or not) and the protestation of the landowner. According to the commonsense principle of proportionality, the more you work, the more you should be paid. But the landowner is right on two counts: he paid the full-day workers exactly what he promised and it is his money to do with as he pleases. The grumblers create the expectation of more pay out of whole cloth. On this score, though, it might be worth meditating on why the landowner specifically requests the manager to pay the latecomers first.

> On its own terms, the parable gets us every time because we can appreciate both the grumbling of the early workers and the protestation of the landowner.

As much as we "get" the parable and are stuck in the paradox of seeing both sides, it is not easy to predict with whom hearers will identify. Because the parable ends with an extended dialogue between the landowner and those who work all day, we are inclined to identify with them. However, there is nothing to keep preachers from casting their hearers in the role of the latecomers who must be celebrating their unexpected windfall and good fortune. (On that score, what might a sermon on Jonah look like in which contemporary Christians were invited to repent and celebrate with the Ninevites?)

The "payment" distributed by the landowner is usually taken to refer metaphorically to God's favor, often specifically to salvation. The "hours of the day" and "laborers" are interpreted along two trajectories: either they represent the historical periods at which various groups come into God's sphere or they represent the points in an individual's life at which he or she might come to saving faith. In the first trajectory, those who start work early might represent the first people of the promise (the Jewish people) while those who join the work crew as the day wears on represent various converted Gentile populations. A more contemporary application might be that the early workers are longtime members of a congregation while the latecomers are new members. According to the second trajectory, the early workers are those who are baptized as infants and who spend their entire life working in the vineyard; those hired on later represent adult converts—all the way up to those who finally repent at the eleventh hour.

Whichever trajectory a sermon follows, it is important to note that from the point of view of reward, there is no proportion or gradation. This corresponds to what we know about God's benefits. Whether the reward is forgiveness or God's blessing or salvation itself, we either have it or we don't. And once you have it, you have it all. The words of absolution are not proportionate but refer to "the entire forgiveness of all your sins." In this way the parable overturns human common sense when it comes to reward. For this reason the last line of the reading is a bit oblique. The line, "the first will be last and the last will be first," is not only the last line of the pericope, it is also the last line of Matthew 19 (v. 30), which immediately precedes the telling of this parable. What can this mean, given that there is no "reversal of fortune" in the parable? It would be one thing if the grumblers were sent away with nothing, but here, the first and the last receive exactly the same (note that this same curiosity will apply to the parable for next week). The clue to pondering this question lies in an important detail: what the grumblers *expect* is more money but what they *grumble about* is that "you have made them equal to us." Is this also Jonah's complaint? This detail gives a bit more credence to the first trajectory and invites us to a homiletical consideration of status and power in the community. In this case the first are not necessarily made last, but the last are made equal to the first. If we pick up the rich "day laborer" imagery from the parable, perhaps it is time that all Christians hear the truth that a Christian is never more than one day old (or, for that matter, ever less than a lifetime old).

204

THE SEASON
AFTER
PENTECOST

HANK J.
LANGKNECHT

To the extent that we understand the landowner to be God, the parable also invites us to consider whether we believe deep down that God really does or really should show partiality. Here we resonate perhaps with Jonah wondering about the incentive to work harder or get at it earlier if all will be rewarded equally in the end. What perhaps all the laborers forget is that the point of the day has not *only* been to get paid (fairly or not) but also to get the grapes harvested. An imaginative sermon approach might be to take the point of view of the landowner whose generosity is inspired to some degree by his joy that the harvest has been accomplished. If we saw the world through God's eyes and shared God's joy at every evidence of the Reign breaking in, is it possible that we could learn to forget which of us played which role?

Isaiah picks up themes similar to those in Jonah, but now through the point of view of someone who is sympathetic to God's point of view. The focus here is on the fact that God's ways are not human ways. But where Jonah bristles and decries God's strangeness, Isaiah seems to celebrate it.

> To the extent that we understand the landowner to be God, the parable invites us to consider whether we believe deep down that God really does or really should show partiality.

Semicontinuous Readings
EXODUS 16:2-15 (RCL)
PSALM 105:1-6, 37-45 (RCL)

The difficulties of the wandering wilderness lifestyle continue to nettle the Israelites and they express their anger to Moses who continues to act in the priestly role as go-between. Once again, the issue is the availability of decent food. In their hunger, the Israelites wish for the slavery they do know rather than the freedom they don't. It is easy for those who have never been hungry to dismiss their complaints as petty. But in fairness to them, they are a large wandering company needing vast natural resources to survive. Why wouldn't they worry? Of course they want all the blessings God is putting before them: freedom, land, and life as God's chosen people. But having their eyes on that future prize only feeds the soul and the communal imagination; it does nothing to fill the stomach. And of course they do not desire to be slaves again in Egypt except that there, at least, they would know that three squares a day were coming. Misery and fulfillment will be part of either life. Which misery is the more bearable misery; which fulfillment is the more fulfilling?

What is being born here is a rich truth about being a pilgrim people: living with God means balancing the tension between promise and hardship. God's anger has not yet resulted in the decree that all of those who witnessed the parting of the Red Sea will die before Israel reaches the promised land (see Num. 14:23). So presumably, all the Israelites expect to get there. But even though the future goal is close chronologically, the people are having trouble keeping vision above belly. One part of God's response is to teach them (us) and test them (us) through the principle of "daily bread." God is growing a people who will come to understand that the final fulfillment of the promise is close neither chronologically nor geographically. God invites us to travel sustained by just one day's worth of bread and the promise (see Hebrews 11 and 12 for a moving sermon excerpt on this very point!).

Psalm 105 was also recited with Exodus 3 on Proper 17 with different verses selected. Here, the selected verses recount the departure from Egypt with the gold and silver jewelry that was lavished upon them by the Egyptians, the pillars of cloud and

> God is growing a people who will come to understand that the final fulfillment of the promise is close neither chronologically nor geographically.

fire, and then God's provenance of quail and water from the rock. There is an emphasis in the psalm on the singing and joy with which they departed Egypt; with that same joyful singing they will accompany their final journey into the land promised to Abraham.

SECOND READING

PHILIPPIANS 1:21-30 (RCL)
PHILIPPIANS 1:21-27 (BCP)
PHILIPPIANS 1:20C-24, 27A (LFM)

Prior to today's lection, Paul has greeted the Philippians, recalled the close bond he feels with them, and assured them that in spite of being imprisoned he still boldly proclaims Christ. In fact, he believes that his witness to Christ is even stronger and gives more glory to God because of his imprisonment. Here again there is a serendipitous resonance between the Exodus reading and this second lesson. The degree to which we bear hardship buoyed by the promise and presence of God bears witness to nonbelievers that our strength comes from God. Paul makes passing mention of rival evangelists who proclaim Christ out of envy and rivalry, but even these Paul celebrates because even out of those dubious motives, Christ is still proclaimed.

In our reading Paul seems to pick up where the reading from Romans last week left off: whether he lives or dies, he is in Christ. Paul's enthusiasm about dying in order to be with Christ sounds a bit foreign to our age and we may hear it as hyperbole, but rhetorically it serves to underline his confidence in the power

206

THE SEASON
AFTER
PENTECOST

HANK J.
LANGKNECHT

of Christ's resurrection to such an extent that the specific circumstances of his life recede in importance.

In the next section of the reading (vv. 27ff.), Paul exhorts the Philippians to live faithfully in a manner analogous to his own, more mindful about the goal and prize than the circumstances of context. Whether I come to you or not, whether your opponents seek to intimidate you or not, stay faithful. It is Christ who is faithful; living faithfully reveals life's exigencies (even opponents) to be the tests—ultimately trivial tests—that they are. In fact, it is a privilege to be tested in this (or any) way; to see whether our trust in the power revealed in Christ's resurrection can sustain us during difficulties. It is a shame, however, that we tend to think primarily of being tested by major traumatic events, or of opponents only in terms of principalities and powers. The reality is that Paul's encouragement to faithful living could be a regular part of how Christians relate to each other in the face of mundane traumas and opponents. Faithful living in marriage, in vocation, or in spiritual disciplines (including regular worship attendance) in the face of the persistent (but decidedly untraumatic) opposition of media, culture, or our own inner lack of resolve is in some ways harder

> The degree to which we bear hardship buoyed by the promise and presence of God bears witness to nonbelievers that our strength comes from God.

than taking a valiant stand against attack. One aspect of this difficulty is that the rich benefits of faithfulness can only be asserted after we have lived them. It is perhaps helpful that the opponents are not mentioned in verse 28 so that the preacher (knowing the context) can supply the identity of our opponents and the nature of their temptations. The preacher can then join Paul in casting a vision of the joy that will be ours when we have stood firm in our callings even as we are exhorted to support one another in the day-to-day challenges to our faithfulness. As Paul will proclaim in next week's reading, it is Christ and the Spirit who give us our victories.

TWENTIETH SUNDAY AFTER PENTECOST

TWENTY-SIXTH SUNDAY IN ORDINARY TIME /
PROPER 21
SEPTEMBER 28, 2008

Revised Common (RCL)	Episcopal (BCP)	Roman Catholic (LFM)
Exod. 17:1-7 or Ezek. 18:1-4, 25-32	Ezek. 18:1-4, 25-32	Ezek. 18:25-28
Ps. 78:1-4, 12-16 or 25:1-9	Ps. 25:1-14 or 25:3-9	Ps. 25:4-5, 6-7, 8-9
Phil. 2:1-13	Phil. 2:1-13	Phil. 2:1-11 or 2:1-5
Matt. 21:23-32	Matt. 21:28-32	Matt. 21:28-32

PRINCIPAL LECTIONARY THEMES

EZEKIEL 18:1-4, 25-32 (RCL, BCP)
EZEKIEL 18:25-28 (LFM)
PSALM 25:1-9 (RCL)
PSALM 25:1-14 OR 25:3-9 (BCP)
PSALM 25:4-5, 6-7, 8-9 (LFM)
MATTHEW 21:23-32 (RCL)
MATTHEW 21:28-32 (BCP, LFM)

"The parents have eaten sour grapes, and the children's teeth are set on edge." On the one hand, this parable is hard to swallow because in individualistic Western cultures, especially where families are strewn about geographically, our friends and coworkers cannot view us through the lens of our families' reputations. On the other hand, none of us is born into neutral circumstances or with a totally clean slate. What our parents ingest how they relate to each other and to us and aspects of their physiology all leave an aftertaste in our mouths. Meditation on the saying, consideration of its truth, and sensory memory of something so sour that it makes the jaw clench would be good preparation for a sermon on this passage in Ezekiel.

God's desire to eliminate the proverb from common use resonates with our sense of fairness (in fact, it's hard to imagine how the community to which Ezekiel preaches thinks it is *unfair*). We affirm that it shall no longer be used by us in Israel and wonder why it ever was. But individualistic (even atomistic) Western

208

THE SEASON
AFTER
PENTECOST

HANK J.
LANGKNECHT

macroculture notwithstanding, in the smaller subcultures in which we dwell (for example, neighborhoods with neighborhood schools, small towns, and congregations) there are informal and insidious ways in which one's family of origin does mark one for success or doom. There may be specific homiletical situations where the promise of God to eliminate inherited guilt or favor is a word in season. At the least, Ezekiel invites us to challenge any arrangement where people are "reduced" to their heritage. For example, Ezekiel's prophecy might open the door to consideration of the relationship between contemporary descendents of white slave owners or members of the Gestapo and the sins of their ancestors. Are they forever culpable? This passage suggests that they are not. Should children born of undocumented immigrants in a country be treated as illegals or innocents?

Another question to pursue is this: Why would Ezekiel's hearers (or contemporary adherents of the proverb) want to cling to it? Are they thereby resisting the reversal of dynasty and fated fortune that is part of God's mission in the world? Beneath all the talk about grapes and teeth, the foundational truth the Ezekiel passage is proclaiming is that God takes no delight in the oppression or death of anyone. God stands by to receive each person as the unreduced singularity that he or she is; God stands by to give life.

> God stands by to receive each person as the unreduced singularity that he or she is; God stands by to give life.

Another aspect of the Ezekiel passage, and one that leans us toward the Gospel reading, is that while backsliders will still bear individual accountability for turning from God, repentance is possible. From the point of view of the individual who may know the sour taste of family burden, it is good news to hear that hope of new life and new direction is always before us. In contrast to the "sour grape" proverb, where the freedom is from the sins of our ancestors, now the freedom we yearn for is from our own past actions. Youthful indiscretions and transgressions do not condemn us forever nor may we ride the coattails of our early zeal for obedience. God's intent to offer this new life resonates nicely with the teaching on forgiveness from Matthew 18:21-35 (Proper 19). It is an invitation to receive each other fresh each day, to acknowledge the reality that people can be stuck in sinful patterns even as we assume that today is a day in which God's power to bring repentance and conversion is present.

Psalm 25 works nicely with the passage from Ezekiel (and the parable in Matthew). The psalm could be the prayer on the lips of a backslider who wishes to move into God's good graces or one who feels the presence of God and wants to keep it that way. "Make me to know your way . . ."; "teach me . . ."; and "lead me." The psalmist stresses the change that can occur in a single lifetime: "Do not remember the sins of my youth or my transgression." The focus on God's action—in fact, really, the psalmist's total dependence on God—is a helpful balance to the tone of Ezekiel and Matthew. Both the prophet and the Gospel writer celebrate God's grace but Ezekiel's talk about people who are wicked and righteous and the parable's suggestion that the two sons act of their own volition puts focus on human action and human response. Hearing them we could be tempted to think that salvation is somehow in our hands. In the psalm, God is the actor and salvation is wholly in God's hands.

The longer (RCL) version of the Gospel reading is in two parts: verses 21-27 narrate a dialogue between Jesus and some religious leaders in the Temple, while verses 28-32 contain a parable with explanation. Making sense of the material in verses 21-27 is a bit difficult on first hearing because the opening question of the religious leaders refers back to certain "things" that Jesus is doing. This first section also includes the testing question that Jesus poses to the leaders about John the Baptist; knowing this gives some context to Jesus' explanation of the parable in verse 32, which is in both the shorter and longer versions of the reading.

It is often the case in Matthew's Gospel that religious leaders are one-dimensional characters who represent unambiguous opposition to Jesus' life and ministry; as a result their questions and challenges to Jesus can seem arbitrary and unnecessarily mean-spirited. Here is a case where knowing what happens in the immediately preceding verses of Matthew casts them in a more reasonable light. Just prior to this reading (in verses 1-17) Jesus entered Jerusalem in grand procession, rebuked and then drove the money changers from the Temple, and performed a host of healings of unclean people—people who should not have been in the Temple to begin with. For the custodians of the Temple to ask, "Who said you could do this?" is quite understandable. However, because the pericope starts with verse 23 and omits the precipitating events, the question seems to come from out of the blue and to be arbitrarily confrontational.

Jesus counters by asking the religious leaders whether John's baptism had a divine or human origin. They quickly discern the no-win nature of the question and so refuse to answer. Jesus refuses to answer back. In one way Jesus' refusal makes no sense. Certainly the leaders' musing reveals that they are driven by (and stymied by) political expedience and concern for their own public image. But why does that get Jesus off the hook? The reader of the whole Gospel of Matthew knows the answer: Jesus has been acclaimed as one who teaches with

> Jesus asks the religious leaders whether John's baptism had a divine or human origin. They quickly discern the no-win nature of the question and so refuse to answer.

and possesses authority (for example, see Matthew 7:29 and 8:9). Conversely, the leaders' inability to respond to a theological question and the reason for their inability strips them of authority. They are chief priests and elders! It is a hard question, but they should be able to bring some wisdom to it—or at the least to explain, in good rabbinic fashion, that there are many sides to the question of

210

THE SEASON
AFTER
PENTECOST

HANK J.
LANGKNECHT

John's baptism and God's will. But they muster no answer and their ruminations reveal the bankruptcy of their leadership: it's about covering their actions and preserving their reputations. As tempting as it might be to preach into this section of the reading from the point of view of Jesus, an approach both more powerful and true would be to explore the ways that Jesus might question the church and its leaders into silence.

The parable (really not quite a parable, more a parable-like question) is a complex gem. Both sons are in the wrong in their own way—the first son treats his father with stark (though honest) disrespect by publicly refusing his order; the second fails to do the father's will. Conversely, both sons are right in their way—one gives the right answer; one does the right thing. Both sons begin as sons, act as sons, and remain as sons; neither is cast from the family. This last detail means a measure of mercy no matter how the preacher frames our identification with the political or theological dynamics between John the Baptist, Jesus, the religious authorities, and the tax collectors and sinners.

In Jesus' explanation, the common antithesis "the first shall be last, the last first" is evoked. Whether "first" and "last" are understood in terms of chronology or honor, the antithesis applies. But even in this explanation, the righteous "last" do go in . . . last. A fruitful area for preaching in this text is the question of why John's message of righteousness and repentance was persuasive to the unrighteous and anathema to the righteous. The text doesn't tell us, but that should not stop preachers from imagining. To the extent that we are identified with the righteous religious, we should want to know why unrighteous sinners will be leading us into the Reign of God.

> A fruitful area for preaching in this text is the question of why John's message of righteousness and repentance was persuasive to the unrighteous and anathema to the righteous.

SEMICONTINUOUS READINGS

EXODUS 17:1-7 (RCL)
PSALM 78:1-4, 12-16 (RCL)

Many of the emotions and relationship dynamics of the wilderness wandering are the same here as in last week's reading from Exodus 16. In the last episode the Israelites were hungry and saw no provision for food; here they are thirsty and there is no water. They still complain to Moses, Moses still demonstrates far more indignation than God (in this episode we also hear Moses' sense that the people are nearing the end of their patience and are ready to stone him), and God, without comment on the state of mind of either the people or Moses, provides.

As noted last week, it is helpful to imagine ourselves as members of a huge wandering company of people and animals who are out of water in the desert. The complaint is not trivial—if anything, lack of water is more terrifying than lack of food. And even though the Israelites have not yet reached Sinai where they will hear the full scope of what God has in store for God's people, even what they are being asked to do and trust here and now, day by day, is considerable.

God hears their complaints and responds and in so doing saves Moses' life or, at the least, lowers Moses' anxiety a bit. In verse 5 God specifies that Moses is to use the staff with which he struck the Nile when he turned the water to blood—the first of the ten plagues (Exod. 7:15). Moses begins his relationship to God with this (or at least "a") staff in his hand, and one of the first signs God performs in the opening conversation with Moses is to turn the staff into a snake—much to Moses' consternation. A staff—a walking stick—is such an ordinary thing, yet when put into the service of God's power it becomes an icon of continuity.

A staff—a walking stick—is such an ordinary thing, yet when put into the service of God's power it becomes an icon of continuity.

The portion of Psalm 78 that is highlighted here focuses specifically on the ways God led them through the sea, using the wonderful image of the water standing in a heap. More discussion of Psalm 78 can be found with the BCP reading from Proper 13.

SECOND READING
PHILIPPIANS 2:1-13 (RCL, BCP)
PHILIPPIANS 2:1-11 OR 2:1-5 (LFM)

Philippians 2 is a well-known, powerful passage of Scripture containing more than a few iconic verses that find their way onto inspirational posters. Lectors who are privileged to serve on this Sunday will be tempted to treat the passage like royalty. The "if then" at the beginning of verse 1, though, reminds us that this reading continues Paul's flow of argument from last week: standing firm in faith as individuals in community means striving side by side and enjoying the privilege and the proud joy of living the struggle. It isn't that Philippians 2 doesn't deserve royal treatment, but there is also power in hearing these grand words in the context of Paul's ongoing conversation.

In verses 1-2 Paul encourages the Philippians to build on every bit of evidence of strength and courage mustered in the community. This means looking everywhere for signs—no matter how mundane—of the working of Christ or the Spirit in the life of the community. When one member supports another or expresses sympathy for another, these small victories are the evidence of the resurrection among us. When they are noticed and celebrated they impel and inspire us and build up the community.

212

THE SEASON
AFTER
PENTECOST

HANK J.
LANGKNECHT

Then in verse 3 Paul exhorts the Philippians and us to kenosis, that same self-emptying obedience-in-trust that will be celebrated in the hymn in verses 6-11. Paul's own language is sufficient to guard us from thinking that he is encouraging an inappropriate giving over of self—as, for example, in horrid cases when victims of oppression or violence are exhorted to accept their plight with humility. Paul is clear that kenosis must be a mutual ethic; it only works if everyone does it. The turn to Christ is strong rhetorically and theologically: rhetorically because it exemplifies the movement toward the highest thing, theologically because Paul knows that sustaining Christian community involves keeping our focus on Christ rather than on ourselves. If all we have are verses 2-5 we will be tempted to race to the bottom so that we can boast of our humility, so that we can be full of empty selves. Paul knows that attention paid to our own faithfulness or sinfulness—our progress or lack—always ends in self-absorption.

When the Christ hymn is read, the words that sing out are "emptied himself," "form of a slave," "humbled himself," "obedient," and "death on a cross." Here the meaning of the cross is not substitutionary atonement or victory over death and the devil; here God exalts the One who exemplifies radical focus on God, denial of prerogative (perhaps a more helpful phrase than denial of self), and obedience to God, all of which witness to absolute trust. Ironically, the language of "exaltation" and "every knee shall bow" and "Jesus as Lord" at the end of the hymn is almost anticlimactic.

> When one member supports another or expresses sympathy for another, these small victories are the evidence of the resurrection among us.

Paul's exhortation to "work out your own salvation with fear and trembling" is not a call to works righteousness (how could anyone think that in this context?); it is a call to obedient living (of a like mind to Jesus). It is also the call to those who have been freed from worrying about where they stand with respect to God for, as Paul proclaims, "it is God who is at work in you."

TWENTY-FIRST SUNDAY AFTER PENTECOST

Revised Common (RCL)	Episcopal (BCP)	Roman Catholic (LFM)
Exod. 24:1-4, 7-9, 12-20 or Isa. 5:1-7	Isa. 5:1-7	Isa. 5:1-7
Psalm 19 or 80:7-15	Psalm 80 or 80:7-14	Ps. 80:9, 12, 13-14, 15-16, 19-20
Phil. 3:4b-14	Phil. 3:14-21	Phil. 4:6-9
Matt. 21:33-46	Matt. 21:33-43	Matt. 21:33-43

Principal Lectionary Themes

ISAIAH 5:1-7 (RCL, BCP, LFM)
PSALM 80:7-15 (RCL)
PSALM 80:7-14 (BCP)
PSALM 80:9, 12, 13-14, 15-16, 19-20 (LFM)
MATTHEW 21:33-46 (RCL)
MATTHEW 21:33-43 (BCP, LFM)

The song of the vineyard in Isaiah 5 is often described as a beautiful, poignant love song. And it is true, the words *love song* appear in verse 1, but to modern ears it seems more like satire, if not comedy, to sing a love song to a vineyard. By the third verse we hear the true intent of the song: it is a lament about a vintner's failed attempt to plant and nurture a vineyard. The careful description of the steps of the process assures the hearer that nothing could have been done differently or more skillfully. In verse 3 we learn that the question "What is to be done?" is being put to God's people, but it is still not clear how the extended metaphor of the vineyard relates to God's people (or even if it is intended to). Who is the vineyard owner? Are we talking about a literal vineyard or is there a spiritual point being made?

Then, in verses 5ff., the singer of the song lays out the plan for this failed project. And again, the steps and their consequences are enumerated carefully, almost ploddingly. The effect is that we hearers feel carried along by the inevitability of it. How can we argue? Of course this is what will happen, what must happen. Then, in verse 6, there is a jarring shift as the singer suddenly eliminates any possibility that this is a mundane agricultural lament: "I will also command the clouds that they rain no rain upon it." Uh oh. Only God commands the rain. And while using the vineyard as a metaphor for God's land or God's people is new with Isaiah, it is still pretty clear that we, God's people, might be led in the same way that Nathan led David to have our indignation turned back on us. Verse 7 delivers the key to the allegory that resolves the question: God's people, Israel and Judah, are the vineyard, God's "pleasant planting." The sales staff at the nursery assured God that these vines would bear the good fruit of righteous justice provided God followed the care instructions (which God did). But even at that, the vines yielded sour bloodshed and sorrow.

Once the solution has been revealed, we have no choice but to go back and read the allegory again informed by the hard truth that we are the beloved vineyard gone wrong. Isaiah leaves some latitude for hearers (and the preacher) to assign real-world referents to the hill, the cleared stones, the watchtower, the vat, the hedge, the wall, and the briers and thorns. The allegory makes its point without those identifications, but if the preacher is seeking to make contemporary application, the opportunity is there. And since we've agreed all along that everything was done right and the destruction of the vineyard is the only reasonable option, we are left to contemplate God's passion, our failure, and to wonder about the future.

If there is a way into and out of the allegory it is to recall that God *loves* people because it is in God's nature to love. However, God *elects* a people for the sake of God's mission. God lavishes attention on the vineyard so that justice and righteousness might flourish. Within the economy of the intimate relationship of love between God and God's people, the sour grapes could be a failure that becomes part of family lore ("remember that year you spent all that time on that vineyard and got those sour grapes?"). But the vineyard is part of God's mission and the urgency God feels for justice demands that fruit be borne. To put it into modern terms, "God's church doesn't have a mission; God's mission has a church." That is to say, if our focus can be on God's work in the world, then even when our participation in that mission is judged and found wanting the mission still goes on. And is that not the main thing? It is a reminder that we are in covenant with a determined God who wishes the redemption of the world. This is not a question of our salvation but of our fitness for mission. Could God set the church aside in favor of a different mission community? Of course.

> God *loves* people because it is in God's nature to love. However, God *elects* a people for the sake of God's mission.

Psalm 80 dovetails with Isaiah in an intriguing and potentially fruitful way. Isaiah 5:7 is not the end of the story; we know that. The psalm is spoken from the point of view of the nation that knows it is in trouble with God: "Restore us, O God; let your face shine, that we might be saved." God is right to be angry, but the people of the trampled vineyard are relying on the covenant bond in order to persuade God to reconsider the planned destruction. You have done all this careful work—in fact, verses 8-11 of the psalm echo the step-by-step process of planting and nurturing that we heard in Isaiah. Now the vineyard people rise up to ask, "Why destroy us?" and to plead for God to try again, "Restore us, O Lord God of hosts; let your face shine, that we may be saved." Again, the preacher might profit from investigating the tension between God's love for a people for love's sake and God's love for mission's sake.

Jesus, in the passage from Matthew, employs Isaiah's vineyard allegory and then improvises it so that it suits the Gospel's religious landscape. From a strictly poetic standpoint, Jesus weakens the allegory by introducing tenants, slaves, and the absentee landlord. Of course, he does this so that the characters in the allegory will correlate directly with the characters of our history. It sounds odd to our ear when the tenants reason that by killing the heir they would inherit the property. A bit of reflection suggests that the only way this makes sense is if they are assuming (or acting as if) the owner is dead so that "squatter's rights" would kick in. Jesus' purpose is not to create a watertight allegory (an extremely difficult task) but to make sure his opponents get the point. Which, according to verse 45, they do.

> Jesus' purpose is not to create a watertight allegory but to make sure his opponents get the point.

The allegory and the explanation of it have the unfortunate effect of encouraging a supercessionist reading—that is, that the prominent place of the former tenants (the Jews) has now been superceded to new tenants (the Christians). Preaching that presents anything like this naïve equation about the relative roles of Jews and Christians is irresponsible. This is especially true insofar as Matthew tends to treat the religious leaders as one-dimensional enemies of Jesus and God's Reign. Congregations that use the lectionary read in its fullness could be reminded of the readings from Romans 9–11 (Propers 13–15) where Paul expresses agony and affection for the situation of the Jews, and comes to a different conclusion.

Jesus' citing of Psalm 118 is a bit awkward in the hearing. The key to the transition is connecting the cornerstone to the son and heir who is killed (rejected) in verse 38. But even at that, the parable ends not with a new vineyard built on the rejected cornerstone but with the same vineyard now run by new management. At the passage end, the religious leaders are facing the same conundrum they mused about when Jesus asked about John the Baptist (Matt. 21:25-27). They are stymied from carrying out their religious and political judgment because they know it won't play well with their public.

216

THE SEASON
AFTER
PENTECOST

HANK J.
LANGKNECHT

As is often the case, the preacher's challenge is leading hearers into this text without settling for the easy (and faulty) assumption that the religious leaders unambiguously represent either the real-life historical leaders whom Jesus encountered or, worse, contemporary Jews. Under the general rule that any group shed in a bad light in the sermon should be identified somehow with the congregation, the preacher would be wise here to challenge the church about its stewardship of God's vineyard, its treatment of God's Word, and (hearkening back to Isaiah) whether the fruit it yields is justice and righteousness for the world.

SEMICONTINUOUS READINGS

EXODUS 24:1-4, 7-9, 12-20 (RCL)
PSALM 19 (RCL)

A lot has happened since the scene we heard last week from Exodus 17. The Israelites have reached Mt. Sinai, been consecrated as God's holy people, and received the Ten Commandments and the first installments of the entire law code. In addition, God has promised them victory so that when their journey ends they will possess the land of Canaan. Now it is time for the covenant to be sealed.

The climax of this portion of the narrative is Moses reading the entire book of the covenant and having the Israelites answering with one voice, "We will do it!" Then follows the sprinkling of the blood of the covenant; the relationship between God and God's people is sealed by the symbol of life: blood. Then Moses and Joshua enter into the glory of God so that the terms can be set in stone.

The semicontinuous reading is not selected to match thematically with the Gospel, but this week there is a resonance. The fact is, the people of God do commit to and then fail to obey the covenant (we remember that Moses will come down the mountain to find the people worshiping the golden calf). We, the people of God, promise to nurture babies who are baptized, we promise to support couples who are married, we promise to honor our pastors and other leaders "for their work's sake." And we fail. Generally, let us hope, we make the vow in good faith; though sometimes we know even as we say "we will, by the help of God," that we won't. Preaching on this passage could take us right into the mystery of our covenant with God—infinite God allied with broken humanity bound together by blood. Were it not for the fact that now it is the blood of the new covenant, how would we stand?

> Preaching on this passage could take us right into the mystery of our covenant with God—infinite God allied with broken humanity bound together by blood.

Psalm 19 opens with a gorgeous anthropomorphism: the heavens and the earth tell about God's glory. The sun comes out to greet the day beaming like a groom after the wedding night. Even though nature uses no words and no speech, still there is a *telling*. But words are also God's gifts; they are the means by which the things that must be told are given shape and brought into conversation with our lives. The law of the Lord is the essence of this gift. The law is perfect; it revives the soul, gives refreshment and enlightenment, and it inspires our rejoicing.

The psalmist is more realistic than the people receiving the law on Sinai. The psalmist knows that no mortal can keep the law. It is God who detects our faults and keeps us from error. Only with God's help are we blameless. This is the necessary corrective for times when we begin to imagine ourselves as God's equal.

SECOND READING
PHILIPPIANS 3:4B-14 (RCL)

In chapter two Paul celebrates the self-emptying of Jesus and exhorts the Philippians to have that "same mind" in themselves. In this reading Paul will testify to his own willingness to empty his own life of prerogatives so that he may have a full relationship with Jesus Christ. The law is holy, just, and good and the elements of his life that Paul is regarding are good things accomplished in service to God. And yet these can be—must be—set aside if he is to live life in Christ. An intriguing rhetorical turn is that Paul regards all gain as *loss*. Paul's argument would be strong enough were he merely to say that his gains are worthless rubbish. But he goes beyond that to say that they are loss, that somehow even good things when they are attached to our striving, our work, our choices actually have us moving backward.

We are invited here into the great mystery. To receive the righteousness that comes from the cross is to trust God unassisted by any resources at all. Even the good things of this life have a negative impact on our trust. On the one hand we may be tempted to accumulate them in order to barter for salvation (works righteousness); on the other we may see them as our due, or more benignly as the fringe benefits of life in Christ (election righteousness?).

> To receive the righteousness that comes from the cross is to trust God unassisted by any resources at all. Even the good things of this life have a negative impact on our trust.

They are neither. When we bear them proudly as marks of our identity, they are relics and remnants of an irrelevant accounting system. Jesus did not count equality with God a thing to be grasped; he gave that up of necessity; this is the essence of the "mind of Christ." The question hangs there: If equality with God was an impediment to obedience, what case can we make to cling to anything?

A powerful sermon on this passage might walk us through verses 4-6 using contemporary categories. The climax would be to suggest that even our identity

218

THE SEASON
AFTER
PENTECOST

HANK J.
LANGKNECHT

as Christians (let alone as Lutherans or as Presbyterians or as Roman Catholics) might be an impediment to trusting in Christ alone. If we are not willing to be stripped of our deepest identity (even our Christian identity), there is a chance that our trust is in that identity and not in Christ.

Paul's rhetoric takes a paradoxical turn in verses 12ff. Having stripped himself of the credentials and prerogatives given by birth or won by his effort, Paul then readopts "goal" and "striving" language. Perhaps this odd turn is Paul's response to a particular false teaching of which he is aware in the community at Philippi. Or it may be that this paradox is the logical conclusion: to rest in *anything—even in his belief that he rests in nothing*—compromises the true goal: to know only Christ and the power of his resurrection.

PHILIPPIANS 3:14-21 (BCP)

This passage continues the paradox of the section just completed insofar as the first main thought ends with ". . . let us hold fast to what we have attained." How odd to talk here about holding fast after waxing so eloquently about kenosis and the affirmation that all gains are losses. A way out of the starkest form of the paradox is to recall that part of what we have attained is that accumulation of Christ's and the Spirit's movement in the community. Mundane, ordinary events become for us evidence of the resurrection life. They come and go, they cannot be collected, they hardly convince us (let alone the world), and yet they nourish and sustain the community in the face of opposition.

In verse 17 Paul contrasts the "ideal group" (those who wish to be identified with him) with those "enemies of the cross of Christ." The terms Paul uses for them are odd: "their god is the belly," "their glory is in their shame," and "their minds are set on earthly things." There is the clear sense that the Philippians will know who he is talking about (even if we do not). Paul's condemnation, though, is a tearful one (here we think again of his agonizing in Romans 9 about his "own people"). It is striking that Paul's condemnation is brief; what other attitude could he have given that he has just taught how even *good things*—honorable lineage, devout study, and hard work—are impediments to unity with Christ. Paul does not spend a lot of time on the opponents; instead he encourages the church to focus on the goal, to look toward the transformation that is coming.

> Paul encourages the church to focus on the goal, to look toward the transformation that is coming.

PHILIPPIANS 4:6-9 (LFM)

See the second reading for the Twenty-Second Sunday after Pentecost, Proper 23 (October 12, 2008), below.

THE SEASON AFTER PENTECOST / ORDINARY TIME

PROPER 23 THROUGH REIGN OF CHRIST SUNDAY AND THANKSGIVING

BEVERLY A. ZINK-SAWYER

There is nothing "ordinary" about Ordinary Time! If we subscribe to the centuries-old Christian belief that every Sunday is "a little Easter" because our weekly gatherings bear witness to the day of Christ's resurrection, then even the Sundays we observe in Ordinary Time are extraordinary. The Scripture texts for the last several weeks of lectionary Year A reflect the extraordinary nature of this portion of the liturgical year as they tell the stories of ordinary people doing extraordinary things. We read of Moses and Joshua and Deborah who led their people against formidable enemies. We hear the words of the prophets who proclaimed an unwelcome message of destruction in the midst of the people's comfort and complacency. We watch the Christians of first-century Thessalonica wrestle with questions of faith not unlike the questions that trouble us as twenty-first-century believers. And we listen as Jesus teaches what it means to live as members of the new kingdom he came to establish on earth. In all these words, we are shown how to live with extraordinary faith in the ordinary circumstances of our own lives because of the God who has been ever faithful to us.

A closer look at the lections that conclude this liturgical year reveals themes of holiness, faithfulness, obedience, and responsiveness—all to be practiced as we live *in* and *into* God's promised kingdom. Texts from the closing chapters of the Gospel of Matthew serve as the primary readings for this portion of Year A. We find Jesus in Jerusalem in the days between his triumphal entry and his crucifixion. Parables and teachings are interspersed between skirmishes with the

220

THE SEASON
AFTER
PENTECOST

BEVERLY A.
ZINK-SAWYER

scribes and Pharisees, all painting a portrait of Jesus' understanding of life in the kingdom of God. The complementary first readings (except for All Saints' Day/ Sunday) are drawn from a variety of First Testament materials including Torah and Wisdom literature but primarily prophetic writings. This emphasis on the prophetic witness is appropriate given the fact that the prophets were proclaiming their own vision of the coming day of the Lord, a vision not unlike the vision of the kingdom of God proclaimed by Jesus. These themes are echoed in the emotional expressions of the psalms that serve as commentary on the first readings. The psalmist articulates our hopes, fears, and thanksgivings as we seek to find our place in the vast kingdom of God. The second readings for this period are drawn primarily from Paul's first letter to the Thessalonians and read in a continuous fashion. They relate the struggles of a young community of believers trying to live out their faith amidst cultural hostility and theological doubts.

The Revised Common Lectionary offers an optional text for each week's first reading that provides a series of semicontinuous lections related to the wilderness journey of the Israelites and their conquest of Canaan. This optional stream of readings might well provide several weeks of "teachable moments" for preachers seeking to increase the biblical knowledge of their congregations. Indeed, the most common concern I hear voiced by preachers these days has to do with the so-called biblical illiteracy of many church members: the lack of familiarity with basic names, stories, and concepts from the Bible. In response to this postmodern dilemma, Christian preachers and teachers continually search for new ways of teaching the old stories. The texts about Moses, Joshua, Deborah, and the triumphs and tragedies of the people of Israel that comprise this period Ordinary Time tell of a God who continues to love us and lead us even when our faithfulness wavers. In addition, these stories of Israel's journey and settlement lend themselves to a sermon series focused on such topics as the faithfulness of God, great leaders of Israel, or our human response to God's goodness. Many preachers have discovered great interest among their listeners in series of sermons on an announced set of topics. The second and Gospel readings might also give rise to such a series as the preacher looks at lessons learned from the church at Thessalonica or Jesus' teachings on righteous living as members of the kingdom of God.

The final weeks of the liturgical year include three days dedicated to special observances.[1] The first festival day is November 1, All Saints' Day, which may be celebrated with a special service on November 1 or observed the following day during Sunday worship. The texts for all three lectionaries for that day hold before us examples of what saintly living looks like according to Scripture. The liturgical year culminates in the celebration of Christ the King or Reign of Christ Sunday. In beautiful scriptural images we are invited to renew our faith in the One who

221

THE SEASON
AFTER
PENTECOST

———

BEVERLY A.
ZINK-SAWYER

reigns triumphant over all and empowers us to live faithfully in his name. Thanksgiving Day, the final of the three special days, occurs this year between the end of one liturgical year and the beginning of another, not an inappropriate time to pause to give thanks for God's care for us in all times and seasons.

Through these weeks of this final portion of the church year, we hear the question: How shall we then live until the promised day of the Lord? From these words and experiences across Scripture, we hear the answer: we are to live faithfully, joyfully, and responsibly. As preachers, we have the great gift of proclaiming, even on the "ordinary" days, the good news of all that God has done for us. How extraordinary!

Note

1. Commentary on the texts for Reformation Day/Sunday, celebrated primarily in Lutheran churches on October 31 or on the immediately preceding Sunday, which has previously been included in the seasonal volumes of *New Proclamation*, may now be found in *New Proclamation Commentary on Feasts: Holy Days and Other Celebrations*, ed. David B. Lott (Minneapolis: Fortress Press, 2007).

TWENTY-SECOND SUNDAY AFTER PENTECOST

TWENTY-EIGHTH SUNDAY IN ORDINARY TIME / PROPER 23

OCTOBER 12, 2008

Revised Common (RCL)	Episcopal (BCP)	Roman Catholic (LFM)
Exod. 32:1-14 or Isa. 25:1-9	Isa. 25:1-9	Isa. 25:6-10a
Ps. 106:1-6, 19-23 or Psalm 23	Psalm 23	Ps. 23:1-3a, 3b-4, 5-6
Phil. 4:1-9	Phil. 4:4-13	Phil. 4:12-14, 19-20
Matt. 22:1-14	Matt. 22:1-14	Matt. 22:1-14 or 22:1-10

The texts for today remind us of our faithful God who provides deliverance from danger and oppression and who invites us to feast at the table of grace. That same God, however, expects our faithful response in return.

FIRST READING

EXODUS 32:1-14 (RCL)

The Exodus story of the golden calf is one of the most memorable stories to emerge from the wilderness journey of the Hebrew people. Perhaps it is so memorable because we see our own nature reflected in the behavior of the ancient Israelites gathered at the base of the mountain while Moses, their leader, is on Mt. Sinai in conversation with God. It is a story of human impatience, selfishness, ingratitude, and fear—human qualities, unfortunately, that are timeless.

The incident occurred in the middle of the exodus from Egypt to the promised land. Many hardships had been encountered and transcended, including hunger and thirst. Complex laws, including the Ten Commandments, had been given by God and received by the people. A covenant between God and the people had been marked by a blood sacrifice. When Moses presented the book of the covenant to the people, they responded, "All that the LORD has spoken we will do, and we will be obedient" (24:7). Moses sealed the deal by taking blood from sacrifices offered to the Lord and dashing it first against the altar and then on the people, saying, "See the blood of the covenant that the LORD has made with you in accordance with all these words" (24:8). From that moment, the centrality of the covenant for the identity of the Israelites became evident, giving rise to the construction of the tabernacle and the ark of the covenant along with the ritual practices that accompanied them. Thus the flagrant violation of the covenant by the people as demonstrated in the golden calf incident represents more than disobedience; it is a rejection of the very purpose and identity of the people called and cared for by Yahweh.

The story is particularly interesting—and "preachable"—because of its portrayal of the nature of both human beings and God. Though we are separated from this story by millennia, the human proclivities that drive the Israelites to act "perversely" (v. 7) are well known to us, making it easy to find homiletical analogies to life today. The first unit of the chapter (vv. 1-6) relates the exchange between the people of Israel and Aaron, their designated leader, in the absence of Moses. When Moses "delayed to come down from the mountain," the people grew impatient and demanded that Aaron "make gods" (v. 1) for them. With the gold gathered from their jewelry, the image of a calf was cast and worshiped by the people, complete with an altar, burnt offerings, and a festival. Perhaps the ultimate insult to the Lord was the declaration that this graven image was the one who had delivered the people from the land of Egypt (v. 4).

> This story reminds us that not all objects of our spiritual longing are equal; many are, in fact, idolatrous and even dangerous.

We see in this incident the human longing to acknowledge a power beyond human ability, a longing to worship and put our trust in something mysterious and greater than ourselves. Some might call this the human quest for spirituality. This story reminds us that not all objects of our spiritual longing are equal; many are, in fact, idolatrous and even dangerous. Yet we can point to numerous idols in our own contemporary context—money, power, possessions—that claim our loyalty in perhaps a less obvious but more insidious way. The Israelites' willingness to ignore the covenant and worship an idol was prompted by impatience and fear: impatience in "waiting on God" to care for them in God's own time and way, and fear that they had been abandoned. How often do we grasp for ephemeral things because we, too, are impatient and fearful?

Perhaps the most unusual dimension of this story, however, is its portrayal not of humanity but of God. The God represented in this text is One who displays amazingly human emotions. In the face of the disobedience of the people and their disregard for the covenant relationship, God expressed anger and disappointment. "Now let me alone," God implored Moses, "so that my wrath may burn hot against them and I may consume them" (v. 10). The implication is a God who is seething with anger to the point of desiring single-minded, solitary

> God hears our prayers and answers them in ways that are often surprising and far more generous than we could ever imagine.

224

THE SEASON
AFTER
PENTECOST

BEVERLY A.
ZINK-SAWYER

concentration on the betrayal that has occurred. How ungodly a response—and how human! Rather than instilling within us fear of a vengeful, angry God, however, these characteristics should comfort us with the realization that we, indeed, have been made in the image of a God who feels as deeply as we have been created to feel—and feels not only the negative emotions of anger and disappointment expressed in this text but positive emotions such as love and forgiveness. Those positive emotions are revealed in the surprising twist in the story when, the text declares, "the Lord changed his mind about the disaster that he planned to bring on his people" (v. 14), acquiescing to Moses' plea. Here we are reminded of the power of our intercessions on behalf of ourselves and others. God hears our prayers and answers them in ways that are often surprising and far more generous than we could ever imagine.

ISAIAH 25:1-9 (BCP, RCL ALT.)
ISAIAH 25:6-10A (LFM)

This reading from Isaiah sets forth some of the themes that will unfold in other lections for the day, especially the themes of God's care for God's people and of the sumptuous eschatological feast that demonstrates God's goodness. The context of the reading is the preexilic community of Isaiah of Jerusalem, or "First Isaiah," as opposed to the exilic community of later chapters of the prophetic book. The opening verses of the passage (vv. 1-5) form a unit that praises God for God's faithfulness in delivering the people from their enemies. The implication is that God has destroyed the dwelling place of those who wished the people of the Lord harm, making their "city a heap, the fortified city a ruin" (v. 2). The "palace of aliens" has been destroyed and "will never be rebuilt" (v. 2). The result of God's work of deliverance is that God will be glorified by the "strong peoples" who recognize God's righteousness and feared by the "ruthless nations" who do not (v. 3). The beautiful metaphorical language praising God that closes the unit draws on meteorological images, describing God as "a shelter from the rainstorm and a shade from the heat," the One who protected the people from "the blast of the ruthless" that came "like a winter rainstorm," from "the noise of the aliens" that descended "like heat in a dry place" (vv. 4-5). God's care came like "the shade of clouds," subduing the heat of the ruthless (v. 5). Such images evoke moments when God shelters *us* from the storms of life and perhaps even from ruthless enemies.

> Perhaps the most beautiful—and compelling—image of the text is the promise that God "will wipe away the tears from all faces."

Once the people are safe, God gathers them on the "mountain [of] the Lord of hosts," welcoming them to a "feast of rich food" and "well-aged wines" (v. 6). But such a lavish banquet is only a prelude to the ultimate demonstration of God's goodness, for God promises to destroy every-thing that threatens to harm God's people, including the final enemy of death (v. 7). "All peoples" are invited to this eschatological banquet, making the promise one that extends down through the ages to all who trust in the Lord, including us. Perhaps the most beautiful—and compelling—image of the text is the promise that God "will wipe away the tears from all faces" (v. 8). What a promise! What a hope we have in our faithful God when our faces are stained with tears of dis-appointment and fear. We who gather regularly at the Lord's table are reminded of the promise of the heavenly banquet to come, and we glimpse at that table the work of our faithful God who has "swallow[ed] up death forever" and who "wipe[s] away the tears from all faces."

RESPONSIVE READING
PSALM 106:1-6, 19-23 (RCL)

Psalm 106 is a lengthy recitation of the history of the Israelite people. Like any historical account, it emphasizes particular episodes and events in that history and offers its own critical commentary on the various people and events involved. The opening verses invite the community to give praise to the Lord because of the "steadfast love" and "mighty doings" (vv. 1, 2) of the Lord. The verse that follows this brief declaration of praise quickly shifts from the works of the Lord to the response of the people, stating the "happy" condition of "those who observe justice" and "do righteousness" (v. 3). The complementary nature of divine work and human responsibility echoes the message of the first reading from Exodus. Once the goodness of God and the character of the righteous are established, the psalmist turns to a personal request for God's favor. Anticipating the verses that follow, which recount God's deliverance of the people of Israel, the psalmist petitions God for a similar display of favor and deliverance (v. 4), hoping to share in the joy and praise of God's people (v. 5) while acknowledging their sin (v. 6).

The concluding verses of today's lection recount the incident of the golden calf described in the first reading from Exodus. By their action, the psalmist says, the people exchanged "the glory of God for the image of an ox that eats grass" (v. 20). They "forgot God, their Savior," the One "who had done great things" and "wondrous works" and "awesome deeds" for the Hebrew people (vv. 21, 22). The final verse of the passage remembers Moses, who "stood in the breech" (v. 23) lest God destroy the people.

226

THE SEASON
AFTER
PENTECOST

BEVERLY A.
ZINK-SAWYER

PSALM 23 (BCP, RCL ALT.)
PSALM 23: 1-3A, 3B-4, 5-6 (LFM)

The familiar and beloved "shepherd psalm" appears elsewhere in this year's lectionary (see Christ the King/Reign of Christ Sunday, below.) In the context of today's readings, it functions as a reiteration of the sovereignty and care demonstrated by God for God's people. God the Shepherd destroys our enemies, even the ultimate enemy, death.

SECOND READING

PHILIPPIANS 4:1-9 (RCL)
PHILIPPIANS 4:4-13 (BCP)
PHILIPPIANS 4:12-14, 19-20 (LFM)

This text from Paul's letter to the Philippians includes his final words of encouragement, advice, and exhortation to the people of the church at Philippi. The passionate feelings of the apostle for the members of that congregation are evident from the opening verse in which he describes the readers as "my brothers and sisters, whom I love and long for, my joy and crown" (v. 1). Perhaps those deep feelings are the reason he begins his exhortations by urging two of the members, Euodia and Syntyche, women who had "struggled beside [Paul] in the work of the gospel," to "be of the same mind in the Lord" (vv. 2-3). The feelings of affection Paul has for this community and the good work he has observed them doing must not be threatened by any personal disagreements.

Paul's exhortations invite the community to demonstrate several qualities becoming of Christian believers. Those qualities begin where we must always begin as God's beloved people: rejoicing in our relationship with the Lord (v. 4). Other qualities include gentleness, trust, and persistent prayer. Paul encourages us to "let [our] requests be made known to God" (v. 6), bringing to mind the fervent plea of Moses on behalf of the people in the first reading, the plea that caused God to refrain from destroying the people. We will never know precisely how prayer works for us or for God, but Paul indicates that, through our prayers, "the peace of God, which surpasses all understanding," becomes real to us, guarding our "hearts" and our "minds in Christ Jesus" (v. 7).

> In an age when we seem to be surrounded by discontent, Paul's words are a welcome reminder of what it means to be a Christian in the twenty-first century.

Two of the lections include Paul's words of thanks to the Philippians for supporting his ministry as well as his statement on contentment. In an age when we seem to be surrounded by *dis*content, Paul's words are a welcome reminder of what it means to be a Christian in the twenty-first century. Few people today appear to be satisfied with what they have, no matter how much it is, and are driven to pursue more and more no matter the cost. All communities of faith have within them examples of people who live faithful lives that challenge the cult of acquisitiveness. The preacher might lift up such exemplary lives of simplicity and trust, reminding the listeners that "God will fully satisfy every need" of ours "according to his riches in glory in Christ Jesus" (v. 19).

The Gospel
MATTHEW 22:1-14 (RCL, BCP, LFM)
MATTHEW 22:1-10 (LFM ALT.)

Matthew's parable of the wedding banquet continues the day's themes of God's graciousness and our faithful response. It portrays the kingdom of heaven in an allegorical story of a king who gave a wedding feast for his son. The narrative begins when the king sends his servants out to issue invitations to the guests. The first surprise of the story is that the invited guests refuse to come. Undaunted, the king sends out more servants with the message that the dinner has already been prepared. But again the invitees refuse, this time mocking the servants and even mistreating and killing them. Enraged by the response, the king fights back, destroying the murderers, burning their city, and declaring that the invitees were not worthy anyway. He sends his servants out a third time to gather "all whom they found, both good and bad," until the wedding hall is filled.

Given the context of Matthew's Gospel, the story is more of an allegory than a parable. It recounts the historical events of Israel's rejection first of the prophets and then of the missionaries who carried the Christian gospel. The destruction of Jerusalem by Rome in 70 C.E. is echoed in the burning of the city, and the final act of opening the kingdom to the Gentile community is portrayed in the extension of the banquet invitation to unexpected guests. One of today's Gospel lections ends at this point, portraying a kingdom of heaven in which the "guests" are a mixed lot of the least and the last. The parable becomes, then, a story of the abundant grace of God that welcomes all whether or not they are worthy of that grace. That in itself is a message worth preaching and one in which we all can find ourselves. None of us feasts at the banquet of God's grace

> The parable becomes a story of the abundant grace of God that welcomes all whether or not they are worthy of that grace.

because we are worthy or because we first chose a place at the table. We have, instead, *been chosen by* God and made worthy to be part of the kingdom solely by God's grace and generosity. Such an interpretation of the text is timely for

228

THE SEASON
AFTER
PENTECOST

BEVERLY A.
ZINK-SAWYER

the Christian community that even today makes judgments about those who are worthy or unworthy to participate in the church.

The other lections, however, add the bizarre "second" parable that distinguishes Matthew's version of the story (as opposed to those that appear in the Gospels of Luke and Thomas). It is a harsh story about a guest who was not properly dressed and who is consequently cast "into the outer darkness" (v. 13) for his sartorial blunder. The transgression seems innocent and the punishment severe. What this addendum seems to convey to the Matthean community—and to the church today—however, is that even though we are graciously welcomed to the banquet feast of the kingdom, there are certain "table manners" that are expected of us. God's graciousness invites an appropriate response, just as God's covenant with the ancient Israelites demanded their faithfulness, and just as the new life in Christ described by Paul to the Philippians demanded certain qualities of behavior. There is no "cheap grace" in this kingdom—only grace freely given *and* freely accepted by our joyful, faithful response.

TWENTY-THIRD SUNDAY AFTER PENTECOST

TWENTY-NINTH SUNDAY IN ORDINARY TIME / PROPER 24
OCTOBER 19, 2008

Revised Common (RCL)	Episcopal (BCP)	Roman Catholic (LFM)
Exod. 33:12-23 or Isa. 45:1-7	Isa. 45:1-7	Isa. 45:1, 4-6
Psalm 99 or Ps. 96:1-9 (10-13)	Psalm 96 or 96:1-9	Ps. 96:1, 3, 4-5, 7-8, 9-10
1 Thess. 1:1-10	1 Thess. 1:1-10	1 Thess. 1:1-5b
Matt. 22:15-22	Matt. 22:15-22	Matt. 22:15-21

Today's lections portray a God whose power and purposes sometimes are made manifest through unlikely people and in unexpected ways. Earthly kings, leaders, and laws hold temporal sway over our lives, but ultimate power over all things belongs to God, who invites our faithful and grateful response.

FIRST READING

EXODUS 33:12-23 (RCL)

The conversations between God and Moses go on as Moses perseveres in leading the Israelites from Egypt to the promised land. The people continue to bicker, complain, and disobey, and Moses continues to intercede on their behalf for God's mercy. Last week's reading told the story of the people's sin when they constructed a golden calf that became the object of their worship in place of the one true God. The people had become restless and had begun to doubt the power and promises of God. So once again, as he had done on several previous occasions, Moses bailed them out of their transgression by convincing God to refrain from destroying them. Today's reading reveals something of Moses' *own* frustration with God's reliability as he pleads with God for some assurance that this journey they are on will come to fruition.

God grants Moses that assurance in word and in action. "My presence will go with you, and I will give you rest," God assures him (v. 14). To demonstrate that assurance, God reminds Moses of God's special name, YHWH (v. 19), given

230

THE SEASON
AFTER
PENTECOST

BEVERLY A.
ZINK-SAWYER

previously and exclusively to Moses (3:15). But now God deepens the relationship with Moses, inviting Moses to see not God's face ("for no one shall see me and live," v. 20) but to see God's back as God's glory passes by Moses while he is sheltered in the cleft of a rock.

A sincere parishioner once asked me in the middle of a Bible study if people of the First Testament were holier than we are today. To read the stories of characters who regularly conversed with God, received revelatory visions, and were empowered to perform miracles would make one think that, indeed, we are lacking some holy quality since few modern people—even very faithful people—have such experiences. Perhaps the answer is related less to our holiness than to our ability to see beyond what we expect to see. Perhaps in our scientific, skeptical age we are less willing or able than people who lived before us to see the hand of God in our lives and world. The word of assurance in this text is that God hears and responds to our earnest prayers as surely as God responded to Moses, saying, "My presence will go with you, and I will give you rest" (v. 14). That is the comforting word God continues to speak even today in our moments of frustration and doubt.

> The word of assurance in this text is that God hears and responds to our earnest prayers as surely as God responded to Moses.

ISAIAH 45:1-7 (RCL alt., BCP)
ISAIAH 45:1, 4-6 (LFM)

This text from the prophet Isaiah comes from the section of the book attributed to Second or Deutero-Isaiah (chaps. 40–55). These chapters relate the resettlement of the Israelites after their return from decades of exile in Babylon. Cyrus, the king of Persia, who allowed the Jews to return to their homeland after he conquered Babylon, is the subject of the opening of the text. This non-Jewish leader is surprisingly described as the Lord's "anointed" (v. 1), the term referring to the Messiah. The text unfolds a series of promises that God makes to Cyrus, including promises that God will "subdue nations" and "level the mountains" to allow Cyrus to accomplish his work. But God makes it clear that the accomplishments promised to Cyrus are in fact the work of God through him, and the knowledge and power given to Cyrus are the proof that it is in fact the God of Israel who calls Cyrus by name (v. 3).

> God sometimes works through those who do not know God, whether by choice or by ignorance.

Inherent in this text are several reminders of the nature and ultimate power of God. God is the One who anoints, empowers, and calls Cyrus by name, indicating an intimate, divine relationship. This is the Lord, Cyrus is told, "and there is no other; besides me there is no god" (v. 5). This is the God who forms light and darkness, who makes weal and creates woe, who does "all these things" (v. 7). What we overhear in this conversation with Cyrus is a reiteration that there is one God who creates and controls all things. God is Lord of all that we are and have and the One to whom we owe our ultimate allegiance. One other dimension of this text is interesting. God declares to Cyrus: "I surname you, though you do not know me. . . . I arm you, though you do not know me" (vv. 4, 5). Here we are reminded that God sometimes works through those who do not know God, whether by choice or by ignorance. But even those of us who acknowledge faith in God are sometimes blind to God's power and presence in our lives. Nevertheless, God's work in us, through us, and for us never ceases, so that all may know the Lord (vv. 6-7).

Responsive Reading
PSALM 99 (RCL)

This psalm of praise is one of a series of "enthronement psalms" celebrating the reign of God as king. Proof of God's goodness and worthiness of worship is presented through a list of the qualities of God, including God's holiness, love of justice, and establishment of equity. Added to those qualities making God worthy of praise is the fact that God answered the cries of his priests Moses, Aaron, and Samuel (v. 6). God spoke to them, forgave them, and even avenged their wrongdoings (v. 8), and they in turn kept God's decrees (v. 7). The psalm expresses the theme within today's lections of a sovereign God who remains faithful to us even as we are called to faithfulness to God, who hears and answers our prayers, and who works through human agents by blessing them with divine power.

PSALM 96:1-9 (10-13) (RCL alt.)
PSALM 96 or 96:1-9 (BCP)
PSALM 96:1, 3, 4-5, 7-8, 9-10 (LFM)

Psalm 96 also is numbered among the enthronement psalms offering praise to God who reigns as king over all things. In this particular psalm, all things include the peoples and the nations of the world but goes beyond those to call all of creation to praise God. The heavens, the earth, the sea, the field, and the trees of the forest together will rejoice and sing for joy. Thus we are reminded of our unity with all creation in the presence of God. The close of the psalm anticipates the coming of the Lord "to judge the earth" (v. 13). The ominous nature of such an event is tempered by the conviction that God "will judge the world with righteousness, and the peoples with his truth" (v. 13).

232

THE SEASON
AFTER
PENTECOST

BEVERLY A.
ZINK-SAWYER

SECOND READING

1 THESSALONIANS 1:1-10 (RCL, BCP)
1 THESSALONIANS 1:1-5B (LFM)

The Christian community at Thessalonica, the capital city of Macedonia, found itself at the center of a number of cultural and religious conflicts. As a major city of the Roman Empire, it reflected Roman interests and values, interests and values that were likely to come into conflict with the interests and values of the fledgling Christian church. Not least among the sources of conflict was the question of allegiance to the Roman emperor versus allegiance to Christ as Lord. Thus Paul's letters address the struggles of the Thessalonian Christians as they figured out how to live out their new faith in the midst of an often-hostile culture. The letters also hold forth the hope of Christ's coming again since, at the time of their writing around 50 or 51 C.E., the Thessalonian church was not far removed from Jesus' resurrection and promise to return. Given the difficulties of living as Christians in the Roman world, the Thessalonians and other early believers longed for the day when Christ would return in glory to establish the kingdom of God on earth.

Paul's first letter to the Thessalonians begins as we might expect such a letter to begin: with the identification and greetings of the writers. It follows the standard form for a letter of its day in the opening salutation. Paul, Silvanus, and Timothy greet the church at Thessalonica in the name of God and the Lord Jesus Christ. While probably authored by Paul, he writes on behalf of all three of them, indicating their close companionship and work in ministry. Paul offers thanksgiving to God for the members of the church community and for their "work of faith and labor of love and steadfastness of hope" in the Lord (v. 3). When understood in the context of the challenges that faced this church, Paul's commendation is particularly poignant. He then reminds the people of their divine election, of the fact that God has "chosen" them (v. 4). Perhaps the reminder of having been chosen mitigates whatever struggles and persecutions they faced. The proof of their "chosenness" was in the ways in which the gospel message took root among them. They not

> Paul seems to indicate that the holistic work of the gospel was made manifest in the faithful living of the Thessalonian church.

only heard the "word," but they received it "in power and in the Holy Spirit and with full conviction" (v. 5). Paul seems to indicate that the holistic work of the gospel was made manifest in the faithful living of the Thessalonian church.

That living out of the gospel is confirmed in the following verses. "In spite of persecution," the Thessalonians "received the word with joy inspired by the Holy Spirit" and "became an example to all the believers in Macedonia and Achaia" (vv. 6, 7). The faith of the Thessalonians became known far and wide in the Roman world. Reports about their church had returned to Paul, confirming his own experience of welcome among the community and his witness of their conversion from idol worship to the worship of God.

The message to the first-century Thessalonians is a message equally relevant for the twenty-first-century church. Some Christians live under the threat of physical, or at least social, persecution. For most of us in the Western world, however, the threats to our faith are less obvious but more insidious. We live in a culture and in subcultures that are often apathetic or even hostile to Christian faith. Some contemporary scholars have characterized us as "exiles" within our own homeland, using the First Testament exilic imagery. Paul's words encourage us to hold fast to our faith in spite of worldly challenges and to seek "joy inspired by the Holy Spirit," so that we might become an example to others.

THE GOSPEL
MATTHEW 22:15-22 (RCL, BCP)
MATTHEW 22:15-21 (LFM)

The confrontations between Jesus and the Jewish leaders continue during his final days in the city of Jerusalem. This particular encounter was a deliberate attempt to trick Jesus into saying something that would be worthy of action on the part of the authorities who "wanted to arrest him" (21:46) because of his dangerous teachings that threatened the status quo and his popular appeal among the people. So "the Pharisees went and plotted to entrap him in what he said" (22:15), showing their determination to get Jesus to hang himself, as it were, by his own words. In their quest to entrap Jesus, the Pharisees enlisted strange bedfellows: the Herodians. Ordinarily the Pharisees, devout Jews who lived every letter of the law (and were not sympathetic toward Rome), and Herodians, Jews who were aligned with the Roman leader Herod Antipas, would make unlikely allies, but here we find them united in their common contempt for Jesus. The "test" to which they put Jesus would reveal the usefulness of having both Pharisaic and Herodian witnesses to his answer since it would be difficult for Jesus to respond in a way that pleased both.

The test was preceded by transparently insincere words of flattery. Declaring their awareness of Jesus as one who is sincere, who teaches the way of God with truth, and who regards everyone impartially, they zing him with a question about the payment of taxes. "Is it lawful to pay taxes to the emperor, or not?" (22:17). Any answer would anger some of the questioners and perhaps even put Jesus' life in jeopardy. At its core, the question had nothing to do with taxes; instead, it had everything to do with Jesus' regard for Rome and the emperor. He was

234

THE SEASON
AFTER
PENTECOST

BEVERLY A.
ZINK-SAWYER

asked, essentially, if he supported the Roman government or not. To answer *no*, he would be branded a political insurgent; to answer *yes*, he would renounce his Jewish heritage and mission and alienate his own Jewish people.

In his inimitable way, Jesus discerned the trap and along with it the "malice" (v. 18) of the questioners and asked for a coin, a symbol of the domination of Caesar and a fact of Jewish life in first-century Palestine. Rather than let himself be caught in the trap by yielding to either side, Jesus left the questioners "amazed" (v. 22) when he pointed to the image of the emperor on the coin, declaring, "Give therefore to the emperor the things that are the emperor's, and to God the things that are God's" (v. 21). Jesus' answer reiterates the inextricability of the various dimensions of our lives and respects the temporal worlds in which we live while acknowledging the ultimate sovereignty of God. His pronouncement on the question, giving this incident the designation of a "pronouncement story" in Gospel literature, silenced the authorities, and "they left him and went away" (v. 22).

> Jesus' answer reiterates the inextricability of the various dimensions of our lives and respects the temporal worlds in which we live while acknowledging the ultimate sovereignty of God.

Perhaps the most important thing to remember when interpreting and proclaiming this text is what it does *not* say. A number of interpreters of this text through Christian history have turned to it to defend the doctrine of separation of church and state. Jesus' answer to the Pharisees and Herodians, however, cleverly declares precisely the opposite. The reality is that no matter who we are or when or where we live, every human being exists in what might be described as concentric spheres of identity. We live in nuclear and extended families and in neighborhoods and states and nations. We live under the influence of religious, political, and philosophical loyalties. Jesus acknowledged the reality—and the legitimacy—of one of those spheres when he told his questioners to give to the emperor the things that are the emperor's, including imposed taxes. But the second half of his pronouncement—that we give to God what belongs to God—indicates the ultimate location of our loyalties since God, as declared in the psalms for today, is king and ruler over all things. Thus the question of separation of the spheres in which we live is moot since God remains Lord of all.

TWENTY-FOURTH SUNDAY AFTER PENTECOST

THIRTIETH SUNDAY IN ORDINARY TIME / PROPER 25

OCTOBER 26, 2008

Revised Common (RCL)	Episcopal (BCP)	Roman Catholic (LFM)
Deut. 34:1-12 or 　Lev. 19:1-2, 15-18	Exod. 22:21-27	Exod. 22:20-26
Ps. 90:1-6, 13-17 or 　Psalm 1	Psalm 1	Ps. 18:2-3a, 3b-4, 47, 51
1 Thess. 2:1-8	1 Thess. 2:1-8	1 Thess. 1:5c-10
Matt. 22:34-46	Matt. 22:34-46	Matt. 22:34-46

The practice of true holiness and obedience to God are themes of the lections for this week. The people of Israel are called to holiness through reminders of their covenant relationship with God and God's continual care for them. They witness the culmination of a holy life with the death of their leader, Moses. Jesus reiterates the call to holiness in the words of the *Shema*, the command to love God with our whole being and to manifest that love in our love for others.

FIRST READING

DEUTERONOMY 34:1-12 (RCL)

The decades of traveling through the wilderness were coming to an end for the Hebrew people. The long-awaited promised land was finally in sight. Moses climbed "from the plains of Moab to Mount Nebo, to the top of Pisgah, which is opposite Jericho" (v. 1). From there he must have had a breathtaking view of the land promised so long ago to Abraham. The view was bittersweet, however, since we know by this point in the story that Moses will not be the one leading the people to settlement in the promised land. We do not know exactly why Moses is denied the one thing he must have desired most as he endured the hardships of his monumental leadership task. Not only did he have to face the same challenges of wilderness life that the people did, but added to those were layers of responsibility, not the least of which was serving as the mediator between the often-disgruntled people and an often-angry God. Nevertheless, there are several

236

THE SEASON
AFTER
PENTECOST
─────────
BEVERLY A.
ZINK-SAWYER

references earlier in Deuteronomy (1:37; 3:27; 4:21) that point to the eventual disallowance of Moses' entry into the promised land. Whether it was God's anger at Moses for Moses' disobedience or for the disobedience of the people, the consequence of disobedience to God was severe.

This text recounts the end of the journey for Moses. Moses ascends to the top of Pisgah to view "the whole land": Gilead, Naphtali, Ephraim and Manasseh, Judah, the Negeb, and the valley of Jericho (vv. 1-3). He was allowed to drink in with his eyes a sight that we can only imagine given the years of hardship and anticipation that preceded that dramatic moment. Then there in the land of Moab, the text tells us quite matter-of-factly, Moses died. There is no cause of death other than that it occurred "at the LORD's command" (v. 5). In fact, the Deuteronomic narrator notes that Moses' "sight was unimpaired and his vigor had not abated" (v. 7). The Israelites had simply reached the brink of the promised land, and Moses had fulfilled his God-given purpose. He was buried in Moab where the people mourned his death for thirty days. Then Joshua, God's chosen successor to Moses, began his work as the people's leader, "full of the spirit of wisdom" that had been conveyed to him through Moses' hands (v. 9). An affirmation of the uniqueness of Moses concludes the text. He was unparalleled as a prophet in Israel, given divine ability to perform "signs and wonders" and "terrifying displays of power" (vv. 11, 12), first in the sight of Pharaoh and then "in the sight of all Israel" (v. 12).

There are many poignant dimensions of this report of the end of Moses' life and work. We cannot read it without a sense of indignation that Moses, who had to put up with so much from the people *and* from God, was denied the only appropriate reward for his faithfulness. We are reminded once again in this story that life—even life lived in faithfulness to God—is sometimes unfair. We are also reminded that our choices, especially choices for disobedience no matter how well intended even *they* may be, have consequences. But there is also a note of hope in this text: hope that the people, who have been led and shaped by Moses, will now honor his memory as they are led by Joshua and shaped by the law God gave through Moses. As Patrick Miller suggests, "Israel henceforth will not be led by a great authority figure but by the living word of the torah that Moses taught and that goes always with the people in the ark (10:1-5), God's word in the midst of the people."[1] It is appropriate, then, that the leading of the people by torah should begin at this point since the Torah, the five books of Moses, comes to a close with this text. Like the people of Israel, we, too, have God's law—God's word that shapes and leads us on our own journeys.

> We cannot read this text without a sense of indignation that Moses, who had to put up with so much from the people *and* from God, was denied the only appropriate reward for his faithfulness.

LEVITICUS 19:1-2, 15-18 (RCL ALT.)

Like most of the book of Leviticus, chapter 19 is a list of laws or rules setting forth human behavior. This particular chapter begins a section of the book that has been identified as the "Holiness Code," so named for the opening verses in which God commands the people to be holy as God is holy. The manifestation of holiness occurs not only through laws governing personal behavior but also through laws governing community conduct, including social, ethical, and cultic practices. Such is the focus of verses 15-18. They require the people of Israel to act with justice and impartiality in rendering judgments and to refrain from slander, hate, and vengeance, instead loving one's neighbor as oneself.

"Holiness" is not a term we use often in the community of faith today. In fact, most of us would be hard-pressed even to define holiness. Yet we all know what it looks like when we see it. Who has *not* witnessed a truly "holy" life, even as we struggle to live such a life ourselves? The preacher of this text might explore ways in which individuals and communities of faith can live into holiness, pointing to examples and qualities of a holy life.

EXODUS 22:21-27 (BCP)
EXODUS 22:20-26 (LFM)

The importance of laws in shaping the life of the people of Israel continues in this text from Exodus. The people are reminded throughout the Torah that their covenantal relationship with God is made manifest through specific expressions of personal and communal behavior. This particular set of laws relates to social and religious practices. Verse 20 reiterates the supremacy and uniqueness of the one, true God, the giver of the law. God promises to destroy anyone who shows loyalty—in this case, through sacrifices—to any god "other than the Lord alone" (v. 20). The rest of the laws in this collection relate to the treatment of others: resident aliens, widows and orphans, and those forced to borrow money due to their poverty.

Laws such as those set forth in this text remind us of the tangible way in which we live out our love for and loyalty to God. The mistreatment of others, especially "the least of these," as Jesus once described the needy, is, in reality, the mistreatment of God. Thus, as we are often reminded in Second Testament texts, a true test of our faithfulness to God is in how we treat others. Although the laws

> The mistreatment of others, especially "the least of these," as Jesus once described the needy, is, in reality, the mistreatment of God.

of the Torah often seem obscure and strange to our modern sensibilities, the intention of those laws continues to be essential to the well-being of religious

238

THE SEASON
AFTER
PENTECOST

BEVERLY A.
ZINK-SAWYER

communities today. We would be wise to heed these ancient laws as we seek to shape faithful lives. The issues of poverty, of those who are left behind by our social services, and especially of the treatment of aliens residing in our midst are timely and crucial issues for twenty-first-century communities of faith.

RESPONSIVE READING
PSALM 90:1-6, 13-17 (RCL)

Psalm 90 bears the heading, "A Prayer of Moses, the man of God," the only psalm to carry such attribution. Keeping the life—and, as noted in the first reading from Deuteronomy, death—of Moses in mind places this psalm in a particular interpretive framework. The first two verses declare the certainty of God's power and presence. God is acknowledged as the Creator, the One who brought forth the mountains and formed the earth. Before anything was, there was God; and God will continue to be after everything else ceases to exist. This is the God who remains the same "from everlasting to everlasting" (v. 2). That declaration offers us a word of assurance: the assurance that God will neither forsake us nor change despite all the ephemeral and mutable dimensions of our lives. Not only will God be with us, but we have hope that God will continue to serve as "our dwelling place" (v. 1), a place of safety and comfort, as God has served for generations past. These characteristics of God become more significant when considered in light of our human frailty and the fleeting nature of life (vv. 3-6).

With the assurance of God's faithfulness, the psalmist moves from praise to petition in the second section of this lectionary text (vv. 13-17). Because we know that God is eternal, unchanging, and faithful, we, like the psalmist, can bring before God our desires and our questions. We, also, seek to be satisfied by God's "steadfast love" (v. 14) and granted "the favor of the Lord our God" (v. 17). The final petition asks God to "prosper the work of our hands" (v. 17), reminding us that all that we are and are able to do come from the goodness of God.

PSALM 1 (BCP, RCL ALT.)

The opening psalm sets forth the contrasting life experiences of those who are considered to be "happy" (or blessed) and those considered to be "wicked." The happy are not tempted by the alluring ways of the "wicked" or of "sinners" (v. 1). Instead they spend their time delighting in and meditating on "the law of the LORD" (v. 2). The law provides a secure foundation and a constant source of nourishment for those who are steeped in it, much like "trees planted by streams of water" (v. 3) that flourish because they are securely rooted and continually fed.

In contrast, the wicked are not so rooted, leaving them vulnerable to wind and to righteous judgment.

This psalm makes a bold assertion about the consequences of righteous versus wicked behavior. The "happy" prosper while the "wicked" perish. That is the way we would like life to be, but we all know that reality is quite different. Is the psalmist merely naïve? No. The psalmist appears to be unhindered by human shortsightedness and instead sees beyond the obvious to a time and ways that the blessed really do prosper and the wicked perish. Ultimately we are called to stand firmly rooted among the righteous where the Lord watches over us.

PSALM 18:2-3A, 3B-4, 47, 51 (LFM)

Psalm 18 is a song of royal thanksgiving, a psalm of praise offered to God following a kingly victory. God is affirmed as the psalmist's "rock," "fortress," "deliverer," "shield," and "stronghold" (v. 2), images conveying qualities of unfailing strength. Even in the presence of "enemies" (v. 3) and encompassed by "the cords of death" and "the torrents of perdition" (v. 4), the psalmist prevailed and was granted vengeance (v. 47) because of the power of God. The closing verse of the text affirms the continuation of the king's dynasty through "David and his descendants forever" (v. 50).

SECOND READING
1 THESSALONIANS 2:1-8 (RCL, BCP)

As the readings in Paul's letters to the Thessalonians continue, Paul recounts the origins of the church at Thessalonica. He reminds the Thessalonian church that it emerged out of his own hardships and perseverance. He recalls having "been shamefully mistreated at Philippi" (v. 2), suggesting perhaps that he and his colleagues were not unprepared for what might be similar treatment in Thessalonica. Given the less-than-welcoming atmosphere in Thessalonica for the Christian gospel (see the discussion of last week's second reading), it is not surprising that Paul would anticipate yet more shameful treatment in another city. The success of the Thessalonian church, however, proved that the mission of Paul, Silvanus, and Timothy to Thessalonica "was not in vain" (v. 1).

Paul attributes the success of their mission to their "courage in our God to declare to you the gospel of God in spite of great opposition" (v. 2). God, Paul acknowledges, was the source of their ability to prevail despite the challenges they faced. That said, he goes on to put to rest what might have been accusations made against him and his colleagues that their work was the result of less than pure motives. He defends their ministry among the Thessalonians as a response

240

THE SEASON
AFTER
PENTECOST

BEVERLY A.
ZINK-SAWYER

to God's call. It was God who "entrusted [them] with the message of the gospel," and it was "to please God who tests our hearts" that they preached and "not to please mortals" (v. 4). Paul appeals to the Thessalonians as witnesses to the fact that he and his companions did not attempt to deceive them "with words of flattery or with a pretext for greed" (v. 5). Nor did they seek human approval—only divine.

Perhaps the most poignant dimension of this text is Paul's assertion that he and his companions demonstrated their concern for the Thessalonians by treating them gently, "like a nurse tenderly caring for her own children" (v. 7). Their feelings for the people of Thessalonica were so deep that they were moved to share with them "not only the gospel of God but also our own selves" (v. 8). Such nurturing, maternal imagery is not what we usually associate with the writing of Paul, but here we get a glimpse of the depth of feeling he had for those who shared in the work of the gospel. His words challenge us as pastors and leaders of churches today as we minister amidst what are often fractious

> Caring deeply for the people with whom we minister and helping them learn to care for one another is the only way in which the work of the church will prosper.

communities of faith. Caring deeply for the people with whom we minister and helping them learn to care for one another is the only way in which the work of the church will prosper.

1 THESSALONIANS 1:5C-10 (LFM)

See the commentary for the Twenty-Third Sunday after Pentecost (Twenty-Ninth Sunday in Ordinary Time/Proper 24), October 19, 2008, above.

THE GOSPEL
MATTHEW 22:34-46 (RCL, BCP)
MATTHEW 22:34-40 (LFM)

The sparring between Jesus and the religious leaders in Jerusalem continues during the last days of his life. Each time the Pharisees or Sadducees pose a question meant to trick Jesus into incriminating himself, he answers it unexpectedly, leaving the witnesses "amazed" (22:22) and "astounded" (22:33). He had cleverly responded to questions about paying taxes and about the resurrection of the dead. Now the Pharisees are back, and they have brought with them a "big gun," a lawyer who was one of their number. The lawyer's question was befitting of his profession: "Teacher, which commandment in the law is the greatest?" (v. 36). As we have discerned from even brief lections drawn from the Torah such as today's first readings, the commandments contained in the Law of Moses were numerous, complex, and specific. Thus the question the lawyer posed to Jesus was all but impossible to answer given the hundreds of laws Jesus would have to comb through mentally to arrive at an answer. Not only did Jesus have to contend with the vastness and complexity of the law, but to privilege one injunction above all others would be tantamount to heresy and perhaps finally give the Jewish leaders the evidence they needed to condemn Jesus.

In his great wisdom, Jesus once again responded immediately and cleverly, thwarting the Pharisaic scheme. Out of all the laws he identified the one on which, he implied, all others depended. He quoted the *Shema* set forth in Deuteronomy 6:5, commanding our love for God. By naming this law as the one that stands above all others, Jesus made it clear that all that we are and all that we are able to do (including keeping all the other laws) grows out of our relationship to God. That relationship precedes and supercedes everything else. Jesus did not stop with that one commandment, however, but attached to it a necessary second part. We demonstrate our faithfulness to the greatest commandment by our love for our neighbor, citing a commandment from the Holiness Code recorded in Leviticus 19. By juxtaposing these two commandments, Jesus makes the bold claim that love for neighbor is the ultimate expression of love for God, taking precedence over any number of other expressions. The message for us is clear, especially in an era in which love for neighbor can easily become lost in our assiduous attempts to pursue personal piety. Jesus reminds us of our obligation to God and its expression through our obligation to the community.

> Jesus reminds us of our obligation to God and its expression through our obligation to the community.

In the second part of the text, Jesus turns the tables and poses a question to the Pharisees. He asks them about their understanding of the Messiah, subtly inquiring about their understanding of *him*. They answered from their tradition, identifying the Messiah as the son of David. Jesus challenged their answer, and in doing so proved that he knew not only the Torah but also the Writings as he quoted from Psalm 110. This Matthean portrayal of Jesus places him squarely within traditional Judaism, literally rendering the Pharisees speechless, who from that day did not "dare to ask him any more questions" (v. 46). The obscure nature of this exchange does not lend itself easily to homiletical interpretation, but the question of Jesus' identity continues to be an important question for us today. That question also brings us back to the first part of this lection, for if we acknowledge Jesus as Lord of our lives, we will live in a way that honors God and all of God's creation—in other words, we will love God, our neighbor, and even ourselves.

Note

1. Patrick D. Miller, *Deuteronomy*, Interpretation, a Bible Commentary for Teaching and Preaching (Louisville: John Knox Press, 1990), 244.

ALL SAINTS DAY /
ALL SAINTS SUNDAY

NOVEMBER 1, 2008
(OR TRANSFERRED TO NOVEMBER 2, 2008)

Revised Common (RCL)	Episcopal (BCP)	Roman Catholic (LFM)
Rev. 7:9-17	Sir. 44:1-10, 13-14 or 2:(1-6) 7-11	Rev. 7:2-4, 9-14
Ps. 34:1-10, 22	Psalm 149	Ps. 24:1-2, 3-4, 5-6
1 John 3:1-3	Rev. 7:2-4, 9-17 or Eph. 1:(11-14) 15-23	1 John 3:1-3
Matt. 5:1-12	Matt. 5:1-12 or Luke 6:20-26 (27-36)	Matt. 5:1-12a

All Saints Day provides an opportunity for the church to look both backward and forward. We look back in thanksgiving for those who lived the life of faith before us and now live eternally with God. But we also look forward to the vision painted in the Second Testament of what we as the community of faith today might be.

FIRST READING
REVELATION 7:9-17 (RCL)
REVELATION 7:2-4, 9-14 (LFM)

The bizarre, apocalyptic revelation of John seems an unlikely place to turn for a text celebrating the saints of the church. Nestled in the description of the calamities provoked by the Lamb's opening of the seven seals, however, is a tribute to the "servants of our God" (v. 3) who are marked on the forehead with "the seal of the living God" (v. 2) in order to protect them from the coming devastation of the earth to be unleashed by the opening of the sixth seal (6:12—7:3). The number of those who are "sealed" with the mark of God is stated to be 144,000, according to what John "heard" (v. 4). That verse—and the number it proposes—has proved to be problematic for Christians through the centuries of the church as believers try to determine who is included among those whom God has chosen to welcome into the kingdom of heaven. Some traditions have taken the "sealing" of the 144,000—twelve thousand people representing each of the twelve tribes of Israel—literally, believing that there will be a limited number of believers received into heaven. Other traditions, like my own Calvinist Presbyterianism, have, at least in the past, promoted the doctrine of election that, while avoiding prediction of numbers, declared that only a group of elect souls predestined by God would be saved.

Biblical tradition, of course, reveals that any use of the number twelve is symbolic of completeness. With that symbolism in mind, the "one hundred forty-four thousand" (v. 4) represents not a fixed number but a large, indeterminate number. Thus, rather than a text of exclusion, this really is a text of *inclusion*: inclusion of "a great multitude" (v. 9) of the faithful whom God has gathered. The importance of the multitude is not its size. It is, indeed, a group so large "that no one could count" (v. 9). More notable than that is the multitude's composition: "from every nation, from all tribes and peoples and languages" (v. 9). This is good news for all of us, for it is clear that there is a place for all God's children in this heavenly gathering.

> Rather than a text of exclusion, this really is a text of inclusion: inclusion of "a great multitude" of the faithful whom God has gathered.

The diversity of the multitude is especially important in light of the description of the multitude's activity that follows. This text speaks of the liturgical practice of the faithful in heaven. Those gathered from all peoples and places become united in an act of worship before the Lamb. They raise their voices in praise, fall on their faces before the throne of God, and sing—practices not unfamiliar to any worshiping community. Even their garments reflect the liturgical significance of the moment: they are "robed in white" (vv. 9, 13), reflecting the baptismal practice of the early church that clothed catechumens in white robes symbolizing new life. Thus this text offers a glimpse of heavenly worship, a glimpse that provides a model for our earthly worship. Certainly our worship practices in many ways already reflect the heavenly worship portrayed here, but the composition of our "multitudes" that gather each Sunday falls, in most cases, far short of the image of diversity presented in this text. This vision of the saints of God gathered in God's presence reminds us of the diversity within the community of saints but also the unity of faith that transcends that diversity, the diversity within unity we are called to reflect as the community of faith still on earth.

If that is the word of challenge in this text, there is also a word of comfort. The saints who have fought the good fight and remained faithful unto death, those "who have come out of the great ordeal" and "washed their robes and made them white in the blood of the Lamb" (v. 14), are promised a future safe in the presence of God. They will "hunger . . . and thirst no more" (v. 16); the Lamb "will be their shepherd" and

> The saints who have fought the good fight and remained faithful unto death are promised a future safe in the presence of God.

244

THE SEASON
AFTER
PENTECOST

BEVERLY A.
ZINK-SAWYER

"guide them to springs of the water of life, and God will wipe away every tear from their eyes" (v. 17). This is the word of hope into which we live as people and communities of faith. No matter what ordeals befall us, we have a God who fills all our needs and reaches down to wipe every tear from our eyes until we are gathered with all the saints to worship before the throne of God.

SIRACH 44:1-10, 13-14 (BCP) OR 2:(1-6) 7-11 (BCP ALT.)

Sirach, known also by the Greek name Ecclesiasticus, stands in the wisdom tradition of ancient Israel. Probably written sometime between 200 and 180 B.C.E. by Ben Sira, a wise teacher who lived in Jerusalem, it sets forth a rationale for a life lived in faithful obedience to God. Such a life is characterized by particular qualities of behavior, including honesty, hard work, perseverance, wise choices, and careful speech. The second chapter conveys instruction from a parent to "my child" (v. 1), inspiring the child to find hope and direction in a relationship with and fear of the Lord, similar to instructions found in the book of Proverbs.

Chapter 44 recounts the work of the heroes of Israel's past, opening with the familiar phrase, "Let us now sing the praises of famous men" (v. 1). This list of heroes is notable for the variety of gifts attributed to them, including the gifts of leadership, wisdom, writing, wealth, and even music. All of them "were honored in their generations" (v. 7) and some have left the legacy of "a name" (v. 8) that continues to be praised. Still others have been forgotten and "have become as though they had never been born" (v. 9). Yet even they, the author asserts, "were godly men, whose righteous deeds have not been forgotten" (v. 10). The bodies of these faithful people "are buried in peace" (v. 13), but their glory, their offspring, and their names live on "generation after generation" (v. 14). This text calls us to remember *all* the saints and the many and varied gifts they shared and left for us to emulate.

> This text calls us to remember all the saints and the many and varied gifts they shared and left for us to emulate.

Our tendency is to compare legacies and honor those whose work was extensive and most visible. Often, however, the greatest legacies are left in small and quiet ways.

RESPONSIVE READING
PSALM 34:1-10, 22 (RCL)

This psalm is a tribute to the responsiveness of God to our cries for help and salvation. The first six verses are written in the first person, offering the psalmist's personal testimony to the words spoken. The opening three verses express the psalmist's own praise to God and invite others to join in that praise, but it is the following three verses that testify to why the psalmist was moved to praise. Those verses (vv. 4-6) and the personal testimony within them give hope to those of us reading these words many centuries later. Here is an obvious connection to the inclusion of this psalm on All Saints Day. Our own faith comes not so much from intellectual assent to a theory about God's goodness but from personal testimony to how God has been faithful in the lives of believers. We can trust that God will deliver *us* just as God "answered" and "delivered" (v. 4), "heard" and "saved" (v. 6) the psalmist. We are invited by the psalmist—and by all the faithful people who have gone before us—to "taste and see" (v. 8) for ourselves that the Lord is good. We are challenged by our ancestors in faith to "seek the LORD" and discover, as they did, that we then will "lack no good thing" (v. 10). The final verse of the psalm, included in today's reading, reiterates the assurance of our redemption when we "take refuge" (v. 22) in the Lord.

PSALM 24:1-2, 3-4, 5-6 (LFM)

Used as a hymn as the community entered the Temple for worship, this processional psalm acknowledges the greatness of God as Creator and the frailty of our humanity in comparison. The first couplet in this lectionary text declares that all of creation belongs to God: the earth with its seas and rivers, and the world with its many inhabitants. Cognizant of God's omnipresence, the second couplet asks if any worshiper is worthy in comparison even to approach the "holy place" of God (v. 3). While never being fully worthy to stand in the presence of God, we are assured that we can at least prepare ourselves through cleanliness of hand and heart. The reference to "clean hands" (v. 4) implies the ritual practices of cleansing before entering the Temple. In a similar but metaphorical way, we are commanded to come into God's presence with clean hearts as well—hearts that reject what is false and deceitful. The good news for us as the gathered community is that those who approach God with such sincerity, imitating the saints who have gone before us, will be welcomed, blessed, and granted God's salvation (vv. 5-6).

PSALM 149 (BCP)

Praise to God is the theme of this communal psalm. The psalmist makes reference to the "assembly of the faithful" (v. 1) and calls Israel, "the children of Zion," to "rejoice in their King" (v. 2). The people are commanded to demonstrate their praise "with dancing" and with music made on the "tambourine and lyre" (v. 3). Such references in the psalms and other First Testament materials have become

246

THE SEASON
AFTER
PENTECOST

BEVERLY A.
ZINK-SAWYER

important examples for some of our own contemporary worship practices, including liturgical dance and instrumental music. Worship leaders who are challenged by congregations for including these "innovative" practices can defend them by reclaiming the ancient and historic practices mentioned here.

The psalm takes an interesting turn in verse 4, implying that God blesses "the humble with victory." The idea of "victory" is elaborated in the following verses when the people are encouraged to hold "two-edged swords" (v. 6), to "execute vengeance on the nations and punishment on the peoples," binding their leaders and bringing judgment upon them (vv. 7-9). "This," the psalmist declares, "is glory for all [God's] faithful ones" (v. 9). Beyond these undeniably harsh words of violence and vengeance lies the reality of a God who leads God's people to victory over all the things that threaten to harm them.

SECOND READING
1 JOHN 3:1-3 (RCL, LFM)

The first letter of John is probably best known for its depiction of God's love for us and the kind of love we are to show to each other because of that prior divine love. What is often forgotten in reading this letter is that it grew out of a situation characterized by anything *but* love: a late-first-century church or group of churches that were torn apart by disagreement and eventual schism. The dispute emerged over the passing of the faith from first- to second-generation believers, not an unusual time for disagreement. The letter seeks to get at the essentials of Christian faith, the bottom-line beliefs that express what difference faith in Jesus Christ makes for those who believe in him. Among those essentials is the recognition that, no matter what befalls us or how we are treated by the world, we remain the "children of God" (v. 1). In this earthly life, we are not privileged to understand precisely what that designation means. It offers us hope, however, for this world and for the world to come. In the meantime, we are to "purify" ourselves, "just as [God] is pure" (v. 3).

> The letter seeks to get at the essentials of Christian faith, the bottom-line beliefs that express what difference faith in Jesus Christ makes for those who believe in him.

The reference to purity echoes the Gospel lesson, the Beatitudes, in which a portrait of those who are "blessed" by God—those who are called "children of God," as this epistle text and as one of the Beatitudes put it—is painted as encouragement for the perseverance of the faithful. In both texts we find both present and future dimensions: the blessings that come from the present realization that we are God's children, and the hope that one day we will be like God and see God and dwell eternally in God's presence, as do the saints we celebrate today.

REVELATION 7:2-4, 9-17 (BCP)

See the comments on today's first reading, above.

EPHESIANS 1:(11-14) 15-23 (BCP ALT.)

This text appears at the close of the liturgical year on Christ the King/ Reign of Christ Sunday in the Revised Common Lectionary (see the comments on the second reading for that day). In that context, the interpretive emphasis is on the exaltation of Christ portrayed in verses 20-23. In the context of All Saints Day, however, a different emphasis emerges as we focus on those who are called and marked by Christ and blessed as his people. The larger text (vv. 11-14) begins with a reference to the "inheritance" (v. 11) we have obtained through our connection to Christ. The idea of inheritance (repeated again in verses 14 and 18) and reference to the "saints" (*hagioi*) in verses 15 and 18 make this an appropriate text for this day. There is also a reference to believers who "were marked with the seal of the promised Holy Spirit" (v. 13), connecting to the mark sealed on the foreheads of the servants of God described in the first reading from Revelation. Gathering up these themes and references creates a picture of the community of saints, living and dead, who have been called and marked by God and who always live under the protective power of God the Father and Christ the exalted Son.

THE GOSPEL
MATTHEW 5:1-12 (RCL, BCP)
MATTHEW 5:1-12A (LFM)
LUKE 6:20-26 (27-36) (BCP ALT.)

The Matthean and Lukan renditions of the Beatitudes of Jesus comprise the Gospel lessons for this All Saints Day. The list of qualities of the ones whom God has blessed is descriptive in nature, declaring that God has granted God's favor to those who exhibit certain qualities. But this list is also *prescriptive*, offering guidance for those of us hearing these words generations later. It gives us a clear sense of the qualities we are to emulate as those who call ourselves God's people today. The descriptive qualities of God's blessed people and the prescriptive challenge set before us to strive for those qualities come together in the examples of faith we celebrate on this All Saints Day. It is an appropriate text, then, for the day when we remember those who embodied the qualities described here and who now are blessed by dwelling in the eternal presence of God.

248

THE SEASON
AFTER
PENTECOST

BEVERLY A.
ZINK-SAWYER

As is usually the case in the Gospels, the location of Jesus' teaching is significant. Matthew's Gospel places the Beatitudes very early in Jesus' ministry. He had barely emerged from his temptation in the wilderness, begun his public ministry, and called the first disciples when "his fame spread throughout all Syria, . . . And great crowds followed him from Galilee, the Decapolis, Jerusalem, Judea, and from beyond the Jordan" (4:24-25). Sometimes Jesus turned *to* the crowds to teach; at other times, such as this one, he turned *away from* the crowds for a private moment with the disciples. But the mountain to which Jesus and the disciples withdrew represented more than a change in venue. It appears to be a deliberate move, symbolic of the new law embodied in Jesus. The location enhances Matthew's effort to portray Jesus as the fulfillment of First Testament promises, the one who carries on and completes the Jewish hope for the Messiah, the new Moses climbing another mountain to convey God's *new* law for the people. (In Luke's version, Jesus came down to a level place. The "blessings" are only three in number and more eschatological in nature and followed by a series of "woes." In both texts, he turns away from the crowds and speaks to the disciples.)

The new law, or, perhaps more appropriately, the new way of *being* that Jesus proclaims in the Beatitudes of both Gospels, is a reversal of the usual way of living in the world. The world would write a different version of the Beatitudes, declaring that we are blessed when we are rich in things, when we are filled with all the good food we can eat, when we are bold, when we laugh, and when we "grab for all the gusto we can," as an ad put it some years

> The new law, or, perhaps more appropriately, the new way of being that Jesus proclaims in the Beatitudes of both Gospels, is a reversal of the usual way of living in the world.

ago. But the blessing bestowed upon the children of God, as seen in the lives of the faithful saints we honor today, is not something we earn or something that would have any value according to the world's standards of measurement. We are worthy to be called God's children and promised reward in heaven not because of what we have accumulated or how the world views us but because God has deemed us worthy of blessing.

TWENTY-FIFTH SUNDAY AFTER PENTECOST

THIRTY-FIRST SUNDAY IN ORDINARY TIME / PROPER 26
NOVEMBER 2, 2008

Revised Common (RCL)	Episcopal (BCP)	Roman Catholic (LFM)
Josh. 3:7-17 or Mic. 3:5-12	Mic. 3:5-12	Mal. 1:14b—2:2, 8-10
Ps. 107:1-7, 33-37 or Psalm 43	Psalm 43	Ps. 131:1, 2, 3
1 Thess. 2:9-13	1 Thess. 2:9-13, 17-20	1 Thess. 2:7b-9, 13
Matt. 23:1-12	Matt. 23:1-12	Matt. 23:1-12

Images of true and false leaders are juxtaposed in this week's readings. True leadership is modeled by Joshua, who leads the Israelites into the promised land, by Paul and his companions, who served the church at Thessalonica, and by Jesus, who lived and taught the virtues of humility. In contrast to those examples, the prophets Micah and Malachi warn the people against leaders who preach one thing but practice another.

FIRST READING
JOSHUA 3:7-17 (RCL)

After years of deprivation and hardship on their journey through the wilderness, the Israelites finally arrive at the day promised by God for generations: the day they step foot on the promised land. The Lord announced to Joshua that the day had come for him to take the people across the Jordan River to occupy Canaan. Notable in the opening verses of the text is the fact that God is in charge of the entire process. It was God who chose the day, "This day" (v. 7), for the final step of the long journey, and it was God who had appointed Joshua as the one to complete the work Moses had begun. The faithfulness of God in leading the people across the Jordan River became an essential part of Israel's common memory, celebrated in the texts and liturgical practices that would define them for the rest of their history.

250

THE SEASON
AFTER
PENTECOST

BEVERLY A.
ZINK-SAWYER

Acting in response to the prompting of God, Joshua orchestrated the entrance to the promised land. The crossing of the river had distinctive liturgical qualities, most of which revolved around reverence for and protection of the ark of the covenant. The ark represented the very presence of God, "the Lord of all the earth" (v. 11), for by the ark's safe arrival in the new land, the people would "know that among you is the living God" (v. 10) and God was certain to give them conquest over the present inhabitants of the land. Thus the success of the settlement in Canaan depended upon the safety of the ark. That safety was ensured by the appointment of twelve men, one representing each tribe of Israel, to serve as priests who would bear the ark into the new land.

Reminiscent of the crossing of the Red Sea earlier in the Israelites' history (Exodus 14–15), the flowing waters of the Jordan River are held back as soon as the priests carrying the ark step into it. The stanched flow of the river would have been particularly miraculous at the time of the crossing, "the time of harvest" (v. 15), when the river was full from the winter rains and mountain snowmelt. Other than the damming of the river, however, the monumental event of crossing into the promised land occurred with limited struggle and little fanfare. What fanfare there was revolved around the transport of the ark. The people followed the priests to the river and crossed into Canaan while the priests stood and held the ark in the dry riverbed.

This brief story became central to the life and faith of Israel in the promised land. Its significance lies in the text's portrayal of trust enacted and promises fulfilled. God kept the covenant made many generations before with Abraham, and the people retained faith in that covenant by means of their obedience through long years of struggle. Joshua trusted God's faith in him to carry on the tradition of leadership established by Moses. The priests trusted God to use them to provide safe passage for the people and, more importantly, the very presence of God in the form of the ark. This is a story above all else of a God who loves us enough to make a way for us when there appears to be no way. It should bring to mind those times in our lives when such a way opened miraculously before us and we were led safely into a new place. We remember and celebrate God and God's faithfulness through our own liturgical practices as we gather to worship as God's faithful people today.

> This is a story above all else of a God who loves us enough to make a way for us when there appears to be no way.

MICAH 3:5-12 (RCL ALT., BCP)

In this text, the prophet Micah denounces those who seek to lead the people by means of deceit and empty promises. The Lord warns the people through Micah to be alert to leaders who seek to lead them astray by their beautiful but deceptive rhetoric, including the promise of "peace" (v. 5). Such false prophets told the people what they wanted to hear rather than confronting the harsh realities of human corruption evident around them. In the meantime, the nation moved ever closer to destruction as Micah anticipated the day when "the sun shall go down upon the prophets" and "the seers shall be disgraced" (vv. 6, 7). The greed of the "rulers" and "priests" and "prophets" (v. 11) would lead to the destruction of Jerusalem, which "shall become a heap of ruins" (v. 12) as a result of corrupt leadership. In contrast, Micah, filled with "power" and "with the spirit of the LORD," offered a more truthful vision of reality, daring "to declare to Jacob his transgression and to Israel his sin" (v. 8). Micah does not shrink from the prophetic calling but seeks to be a voice of truth amidst the barrage of falsehoods.

Despite our distance from the ancient days of Micah, we can relate to the abuses he decries. In recent decades we have witnessed a number of notable scandals involving well-known political and religious leaders. We place enormous trust in those who hold positions of leadership in society and church— trust that political leaders will act not out of self-interest but on behalf of the common good, and trust that religious leaders will both embody and proclaim the truth of God. Yet time and again we are reminded of the humanity of our leaders who often, for whatever reasons, disappoint us by their pursuit of power and greed. Micah's timely message warns us to beware of those who would lead *us* astray with their enticing rhetoric, with words we wish to hear rather than words we perhaps *should* hear, resulting in our proclivity for following false prophets. Such misplaced faith will only lead to our own destruction.

> Micah's timely message warns us to beware of those who would lead *us* astray with their enticing rhetoric, with words we wish to hear rather than words we perhaps *should* hear.

MALACHI 1:14B—2:2, 8-10 (LFM)

Condemnation of those who provide false leadership continues in this reading from the prophet Malachi, although in this text it is specifically the religious leaders who are condemned. Malachi, who prophesied after the return of the exiles to Jerusalem and the dedication of the Second Temple (515 B.C.E.), is primarily concerned with the purity of liturgical practices. The reading opens with the declaration of God as "a great King" and the one whose "name is reverenced among the nations" (1:14b). The establishment of God's identity and universal acclaim precede a denunciation of human priests who are unwilling to recognize God's glory. As a result, they and the "blessings" (2:2) granted to them through the priestly line will be cursed. They have "corrupted the covenant of Levi" and, even worse, "caused many to stumble by [their] instruction" (2:8).

252

THE SEASON
AFTER
PENTECOST

BEVERLY A.
ZINK-SAWYER

Malachi reminds us of the responsibilities inherent in religious leadership. In these warnings to religious leaders, however, the community of laity may overhear its own call to accountability both in terms of its own faithful practices and in terms of a demand for honesty among those entrusted with leadership.

RESPONSIVE READING
PSALM 107:1-7, 33-37 (RCL)

This psalm invites the community's thanksgiving to God for redemption from various difficulties. The "redeemed of the LORD" have been saved "from trouble" (v. 2) and "gathered in" from north, south, east, and west (v. 3). The "trouble" from which God saved the people is elaborated in verses 4-7 and is reminiscent of the plight of the Israelites as they journeyed to the promised land. "Some wandered in desert wastes" (v. 4), the psalm declares, "hungry and thirsty" (v. 5) until they "cried to the LORD in their trouble" (v. 6). God "delivered them from their distress" (v. 6) and "led them by a straight way" to "an inhabited town" (v. 7). The second set of verses provides what appears to be a description of the new place to which God has led the people: a place of "springs of water" (v. 33) and "fruitful land" (v. 34), contrasting this abundance with the hunger and thirst that plagued the people before deliverance. The psalm brings to mind the crossing into Canaan described in the first reading as God's ultimate act of redemption on behalf of the people of Israel. After many years of hunger and thirst, the people are led safely into a place of abundance.

PSALM 43 (RCL ALT., BCP)

In contrast to the communal praise of Psalm 107, Psalm 43 expresses the feelings of an individual standing in the presence of God. The psalmist seeks God's deliverance from "those who are deceitful and unjust" (v. 1), commenting on the false leaders of the first reading from Micah. In the midst of "the enemy" (v. 2), God is petitioned for "light" and "truth" (v. 3) to lead the way. Such light and truth will lead to the worship of God in the Temple of Jerusalem, God's "dwelling" on God's "holy hill" (v. 3), with an implied offering on "the altar of God" and praise "with the harp" (v. 4). The concluding verse conveys a conversation within the psalmist's own soul as the psalmist finds hope and help in God.

PSALM 131:1, 2, 3 (LFM)

Psalm 131 falls within the group of psalms (120–134) known as "Songs of Ascent" assumed to have been used by the faithful on their journeys to worship in Jerusalem. It expresses a sense of humility that stands in sharp contrast to the arrogance of those described in the first reading from Malachi. The psalmist takes a humble stance with a "heart not lifted up" and eyes "not raised too high" and the avoidance of "things too great and too marvelous for me" (v. 1). Maternal imagery of "a weaned child with its mother" is used in verse 2 to convey the sense of calm that has overtaken the psalmist. In the final verse, the psalmist invites all of Israel to find similar peace through "hope in the LORD" (v. 3).

SECOND READING
1 THESSALONIANS 2:9-13 (RCL)
1 THESSALONIANS 2:9-13, 17-20 (BCP)
1 THESSALONIANS 2:7B-9, 13 (LFM)

This text is an extension of last week's second reading as Paul continues to defend his ministry among the Thessalonians. In the previous text, he defended the pure motives he and his colleagues had in bringing the gospel to Thessalonica. In today's reading, he points to additional evidence of their good intentions by reminding the Thessalonians of their "labor and toil" and how they "worked night and day" (v. 9) lest they be a burden to the community. Indeed, the "pure, upright, and blameless" (v. 10) conduct of the apostles reflected their consideration for the believers. Paul then employs the paternal image of a father dealing with his children to describe the "urging," "encouraging," and "pleading" they did to bring the Thessalonians to "a life worthy of God" (v. 12) and the acceptance of their message "not as a human word but as what it really is, God's word" (v. 13). The closing verses of chapter 2 express Paul's regret concerning a forced separation—perhaps for political reasons—from Thessalonica. He reaffirms his affection for the church by declaring it "our glory and joy" (v. 20).

This text raises interesting points to ponder. The parental image of verse 11 reminds us of the image of the church as a family. As he does in last week's lection, Paul conveys deep and intimate feelings for the community at Thessalonica and encourages them in a loving way in this portion of the letter. The object of his heartfelt pleading with the congregation is "a life worthy of God" (v. 12). What might such a life look like for us, and how might we obtain it? Paul also reminds us that we are shaped

> Paul reminds us that we are shaped by God's word—but God's word, he says, is different from a human word.

by God's word—but God's word, he says, is different from a human word. It is easy to blur the distinction between words that are human and words that are divine. The preacher might explore the characteristics and discernment of God's word to us, for it is evidence of the work of that word in us that will lead to our own glory and joy.

THE GOSPEL

MATTHEW 23:1-12 (RCL, BCP, LFM)

Yet another among the skirmishes between Jesus and the religious authorities during his last days in Jerusalem, this exchange is particularly sharp in its rhetoric directed against the scribes and the Pharisees. It is a very public confrontation as Jesus speaks not just to the religious leaders or to the disciples, as he does in earlier texts, but "to the crowds and to his disciples" (v. 1). It appears that Jesus wishes for the scribes and Pharisees to overhear his words of condemnation before addressing them directly (beginning with verse 13).

Jesus sets up his words of warning by establishing the credibility of the scribes and Pharisees. He notes that they "sit on Moses' seat" (v. 2), implying that they are responsible for communicating the Law of Moses to the people. This makes any abuse of their position and power even greater, for they have been entrusted with the religious nurture of the community both by God and by a long tradition of leaders commissioned to pass on the Jewish faith. Sadly, while they know the law better than any others in the community, "they do not practice what they teach" (v. 3). Jesus is careful, however, to distinguish the legitimate teachings of the religious leaders from their negligent behavior. "Do whatever they teach you and follow it" (v. 3), Jesus tells his listeners, confirming that even the teachings of corrupt leaders remain righteous. The law is not compromised despite the abuses of its purveyors. The flaw was not in the law itself, which the people should continue to obey, but in the inability of certain leaders to remain faithful to it. Jesus then enumerates various ways in which abuse of the law was evident in the actions of the scribes and Pharisees. Those abuses included the addition of burdensome interpretations to the already-complex law, ostentatious displays of piety and ritual practices, and the cultivation of special recognition in deference to their religious roles.

In verse 8, Jesus shifts his discourse from condemnation of the religious leaders to instruction intended for the crowds and disciples. They are told not to seek the honorable human titles of "rabbi" or "father" or "instructor," for those

> Jesus is careful to distinguish the legitimate teachings of the religious leaders from their negligent behavior.

titles belong only to God, the "one Father—the one in heaven," and to "the Messiah" (v. 9). Rather than seeking human adulation, Jesus challenges his listeners to practice humility and servanthood, for only those "who humble themselves will be exalted" (v. 12).

In order to understand the impact and intention of Jesus' words, we must juxtapose them next to many other words of Jesus through the Gospels, words that call believers to humility and to lives of faithful service freely given on behalf of others. Matthew's Gospel speaks to believers struggling to understand how to live out their faith following the destruction of the Temple in Jerusalem and amidst escalating conflicts over traditional Jewish and new Christian practices. Here and elsewhere in Matthew, especially in the Beatitudes and the whole Sermon on the Mount, Jesus creates a vision of the community of faith as he intends it to be. That community is marked by qualities of humility, generosity, and equality.

> Jesus creates a vision of the community of faith as he intends it to be, marked by qualities of humility, generosity, and equality.

TWENTY-SIXTH SUNDAY AFTER PENTECOST

THIRTY-SECOND SUNDAY IN ORDINARY TIME / PROPER 27
NOVEMBER 9, 2008

Revised Common (RCL)	Episcopal (BCP)	Roman Catholic (LFM)
Josh. 24:1–3a, 14–25 or Wisd. of Sol. 6:12–16 and Amos 5:18–24	Amos 5:18–24	Wisd. of Sol. 6:12–16
Ps. 78:1–7 or Wisd. of Sol. 6:17–20 and Psalm 70	Psalm 70	Ps. 63:2, 3–4, 5–6, 7–8
1 Thess. 4:13–18	1 Thess. 4:13–18	1 Thess. 4:13–18 or 4:13–14
Matt. 25:1–13	Matt. 25:1–13	Matt. 25:1–13

As we move toward the close of the liturgical year, we encounter texts that speak of our ultimate hope in the promised day of the Lord and ways in which we can live faithfully in the meantime. We are reminded that we are not to be concerned about the details of the Lord's coming—neither its timing nor form. Instead, we are to continue to live out our promises to God and others.

FIRST READING
JOSHUA 24:1-3A, 14-25 (RCL)

By this point in the book of Joshua, the people of Israel had settled into a life very different from the nomadic existence of their ancestors who had traversed the wilderness. The exigencies of sheer existence that had consumed the attention of the Israelites who followed Moses and, later, Joshua into the promised land were replaced by concerns about the conquest and division of land and the dangers of syncretism as the Israelites came into contact with foreign peoples and practices. The temptations facing the Israelites in Canaan were different from but no less significant than the temptations that had plagued their wilderness journey.

One of those temptations—the temptation to abandon the God who had brought the people of Israel out of the land of Egypt and had entered into a covenant relationship with them—was both old *and* new. It was old in the sense that the people had repeatedly become discouraged and disobedient on their journey, sometimes provoking the wrath of God as well as the wrath of their leader, Moses. But the temptation to turn from God was also new in that along with the comfort of settlement in the promised land came a sense of complacency. Now that they had achieved the goal of a settled life in the land promised to their ancestors, there was less uncertainty to keep them faithful to the God and commitments of the past. There is something about human nature that draws us to faith when we are in need but resists those same commitments when we seem to be prospering on our own. It is the same dimension of human nature that causes people to flock to churches in times of war and community crisis only to disappear after the crisis has abated. The Israelites stayed close to God when their need for God's provisions was great, but once they had obtained a degree of comfort

and security in their new land, they were in danger of becoming complacent and drifting away from God.

In order to ensure the faithfulness of the people in the face of their success, Joshua called for a communal renewal of the covenant with God. He gathered the people before their leaders and reminded them of the great work God had done in fulfilling the promises made to Abraham. As he and other leaders of Israel had done and would later do, Joshua spoke the words of the Lord, recounting the history of the people's journey and conquest and making clear the mighty acts of God along the way. In light of that dramatic summary of events, Joshua put before the people the choice between faithful service to the God who had redeemed them, or service to ancient and foreign gods. Joshua made his own choice clear in

the familiar words of verse 15: "But as for me and my household, we will serve the LORD." The people added their assent to Joshua's choice, remembering all that God had done for them. That was not enough, however, for Joshua pressed them, as if he were asking, in the parlance of a recent television game show, "Is that your final answer?" The "holy" and "jealous God" (v. 19) who had saved them would not tolerate their fickleness should they find other gods more attractive. But the people held firm to their decision, bearing witness to their own commitment. As testimony to this act of commitment, "Joshua made a covenant with the people that day, and made statutes and ordinances for them at Shechem" (v. 25).

This text reminds us of the choices we face and the commitments we are called to renew as we meet the challenges of each day. Some years ago, before I was married, I read an article by a marriage counselor who made the point that couples don't say "I do" just one day of their lives. Instead, even the strongest

258

THE SEASON
AFTER
PENTECOST

BEVERLY A.
ZINK-SAWYER

marriages demand that spouses say "I do" again and again and again as they live out the realities of life together. I found that idea interesting, but it didn't mean a whole lot to me—until I got married myself. And now I realize how true that writer's words are. Marriage is a commitment that doesn't mean much until you experience the joys and sorrows, the plenty and want, the sickness and health that mark the seasons of life. The same is true of our commitment to God. It is only when tested in the fires of life—even the "fires" of comfort and complacency—that our commitment reveals its true mettle. And while in some ways the commitment to be faithful to God is difficult to keep, especially when we "see the sights that dazzle," as an old hymn puts it, it really makes life simpler, for all the decisions we are called to make are rooted in that prior decision to remain faithful to God.

AMOS 5:18-24 (RCL ALT., BCP)

The text from Amos, identified as a shepherd of Tekoa who prophesied during the first half of the eighth century B.C.E., warns of the coming "day of the LORD." The prevailing expectation for the long-promised day of the Lord was filled with hope and anticipation. It was believed that God would rescue God's people with great fanfare and drama, a cause for great rejoicing. It certainly was *not* envisioned as a day of accountability and distress as portrayed in these words of woe. This less sanguine account of the day of the Lord, however, sets us up for the eschatological themes that mark the conclusion of the liturgical year and the beginning of Advent.

The words of this text reflect the theme of the prophet: a warning of the judgment that will come upon Israel for its failure to remain faithful to God. In its pursuit of prosperity, the nation had neglected its spiritual and ethical responsibilities. Throughout this prophetic book, Amos calls the people back to their original commitments to God. In doing so, he echoes the sentiments of other prophets as well as the words of Jesus in the Gospels, all of whom remind us of the necessity of congruence between our words and actions. Here Amos reminds his own people—and *us*—of the relationship between our liturgical practices and our social witness. He challenges us to move beyond the confines of temple or church into the places that are devoid of justice, for in such witness we reveal our true commitment to God.

> Amos reminds his own people—and *us*—of the relationship between our liturgical practices and our social witness.

WISDOM OF SOLOMON 6:12-16
(RCL ALT., LFM)

The Wisdom of Solomon, a deuterocanonical/apocryphal book attributed to King Solomon, addresses the Jewish community scattered beyond the geographic bounds of Israel. In such foreign contexts, it was not easy to remain faithful to the practices that shaped the people before the Diaspora. As a result, the temptations to yield to the ways of the dominant Hellenistic culture were great. This text reflects a common understanding of wisdom as personified in a woman, an understanding familiar to us from the book of Proverbs. The writer challenges the Jews, no matter where they reside, to pursue Wisdom as a source of the true and godly life. What is interesting and reassuring in this text is the fact that Wisdom may indeed be "found by those who seek her" (v. 12). Wisdom—that is, knowledge of the right paths to travel and the right things to do—is not as elusive as we might think. Instead, for "those who love her" (v. 12), Wisdom is "found sitting at the gate" (v. 14) and "graciously appears to them in their paths, and meets them in every thought" (v. 16). If we think of Wisdom in terms of the knowledge and presence of God, we are assured that God is wherever we happen to be, waiting patiently and graciously to lead us in God's righteous ways.

RESPONSIVE READING
PSALM 78:1-7 (RCL)

The psalmist calls the people together as a teacher gathering a class. The "teaching" (v. 1) to be shared is a recitation of Israel's history in the form of a "parable" (v. 2), as occurred at Shechem as described in the first reading, so "that the next generation might know" (v. 6) the mighty acts of God on behalf of the people of Israel. The teaching includes the "decree" and "law" (v. 5) established by God and the covenant made with their ancestors for all generations. Included in the teaching, however, are not just the "glorious deeds" and "wonders" (v. 4) of the Lord but also "dark sayings from of old" (v. 2), things that the people might want to forget. Instead, "they will not hide them from their children" (v. 4), indicating that even the dark moments of our past can enlighten the future. The honesty and self-awareness expressed in this psalm are qualities worthy of note, encouraging us to acknowledge our mistakes lest we repeat them. Only by remembering both the good times and the bad can we "set [our] hope in God" (v. 7) who is ever faithful.

WISDOM OF SOLOMON 6:17-20 (RCL ALT.)

The alternate first reading from Wisdom of Solomon continues in this text. The first reading established the availability of Woman Wisdom for those who seek her. This text sets forth a rationale for *why* one should seek Wisdom, with each benefit building upon the previous one. Wisdom begins with a desire for instruction, which reveals a love of Wisdom, which indicates one's obedience to Wisdom's laws, which results in the assurance of immortality, which ultimately "brings one near to God" (v. 19) and the "kingdom" (v. 20).

PSALM 70 (RCL ALT., BCP)

This psalm appears in almost identical form as part of Psalm 40 (vv. 13-17). In both versions, the psalmist prays for deliverance and with it the condemnation of those who seek to do the psalmist harm. "All who seek [God]" are called to "rejoice" and declare that "God is great!" (v. 4). The psalm ends with an acknowledgment of the psalmist's condition as "poor and needy" and the assurance of God as "my help and deliverer" (v. 5). In these words we find a range of human emotions not unfamiliar to us, including a cry for help, a call for vengeance, an eruption of praise, and an acceptance of the frailty of humanity in the face of God's power.

PSALM 63:2, 3-4, 5-6, 7-8 (LFM)

Having "looked upon [God] in the sanctuary" (v. 2), the psalmist is moved to a beautiful and personal hymn of praise. The evidence of God's "power and glory" (v. 2) and "steadfast love" (v. 3) leads to the liturgical acts of praise and blessing and the lifting of hands in petition. God has filled the psalmist "as with a rich feast," evoking the psalmist's praise "with joyful lips" (v. 5). A beautiful image of the safety and shelter offered to us by God appears in verse 7 when the psalmist sings for joy "in the shadow of [God's] wings." The soul of the psalmist "clings to [God]," upheld by God's "right hand" (v. 8). We are reminded in this psalm of our own need and longing for God, expressed so well by Saint Augustine in his words, "Our hearts are restless until they rest in thee."

1 THESSALONIANS 4:13-18 (RCL, BCP, LFM)
1 THESSALONIANS 4:13-14 (LFM ALT.)

The *parousia*, the second coming of Christ, was foremost in the minds of first-century Christians. They struggled to hold on to a tenuous faith in the face of persecution, secular temptations, and the hostility of the culture around them. Doubt and confusion about the teachings of Christianity had begun to seep into the community, especially among the newest converts. In an effort to shore up the faith of the church at Thessalonica, Paul offers a word of hope regarding those who have already died and who, the Thessalonians feared, might not then be able to partake in the promised day of Christ's coming. The result is a passage of this first letter to the Thessalonians that some regard as the most important passage of Paul's letters to that church. Perhaps the significance of Paul's words lies in their timelessness, for they speak to all of us who are both Christian and mortal. It was the hope of the resurrection and the promise of eternal life that gave the early Christian community its identity even as those beliefs shape our identity as the church today. Indeed, as Paul put it, because of Christ's resurrection we do "not grieve as others do who have no hope" (v. 13).

In answering the Thessalonians' concern, Paul shares his vision of what the day of resurrection will look like. Upon the Lord's command, "with the archangel's call and with the sound of God's trumpet" (v. 16), the Lord will descend from heaven to receive first believers who have died and then those still alive. What is most important in this vision of Paul is his declaration at the end of this text when he states that we all "will be caught up in the clouds together with them to meet the Lord in the air; and so we will be with the Lord forever" (v. 17). That is the crux of the text and the word of hope that speaks even to those of us who await Christ's second coming almost two millennia after these words were written.

The Christian community continues to express widely divergent views of just what Christ's second coming will look like and how faithful Christians, living and dead, will participate in that day. In proclaiming this and similar eschatological texts, we would do well to remember that Paul's intention in these words to the Thessalonians was to offer encouragement and hope, *not* to provoke fear and dread and speculation. Two thousand years after the first coming of Christ, we still await the promised second coming. The precise time and form of the *parousia* remain a preoccupation of some groups of Christians. Our call, however, is not to spend our precious time on earth with eyes focused on the heavens but instead to live fully and faithfully in the moment and in the world God has given us.

> Paul's intention in these words to the Thessalonians was to offer encouragement and hope, not to provoke fear and dread and speculation.

262

THE SEASON
AFTER
PENTECOST

BEVERLY A.
ZINK-SAWYER

THE GOSPEL
MATTHEW 25:1-13 (RCL, BCP, LFM)

The preoccupation of the early church with the *parousia*, and particularly its delay, continues to be evident in this Gospel text from Matthew. The parable of the wise and foolish bridesmaids opens a series of three parables at the conclusion of Jesus' public ministry in Matthew 25. All three parables offer commentary on the questions of what the day of the Lord's coming will look like and when it might occur.

The parable that comprises today's Gospel reading portrays an impending wedding celebration. In characteristic style, Jesus introduces the parable with a reference to the kingdom of heaven, telling his listeners, "Then the kingdom of heaven will be like this" (v. 1). Ten bridesmaids prepare to welcome the groom (probably an allegorical reference to Jesus), taking with them lamps to light the way. Early on, the parable identifies the bridesmaids as "wise" and "foolish," with five of each, the description based on their supply of oil. The amount of oil they carried might not have posed a problem except for the fact that the bridegroom was delayed. When he finally arrives, after the bridesmaids had fallen asleep, the "wise" were prepared to do their appointed job and meet him while the "foolish" futilely tried first to borrow and then buy additional oil. By the time the foolish ones had replenished their supply, the wedding banquet had begun, and they were shut out of the festivities. With this story in mind, Jesus admonishes his listeners to "Keep awake therefore, for you know neither the day nor the hour" (v. 13).

The parable seems to exude harshness, judgment, and a clear lack of concern for sharing our abundance with others. In other words, it seems to be contrary to the many things Jesus taught according to the previous twenty-four chapters of Matthew. The parable's intent is not to contradict the faithful practices encouraged by Jesus but instead to discourage unhelpful preoccupation with things not given to us to know, including the time of the ultimate culmination of his ministry in the promised kingdom of heaven. While it is not for us to know *when* that culmination will occur, it *is* our responsibility to remain watchful and faithful—qualities portrayed in the preceding verses in Matthew (24:36-51)—until the promised day of the Lord. In discerning what it means to be watchful and faithful, we are brought back to all those earlier teachings of Jesus, allowing those teachings and this seemingly harsh eschatological vision to coexist. The time for generosity and sharing is *not* at the moment of the kingdom's coming but *now* as we live gratefully and gracefully in the sure and certain hope of the coming of the Lord.

> The parable's intent is not to contradict the faithful practices encouraged by Jesus but instead to discourage unhelpful preoccupation with things not given to us to know.

TWENTY-SEVENTH SUNDAY AFTER PENTECOST

THIRTY-THIRD SUNDAY IN ORDINARY TIME / PROPER 28

NOVEMBER 16, 2008

Revised Common (RCL)	Episcopal (BCP)	Roman Catholic (LFM)
Judges 4:1-7 or Zeph. 1:7, 12-18	Zeph. 1:7, 12-18	Prov. 31:10-13, 19-20, 30-31
Psalm 123 or Ps. 90:1-8, (9-11), 12	Psalm 90 or 90:1-8, 12	Ps. 128:1-2, 3, 4-5
1 Thess. 5:1-11	1 Thess. 5:1-10	1 Thess. 5:1-6
Matt. 25:14-30	Matt. 25:14-15, 19-29	Matt. 25:14-30 or 25:14-15, 19-21

The themes of waiting, watching, and preparedness continue in the readings for this next-to-last Sunday of the liturgical year. Hope for the promised day of the Lord is expressed in both First and Second Testament texts. While that day may "come like a thief in the night," as Paul suggests, those who have been faithful caretakers of God's gifts will be granted the joy of salvation.

FIRST READING
JUDGES 4:1-7 (RCL)

The struggles of the Israelites to settle into the land of Canaan continue in this text from the book of Judges. Early in the book, we read of the chaos that ensued among the tribes of Israel after the death of Joshua and their inability to conquer the nations inhabiting Canaan because of their perpetual unfaithfulness to God. Left to their own devices without an identifiable leader (as Moses and then Joshua had been), the people grew fractious and disobedient. They "did what was evil in the sight of the LORD and worshiped the Baals; and they abandoned the LORD, the God of their ancestors" (2:11-12). In response, "the anger of the LORD was kindled against Israel, and he gave them over to plunderers who plundered them, and he sold them into the power of their enemies all around" (2:14). Moved by the distress of the people, however, as was so often the case, God in God's mercy "raised up judges, who delivered them out of the power of those who plundered them" (2:16). Thus began a cycle of disobedience, punishment, repentance, forgiveness, and new leadership that characterized generations of Israelite history.

264

THE SEASON
AFTER
PENTECOST

BEVERLY A.
ZINK-SAWYER

It is in the midst of one of these cycles that the events of today's reading take place. This would be just another story in the historical narrative of the judges of Israel except for the fact that this judge is a *woman*. Deborah, "a prophetess, the wife of Lappidoth" (v. 4), is chosen by God to judge the people and, with the help of her military commander, Barak, lead them against King Jabin of Canaan and his army commander, Sisera. We have in this text a stunning example from the First Testament of the power of women anointed by God. Deborah's work as a prophetess, judge, and military leader enable the Israelites to vanquish yet another enemy in their conquest of Canaan. The lection ends with God's promise to give Sisera into the hands of Barak, but the story that follows tells of the decisive triumph of Barak and Deborah *together* over King Jabin. Equally notable is the fact that Deborah's success is aided by the brave if gruesome effort of another woman, Jael, who secures the promised victory by driving a tent peg into the head of Sisera. The bravery of these two women and the stunning victory they provoke is recounted in the "Song of Deborah" that comprises chapter 5. Throughout the history of Israel and into the life of the church today, Deborah, along with other female prophets and leaders, has been celebrated as an example of how God chooses and uses women for divine purposes.

> We have in this text a stunning example from the First Testament of the power of women anointed by God.

ZEPHANIAH 1:7, 12-18 (RCL ALT., BCP)

This text from the prophet Zephaniah, written sometime during the reign of King Josiah in the seventh century B.C.E., conveys a message not unlike last week's first reading from Amos that portrayed a dark vision of the day of the Lord. Zephaniah calls for silence in the face of the promised day (v. 7), but it turns out to be an ominous silence that bespeaks the devastations rather than the celebrations to come. While the people expected a joyful deliverance, Zephaniah warns that God "will punish the people who rest complacently on their dregs" (v. 12). Those who have been preoccupied with accumulating wealth and building houses and planting vineyards will not enjoy the fruits of their labors and will not escape the wrath of the Lord to come. The real problem was not what the people had done in terms of becoming complacent and acquisitive but what they had *not* done: remain faithful to God. They had pursued other attractions and put their trust in other things, abandoning the one thing—obedience to God—that would grant them true security. The people had stored up their "treasures on earth" rather than in heaven, as Jesus put it in the Sermon on the Mount. The warning extends to us, to those who live in a time and place where it is easy to rest complacently on our wealth and accomplishments, forgetting our allegiance to the One who was and is and is to come.

The "Ode to a Capable Wife" concludes the book of Proverbs. It is a fitting conclusion in that it brings the collection of wisdom sayings full circle to its early portrayal of Woman Wisdom, the one to be sought and valued as the means to a godly life. The ode takes the form of an acrostic poem with each line beginning with a letter of the Hebrew alphabet in order. The verses of the lection attest to the value and trustworthiness of the capable wife and praise her industriousness. She cares for her family through her handwork and also opens her hands in service to the poor and needy. She runs her household with great ability and commitment. For all of her attributes and for the good work she does, she is praised not only by her family but by the community as well. Thus we find in this description qualities of faithfulness to be desired and emulated not unlike the faithful qualities of Woman Wisdom.

Upon first glance, this First Testament portrayal of woman appears to stand in stark contrast to that of the Revised Common Lectionary's first reading for today from Judges. Deborah, the judge and military hero, exhibited qualities that would seem to be quite antithetical to those of the capable wife. Another look, however, reveals more similarities than differences between the two women. The wife of Proverbs 31 fulfills her vocation with diligence, dedication, and determination. She also demonstrates sincere care for her family and people of the greater community. In all her work, she "fears the LORD" (v. 30) and is deserving of praise "in the city gates" (v. 31). Deborah demonstrated similar qualities as she responded to God's call (surely an example

> The wife of Proverbs 31 fulfills her vocation with diligence, dedication, and determination.

of her fear of the Lord), risked her life for her people, and ruled with wisdom and courage. Her good work was praised "in the city gates" through the song recorded in Judges 5. Both portrayals of strong and godly women provide a challenge to *all* of us—men and women alike—to exhibit similar qualities as we live out our own vocations and relationships in obedience to God.

RESPONSIVE READING
PSALM 123 (RCL)

Psalm 123 invites us to "lift up [our] eyes" (v. 1) in order to receive the goodness and mercy of God. The images used to express our relationship to God are images of a subordinate individual to his or her superior. Our eyes look to God as a servant to his master or a maid to her mistress (v. 2), hoping, as they do, to find mercy. Implicit in these images is the expectation that the one in the superior

266

THE SEASON
AFTER
PENTECOST

BEVERLY A.
ZINK-SAWYER

position in the relationship—God, in the psalmist's case and ours—can be trusted to dispense mercy. Thus the psalmist petitions God to "have mercy upon us, for we have had more than enough of contempt" (v. 3). The reason for the petition is elaborated in the final verse when the psalmist refers to the "scorn of those who are at ease" and "the contempt of the proud" (v. 4). The psalmist reveals nothing more about the nature of the affliction, but it is not hard to imagine people and situations that might prompt us to cry out to God in a similar way.

In those times when we feel overwhelmed by the rejection of others, especially as we try to pursue what is just and right, we can be assured that God returns our gaze with mercy. Indeed, there is something compelling about looking into the eyes of another. Perhaps the eyes truly are "the window on the soul," as has been suggested, for it is impossible to look into someone's eyes and not see the depths of his or her true emotions, things we often miss in outward appearances and actions. This psalm invites us to explore all that can be revealed when we look deeply into each other's eyes and then lift our human eyes heavenward to God.

PSALM 90:1-8, (9-11), 12 (RCL ALT.)
PSALM 90 OR 90:1-8, 12 (BCP)

This psalm appeared a few weeks ago as the responsive reading for the Twenty-Fourth Sunday after Pentecost in the Revised Common Lectionary. In that context, these words attributed to Moses provided a response to that day's first reading from Deuteronomy recounting the death of Moses. In the context of today's lections, it offers commentary on the reading from Zephaniah with its vision of the day of the Lord. The psalm records a private conversation between the psalmist and God in which the psalmist acknowledges the eternal presence and greatness of God in the face of human mortality. Juxtaposed with the words of Zephaniah, the psalm affirms the power of God who created all things but can just as easily "sweep them away" (v. 5) like a dream. We and all of creation exist by the word and will of God for whom "a thousand years . . . are like yesterday" (v. 4). We cannot help but be struck by this portrayal of God's might and the ephemeral nature of the things that seem so lasting and secure to us. It puts our human worries into cosmic perspective. Perhaps the most significant word of this text for us, however, comes in verse 12 when the psalmist asks God to "teach us to count our days that we may gain a wise heart." Only by the grace of God can we learn to live each day we have been given fully and faithfully.

PSALM 128:1-2, 3, 4-5 (LFM)

267

TWENTY–SEVENTH
SUNDAY AFTER
PENTECOST
———
NOVEMBER 16

The psalmist paints a picture of the ideal life and home. A theme of the psalm is that the "happy" (v. 1) and "blessed" (v. 4) life is built upon fear of the Lord. That concept echoes the first reading from Proverbs in which the capable wife is described as one "who fears the LORD" (Prov. 31:30). Personal prosperity as defined by happiness, plenty, and a pleasant family life issues from a right relationship with the Lord. The text closes with a blessing upon the individual and upon the future of the community as represented by "the prosperity of Jerusalem" (v. 5).

SECOND READING

1 THESSALONIANS 5:1-11 (RCL)
1 THESSALONIANS 5:1-10 (BCP)
1 THESSALONIANS 5:1-6 (LFM)

Paul's acknowledgement of the Thessalonians' interest in the *parousia* continues as he moves toward the close of his first letter to the church. The first three verses of the chapter remind the readers of the unknown nature of the day of the Lord. As in other recent lections, Paul expresses in this text a sense of confidence in the Lord's coming, but along with that confidence is the firm belief that the time and nature of that event cannot be discerned—nor should those questions preoccupy the thoughts of believers. Using the image of a "thief in the night" (v. 2), he reiterates the dramatic, unexpected nature of the day of the Lord. To the image of the thief in the night he adds the image of a pregnant woman suddenly struck by labor pains. In the midst of "peace and security," Paul warns, will come "sudden destruction" (v. 3).

Paul's intention in this text is *not* to instill fear in the believers at Thessalonica about the Lord's coming, however. His intention is just the opposite: to offer hope and encouragement. The faithful Thessalonians "are not of the night or of darkness" but "are all children of light and children of the day" (v. 5). The unfaithful may "fall asleep" (v. 6) and "get drunk at night" (v. 7), rendering them unprepared for the coming of the Lord as the foolish bridesmaids of last week's Gospel reading. But those who trust in the Lord will remain awake and sober, armed with "the breastplate of faith and love, and for a helmet the hope of salvation" (v. 8). Indeed, Paul reminds his readers, God's plan for them is "salvation

> Paul's words here offer a corrective for preaching that emphasizes the darkness of impending destruction rather than the light of salvation hope.

through our Lord Jesus Christ" and not "wrath" (v. 9). With this reassurance, the Thessalonians should "encourage one another and build up each other" (v. 11).

268

THE SEASON
AFTER
PENTECOST

BEVERLY A.
ZINK-SAWYER

Even today preaching on eschatological themes and texts is intended more often to provoke fear than to instill faith. Paul's words in the final chapter of 1 Thessalonians offer a corrective for preaching that emphasizes the darkness of impending destruction rather than the light of salvation hope. That is not to say that we should minimize the cosmos-shattering dimensions of God's future as portrayed in so many biblical texts. It *is* to say that for those who put their trust in the Lord, who live as children of the light, that future can only be one of hope. In the meantime, the church is called to "encourage one another," "build up each other," and do the faithful work God has called us to do here and now in the world God has created and redeemed in Jesus Christ.

THE GOSPEL
MATTHEW 25:14-30 (RCL, LFM)
MATTHEW 25:14-15, 19-29 (BCP)
MATTHEW 25:14-15, 19-21 (LFM ALT.)

The second of the three parables that comprise Matthew 25 serves as the Gospel reading for today. As with the other two parables, this one, the parable of the talents, points to the *parousia* and offers yet another glimpse of the kingdom of heaven. The parable tells the story of a man who heads off on a journey, leaving the care of his property in the hands of his servants—a not-uncommon scenario. What *is* uncommon in this story is the fact that the "property" (v. 14) he entrusts is an enormous amount of money. He gives to each of three servants a different number of "talents," a monetary unit representing an average of fifteen or twenty years of work. As in many of Jesus' parables, the hyperbole of such unbelievable amounts of money sets up the story's intended effect. The discrepancy in the distribution of talents, Jesus tells us, has to do with the "ability" (or *dynamis*, "power," v. 15) of each servant. The property owner leaves, upon which two of the servants go off and invest their coins, doubling the investment, while the third hides his coin in the ground for safekeeping. When the owner returns, he praises the wise investors and rewards them with greater responsibility, but he is infuriated by the inertia and fear of the third, overly cautious servant. The hyperbole of the parable continues in the description of the "wicked and lazy" (v. 26) servant's fate: he is cast "into the outer darkness, where there will be weeping and gnashing of teeth" (v. 30).

Interpreters through the centuries of the church have tried to allegorize this parable as a story about Jesus' relationship to his followers after the resurrection

> Faithful living in the meantime—in the time God has given us on earth—should be characterized more by engagement and even risk than by fear and inactivity.

or turn it into a lesson on the use of our abilities. While it may have elements of both, it is primarily a lesson on how we are to live as people of faith until the promised day of the Lord. When read in light of the other lections for the day, we see that we are called to live courageously (as Deborah), responsibly (as the prophets), industriously (as the capable wife), and hopefully (as the psalmist and the Thessalonians). As Paul Simpson Duke suggests, "Jesus' point seems to be that the worst we can do is nothing."[1] Faithful living in the meantime—in the time God has given us on earth—should be characterized more by engagement and even risk than by fear and inactivity. "The parable proclaims joyous freedom under great grace," according to Duke.[2] This vision of the life God intends for us is captured in the words of Irenaeus, theologian of the second century: "The glory of God is a human being fully alive." As we consider what it means to live fully with the blessings God has bestowed upon us, "we may rightly cast an eye to the ending that will take us all, and to the hope that eternity rings with God's gladness over all who took the trustful risk."[3]

Notes

1. Paul Simpson Duke, *The Parables: A Preaching Commentary* (Nashville: Abingdon, 2005), 54.

2. Ibid., 56.

3. Ibid.

CHRIST THE KING /
REIGN OF CHRIST

LAST SUNDAY IN ORDINARY TIME / PROPER 29
NOVEMBER 23, 2008

Revised Common (RCL)	Episcopal (BCP)	Roman Catholic (LFM)
Ezek. 34:11-16, 20-24	Ezek. 34:11-17	Ezek. 34:11-12, 15-17
Psalm 100 or 95:1-7a	Ps. 95:1-7	Psalm 23
Eph. 1:15-23	1 Cor. 15:20-28	1 Cor. 15:20-26, 28
Matt. 25:31-46	Matt. 25:31-46	Matt. 25:31-46

We have reached the culmination of the liturgical year on this Christ the King Sunday. Perhaps the less monarchical, less patriarchal designation "Reign of Christ" Sunday used by many traditions today best captures the significance of the day, for it is not only the triumphant person and work of Christ that we celebrate but his assurance that his continuing reign means peace and justice for all his people.

FIRST READING

EZEKIEL 34:11-16, 20-24 (RCL)
EZEKIEL 34:11-17 (BCP)
EZEKIEL 34:11-12, 15-17 (LCM)

The reading from the book of the prophet Ezekiel sets forth several of the themes that recur in the texts for this celebratory Sunday, including the themes of shepherd and sheep, of judgment and comfort, of doom and restoration, and of the One who rules over all and will set all things right. Chapter 34 occurs early in the third division of the book of Ezekiel (chaps. 33–39) and signals a decided shift in the tone of the prophet from impending destruction to the hope of restoration. The fall of Jerusalem in 587 B.C.E. (noted in 33:21) and Israel's long years in exile tempered the prophet's message. The opening verses of the chapter (vv. 1–10) castigate the "shepherds" or leaders of Israel for their self-serving behavior and their failure to protect those whose care had been entrusted to them. In light of this abdication of responsibility on the part of those whom God had placed over the people as shepherds, God, through the prophet, declares the establishment of a new order in which God will take over as shepherd of the sheep, fulfilling the duties neglected by the once-trusted human leaders (vv. 11-14).

The new divine shepherd will do for the distraught, exiled people all that their human leaders did *not* do. Gentle care for and personal involvement with the sheep are among the qualities of the shepherd described in today's text. God will "seek out," "search for," and "rescue" the sheep. The sheep will be "gathered" and brought to a safe place—"their own land"—from the places to which they had been "scattered" on the dark day of exile. In contrast to the time of want caused by the greediness of the false shepherds, God's reign as shepherd will bring about "good grazing" on "rich pasture." Echoing the familiar image from Psalm 23, God will make the sheep "lie down" in a place of safety and abundance. Those who are lost will be found, those who are injured will be healed, and those who are weak from their abusive ordeal will be strengthened.

> In contrast to the time of want caused by the greediness of the false shepherds, God's reign as shepherd will bring about "good grazing" on "rich pasture."

Into the midst of this pastoral image, however, a clear note of judgment is inserted. The One who will feed the hungry will also destroy "the fat and the strong." The fat and the strong will be fed not with good things but "with justice." Anticipating the dimension of judgment inherent in the day's Gospel text from Matthew, this first reading makes it clear that there are consequences for one's actions and inactions. How we treat those entrusted to us, and even those whose paths we simply cross in the living out of daily life, will be judged by the One who has chosen to care for us all.

That One is the subject of the remainder of the text. God will take charge of the judgment among the sheep but will not leave the people without a shepherd to serve as God's representative in a more immediate and tangible way. God's "servant David" will feed and care for the people in their day of restoration and will serve as their "prince."

Images for preaching this ancient text are abundant. Even those of us who have never experienced physical exile have experienced various kinds of spiritual and emotional "exile" that make us long for the promises of a God who searches us out, heals our injuries, and restores us to new life. We can also relate to "shepherds," be they political leaders, family members, or other persons of authority, who have failed us and made us desire the kind of shepherd we see God to be in this text. And lest we try to abdicate our *own* responsibility for those around us, Ezekiel calls us to moral and ethical responsibility within the communities we inhabit, anticipating the vision portrayed in the Gospel text from Matthew.

272

THE SEASON
AFTER
PENTECOST

BEVERLY A.
ZINK-SAWYER

RESPONSIVE READING

PSALM 100 (RCL)

Psalm 100, one of the best-known and most beloved of the psalms, ushers us into the very presence of God as the community gathers to worship. It is a psalm of thanksgiving, and unlike many psalms, there is no shift in mood in this one—no dark images or anguished lament. Instead, it is focused solely on God, the object of the community's worship. Most of the verses begin with commands to the community ("make," "worship," "come," "know," "enter," "give thanks"), commands that we as the community of faith today should heed as we continue to be so bold as to approach God in our corporate worship.

Commentary on the text of the first reading from Ezekiel occurs in the implied image of God as our shepherd. The one praised and worshiped in this psalm is the True Shepherd of the sheep, including us, described by Ezekiel. This shepherd made us and continues to claim us and care for us. One of the contemporary confessions of the Presbyterian Church states, "In life and in death we belong to God." A similar confession of faith is made when we recite this psalm. We are affirming with sure and certain knowledge that God, who made us and gathers us into God's presence, will not abandon us no matter where we might stray. Such personal connection to the sheep brings to mind the promises made in Ezekiel's oracle that God will seek us, heal us, and restore us to new life.

This psalm conveys attitudes toward worship that we as God's present-day "sheep" would be wise to remember. First of all, it serves as a reminder that worship is about God and not about us. God is the Creator, Redeemer, and Sustainer, the One who has reached out to us and provides for all our needs. In the face of such love, we can only respond with praise and thanksgiving. Second, the psalm reminds us that worship of God, whether expressed privately or corporately, should be conducted in a spirit of joy, gladness, and thanksgiving. While the circumstances of our lives might contradict those feelings, the assurance that God's "love endures forever" and God's faithfulness extends "to all generations," even ours, should compel us always to enter God's presence with hope and joy.

> The psalm reminds us that worship of God, whether expressed privately or corporately, should be conducted in a spirit of joy, gladness, and thanksgiving.

PSALM 95:1-7 (BCP)
PSALM 95:1-7A (RCL ALT.)

The images of both king and shepherd are evident in this liturgical psalm. Like Psalm 100, it opens with an invitation to the community of faith to approach with joy and thanksgiving the One who assures our salvation. The text then moves to a declaration of the qualities that make God worthy of our praise, including the implied declaration of God as shepherd (v. 7). Unlike Psalm 100, however, this hymn declares God's ultimate authority above all other powers and invokes images from creation to express the vastness of God's reign. The God praised is "a great King above all gods" whose hand holds "the depths of the earth" as well as "the heights of the mountains." Despite the extent of God's power and responsibility, God's hand nevertheless reaches out to us, God's "people," God's "sheep." The images of God as all-powerful King and caring Shepherd stand in juxtaposition in this psalm, calling us to praise the all-powerful One who even provides for our lowly needs. The final phrase of the text challenges us to "listen to his voice" (v. 7)— a word to be heeded today and always.

PSALM 23 (LFM)

The qualities of the caring shepherd portrayed in the Ezekiel text are magnified in this familiar and comforting psalm. The psalm opens with a brief affirmation that "the Lord is my shepherd" and then moves quickly to ways in which that assurance is manifested by means of God's relationship with the believer. The images of green pastures, still waters, right paths, and restoration hearken back to the promises God made through the prophet Ezekiel. As the True Shepherd, Ezekiel declared, God would feed and quench the thirst of the people and restore them to safe places after they had been scattered and led astray by the false shepherds. Perhaps the most powerful declaration of this psalm is the simple phrase "I shall not want" that follows the opening affirmation of God as shepherd. Countless sermons could be constructed based on that one verse alone! As human beings we are prone to want: to want for basic needs of food and shelter and love, and, once those needs are satisfied, to want for more and more in what often becomes a devastating escalation of selfish desires. Hard as it is to believe at times, the psalmist assures us that, with God as our shepherd, all our wants will be satisfied.

The rest of this powerful psalm presents scenarios of danger in which we find that we are safe because of God's shepherding presence. Even in the darkest valleys through which we all are called to walk at some point in our lives, just enough light shines so that we are able to see the outline of the familiar shepherd's accoutrements of rod and staff. If we are attentive, we might even feel them prodding us into faith. Even when we are forced to dine in dangerous places, the reassuring

> This powerful psalm presents scenarios of danger in which we find that we are safe because of God's shepherding presence.

flow of oil upon our heads empowers us to endure. With such experiences of God's power and presence, we can say with confidence that all our future days

274

THE SEASON
AFTER
PENTECOST

───────

BEVERLY A.
ZINK-SAWYER

will be lived with the assurance of God's gifts of goodness and mercy. Scholars suggest that a more accurate rendering of "follow" would be "pursue," conveying the sense of God's refusal to let us go (such as the pursuit of the believer in Francis Thompson's poem, "The Hound of Heaven"). Again we are reminded of Ezekiel's True Shepherd who pursues the scattered sheep in far and dangerous places. Such assurance keeps us forever in "the house of the LORD" (v. 6), that is, forever in the presence of God.

SECOND READING
EPHESIANS 1:15-23 (RCL)

In this text from the first chapter of the letter to the Ephesians, Paul prays that the "saints who are in Ephesus" (v. 1) might be strengthened in their faith by the heavenly vision of Christ who reigns over all things. The text appears earlier in this lectionary cycle (see the discussion of the second reading for All Saints' Day, above), but it has special significance when read in the context of Christ the King Sunday. Although the monarchical image of Christ as King is not explicitly stated, the writer implies that Christ functions in such a role because God has put God's "power to work in Christ" (v. 20), placing him "far above all rule and authority and power and dominion" (v. 21).

The primary declaration of this text in the context of the celebration of Christ as King is the truth that Christ is Ruler over *all* things in heaven and on earth,

> The primary declaration of this text in today's context is the truth that Christ is Ruler over *all* things in heaven and on earth, both now and forever.

both now and forever. There is something greatly comforting for us in this declaration, for we live in the knowledge that, no matter what other claims compete for our loyalty, our only and ultimate hope is in the One whom God has seated "in the heavenly places." As Paul puts it elsewhere, *nothing* can separate us from the love of God—and, according to this text, the *power* of God—in Christ Jesus. No matter what powers threaten to destroy us personally or corporately, we see by faith beyond them with the "eyes of [our] hearts enlightened" by the "fullness of him who fills all in all" (v. 23).

1 CORINTHIANS 15:20-28 (BCP)
1 CORINTHIANS 15:20-26, 28 (LFM)

Since the first Easter Day, Christian believers have debated precisely what Christ's resurrection from the dead looked like and, even more importantly, what it means for us. In the verses immediately preceding this text from his first letter to the Corinthians, Paul sets forth a logical argument directly connecting Christ's resurrection to the content of Christian faith and to the hope of Christian believers. He then makes a bold declaration of the fact that "Christ has been raised from the dead" (v. 20), providing us poor humans who have followed Adam into sin and mortality hope for being "made alive in Christ" (v. 22).

This text is most often heard in the context of funerals or as part of Easter celebrations. It has even been popularized by means of a chorus in Handel's "Messiah." Today's Christ the King context shifts the emphasis of the text from Paul's argument for the reality of Christ's resurrection to a declaration of Christ as ruler over all things—not just "every ruler and every authority and power" (v. 24), but even the "last enemy," death. The "kingdom" is mentioned specifically in eschatological terms: in the end, when he has demonstrated his reign over all things, Christ "hands over the kingdom to God the Father" (v. 24). In the meantime, we live lives that are often tormented by Christ's enemies, the powers of this world. But our lives are also lives of faith, knowing that because of Christ's resurrection and reign, those powers can never destroy us.

THE GOSPEL
MATTHEW 25:31-46 (RCL, BCP, LFM)

Jesus' teaching in the Gospel of Matthew culminates in three parables that comprise chapter 25 and serve as his final words before the events that lead to his arrest and crucifixion. The third of the three stories, while often referred to as a parable, is better described as an apocalyptic vision of the final judgment when Christ will reign in power as king of all heaven and earth. The image of king presented by Matthew brings us full circle from the Ezekiel passage in that both texts portray a shepherd king who cares for all his people/sheep, especially those who have been afflicted by hunger, poverty, neglect, or abuse. In addition, the shepherd king in both the first reading and Gospel lessons is responsible for judging the behavior of the flock. The Ezekiel text clearly predicts destruction to fall upon those who benefited from the abuse of the weak and injured. Indeed, the entire flock, Ezekiel proclaims, shall stand before God to be judged for their treatment of their fellow sheep.

This text from Matthew anticipates a similar moment of judgment: judgment between the "sheep" and the "goats," that is, between those who were attentive to the needs of "the least of these," the "members" of the king's family, and those who ignored them (vv. 40, 45). Scholars continue to debate the precise meaning of the "nations" (*ethnē*, v. 32) who are judged and "the least of these who are members of my family" (*adelphoi*, v. 40) who are served by the faithful

276

THE SEASON
AFTER
PENTECOST

BEVERLY A.
ZINK-SAWYER

sheep. Are the "nations" political entities, or a more specific group of Gentiles (the usual translation), or individuals? Does the "least of these" include *all* who are in need or only those within the Christian community or, even more specifically, those to whom Christian missionaries were sent? Most interpreters today believe the integrity of the text is maintained by extrapolating to *all* believers and *all* the needy in light of Jesus' own ministry.

The reactions of both the blessed and the accursed in the text provide an interesting focus for preaching. The blessed are surprised at their welcome into the kingdom. They are curiously unaware of how the king's judgment was rendered and what acts led to their inclusion among the sheep. The king then apprises them of their righteous treatment of himself as represented in the needy of the world. Likewise the condemned are baffled by how they landed among the goats. "If only we had known it was you in all those needy people!" they argued before the king. The goats in the parable are condemned not because of any sin of *commission* but because of the sin of *omission*, the sin captured in the prayer of confession that asks God to forgive those things we have *not* done that we *ought to have* done. The king implies that the goats should not have needed neon signs directing them to the right thing to do. By this point in the Gospel, they had all the signs they needed by means of the example of Jesus himself, the ultimate standard for Christian behavior.

> The blessed are surprised at their welcome into the kingdom. Likewise the condemned are baffled by how they landed among the goats.

There is a danger of reducing the challenge of this text to a theology of works righteousness. Putting this story in the context of all of Jesus' teachings, it should become clear to the reader that we do acts of love and compassion not to *earn* a place among the righteous sheep or even a place in heaven but *in response to* what God has already done for us in Christ. Because God first loved us in Jesus Christ, we are free to love others—no, we are *compelled* to love others because we know no other way to respond to God's amazing love. We see the ultimate expression of that love in the incarnation, the anticipation of which begins next Sunday with the First Sunday of Advent. The notion in this text of the surprising places and faces in which we see Christ sets us up nicely for the season of Advent, for what could be more surprising than a God who comes to dwell with us in the form of a poor, helpless child born in obscurity to peasant parents? Indeed, God came to us as "one of the least of these"—and still does.

THANKSGIVING DAY

NOVEMBER 27, 2008 (U.S.A.) /
OCTOBER 13, 2008 (CANADA)

Revised Common (RCL)	Episcopal (BCP)	Roman Catholic (LFM)
Deut. 8:7-18	Deut. 8:1-3, 6-10 (17-20)	Deut. 8:7-18 or
		Sir. 50:22-24 or
		1 Kgs. 8:55-61
Psalm 65	Psalm 65 or 65:9-14	Ps. 113:1-8 or Ps. 138:1-5
2 Cor. 9:6-15	James 1:17-18, 21-27	1 Cor. 1:3-9 or
		Col. 3:12-17 or
		1 Tim. 6:6-11, 17-19
Luke 17:11-19	Matt. 6:25-33	Luke 17:11-19 or
		Mark 5:18-20 or
		Luke 12:15-21

Thanksgiving Day provides an opportunity for communities of faith to gather to acknowledge God as the source of the goodness and grace we experience. The texts for the day focus on themes of gratitude, abundance, and generosity and call us to create a lifestyle of thanksgiving centered on God rather than on material possessions or national pride. We are challenged to live in gratitude for the abundance freely bestowed upon us, but we are also challenged to cultivate generosity as the expression of our thanks to God for all God's gifts.

FIRST READING

DEUTERONOMY 8:7-18 (RCL, LFM)
DEUTERONOMY 8:1-3, 6-10 (17-20) (BCP)

The Israelites continue to journey toward the promised land. They have been reminded of their status as the "chosen" people of God (chap. 7). They were chosen not because they "were more numerous than other people"—in fact, they "were the fewest of all peoples" (7:7). Instead, they were chosen "because the LORD loved [them] and kept the oath that he swore to [their] ancestors" (7:8). This reminder is followed by a list of the things God promised to do for the people of Israel in response to their faithful obedience (7:12-26). Those promises included

277

278

THE SEASON
AFTER
PENTECOST

BEVERLY A.
ZINK-SAWYER

progeny, agricultural prosperity in the form of livestock and food, protection from disease, and the destruction of the nation's enemies. However we view it, this is a picture of abundance—abundance of material goods and peace of mind—that God paints for the chosen people.

That picture of abundance is applied to the vision of settlement in the promised land in chapter 8. After a reminder to the people to remain faithful to the commandments God had given them (vv. 1, 6) and to remember the "long way" through which God had led them through their "forty years in the wilderness" (v. 2), a portrait of the abundant land promised to them is offered. The "good land" is a land overflowing with water and sources of nourishing food, a land where the people "may eat bread without scarcity" and "lack nothing" (v. 9), a land rich in minerals such as iron and copper. This promise of abundance stands in stark contrast to the deprivation the people have endured on their journey. The caveat with which it comes, however, is the reminder that all those good things would result *not* from any work of the people but from the goodness of God. If they remain faithful and keep their part of the covenant, God will bless the people with abundance and prosperity. The faithfulness of the people must not end, however, when they occupy the promised land. Instead, they are called to remember God in their prosperity even as they called upon God in their time of want.

> The people are called to remember God in their prosperity even as they called upon God in their time of want.

This text is particularly appropriate for contemporary believers who celebrate Thanksgiving Day. North Americans are blessed to live in lands of abundance not unlike the promised land, and, in terms of the rest of the world, we are blessed with the gift of prosperity. Yet many people in our nations have succumbed to the danger of forgetting God in our prosperity. It is human nature to call upon God in our times of need but to fail to acknowledge God in our times of success. On Thanksgiving Day we have the opportunity to remember that the blessings we enjoy are *not* our own doing but gracious gifts of God. As our ancestors in faith were humbled by the gift of manna, so we are called to be humbled in the face of God's provisions for us today.

SIRACH 50:22-24 (LFM ALT.)

These verses conclude a hymn of praise to the high priest, Simon. After accepting the offerings and songs of the people, Simon blessed them by means of this prayer of praise to God. He describes God as the One "who everywhere works great wonders, who fosters our growth from birth, and deals with us according to his mercy" (v. 22), and he petitions God to "give us gladness of heart" and "peace" (v. 23) throughout our days. The God portrayed in this text is the source of all good things and thus worthy of our unending thanksgiving.

1 KINGS 8:55-61 (LFM ALT.)

This text from the first book of Kings occurs at the end of a narrative describing the dedication of the Temple. The priests and people had gathered to mark the solemnization of the first permanent home for the ark of the covenant and all the artifacts and rituals that accompanied it. After a speech reminding the people of the salvific work of God and promise of a "house" for the Lord (8:14-21) and a prayer dedicating the Temple to the work of God (8:22-53), Solomon raises his hands to bless the assembly of Israel. In this blessing Solomon again reminds the people of God's faithfulness to them as demonstrated in the promises kept to Moses and their ancestors. But Solomon leaves the people with more than a reminder of the past, for he also calls them to continue to honor their covenantal relationship with God by "walking in [God's] statutes and keeping [God's] commandments" (v. 61). By such faithfulness "all the peoples of the earth may know that the LORD is God; there is no other" (v. 60).

RESPONSIVE READING

PSALM 65 (RCL, BCP)
PSALM 65:9-14 (BCP ALT.)

Psalm 65 offers praise to God for expressions of God's deliverance in various circumstances of life. In the first stanza (vv. 1-4), the psalmist acknowledges God's faithfulness in answering prayer and forgiving transgressions. The prayers and petitions for forgiveness appear to be lifted up in a liturgical context as evidenced by references to God's "courts" and "house" and "holy temple" (v. 4). The second stanza (vv. 5-8) moves to larger venues of God's power. God's goodness is not limited to the Temple but pervades "all the ends of the earth" and "the farthest seas" (v. 5). The mountains bear witness to God's might, and the roaring seas and waves and peoples are silenced by God's power (vv. 6-7). Even those "who live at earth's farthest bounds are awed by [God's] signs" (v. 8), inferring that none can escape evidence of God's work.

The final stanza of the psalm (vv. 9-13) "portrays the world as the farm of God," according to James L. Mays.[1] Through beautiful agricultural images calling to mind the images of the promised land presented in the first reading, we are reminded that God is the One who softens the earth with showers, who causes the pastures of the wilderness to overflow and the valleys to deck themselves with grain. These good gifts of the earth "shout and sing together for joy" (v. 13), something we as the people of God are called to do in response.

> We are reminded that God is the One who softens the earth with showers, who causes the pastures of the wilderness to overflow and the valleys to deck themselves with grain.

PSALM 113:1-8 (LFM)

Praise is offered to the Lord in this psalm with no chronological or spatial limitations. The Lord's name is blessed "from this time on and forevermore" and "from the rising of the sun to its setting" (vv. 2-3). The psalmist declares that "the LORD is high above all nations, and his glory above the heavens" (v. 4). Despite—or perhaps because of—this greatness, God, who is "seated on high" looks "far down on the heavens and the earth" (vv. 5-6). On the earth God sees the poor and the needy and has compassion upon them, lifting them up from the dust to "sit with princes" (v. 8). This great God of all time and space nevertheless cares for us and our needs.

PSALM 138:1-5 (LFM ALT.)

As in Psalm 113, the attentiveness and greatness of God are juxtaposed in this psalm of praise. We overhear the psalmist in personal prayer, offering thanks and praise to God for God's love and faithfulness. The psalmist called, and God answered, increasing the psalmist's "strength of soul" (v. 3). From this personal testimony the psalmist moves to call "all the kings of the earth" (v. 4) to praise God, for "great is the glory of the LORD" (v. 5). In this call to the kings we are reminded that even the rulers who hold temporal power on earth are subject to the greatness of God who rules over everyone and everything.

SECOND READING

2 CORINTHIANS 9:6-15 (RCL)

The themes of thanksgiving, abundance, generosity, and reciprocity that characterize the readings for Thanksgiving Day are brought together in this text from Paul's first letter to the church at Corinth. The larger context for Paul's words is a discourse on the centrality of generous giving in the new Christian life, but the more specific context for this teaching is the immediate need of the Jerusalem church. The Christian community in Jerusalem, the "mother church" as it were, was in financial difficulty. A famine that afflicted the area as well as their own extreme generosity had depleted their resources, so Paul appealed to what he knew was the faithful and generous nature of the church at Corinth to assist with a collection he initiated for the suffering Christians in Jerusalem. To ensure a generous response from the Corinthians, Paul cast his appeal in terms a general statement on Christian giving.

We are expected to sow bountifully, give cheerfully, and share abundantly in order to continue to be supplied out of the abundance of God.

Central to Paul's philosophy of Christian giving is the realization that God is the source of all our blessings, but along with those blessings comes responsibility. We are expected to sow bountifully, give cheerfully, and share abundantly in order to continue to be supplied out of the abundance of God. This is not an appeal to works righteousness; instead, Paul makes it clear that through our generosity we "glorify God" and demonstrate our "obedience to the confession of the gospel of Christ" (v. 13). Yes, Paul says, sowing bountifully will enable us to reap bountifully. But the replenishment of our bounty comes in response to our faithfulness and for the purpose of continued generosity. As we give, more will be given to us as a sign of God's grace and our response to God's "indescribable gift" (v. 15).

JAMES 1:17-18, 21-27 (BCP)

This text from James conveys the idea that not only do the gifts we have to share come from God but our ability to share them also comes from God. We who have been blessed so graciously by God, who have been born "by the word of truth," now lead the way to belief for others as "a kind of first fruits" of God's new creatures (v. 18). In order to fulfill that exemplary role, we must rid ourselves "of all sordidness and rank growth of wickedness" (v. 21) and instead demonstrate the qualities of new life in Christ as "doers of the word, and not merely hearers" (v. 22).

1 CORINTHIANS 1:3-9 (LFM)

Following the salutation of the first letter to the Corinthians, Paul gives thanks for the gifts that God has given to the church at Corinth: gifts including grace, Christian speech and knowledge, testimony to Christ, and spiritual gifts. Verses 7-9 anticipate a time when those gifts will be tested as the community waits for "the day of our Lord Jesus Christ" (v. 8). Paul's initial acknowledgment of the gifts given to the Corinthians becomes poignant in light of the divisions in the church he addresses head-on in subsequent chapters. Once he has established the blessings bestowed on the Corinthians, Paul is justified in calling them to a more faithful response to God's goodness.

COLOSSIANS 3:12-17 (LFM ALT.)

The letter to the Colossians addresses the place and role of Christians in the world. In the text immediately preceding this one, practices characteristic of pre-Christian life—including anger, slander, and lies—are condemned. Along

282

THE SEASON
AFTER
PENTECOST

BEVERLY A.
ZINK-SAWYER

with faith in Jesus Christ comes a new way of being in the world, portrayed in this beautiful text in terms of the act of clothing oneself, an image enacted by the early church through the white garments of baptism. Those who have been born anew in Christ put on new clothes that convey new qualities of life such as compassion, kindness, forgiveness, and love. Peace will dwell within the hearts of individual believers and within the community, all of whom are called to "be thankful" (v. 15). The text closes with images of teaching, singing, and thanksgiving, pointing to a liturgical response to the new life in Christ.

1 TIMOTHY 6:6-11, 17-19 (LFM ALT.)

In his first letter to Timothy, Paul extols the virtues of contentment. The opposite of contentment, he warns, the pursuit of riches, will only result in hardship and ruin, for "the love of money," as is still often quoted today, "is a root of all kinds of evil" (v. 10). Instead, the godly person pursues qualities such as righteousness, faith, and love. Anything else, including riches, provokes precarious hope. Only trust in God, which issues in generosity and good works, provides "the treasure of a good foundation for the future" (v. 19).

THE GOSPEL
LUKE 17:11-19 (RCL, LFM)

Luke records the story of Jesus' healing of ten men with leprosy. It is one of the many significant incidents in Jesus' ministry that occurs while he is on his way somewhere, in this case to Jerusalem. He passes through an unnamed village and is approached by ten lepers. They keep their distance from him, however, knowing by this time the rules that governed the lives of lepers, including complete social ostracism due to their "unclean" condition. Jesus responds to the lepers, but the text notably states that Jesus "saw them" (v. 14) rather than heard them. The text echoes other Gospel stories in which Jesus saw the plight of the needy and had compassion upon them. The act of seeing the need of the lepers prompted Jesus' command that they go to the Temple to show themselves to the priests. In the process of responding to that command, "they were made clean" (v. 14). There is no argument on the part of the lepers, and no dramatic action on the part of Jesus. Jesus commands, they follow, and they are healed. The immediate and faithful response of the lepers indicates something about their trust in Jesus' ability to make them well, a trust that becomes a model for us.

Just as Jesus "saw" the plight of the lepers, one of them "saw that he was healed" (v. 15) and turned back to offer thanks to Jesus. Luke, the Gospel writer who presented the parable of the Good Samaritan several chapters earlier, notes that the thankful leper was a Samaritan, one who lived with the double ostracism of his unclean status as a leper and his heritage as a despised Samaritan. Yet just as the Samaritan in the parable turned out to be the good one, so this Samaritan turns out to be the faithful and grateful one. Jesus asked about the others who were probably on their way to the Temple as commanded and noted that it was only "this foreigner" (v. 18) who took time to give thanks. It is this recognition that our healing, our restoration to new life in both body and soul, is always the work of God's grace that provides the message of this text on Thanksgiving Day. Our only appropriate response to that grace is to turn to the Lord to offer gratitude.

> Recognizing that our healing, our restoration to new life in both body and soul, is always the work of God's grace provides the message of this text on Thanksgiving Day.

MATTHEW 6:25-33 (BCP)

This portion of Jesus' Sermon on the Mount as recorded by Matthew offers an antidote to human anxiety. Such an antidote was essential for Matthew's community as it faced uncertainty and deprivation following the fall of Jerusalem. But the words of the text are no less essential for us today in an era characterized by unprecedented anxiety. This short lection includes several of the most memorable phrases and images of Scripture. Jesus says, "Do not worry about your life" (v. 25), reminding us that life is more than the tangible, temporal needs of the body for food and drink and clothing. His argument for this assurance is made by pointing to the "birds

> If God's constant care for creation extends to animals and birds, surely God will care for humanity.

of the air" (v. 26) whom God feeds and the "lilies of the field" (v. 28), which God clothes. If God's constant care for creation extends to animals and birds, surely God will care for humanity. To think otherwise is to be "of little faith" (v. 30). Rather than spending our time worrying about our needs, Jesus commands us to "strive first for the kingdom of God and his righteousness" (v. 33). Then everything else will fall into place. On Thanksgiving Day we are reminded of the ever-present care and generosity of God and moved to offer our thanks.

MARK 5:18-20 (LFM ALT.)

These verses from Mark's Gospel conclude the story of Jesus' healing of the Gerasene demoniac. The man who was healed begs to follow Jesus across the

284

THE SEASON
AFTER
PENTECOST

———

BEVERLY A.
ZINK-SAWYER

sea from the Gentile area of the Decapolis to Jewish territory. The healing had disturbed the community enough to make them "beg Jesus to leave their neighborhood" (v. 17). Perhaps unsure of his own fate if he remained among them, the healed man sought refuge with Jesus. But Jesus sent him back into the Decapolis to proclaim "how much Jesus had done for him" (v. 20), provoking the amazement of everyone. The former demoniac became a witness to the power and grace of God in Jesus Christ. Although we might experience transformation in less dramatic ways, we are nevertheless called to be witnesses to God's work in our own lives and communities.

LUKE 12:15-21 (LFM ALT.)

The parable of the rich fool serves as a cautionary tale against greed and acquisitiveness. A rich man is overwhelmed by a great harvest, prompting him *not* to share his abundance but to build bigger barns in order to hoard it for himself. The idea of overwhelming wealth with no thought for the poor is particularly galling in Luke's Gospel, which is ever mindful of the poor and neglected. As the rich man settles into a smug sense of security for what he expects to be "many years" (v. 19), God disturbs him and demands his life (or, according to the Greek, his "psyche," soul), leaving him with nothing. In this portrayal of the rich fool, there is no sense of gratitude, no move toward generosity, and no acknowledgment of God as the source of his abundance—there is only selfishness and greed. Rather than being lured into the false security of the rich man, as we might be tempted by the world in which we live, Jesus implores us to be "rich toward God" (v. 21). Indeed, on Thanksgiving Day we are reminded that true wealth and security rests in God alone.

Notes

1. James L. Mays, *Preaching and Teaching the Psalms*, ed. Patrick D. Miller and Gene M. Tucker (Louisville: Westminster John Knox, 2006), 46.

MARCH 2008

Sunday	Monday	Tuesday	Wednesday	Thursday	Friday	Saturday
						1
2 4 Lent	3	4	5	6	7	8
9 5 Lent	10	11	12	13	14	15
16 Palm Sunday / Passion Sunday	17 Monday of Holy Week	18 Tuesday of Holy Week	19 Wednesday of Holy Week	20 Maundy Thursday	21 Good Friday	22 Holy Saturday / Easter Vigil
23 Easter Sunday	24	25	26	27	28	29
30 2 Sunday of Easter	31					

APRIL 2008

Sunday	Monday	Tuesday	Wednesday	Thursday	Friday	Saturday
		1	2	3	4	5
6	7	8	9	10	11	12
3 Sunday of Easter						
13	14	15	16	17	18	19
4 Sunday of Easter						
20	21	22	23	24	25	26
5 Sunday of Easter						
27	28	29	30			
6 Sunday of Easter						

MAY 2008

Sunday	Monday	Tuesday	Wednesday	Thursday	Friday	Saturday
				1 Ascension of the Lord	2	3
4 Ascension of the Lord / 7 Sunday of Easter	5	6	7	8	9	10
11 Day of Pentecost	12	13	14	15	16	17
18 Holy Trinity Sunday / 1 Sunday after Pentecost	19	20	21	22	23	24
25 2 Sunday after Pentecost	26	27	28	29	30	31

JUNE 2008

Sunday	Monday	Tuesday	Wednesday	Thursday	Friday	Saturday
1	2	3	4	5	6	7
8 3 Sunday after Pentecost	9	10	11	12	13	14
15 4 Sunday after Pentecost	16	17	18	19	20	21
22 5 Sunday after Pentecost	23	24	25	26	27	28
29 6 Sunday after Pentecost	30					
 7 Sunday after Pentecost						

JULY 2008

Sunday	Monday	Tuesday	Wednesday	Thursday	Friday	Saturday
		1	2	3	4	5
6	7	8	9	10	11	12
8 Sunday after Pentecost						
13	14	15	16	17	18	19
9 Sunday after Pentecost						
20	21	22	23	24	25	26
10 Sunday after Pentecost						
27	28	29	30	31		
11 Sunday after Pentecost						

AUGUST 2008

Sunday	Monday	Tuesday	Wednesday	Thursday	Friday	Saturday
					1	2
3	4	5	6	7	8	9
12 Sunday after Pentecost						
10	11	12	13	14	15	16
13 Sunday after Pentecost						
17	18	19	20	21	22	23
14 Sunday after Pentecost						
24	25	26	27	28	29	30
15 Sunday after Pentecost						
31						
16 Sunday after Pentecost						

SEPTEMBER 2008

Sunday	Monday	Tuesday	Wednesday	Thursday	Friday	Saturday
	1	2	3	4	5	6
7 17 Sunday after Pentecost	8	9	10	11	12	13
14 18 Sunday after Pentecost	15	16	17	18	19	20
21 19 Sunday after Pentecost	22	23	24	25	26	27
28 20 Sunday after Pentecost	29	30				

OCTOBER 2008

Sunday	Monday	Tuesday	Wednesday	Thursday	Friday	Saturday
			1	2	3	4
5 21 Sunday after Pentecost	6	7	8	9	10	11
12 22 Sunday after Pentecostt	13 Thanksgiving Day (Canada)	14	15	16	17	18
19 23 Sunday after Pentecost	20	21	22	23	24	25
26 24 Sunday after Pentecost	27	28	29	30		

NOVEMBER 2008

Sunday	Monday	Tuesday	Wednesday	Thursday	Friday	Saturday
						1 All Saints Day
2 All Saints Sunday / 25 Sunday after Pentecost	3	4	5	6	7	8
9 26 Sunday after Pentecost	10	11	12	13	14	15
16 27 Sunday after Pentecost	17	18	19	20	21	22
23 Christ the King 30	24	25	26	27 Thanksgiving Day (USA)	28	29